Man-eaters,
mambas and
marula madness

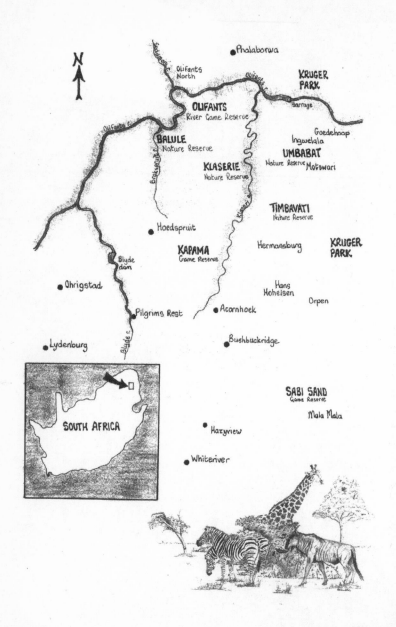

Man-eaters, mambas and marula madness

A game ranger's life in the lowveld

Mario Cesare

Jonathan Ball Publishers
Johannesburg and Cape Town

For my wife Meagan, whose patience and support,
despite being severely tested at times, is unwavering.

© Text and maps – Mario Cesare, 2009
© Illustrations – Melodie Ahlers, 2009
© The copyright holder for each photograph is
   credited in the caption.

Originally self-published in 2009 by
the author under the title *Olifants*.

The revised and updated edition published in
trade paperback in 2011 under the title
Man-eaters, Mambas and Marula Madness by
JONATHAN BALL PUBLISHERS
(A division of Media24 Pty Ltd)
PO Box 33977
Jeppestown
2043

The B format edition was published in paperback in 2011
The limited edition reprinted in 2013

ISBN 978-1-86842-461-0

Cover design by Michiel Botha, Cape Town
Cover photo of Olifants River by N Hulett
Front cover photo of Little Bee-eater by Tom Tarrant
Background photo by E Cesare
Maps by Jan Booysen, Pretoria
Typesetting by Triple M Design, Johannesburg
Set in 10.5/14 pt ITC Stone Serif Std
Printed and bound by Digital Action, Cape Town

Contents

OLIFANTS RIVER GAME RESERVE

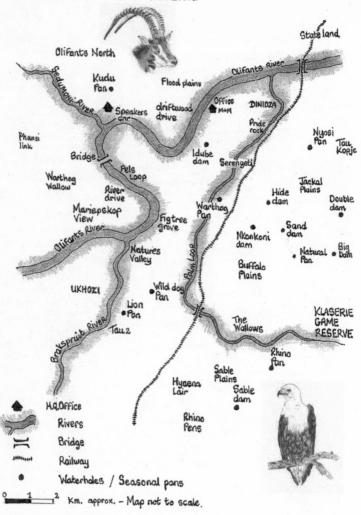

H.Q.Office

Rivers

Bridge

Railway

Waterholes / Seasonal pans

0   1   2   Km. approx. - Map not to scale.

Reserve HQ co-ordinates:
24° 07' 12. 23'S 31° 01' 50.43'E

Foreword

I get the feeling that a deep fascination for the African bush and its wildlife is something universal, something tightly wrapped in the DNA of all mankind. Or is this just the cloistered view of a South African who can't remember better times than his visits to the Kruger National Park, or the Timbavati, and who holds the belief that a bushveld experience seems always to be the highlight for any of our foreign visitors lucky enough to get there?

The question to ask, I guess, is why this is so.

Is it the silence, the tranquillity, the sense of something unspoiled, the excitement of being privy to the unexpected, to the sudden and often explosive raw rhythms of nature? I suspect we could come up with a heap of theories that tie back to the mainstream of man's primitive origins, our disenchantment with the concrete sprawl of our modern cities, the ugliness of the relentless development we see around us and the crowded tempo of modern life.

And it would all be unimportant.

The fact remains. The bushveld is a place where I, and most people I know, are most at peace and very happy to be in.

The bushveld is also where I first met Mario Cesare, under a Mopane tree, where we tested fly rods and compared casting styles, somewhere back in the 1980s. But that day is a convoluted story all on its own. The important thing is that we still share a friendship and a few common passions – fly fishing, the bushveld and wildlife. So we have been in each other's company fairly often since we first met, always in remote places, either viewing wild life or fly fishing. And I was quick to understand that Mario's passion for wildlife is underpinned by a deep empathy for it and an incredible understanding of its many huge machinations and its tiniest intricate nuances. It's an understanding the likes of which I have not encountered to the same level in anyone else. I'm tempted to think there are 'naturals' at this sort of thing, just as we know there are naturals in sport, and that Mario is a natural conservationist. I get the sense that a lot of what happens in his head happens naturally, was just fed empirically along the way in his many years deep in the bush aided by his keen powers of observation.

Not that I should even hint that I'm an expert judge of the qualities of conservationists and naturalists. I am working on a hunch here, but it's a hunch backed by my own observations during the many hours I have spent in Mario's company. More importantly, it's backed by the testimony of many people who are knowledgeable about these things and who happen also to know Mario well. I have been alongside Mario on many rivers and streams and if there's one thing I am sure about, it's that I can tell a lot about a person by just quietly watching how they approach a testy fly stream. Mario's approach is studied, observant and skilled. I would guess he's the same in the bushveld around big game as he is in fly streams around trout.

Man-eaters, Mambas and Marula Madness is more than a series of stories about one of the most successful private game reserves in South Africa. It is that in large part, but in many ways it is also the story of Mario's life, as a family man, as a manager with high responsibility, as a committed diplomat and negotiator for the rights of wild animals and as a humble, compassionate and celebrated conservationist. It is a book richly woven with the tapestry of his life experiences, with charming bushveld vignettes from mambas to man-eaters, with humour (conservationists are paid not so much in currency as in sunsets), with wonderfully fresh insights into the intriguing ways of wildlife (you will never forget his touching story of the brotherhood among buffalo bulls), with accounts of the threats posed by fences and poachers, and with his few encounters with the prospect of sudden death.

This is also a book I have long hoped Mario would write. His head is too filled with the mysteries and intricate workings of this aspect of the natural world to let him slip quietly away one day without leaving us – and the generations to come – with a record of his experiences and insights. Fortunately, Mario has always been a committed note keeper and now at last we have much of that in book form. But as good as this book is, I hope there is more Cesare writing to come. *Man-eaters, Mambas and Marula Madness* has left me, as I suspect it will leave you, with precisely that sentiment.

Tom Sutcliffe
April 2010

Introduction

Dr Ian Player, one of the world's most respected conservationists, addressing a gathering of the Game Rangers Association of Africa, once said, 'Keep records of your experiences ... write, write, write!' His advice could not have found a more eager audience than Mario Cesare. Thoroughly inspired and motivated by his words, I have taken notes and documented my observations for as long as I can remember – and finally, I have compiled my thoughts into some semblance of order.

Which brings us to the here and now.

Olifants River Game Reserve, 'Olifants' from here on, is a privately owned Big Five game reserve, unique among lowveld reserves in that it has a perennial river running through it. Over the years I have done my best to keep the shareholders up to date with the happenings in this fascinating place, in their piece of real Africa, and this ongoing task has proved to be as rewarding as it has been challenging. Through the production of regular newsletters, initially with ballpoint and notepaper, then with typewriters and latterly with laptops and PCs, I have been successful to some degree in bringing the Bush they're so passionate about into their offices and homes.

I have never been asked by a secretary or personal assistant to call back later. No matter the profile of the captain of industry, the workload of the busiest professional or the time constraints of a packed commercial or personal schedule, if the shareholders of Olifants just can't take my call at that moment, they will tell me personally. Invariably, this courtesy then includes a brief enquiry as to how things are on the reserve. The shareholders, the 'family' of Olifants, always want to know the latest news from the reserve and I always want to share it with them.

This book is a synthesis of my experiences and this reserve's growth over the years and is peppered with selected features from the newsletters produced from 1993 to 2009. It is presented in no particular order or sequence. It is designed to be picked up and opened on any page at any time and to strike a chord or re-ignite a memory. The topics range from the earliest recollections of my interest in wildlife through a broad spectrum of nature conservation and environmental issues, to tales of my interaction with the bush and its inhabitants mostly viewed from the reserve's perspective. Both the content and the intent range from conventional to controversial. In some cases, I may disturb some of the dust that has gathered on traditional thinking and may seem insensitive on sensitive matters. The intention is not to be provocative, however, but rather to question history, the status quo and alternative futures with an open mind, very much coloured by the realities and the challenges of life on Olifants.

Of course, there are personal and anecdotal recollections of some days in my life as a game ranger, and the nuts and bolts of practical conservation work. I hope these will offer some respite from the more serious moments and will help create a greater awareness of this wonderful reserve and the pivotal role it plays in a greater conservation system.

We know that conservation ecology is not an exact science. Broadly speaking, the basics can be and are successfully practised by some of the most primitive peoples on earth. There is no magic formula, it is practical common sense and the dependence on and respect for the environment that is the key. Nature is patient and forgiving, she will tolerate honest mistakes with remarkable resilience, and providing that we learn from them, we stand to benefit and prosper.

I am the first to admit I am not a scientist. However, of necessity, a smidgen of technical stuff weaves its way in and out of the meandering road map of this book. I have attempted to make this of interest to those of you who do not wear white dustcoats and thick bifocals. Equally, I am not a seasoned author, so although the words that have emerged as this publication may have been typed by my fingers, they come from the heart often with the emotional content unedited and loosely structured. In the end, though, it is my innate desire to share my experiences that has motivated the production of this book.

I have drawn on some 32 years in the bush, including the years spent beyond the borders of this reserve before my arrival in the embryonic Olifants River Game Reserve. I have also drawn on the experiences of many shareholders, and have named them and their individual lodges or reserves and acknowledged their contributions. At the same time, there has been no selection process for inclusion and there are no favourites, no inner circle.

Kobie Krüger coined the apt saying that 'Game Rangers get paid in Sunsets' and I am sure she would agree that these rewards are so often worth sharing. So it was, earlier this year, when I crested one of the higher ridges on Olifants in order to get an uninterrupted view of a particular sunset. It was one of those events which, given my limited vocabulary, frustratingly defied description.

Utterly humbled by the magnificent sight before me, all I could do was grab the radio microphone and blurt out to whoever was out there listening ...

'How's that sunset?'

I hope that as you travel though these pages you may get to see and share what I have seen. I hope that you will be with me in spirit when I once again blurt out 'How's that sunset?' and you will share, through my eyes, all that is Olifants River Game Reserve.

From the 'Magdalena Method' to the Alliance with Olifants North

AUGUST 2001

February 1993 was one of the hottest months we'd known in the last decade that we had worked in the Timbavati bush. The lowveld region had experienced a couple of years of severe drought, yet despite the onset of summer rains with the associated humidity, the vegetation was slow to respond. It appeared to be cautious and lethargic in recovering, as if it didn't want to expose any fragile new growth to the heat, in case it didn't rain again. The reality was, I suspect, that this demonstrated the degree of dehydration experienced in the preceding drought and, in particular, how much soil moisture had been lost.

Meagan had recently given birth to our son Dino, and my daughter Eleana, who was only two years old at the time, had already carved a place deep in her father's heart. Another love of my life, the country of South Africa, was undergoing considerable political change and the sensitive situation that prevailed did very little for the international tourism market. It became extremely difficult to operate an up-market game lodge, which depended almost entirely on this fickle market. So, yet another love of my life, the bush, was offering no more than an uncertain future, apart from the effects of the drought as already mentioned. This was a major motivating factor in our decision to change careers for one less reliant on foreign tourism.

At that point, I seriously considered opting for the perceived job satisfaction and certain job security of a career with Natal Parks Board. This branch of South African National Parks was streets ahead in conservation innovation; they were progressive ... right

1

up my alley, I thought. I duly applied and went through the lengthy interviewing and selection process. One month later, I was offered a post at Cape Vidal, arguably one of the most spectacular of the Park's reserves.

Situated on the north coast, in the heart of Zululand, the reserve boasts a wide range of habitat types, including a marine reserve with some of the best bill fishing on the Northern Natal coastline. Despite the attractions, I had to turn it down for one very practical reason. The salary offered at that level, at that time, meant that Meagan and my dog would both have to go out and find full-time jobs to keep us alive, while I 'researched' the deep sea fishing potential of this magnificent coastal reserve. Not that I would have been able to afford the expensive fishing tackle needed to facilitate this research.

There is a saying, I think in the advertising industry, that 'emotion decides, while reason but censors and hides'. Well, we needed to listen to reason, not to our emotions. We needed to make a 'head' decision. As difficult as it was, we accepted that this was not the time to allow our hearts to rule. Looking back with the benefit of hindsight, all I can say is, thank goodness we didn't listen to our hearts. Realising that a post with a state department would mean slow starvation, this avenue was abandoned.

So, after nine happy years in the Timbavati, we changed career direction, and made the decision to move to Olifants River Game Reserve, taking up the position as General Manager/Warden. This was very much a husband & wife position, and formally, we became 'the management couple'.

Moving home is never easy and getting to the reserve with all our belongings proved to be no exception. The organisers of the Roof of Africa Rally could have learned many a lesson from the reserve's access roads. The physical challenges of the road that took us to our new home proved stressful indeed, with the driver (me) and the navigator (Meagan) having to co-operate to negotiate the route and get through with all of our furniture and the necessities of life intact ... breastfeeding Dino en route was completely out of the question. I remember it took us an hour-and-a-half to drive the 30 kilometres from Hoedspruit to the reserve's office. This same trip now takes only 40 minutes, which includes having to slow down for the 100 or so speed bumps I have since built. Prior to the era of bumps, incidentally, in a particular emergency, I did it in under 30 minutes!

We arrived at noon, and except for the shrill, high-pitched buzz of cicadas, there wasn't a sound or sign of life. The air was thick with that oppressive mood imparted in the movies, when they portray some rundown, deserted, mid-western USA town complete with the shimmering heat making the corrugated iron roofs go 'tick, tick, tick' as they cooled when the sun slipped behind a cloud. All we needed to complete the scene was for a chain saw to suddenly start up! Eventually, I detected movement near the workshop area and found someone 'alive' who explained that everyone was on a lunch break until 2 pm. Nevertheless, he was kind enough to show us to the 'office'.

The 'office' was an old building with as little charm as an old Pofadder railway station house. We learned later that it doubled as a clubhouse, but we learned immediately that it boasted other inhabitants! The pungent smell of bat urine and droppings which had saturated the gypsum ceiling was almost unbearable. A family of warthogs had dug themselves a cool hollow in the only remaining two square metres of lawn under a baboon-ravaged guava tree, and the soil that was meant to support a lawn now transferred dust with each gust of wind into the office and a murky over-chlorinated swimming pool. After cursory introductions and small talk we were told that our accommodation was not ready yet, and we were asked to settle in elsewhere temporarily.

Depressed doesn't begin to describe how we felt at the time; it was the closest we came to turning around and leaving. The temporary quarters, which must have been a product of the same uninspired architect who had given birth to the office, were a nightmare. High ambient temperatures and humidity made living under the corrugated iron roof of these temporary quarters extremely uncomfortable, particularly at night. There were a couple of groaning fans to help add some sluggish movement to the air, but no air conditioning. Apparently no one had told the previous management that this technology was available.

In our temporary 'home' we couldn't unpack properly, which meant we were going to be living out of boxes for a while, not a happy situation for Meagan at all. Then, in my haste to make things comfortable, I forgot to switch our portable colour TV from 12 to 220 volts. When I plugged it into the wall socket, the acrid smoke and burnt plastic smell left me in no doubt that I'd blown it. To further improve our stress levels, the outgoing management were totally uncooperative. They did everything they could to undermine us. At first it was subtle, but as they neared the end of their notice period, it became blatant and obvious. Nevertheless, being made of sterner stuff, we gritted our teeth and eventually overcame the hurdles that were shoved in front of us.

The reality of settling into the routine of a new job and the sudden change of environment, with its associated challenges, was rather harder on Meagan than it was on me. Much of the disruption to my life was cushioned, as I was out in the bush most of the time, learning new boundaries, roads and water points. Despite the maze of the road network, I began to get my bearings and started to feel more settled. At that point, getting to know the reserve in relation to its neighbouring land owners was made a priority.

The inescapable politics of the area and their effect on the reserve were depressingly apparent. The poaching threat, particularly from the smaller properties across the river, was relentless. In the first month alone, we arrested two men armed with a .303 calibre rifle, poaching warthogs and giraffe on the reserve. Their brazen arrogance was evidenced by the fact that even though one particular warthog they shot ran over 200 metres into our property before dying, they followed it in, cut its throat, and bled it out as they dragged it back to their side of the river. There was absolutely no attempt made to conceal the blood trail, which led right up to the point where the carcass was loaded into a waiting car.

I take some satisfaction in reporting that they don't have that rifle any longer and they're a few thousand rand poorer. Oh yes, and perhaps just a teeny bit less arrogant.

In a widely publicised case, another of our neighbours, a man of the cloth, purposely and with the intention to hunt, lured five lions across from our side of the river onto his congregation's worshipping area. He had slaughtered a cow and then, sitting over the bait the carcass provided, systematically shot three of the lions.

Worse was to come ...

During my familiarisation, I was taken to a high point on the reserve to orientate me in relation to our northern neighbour, the farm Magdalena. Lodge 82, with its elevated position and commanding view, was chosen. I remember mentally comparing the view with that of M'bali camp in the Timbavati, from where Meagan and I had recently moved, and there was no comparison. The Olifants River, with its associated riparian trees and the seemingly unspoilt bush to the north, was spectacular. What also made an impression on me was the lack of power lines, telephone lines and railway tracks. And yet, all was not as pristine as it seemed.

From this vantage point, I was shown the extent of the river frontage that Magdalena shared with Olifants. Despite the thick riverine vegetation that straddled both banks of the river, I could see giraffe on the narrow flood plain, as well as what I thought was a small herd of waterbuck near the water's edge. (The floods of 1996 subsequently had a devastating impact on the ecology of this landscape. Most of the huge, magnificent trees that grew on the banks of the Olifants River were washed away. Where they once stood, the river has deposited silt loads up to two metres deep, creating an enormous floodplain habitat.) Returning to the tale at hand, and with Carl Zeiss's assistance, I was able to bring the small herd ten times closer and determine that the 'waterbuck' were in fact donkeys!

Worse still, as they moved about, bells on their necks made a tinkling sound. It was reminiscent of a Swiss chocolate advertisement and I half expected to hear distant strains of Julie Andrews. Another movement close to them revealed a number of scrawny cattle, which appeared to be of Afrikaner-cross-Brahman strain. I turned to the outgoing manager and asked what these domestic animals were doing in a game reserve area.

He explained that the owner of Magdalena, a well-known homeopath, ran a combined cattle and game farm, and added that all the wildebeest across the river had been shot because the cattle would be susceptible to 'snot siekte' which is carried by them. When I asked about the donkeys, I was told that they were used as bait to lure lions across from Olifants whereupon the lions would be shot. This doctor took the concept of prevention being better than cure to new extremes.

The more I learned, the more ruthless the 'Magdalena method' was revealed to be. Any threat to their sable antelope 'breeding programme' was eliminated. Leopard were trapped in cages strategically placed around the 300-hectare sable camp. They were then shot. Hyaenas were also trapped and shot. Wild dog and cheetah were shot on sight without the preamble of trapping. Magdalena's manager at that time, apparently an ex-Nature Conservation official, had been tasked by the reserve's owner with implementing a campaign against Olifants. The apparent reason for this feud was that the developers had promised not to build in front of the Magdalena camp, but went back on their word and did just that. War was then declared. However understandable the reasons for his anger may have been, venting his emotions by taking revenge on innocent animals was cowardly and shameful.

Incidentally, this vendetta was not only aimed at the larger predators. There was apparently no regard for any animals emanating from Olifants. Nyala, which are as beautiful as they're innocent, were among the known casualties of this campaign. Initially I thought this extremely negative picture was being painted by the outgoing manager as a result of sour grapes. I was about to find out how wrong I was.

A few weeks later, I was called to a sighting of 13 lion at Wild Dog Pan. Among them were two beautiful full-maned males, the dominant males of our resident pride. Later that evening the pride moved down to the Olifants River and crossed into Magdalena near Fig Tree Grove. That was to be the last time I'd ever see them.

The following night, seven lions were shot out of this pride, and to add insult to injury, the whole 'hunt' was videotaped prior to the actual shooting. This smacks of the same subhuman mentality evidenced by terrorists in the mould of Al Qaeda when they videotape their innocent victims before and during their execution. The lions were filmed drinking at the cattle troughs, with the cattle clearly visible in the background. A further three must have been shot later, because only three lions returned the following day, one young male and two pregnant females.

The 'Magdalena method' impacted not only on the area's wildlife and its human population, but also on the topography of the land itself. A few months later, not too far from Magdalena's main camp, an airstrip was bulldozed in an ecologically sensitive area. It was in full view of lodges on Olifants (Environmental Impact Assessments and the Green Scorpions were not an issue in those days). Not only was the airstrip totally useless, due to its limited length and steep slope, but the scar it left on the landscape will take hundreds of years to heal. The stated purpose of this airstrip was to fly hunting clients directly in and out of Magdalena as it was going to be hunted commercially. They knew this would upset the majority of the shareholders on Olifants and the so-called airstrip was an ever-present reminder of the underlying threat.

One morning a couple of months later, I received a call from one of our guards, who reported that domestic dogs had crossed the river from the north and were chasing waterbuck on our side of the river. Immediately, I jumped into my vehicle and was off to investigate. Upon arrival at the point where the dogs were alleged to have crossed the river, I unexpectedly came face to face with the Magdalena manager for the first time. He was standing on the opposite riverbank, with his hands on his ample hips, and when he saw me, he cupped his hands around his mouth and bellowed, '*Goeie môre!*' above the roar of the rapids. I reciprocated. After introducing himself, he went on to say that the two Rottweilers responsible for chasing the waterbuck were his and that should I come across the dogs, I was to shoot them if I wanted to.

I told him I didn't think that would be necessary. I felt like telling him who was actually at fault, and who I thought should be shot, but managed to override the surge of my simmering Italian blood and maintained decorum. Thankfully, the dogs returned of their own accord shortly afterwards.

In the ensuing cordial conversation, on a quieter section on the river, I learnt that his boss had given him a list of things to do that would hurt Olifants. However, he said he could see I was a person with whom he could communicate and that perhaps we should bury the hatchet, at least on a managerial level. The only thing I knew for sure at that stage, was *where* the hatchet should be buried, but I kept that to myself.

What glimmer of hope there may have been was soon snuffed out. A few days later I heard that a large nyala bull, one of only 18 individuals on Olifants at the time, had crossed over from our area near lodge 30 and had been shot. Later, its mounted head was to adorn the manager's house and stay there until he left.

These few examples I have shared with you represent the tip of a destructive iceberg the real magnitude of which we will never know. Thanks to the dedication and commitment of the Olifants shareholders, this untenable situation was eventually resolved. Although Magdalena wasn't needed as a property acquisition, it was purchased for another reason – peace of mind. The then Magdalena is now known as Olifants North, and it and its wild-life population are now in safe hands. We can all rest easy when we see the odd vehicle movement or spotlight on the other side of the river, knowing there's no hunter's rifle behind the light. Best of all, no one is going to miss the domestic stock that used to summon in our beautiful bushveld mornings with moos and heehaws. And, when our lions cross over for a visit, we know there's a good chance they will soon be back, and if not, it will be of their choosing.

It goes without saying that, ecologically, the two areas cannot be and should never be separated. An African ecosystem cannot be defined and demarcated completely and utterly.

There can never be 'big enough' in Africa. African mammals need *lebensraum*. Even the Kruger Park's two million hectares are proving 'too small'. The very nature and dynamism of African ecosystems, particularly when tested under drought conditions, demonstrate how precious every hectare is, and to have control over only one bank of a perennial river is in my opinion, no control at all.

Ecological management is now scientifically based and co-ordinated. Co-operation between north and south, especially where game management is concerned, is excellent. Many species share this combined area, with nyala, waterbuck and hippo being but a few examples of how co-operation is vital for management purposes. At present Olifants North boasts four waterbuck to every one south of the river, and therefore, what may seem to be an over-population in their area when looked at in isolation, is in fact high density due to this species favouring the habitat over there. They simply prefer the North, and the game census records over the years show that this has always been the case. Take the two areas as a whole, however, and combine the waterbuck numbers, and a more realistic picture emerges, upon which management decisions can be made. (This is discussed in a little more detail later under the heading 'Management of game populations'.)

This link is just one more in the chain that gives the combined area strength and makes it the paradise it is and the envy of all. It is also no secret that Olifants North comprises habitat that is more suited to black rhino than it is to their white cousins. Considering the excellent holding pens and infrastructure already in place for the introduction of rhino, we will take advantage of this and consider introducing black rhino in the near future. A visit in 2006 by conservationist and author Ron Thompson confirmed the viability of this concept. As controversial as he may be on some conservation management issues, conversely he is an authority on others, and one of these is black rhino.

Ron studied these animals extensively in Zimbabwe, and after having visited our area on a number of occasions, he is convinced that the Commiphora woodland and hill country of Olifants North, Ukhozi and Olifants West, is very suitable black rhino habitat.

Unbeknown to Ron was the fact that in the last 16 years on this reserve I have never seen or received any report of a white rhino in the area or habitat he describes as suited to black rhino. With no obstacle whatsoever to limit their access, white rhino have not been recorded in this hilly habitat near the Olifants River flood plain or the river itself on the reserve. Despite the worst of droughts, during which many species under resource stress frequently roamed areas they normally wouldn't in search of food and water, the white rhinos would not cross the 'Commiphora curtain'. This line can be identified as the ecotone between the relatively flat bushwillow, marula and knobthorn veld, and the hilly rocky Commiphora woodland which characterises the majority of the topography and vegetation type that the Olifants River meanders through. It is quite incredible to see how the white rhino regard this habitat demarcation zone as if it were a fence-line, a solid barrier, which confirms Ron's observation regarding suitable habitat for black rhino.

And so it is in this particular piece of Africa, that over time, natural cycles are played out, no matter the schemes of man. Perhaps we did not know it at the time, but the madness that was Magdalena was to cause the birth of Olifants North as a co-operative and like-thinking neighbour.

And, as if to confirm this, whilst the scar of Magdalena's 'airstrip' is still visible, it fades faster than we might have expected, as have the memories of the bad old days.

The Klaserie Fence is History!

FEBRUARY 2005

The fence between the Klaserie and Balule Nature Reserves was the only remaining hurdle between our game reserve and the Greater Kruger Park's open system. The removal of this barrier would effectively allow game to enjoy unrestricted movement between the Hoedspruit/Phalaborwa road and the Mozambique border. Furthermore, South African National Parks, in co-operation with the Mozambican government, had started a phased removal of the Kruger/Mozambique fence as well. To date, nearly 30 kilometres of fences had been removed, thereby creating the Transfrontier National Park. Hypothetically speaking, the future promised that there would be nothing in terms of fences to stop animals moving eastwards until they reached the Indian Ocean, an east--west migration possibility of well over 400 kilometres! The reality, in 2009, given the most optimistic predictions, is that only about half that distance will be used ... but that is a huge achievement in itself.

The key to becoming part of this progressive conservation initiative was to become a full member of the Association of Private Nature Reserves (APNR). To fulfil the criteria for full membership of APNR, it was clear that we needed to get our house in order. This proved to be a huge challenge and while Balule had a lot going for it ecologically, it was on the political front that a tremendous amount of work still needed to be done. Once compliance was achieved, however, we were assured the fence would be dismantled. This process, which took nearly 18 years of goal-driven single-mindedness, successfully ran its course in 2005.

Understandably, our shareholders and the broader conservation community were waiting with bated breath for any news on our progress with APNR. In an attempt to inform the shareholders of the significance of what had been achieved, I wrote the following article, which appeared in an early 2005 newsletter. I also took the opportunity to throw in a brief history of the initiative's background.

March 2005: I am told that good news doesn't sell newspapers. Disasters, conflicts, scandals and misfortunes are some of the required and essential ingredients needed to cook up the sort of story that sells. When spiced with sensationalism and carefully tuned with well-placed words and a liberal sprinkling of adjectives, the end product is often a dramatic and marketable rendering of the events. Unfortunately, even when the story is far from an accurate reflection of the facts, it can be immensely readable and, for some, a macabre form of entertainment.

Fortunately I am not in the media business where I would be hard-pressed to earn a crust, as this time I can only report *good news*. Admittedly, it has taken a while to get to this point, but timing was all-important. I thought it better to wait until I was able to report back to you with facts and finality rather than with maybes and speculation. I think it was Sir Winston Churchill who said, 'Lies travel the world, while truth is still putting its boots on.'

'Mario, get to the point!' I can hear you saying … well, OK …

The fence is down! I repeat. THE FENCE IS DOWN!

Where and when did this initiative start? Well, of course, it started with the inception of Olifants and the zeal of men with vision who started this reserve back in 1987. The pioneers of Olifants River Game Reserve were not only keen and talented developers, they were also men of ambition with a conservation ethic to match their sales drive. In 1988, the regulations governing developments were less stringent than they are today, so it was fortunate that they were not ecologically naïve, and despite pressing financial priorities, they never lost sight of the bigger picture.

Ian Green and Tim Ham both realised that this area's long-term future and ecological well-being lay in becoming part of a larger open system. Tim was even more of a believer than Ian, in fact, and so confident were they that the removal of the Klaserie fence was an eventual fait accompli, that it became a passionate part of their sales 'spiel'.

The implication was that Olifants would be associated with the prestigious Klaserie Private Nature Reserve, itself soon to have its boundary with Kruger removed. The Balule area at that point was a loose-knit group of relatively small landowners, many of whom were suffering from that ecologically destructive affliction I call the '*Myne* syndrome', a personal interpretation of the 'Mine, all mine!' attitude for which a cure was later found, thank goodness!

Prospective buyers were entertained on Olifants, and were an enraptured, captive audience. In terms of sales and marketing, selling Olifants, even back then, could not have been much of a challenge.

You can picture the scene ... flickering leadwood log fires burning on the banks of the Olifants River when a lion roars in the distance interrupting the conversation. It would have been a welcome distraction that set the mood like no presentation could possibly emulate. With a dram or two of Scotland's finest, this priceless scenario no doubt helped even the most sceptical buyers to shed their urban mindset and put things in perspective. This was no sales gimmick, and they knew it. It is no wonder then, that cheque books seemed to fall out of pockets and the river became a mere trickle compared to the rate at which the ink flowed into contractual signatures. Nowadays, acquiring a piece of the action on Olifants is virtually limited to 'Dead Man's Shoes', so prized is ownership and so limited are the resale opportunities.

The Klaserie fence remained while the Kruger Park's was dismantled, and our neighbours gloated. Undaunted by this, Olifants River Game Reserve was driven then, as it is now, by its enthusiastic shareholders who took the initiative and began to play a leading role in the area. In terms of commitment to conservation and practical wildlife management in particular, we took the lead in Balule, and in relation to other reserves in the lowveld, we were up there with the best.

As a consequence of the Kruger Park removing its fence with neighbouring private reserves, the APNR was formed. Amongst other functions, this body regulates conservation activities within the member reserves. The APNR management plan, which is modelled on the Kruger National Park's master plan, is now regarded as its broad conservation policy document.

I began attending the APNR meetings early in 1993, mostly to stay in the loop, and at the invitation of the Chairman, Mr Paul Geiger, a former senior colleague who was also chairman of the Timbavati Private Nature Reserve at the time. By late 1993, Balule began to attend in an official capacity, yet only as an associate member ... although this proved interesting at times, it was mostly a frustrating relationship. We knew this marriage was celibate and could never be consummated while the fence remained.

In October 1993, Olifants River Nature Reserve was officially proclaimed a Nature Reserve. This achievement owes a debt of thanks to the fortitude and foresight of Theunis Kotzee, then Chairman. Not only did he champion the cause of Olifants, he looked beyond our boundaries and envisaged the inclusion of the surrounding areas to form one large reserve. These areas have since been brought together in a loose-knit federation of independent reserves, collectively known as the Balule Nature Reserve.

Due to some properties within the Balule area being reluctant to remove fences initially, the Olifants region and the rest of Balule at that stage were, for all practical purposes, separate ecological units and were managed independently. However, the Klaserie fence, which proved an effective barrier to game movement, was not going to discourage Olifants from moving forward. Not being full members of the APNR instilled in our reserve a feisty independence. We didn't just lie down and cry 'foul'; we were obliged to manage our reserve intensively. We persevered and although Olifants went on to become one of the most respected examples of conservation in the area, our sights were always on being part of the greater KNP ... the bigger picture!

Andy Dott was chairman of the Balule Nature Reserve committee at the time and except for a couple of years, has kept the chair ever since. He was, and still is, loyally supported by Steven Hearne, another man with vision and selfless commitment. Andy took up where Theunis left off, sunk his teeth in, and persisted, not letting go for one minute. Although Andy had his own unconventional style and a structurally different approach to things, the common goal remained the same – full membership of the APNR and getting the Klaserie fence down. The challenge lay in creating an ecologically and administratively acceptable reserve, which would fit the criteria for inclusion as a full member of the APNR.

Structurally, the Reserve developed as follows:

- Balule Nature Reserve comprises six independently-run regions, which collectively cover an area of nearly 40 000 hectares.
- Each region employs a warden, and has its own regional constitution and committee, which in turn subscribes to the overriding Balule constitution and Balule committee.
- The APNR committee requires that a warden from each of the four private reserves, namely Balule, Klaserie, Timbavati and Umbabat, attend meetings at that level. In 2002, I was elected to represent Balule Nature Reserve as warden, and also chaired the Balule Wardens Committee, to which I was re-elected each year for the next six years.

Despite the foregoing emphasis on structure, fragmentation was, and always will be, Balule's greatest threat. To overcome this inherent negative, everyone concerned worked on the co-ordination and co-operation of activities between the regions through their wardens. The holistic approach to conservation was becoming a reality and Balule was growing. The Balule Wardens Committee played a huge role maintaining the unity between the regions, which required focused effort on my part. My workload was increasing to the point where I had to divide my time between broader Balule issues and the pressing obligations on Olifants, so I opted to hand the reins over to my successor in January 2008.

I still sit on the Wardens Committee where I represent our region, namely Olifants River Conservancy (ORC). The ORC is the largest of the six regions, covering 16 500 hectares, which comprises well over 40 per cent of the total area of Balule.

Essentially, my work was done. I had been a catalyst in the formation of the Balule Wardens Committee, which is now a widely respected body dealing with coalface conservation issues affecting Balule. In my opinion, however, the most important achievement of this committee, besides its all-important unifying role, is its reputation for credibility, its level of commitment and the image it projects of the reserve. Balule had proved to the 'big boys' of the APNR that we were more than worthy of membership. Not only was our house in order, but in terms of diversity of habitat and balanced game numbers, we were a show house with plenty to bring to the table.

All this despite us having a skeleton or two in a cupboard or two. But then, who hasn't?

The combination of Tim Ham's idea, Theunis Kotzee's procedural and formal methods and Andy Dott's zealous 'I also want to play in the team' approaches culminated in the slow but sure erosion of resistance to the removal of the fence. Ultimately it was Olifants' chairman and the newly elected chairman of Balule PNR, Quentin Sussman, who had enough of the 'happy to be along for the ride' complacency and tackled the issue directly. Determined to get unambiguous answers to simple questions, he persisted until there could be only one answer.

On 22 January 2005, the Klaserie Private Nature Reserve called a special meeting of its members to vote on the removal of the fence. The resulting vote in favour of its removal was a resounding 90 per cent. This, I'm sure, was thanks to the recognition of Balule's efforts by the Klaserie's Chairman at the time, Mike Myers, who is a progressive thinker, a man who calls a spade a spade. Without his practical, fair and down-to-earth approach, this might have dragged on for quite a while longer. Even though it had taken 18 years to get to this point, there was no turning back.

And just like the Berlin Wall, the Klaserie Fence came down. No one regrets its passing.

Nothing Achieved ... I'm Happy to Report

JUNE 2005

Ever had the desire to go and look at nothing, to actually go on a drive with no other purpose than to see for yourself that where there used to be something, there is now nothing? Then, having done that surreptitiously for the third or fourth time by yourself, you find excuses to do it a few more times with those with whom you wish to share the experience.

More than 18 years of persistent persuasion and single-minded focus had gone into this project. Finally, after 20 pairs of leather gloves, approximately 80 000 individual wire cuts, many, many days of hard work and being spurred on by a lot of enthusiasm ... 'Nothing' was achieved, definitively and finally.

The warden of the Klaserie Game Reserve and his team, assisted by an equally committed Olifants team, took just over eight days to remove over 20 kilometres of fencing. Another day or two were needed to remove all signs of there ever having been a fence and to neaten things up. I don't know which of the two teams was more eager, but on the day we were meant to start with the dismantling, I rushed to the fence first thing, hoping to beat their team to the post (no pun intended), only to find some 300 metres of fencing had already been removed. Whether they snuck out at 3.00 am or burned midnight oil wasn't important, the message was clear – let's get this dammed thing dismantled and rolled up before anybody changes their minds or finds another reason to procrastinate.

I drove up to the fence line on the last day intending to tidy up, to make sure we had picked up all the fencing debris, bits of wire, the odd dropper and any related sort of stuff, and at the same time collect any tools that had been left behind. Although the bulk of the wire and fence poles had already been removed, I knew that in a task involving so much material, there would always be something that had been overlooked.

In an ironic twist, and despite there being not a strand of fencing left standing for some 23 kilometres, I arrived to find an impala ram thrashing around in a cloud of dust. He had managed to tangle his horns in the only piece of rolled-up fence wire that had been missed the previous day. Of course, we had him out of his predicament in a few seconds.

The fence had made its 'final strand'.

This piece of wire wouldn't give up and performed its function to the bitter end, demonstrating one final time what it was that made conservationists hate it so vehemently. In recognition of its 'roll' in history, this particular roll was finally cut into memento-sized pieces which would forever symbolise mankind's ill-conceived and selfish approach to wildlife management. Packaged in small clear plastic sheaths, these were made available for shareholders to display as conversation-about-conservation pieces.

At a modest, informal celebration to mark the occasion, the wardens from the various reserves and regions concerned, as well as representatives of the Limpopo province's Department of Environmental Affairs and Tourism, got together. The venue was a quiet site on the southern bank of the Olifants River. The 'manne' met a few metres inside the Klaserie Nature Reserve, close to where the old fence between the two reserves used to end. Moving out of the midday sun, we gathered in the generous shade of an enormous acacia overlooking the water. A pod of curious hippo had gathered a little closer to check out the intrusion that was about to disturb their siesta. Across on the northern bank, a couple of elephant bulls had come down to the river, their wet bodies still charcoal grey from their recent bath. Only the tops of their backs and flapping ears were visible as they grazed on the tender shoots of the tall reeds.

The fire that had been prepared earlier soon burned down to

glowing coals, signifying it was time to braai. A chop or two along with some boerewors was thrown on the hot grid, and while these spat and sizzled, a few beers slid out of the cooler and were downed in easy conversation. A happy, jovial atmosphere prevailed, as the informal yet delicious meal that followed was thoroughly enjoyed. (For salad, the guys just had another beer.)

It was only once the food began to settle, that the men became quieter, and their expressions began to take on that faraway look. This soon gave way to a pensive and contemplative mood as the subsequent ceremonial drive along the entire length of this 'nothing' came to an end on the Olifants Game Reserve's southern boundary line, 23 kilometres later. We eased to a stop, and turned the two Land Cruisers to face the way we'd come, then everyone quietly and deliberately climbed down. One of the wardens, a particularly large, burly individual, broke the ice by admitting that the last time he had felt so emotional, was when he held his firstborn son. Another remarked that, in his opinion, this was one of the most positive steps taken in conservation in this area for the last 20 years.

Not able at the time to think of anything appropriately clever or philosophical to say, I just stood there, humbled in quiet understanding of what had been said, while looking at where conservation's equivalent of the Berlin Wall once divided this beautiful environment. Moreover, I was overwhelmed by the sense of relief that game could now move freely in search of grazing and that the system could now function more naturally. Amongst all of us there it was clearly evident that the far-reaching ecological significance of what had been achieved was sinking in. Although the modest ceremony did not reflect the enormity of the achievement, it took nothing away from those of us who were there … we knew.

At this point, the autumn sun was beginning to sink behind the Drakensberg, the beer supply had dwindled, and it was apparent that the dust in the air had begun to irritate a few eyes. So, it was time to break up and go home before somebody opened their 4x4's cubbyhole, reached in past the bullets and binoculars,

19

hauled out the Kleenex and openly started doing what cowboys aren't supposed to.

Who would have thought it? These supposedly rugged, tough men of the bush, actually admitting that they were so emotionally moved ... by 'nothing'.

Real Big Game Country

In the early 1990s, on a beautiful estate overlooking Karkloof Valley in KwaZulu-Natal, Meagan and I had lunch in the magnificent, lush surrounds with an acquaintance and his son, one of the founders of the Phinda Resource Reserve.

At the time, Phinda was in the initial stages of its development. Strategic chunks of land had yet to be incorporated and consolidated into the proposed reserve. People needed to be moved and relocated, boundaries determined, and big game introduced and established – all in all, a very exciting and challenging project.

Our host's son's enthusiasm centred on the wide variety of habitat types found within the area, from sand forest woodland and wetlands to inland lake systems. He expanded by giving an account of the diversity of species that these unique ecosystems already supported and what they could potentially support. It seemed awesome. I listened intently, not wanting to miss a thing. His knowledge of the area was impressive and I couldn't help feeling a touch envious of this wildlife paradise being so vividly described. Then he said something that changed the mood, something which I felt couldn't go unchallenged, or left hanging in the air.

He maintained that the lowveld reserves, when compared with the proposed Phinda area, particularly the mopane and bushwillow of the northern regions, were little more than semi-deserts. He saw them as environments with relatively low carrying capacities and monotonous vegetation. I didn't argue on that point, even though deep down he must have known he was missing something vital in his comparison. Yet, he made no attempt to hide the arrogance of his stated and disparaging position with even a modicum of concession.

Despite all my efforts at restraint, some physical evidence of my need to respond, however imperceptible, must have caught Meagan's eye. Her subtle way of saying 'leave it' was to deliver a sharp kick to my ankle under the table. But I ignored it, giving way to my urge to elucidate and create a fairer comparative insight that would put things in perspective. However, before embarking on this mission, I pulled up both my feet and placed them out of harm's way under my chair.

Without appearing defensive, I explained that the lowveld, particularly the drier mopane veld of the northern lowveld, is 'Big Game Country' and that elephant, for example, are endemic to the region. They occur in healthy viable populations and the areas in which they roam, although relatively dry, are comparatively large and unspoilt. I also told him that from a practical management point of view, the advantage of having endemic big game was invaluable.

I went on to point out that the other side of the coin was typified by the problems being experienced by Pilanesberg and other areas in the North West where closed systems, fences and geographic isolation amongst other factors brought their own headaches. Incidentally, the failed Knysna elephant re-introduction project had not been planned at that time, but ultimately similar problems would be encountered.

I observed that Phinda was surrounded by a human population dependent on subsistence agriculture. Furthermore, I reminded him that having elephant break out of a reserve surrounded by farmland could have serious consequences. These enormous and dangerous animals wreak havoc in crop fields and attempts by farmers to chase them usually ends in tragedy.

On the other hand, the lowveld had a relatively minor and manageable problem in this regard. If, for example, lion moved out of a fenced reserve in the lowveld, they would almost certainly be shot, as would those that escaped from Phinda. The advantage in our situation however, would be that the lowveld lions that were lost would soon be replaced by other wild lions moving in from Kruger, thereby filling the vacuum. We wouldn't need to source semi-tame, badly adjusted cast-offs from breeding projects or safari parks. Far from it, our lions are homogeneous, arrive without any baggage, and are born in an environment where nature had already selected the fittest and strongest for us. The same recruitment process would apply with regard to elephant that break out and get shot.

These examples were but a couple of attributes that I felt made a strong case for comparative values between the regions, albeit without attempting to give an edge to the lowveld 'semi-desert' so disparaged by our lunch partner.

'You need to look beyond the romantic honeymoon,' I said. 'Running a reserve surrounded by poor farmers is going to require a tremendous amount of PR and intensive administration, so, from a practical conservation management perspective, I'm happy I am where I am.'

This thought, that two totally different reserves with two totally different sets of strengths can appeal to different people, may be demonstrated by using any number of comparative examples. From my experience, one particular example springs to mind, Welgevonden as compared to Olifants. Welgevonden, a game reserve situated in the beautiful Waterberg of Limpopo Province, is composed of reclaimed farmland cohesively re-formed to create a 'Big Five' game reserve. It took a tremendous amount of perseverance and commitment to get to that point, yet today it is a significant conservation success story. It is intensively well managed and supported by a solid base of like-minded shareholders.

Species of larger game are well represented to the point that they boast more variety of larger herbivores than the Big Five private reserves adjoining the Kruger Park. The introduction of game and associated teething problems have largely been ironed out. Despite the reserve encompassing a relatively large area, it is still bounded by a fence and surrounded by stock farmers and smaller fenced game farmers. This means there will always be the inevitable ecological problems associated with a closed system. Nonetheless, these problems are being constantly monitored and well managed.

When I try to compare Welgevonden with Olifants, I find it really hard to come up with a finite list of pros and cons … there is something missing, and it's not just the malaria mozzies or the heat. I think the problem is that they might seem similar, but it's like comparing Canadians to North Americans. There are no obvious, discernable differences, yet they are different, that's that.

People who own property in both Welgevonden and Olifants share the same sentiments – they love both, but for different reasons. Both the reserves have their role to play in the greater scheme of things. Our Phinda host was rather too uncompromising in attitude for our liking.

When I was converting my notes for this chapter into something resembling prose, I noted that Olifants was experiencing a period of change, having recently had some of the most rewarding elephant viewing for years. For nearly ten months there had been elephant continually on the reserve, mainly small groups of up to six young bulls. The number of individual sightings recorded by members was over 50, a record for us. There appeared to be about 12 elephant on the greater reserve area at that time, and we thought it would be wonderful if a breeding herd moved in permanently just to boost these numbers a little. That thought was high on our wish list, and it was materialising sooner than expected. The natural recruitment of elephant, endemic to the region, became a reality.

This all highlights how privileged we are: in spite of all our warts and pimples, 'Big Game R Us'. The natural movement of elephant in our reserve demonstrates that despite the fences, railway line, the power lines and people shining spotlights in their faces, they appear to be happy here. Most importantly, they are relatively free to come and go as they wish. Our area may not be as pleasing on the eye as the sand forests and wetlands of northern Zululand, or as dramatically beautiful as the Knysna Forest, but big game animals, especially elephant, are thriving here, and they're here because they want to be.

To Cull or not to Cull, That is the Question

NOVEMBER 2004 ... AD INFINITUM

The increase in elephant numbers and the apparently destructive feeding habits of these magnificent animals has led to fears of habitat destruction. These fears have reached the point where biodiversity being adversely affected is seen as the best scenario and irreversible damage to the environment as the worst. On Balule Nature Reserve the elephant population has risen from a handful to nearly 500 in the space of 14 years, with the last five years having seen the most rapid growth of nearly 400 per cent! Consequently, the sudden impact of these numbers on the reserve's vegetation has been cataclysmic, particularly the woody component.

Sadly, it appears elephant are becoming their own worst ambassadors, and in some reserves where they were previously tolerated in moderate to healthy numbers, now they're not wanted at all. The management of elephant populations by lethal culling was stopped, due in part to pressure groups who love these pachyderms. Unfortunately, as a result of this well-meant action, the numbers have been increasing exponentially while the available habitat dwindles with each day that passes. The resulting situation has now reached the point where it has turned those landowners who were willing to make land available for manageable numbers of elephant, against them.

Recently, many private reserves have gone to great expense and erected elephant-proof fences around their properties in an effort to deny access to all elephant. Sentiment is such that many others, including those vehemently opposed to fences and who campaigned tirelessly for the removal of these barriers, are now seriously considering the same action. The majority of these landowners who are now excluding elephant from their land admit to doing so reluctantly, as they have great empathy with these icons of the African wilderness. But, these same landowners also love the landscape and other wildlife that depends on the bio-diversity which is evidently under threat.

Privately owned and managed reserves are playing an ever-increasing role in conservation outside the National Parks. Most of these reserves rely on income-generating activities for the funding required to maintain their infrastructure. Eco-tourism in its various facets (even including trophy hunting) is regarded as the most reliable source of revenue. The hunting component is, without doubt, the most lucrative, but in terms of the growing anti-hunting sentiment, is becoming less acceptable as a fund-generating option.

We also need to be cognisant of the fact that areas dominat-ed by elephant are losing biodiversity, and as this happens, the areas' attraction and aesthetic appeal also diminish.

Once investors, shareholders and tourists no longer find an area attractive they will go elsewhere. These days, I am hear-ing more and more comments like 'we need to do something about the increasing numbers of elephant' or 'the bush is looking downright depressing' or 'our reserve is beginning to resemble Delville Wood.' Worst of all, these are the murmurings of discon-tent from those with a fundamental love and understanding of these wonderful, intelligent, appealing creatures. These are the people who previously would only ever have uttered the word 'cull' in hushed tones, behind masks at secret meetings in dark places.

Irrespective of the scientifically motivated hypothesis that this is part of a natural cycle in the bigger scheme of things, it re-mains a hard sell. The majority of us humans are by nature not a patient lot. We are rarely far-sighted enough to go through an apparently negative process that may only show the positive eco-logical benefits a few centuries hence.

The reality is that it is 'their' land that the increasing popula-tion of elephant so desperately needs, but from which they are now being excluded. The full impact of the detrimental consequences of this action will take some time to be understood, but it doesn't take rocket science to calculate the results of the fundamental physics at play.

To my mind, given the simplest laws of nature, not only is the status quo unsustainable, in the long term there can be no doubt that the concomitant effects of being denied access to living space and having to focus their feeding on an ever-dwindling habitat, will kill elephants as surely as if they were being culled.

As the numbers of elephant continue to grow, so does the support for alternatives to lethal culling as a means of effective population management. Unfortunately, none of the other proposals put forward to date are able to be practically implemented on the scale necessary. This dilemma is especially evident in the larger reserves, where not hundreds, but thousands of elephant need to be removed.

Almost everyone is in agreement that unless elephant numbers are controlled, they will ultimately destroy themselves by destroying the very system that sustains them. This well-known scenario played itself out in East Africa's Tsavo Reserve, where thousands of elephants starved to death as a result of habitat destruction. Formerly a dense woodland savanna, today Tsavo is an open grassland savanna. As I stated earlier, some may argue that this is the great circle of life in elephant ecology, and there is evidence to suggest that in certain habitats, this argument has merit.

This theory of the great circle of life, for want of a better term, cannot be widely applied, as there are too many variables in play. In our case, here on Olifants, it would be irresponsible to allow nature to take its course. Adopting this policy could have catastrophic consequences for our biodiversity and as many fear, it may become irreversibly damaged. This is a legacy no conservationist would want to leave behind.

Many are of the opinion that nobody and nothing should have the right, for example, to destroy baobab trees that are thousands of years old – or, as is happening, to destroy at a rapid rate all the younger specimens that would have had a remote possibility of succeeding them. In certain parts of Botswana, this cycle of eradication is complete, with not a single baobab tree with a trunk diameter of a metre or less left! Some of the older trees were providing shade and fruit when Cleopatra ruled Egypt.

That observation gives some weight to the immense passing of time involved in us reaching our current untenable situation.

I became disillusioned with conflicting scientific opinion and tired of reading modern research papers, most of which have been concluded in segments of time so fleeting and so disproportionate to the subject as to render them questionable, particularly as references to assist with elephant management. Not prepared to leave this pressing issue at that, I went back in time to when observations were made and objectively relayed without the constraints of time or deadlines, without the motivation of chasing academic qualification, political recognition or scientific correctness. This took me to an era when events were accurately recorded from keen observation as they happened and descriptions were given the detail that modern text leaves for photography to enhance.

In an old hunting book, *A Hunter's Wanderings in Africa*, by Frederick Courteney Selous, I came across a description by him of an area that is virtually as untouched by man today as it was 120 years ago. Presently, more than 30 000 elephant call it home and many of us have either visited, or are familiar with, this reserve. There is ongoing debate amongst conservationists and the area is presently under the spotlight regarding its elephant population management. It is the Chobe National Park, situated in northeastern Botswana.

Selous writes: 'The next day (Sunday) we continued our journey westwards along the southern bank of the Chobe, which here runs nearly due east. As we had been informed, we found that a dense continuous jungle, interspersed with large forest trees, came down in most parts to the water. This jungle-covered land rises in some places abruptly, in others in a gentle slope, leaving along the shore a margin of open ground (from 10 to 100 yards broad), covered with short grass, and formed, no doubt, by alluvial deposit. As we proceeded, traces of the presence of elephants and buffaloes became more and more frequent, we kept a sharp lookout for fresh spoor.'

Since that time there has been no measurable interference by man that could have helped to change the Chobe, or manipulate the habitat in some way. It is clear that Selous does not appear to be describing the same area we presently know. He did not see as many elephant as we see there today; in fact, all he saw were traces of elephant. If one had to randomly mark out a square metre in Chobe today, chances are it will contain evidence of elephant! In total contrast to the jungle and forest trees he repeatedly describes, there is now only stunted scrub and large tracts of pioneer weeds. A few skeletons of what were once magnificent trees stand as stark reminders, indicating where the forest once stood. The short grass plains are now eroded, weed-strewn dustbowls!

Why? The answer is simple. Nature was left to take its course, unchecked! And all this happened in less than 120 years – ecologically speaking, in the blink of an eye. In one paragraph, Selous has unwittingly spoken volumes on the African elephant and its influence on the habitat.

In the controversial debate on elephant control, many supporters of the 'leave it to nature' option will, paradoxically, in the same passionate breath, support the drive to reverse bush encroachment in lowveld reserves. The rapid establishment and aggressive, competitive growth of the encroaching bush continues to threaten the biodiversity of the smaller private reserves in this area. Although these rapid-growing bushes and trees are a form of natural succession in response to over-grazing, fences and/or poor management, if left unchecked, this encroachment eventually chokes seep lines and clearings. The increasing woody vegetation is thirsty, resulting in a drop in the water table. This, in turn, has a negative effect on the quality of the herbaceous layer and its dependent animal species.

The methods employed in eradication and the degree of thinning vary considerably. Most of the clearings are being re-created to resemble as closely as possible the relatively open landscape mosaic seen in aerial photographs in the years prior to fences and domestic animal husbandry. Mostly, the mosaic of mechanical clearing will reflect the landowners' individual needs or taste.

Renowned ecologist RJ Scholes, who conducted an extensive study on bush clearing in the Klaserie Private Nature Reserve, said that we need to remember that the lowveld is a naturally thickly wooded area and if cleared will always try to reach that climax stage. So, once established, these clearings, which are invariably overdone, need to be intensively maintained in order to keep them from reverting to thick bush. Perhaps it is not surprising that many think this is the elephant's role in the ecosystem.

Nowadays it appears it is socially acceptable and quite trendy in conservation circles to champion the fight against bush encroachment. To 'cull' unwanted bushes and trees in an effort to maintain biodiversity or to return the landscape to how it used to be (or, often, how we'd like it to be), to selectively remove trees in the interests of the ecological well-being of a system is totally acceptable. Yet to cull an elephant for the same reasons is anathema. Ironically, those very reserves that created enormous artificial landscapes which they thought should have been created naturally by elephant in the first place, are now doing everything possible to reduce their numbers. For example, nobody ever thought the elephant numbers in the Sabi Sands Reserve would grow from 17 to over 1 000 in 30 years! Needless to say, the elephant are most grateful for, in particular, the beautiful marula and knobthorn trees that were selected to help create these open areas which well-meaning man thought was the right thing to do at the time.

As a result of elephant impact on the larger trees, these clearings bear very little resemblance today to the parkland mosaic they were originally intended to emulate.

And it is going to get worse.

Clearly, anyone with a pragmatic approach to conservation can see there is, in the larger systems, no practical elephant population control option other than culling. In a more hypothetical environment, though, there are only a handful of conservationists out there who don't see contraception as a realistic and eventually viable alternative to culling.

I believe there is an immediate need for extensive exploration of the opportunity of combining the two methods, a balanced mix of culling and contraception, of the bullet and the dart, drug and pill. But the question remains – Who will bell the cat? As

Aesop observed, it's all very well suggesting what should be done, but who will do it?

Traditional elephant culling methods evoke ethical concerns and worldwide emotional reaction. The use of contraception as an alternative to population control of these pachyderms has long been proposed. Initially the proposed contraceptives were hormonal, such as oestrogens, androgens, progesterones and testosterone. But, they produced negative side effects. Amongst others, the contra-indications included prolonged periods when cows were sexually attractive, resulting in mothers being separated from their calves by over-attentive or aggressive bulls. Calf mortality, abortions and other placental complications, as well as cancerous growths, were also observed. It was obvious from this that this avenue had to be abandoned. So the use of hormonal contraceptives was terminated.

The alternative lay with immuno-contraception, namely porcine zona pellucida vaccine (pZp). It is administered intramuscularly, and this basically triggers antibodies, which prevents fertilisation by blocking receptor sites for sperm on the ovum. Tests on a control population have revealed that pZp is effective for twelve months or longer and is completely reversible. The most important advantage of this method is that it can be practically implemented to a relatively large number of elephant in a reasonably short space of time. In practical terms, darts can be administered from a helicopter or a vehicle. Preliminary study on the behaviour of elephant treated with pZp is very encouraging. There is no apparent influence on elephants' social behaviour or migratory patterns, nor is there any change in their external features.

Research results are encouraging and appear to suggest the dart is a truly viable alternative to a bullet. The findings of Delsink *et al.* (2006) – a reduction of as much as 33 per cent in the population growth rate over 10 years – are indeed cause for optimism.

At last it appears there are promising prospects of a solution to the problem of elephant population control. A side issue is that this solution could alter the age structure of the elephant population just as is happening with human populations in some first world countries in Europe. In smaller populations, where intensive monitoring is possible, we may need to select certain cows for breeding on a rational basis.

Research and study in this particular field is ongoing, but it appears that this non-lethal method as a means to effect population control, especially in 'hands on', well-managed reserves, may prove to be a viable option.

I have no doubt that man will help these icons of Africa to avoid self-destruction, and in the process, will help reserves, Olifants included, to maintain their critical biodiversity.

Reflections on Youth and Nature Conservation

Watching a helicopter skilfully herding game into well-prepared capture bomas, you cannot help but stare in awe as the pilot throws the little machine around in amongst the trees. Above the throb of the motor, the occasional 'krrrrrr' can be heard as the rotor blades inevitably clip the highest twigs off the odd knobthorn tree, not unlike the sound of your lawnmower hitting some rough stuff hidden in the grass. The movements, although practised and effortlessly smooth, are dangerously on the edge. At an altitude of a less than 20 metres, there is absolutely no room for error.

As the pilot explained, 'I wear the chopper, it's part of me.' In other words, he didn't fly it, he was one with the machine.

The removal of surplus animals is a last resort and is only employed after scientific, calculated evaluation. Game capture is not a routine part of game management on Olifants, rather it is a facility to call upon as and when required. In fact, we don't budget for, or rely on, income from game capture. The decision and degree of action taken is entirely dependent on ecological motivation. Despite the rational reasoning behind the activity, once the actual mechanics of the capture are in progress, it remains an exhilarating and exciting part of my job as a game ranger and reminds me of why I chose this path.

Press the re-wind button.

As a young schoolkid in suburban Johannesburg, I would take every opportunity to get out into the veld. Thankfully, in those days, the urban sprawl was still contained and in under a

33

15-minute walk from my home I could be in my version of 'Big Game Country'. This piece of savannah bushveld, studded with conglomerate outcrops created by ancient lava flows, resulted in a richly diverse habitat which was home to a healthy number of endemic wildlife species.

Grey duiker, hyraxes, guinea fowl, mongoose and the occasional jackal were common. As if this wasn't enough, in the back of my mind was the old story that the last leopard was thought to have been shot in that area in the early 1950s. Having only recently read Turnbull Kemp's book on leopards, I knew these enigmatic animals were notoriously secretive, so they could be living undetected in my back garden. This added spice to my forays, as I nurtured the thought that, possibly, one or two might still be lurking about. I still wonder now how many large dog paw prints that I saw were rounded off and enlarged slightly, becoming leopard pug marks in my young imagination.

Of course, with such potential for dangerous encounters, I needed to protect myself, so I was armed to the teeth on most occasions. This was serious stuff, so a BSA air rifle and a pocket knife were the bare bones of my armament. The more time I spent in this area, the more I began to understand the basic workings of nature. I learned how and where to find certain animals and plants and would always volunteer to collect animal or plant specimens for school projects. Not surprisingly, I soon became a firm favourite with my biology teachers. One in particular was young and relatively fit and she would often join me on my outings. I will say no more and leave you to paint the picture of student and teacher and youth and nature and ...

These expeditions took me out of the confines of the classroom and into the open air. This was not my only means of escape, either, for in the days prior to TV, videos and CDs, I found much of what I was looking for in the pages of books, which I consumed at a rapid rate. Living in those pages, I would visit other remote areas and learn about their wildlife. I recall that even then I preferred reading factual adventures and experiences by naturalists, explorers and primitive hunters, rather than fiction. My literary taste remains unchanged.

In my imagination, I explored the wildest parts of Africa and far beyond. I went on safari to East Africa with Robert Ruark and there I learned about the horrors of the Mau Mau. I also learned of the arrogant elegance of the Masai whose domestic dogs would later be responsible for transmitting the diseases that completely wiped out the wild dogs *Lycaon pictus* in East Africa.

I followed the Elsa saga and nursed orphan lion cubs in Kenya with the Adamsons. When the weather got too hot, I would monitor a pack of wolves in Siberia and study their social lives, then cross the Bering Straits into Alaska following the caribou migration into the Yukon. Living with the Inuits, I kayaked with them through the pack ice hunting seals while avoiding polar bears. I also learned that the Inuit did more to survive in their environment than the San Bushmen do in theirs. Even today, I read everything I can on Arctic anthropology.

Despite the adventurous life I was leading in the wild world of my imagination, it was back in the cold reality of the classroom, during a lesson called Vocational Guidance, that I realised what I wanted to do and where my future lay.

They say a picture is worth a thousand words. For me, there is much truth in this.

It was the illustration on the cover and not the contents of a journal that grabbed my interest. The journal was loftily titled *'My Loopbaan'* ('My Career'), a cheaply produced publication, thin on content and invariably promoting some technical career opportunity. It was distributed on occasion during vocational guidance and one issue really caught my eye. The cover illustration was strikingly different, promoting a career in nature conservation by picturing a helicopter daringly manoeuvring a group of giraffe in a capture or census operation. The background depicted the typical umbrella thorn savanna of the Serengeti. I'm sure you get the picture and can imagine how deeply it became imprinted on my heart and soul.

As I recall, the artist used blue, beige and white, not exactly the most dynamic, imaginative or attractive colours one would choose to portray a wildlife scene, but somehow the mood and the message was vivid. I knew there and then that someday my future would be in nature conservation.

The next step was to find out how one went about becoming a game ranger and what did one need to get in the queue? I asked everyone I knew but no one could offer a definitive answer.

The broad consensus was that I needed the minimum of a science degree, and that preference was given to married men. Someone explained to me that nepotism was common, so family of those already employed in the Parks stood a better chance than outsiders. Well, that ruled me out. I was only 15 years old and hadn't yet had the guts to ask a girl for a 'real' kiss, let alone approach one with a marriage proposal. Plus, none of my family were employed anywhere near conservation. Most importantly I would only be able to start a degree when I left school in two years' time, which would mean at least another five to six years' delay.

To add to these depressing prospects, one of my siblings' advice wasn't much inspiration either. My eldest brother had just finished his BSc Honours and when I told him I was going to do the same degree, and then go into Nature Conservation, he laughed. He stated I should rather do something else, anything else. He told me that his best friend, who had also just completed his degree, had started working for 'Fauna and Flora' (Provincial Nature Conservation in those days) and the poor chap was sitting on top of a hill counting baboons.

'What a ridiculous job, you must be crazy to do it,' my brother told him. But, this 'crazy' friend of my brother's went on to obtain his doctorate and become the head of the Department of Environmental Affairs and Tourism. The highly respected Dr Feltus Brand came a long way from counting baboons, though sadly he has since passed away.

Some of you may remember an old radio commercial which went something like this: 'Umfolozi, Hluhluwe, Mkuzi, when roads become river beds, what does a game ranger need in country like this? He needs a mind like a map, a four-wheel-drive and the sureness of Shell!' It was broadcast in the early 1970s or thereabouts, and used to get me so choked up that I taped it and played it over and over again. Meanwhile, my more normal friends taped Deep Purple, Black Sabbath and Pink Floyd and played them over and over again. The walls of most of my friends' rooms were decorated with photos of rock stars, sports cars, girls, more girls and mementos of their own sporting successes.

These were all normal reflections of teenage fashions, tastes and emotional leanings of the time. But not where I was concerned. My aberration knew no bounds. On one wall I had painted an African sunset, with umbrella thorn acacias and a dead leadwood tree, complete with characteristically twisted branches. Under the one prominent tree, I had a blazing fire on the go with two men sitting by its side. Finally, to complete the scene, there was a short-wheel-base Land Rover parked close by, its unmistakable profile silhouetted against the orange glow of the sinking sun. In those days it was the only vehicle I wanted, and the bush was the only place I wanted to be. Those soft-top Landies cost exactly R2 080 brand new! I know, because every day for months I took the no 47 bus into town just to go and look at one.

On the other wall was the pelt of an enormous white-tailed mongoose that I found on the side of the road in Zululand. It had no doubt been killed by a vehicle and the pungent musky mongoose smell never washed out of the fur. I didn't care, I got used to it. But nobody else got used to it, and I was often on my own in my room.

I have never allowed the grass to grow under my feet. This has resulted on occasion in my being accused of being impatient or impulsive or both, traits which are only now starting to mellow as the years pass. In my youth, however, it was difficult to control my natural tendencies as it just wasn't in my nature to dream and wait for things to happen. I wanted to be a game ranger as soon as possible: tomorrow, preferably. I had to do something about it, so when I heard on the grapevine that Rhodesia (Zimbabwe) was looking for young tsetse control officers and that becoming a game ranger in that country was a more practical procedure, I bought a return ticket from Johannesburg to Salisbury (now Harare) via Botswana. I was 15 years old and the ticket cost R26. No cents.

Armed with my new passport and the address of the Rhodesian conservation department, I boarded the train, went straight to my compartment and laid claim to the middle bunk. Filled with excitement at being able to look at the bush from this position, I lay on my stomach with my chin on my fist, as the train slowly pulled out of the station

I didn't know what to expect or how to go about my quest, but I needed to do this thing and find out exactly what the situation was. Waving goodbye to my parents, I got the distinct feeling my excitement wasn't shared, as despite their smiles they couldn't hide their concern as I left for a destination far further from home than ever before in my young life.

The train journey took me for the first time through the beautiful bushveld of the western Transvaal and then on through the mopane scrubland of eastern Botswana, where I spied numerous antelope from my middle bunk position. I think my neck has a permanent kink in it to this day from lying on that bunk staring fixedly out of the window. Finally, on the second day, we crossed into Rhodesia and were in Salisbury the following morning.

I stayed with friends of a friend that evening and experienced the warm welcome and generous hospitality that was so typically Rhodesian. Very early the next day, I was given a lift into the central area of town near Causeway, where the head office of the Department of Wildlife was situated. Salisbury hadn't quite woken up yet and nothing was open. To pass the time I hung around a nearby park that had incorporated some indigenous bush into its landscaping. I recollect being absolutely fascinated when I saw a common duiker in the middle of this small, spotlessly clean city. Later, when the offices opened, I walked straight in and along the corridor to a large door bearing the sign 'Director'. I remember that it stood slightly ajar and as I knocked on it, I inadvertently pushed it further open. But I was too shy to walk in so I hung back until a man's voice said, 'Come in ...'

I went in, walked straight up to his desk and introduced myself, telling him without hesitation or pause where I was from and why I was there. He was very relaxed and smiled a lot, obviously having summed up my situation in a matter of moments.

Redrawn by the author from memories of a bedroom wall

An intuitive and empathetic man, he listened to the words that tumbled from my mouth in an unending flow, until he felt it was his turn. He made me feel completely at ease, and proceeded with patience to explain that I would need to get my O-levels and then emigrate to Rhodesia.

Once these formalities were out of the way, I would then be taken on as a Cadet Ranger for two years, after which I'd probably get my own section. His only concern was that I may get lonely in the bush, as there were times when I'd be away from civilisation for up to six months at a time. That is when it dawned on me why married men get preference. Not once did he ask why I hadn't made an appointment to see him or detail the expected norms of interview and assessment. I was so obviously completely naïve in the ways of accepted procedures, he understood that the desperately keen face in front of him meant no disrespect through lack of protocol. Hell, I was keen, and he could see that. But, the doors to my new life as a game ranger were going to remain closed for a while longer, that was obvious even through my heavily rose-tinted sunglasses.

Returning to South Africa a few days later, much to the relief of my parents, I put my head down and focused on my schoolwork, knowing now there were no shortcuts, yet comforted by my new knowledge of alternatives. Political developments in Rhodesia at the time didn't bode well for that country's future, and I was soon to realise that emigration wasn't an option. I wouldn't be going north.

My father remained worried about my all-consuming passion. As a restaurateur and chef, he never understood what I saw in the African bush, though my mother did, as she had grown up in the country. My Aunt Joan, who had recently visited and thoroughly enjoyed Mala Mala, had gained some firsthand experience of what was driving this fervour I had for the bush and extended a helping hand. Knowing full well I was far too young and underqualified, she helped me compile an application for employment at Mala Mala, which was duly posted off. Bless her heart, she needed to do something to give me hope and to shut me up for a while. Nothing came of her endeavours and on many an occasion my father would take me aside and say, 'You must-a open-a da ristorante, Mario; me, I teach-a you to cook-a da food.'

All credit to my father, he did teach me to cook a little. But, as I came to understand the effects of the demanding work and late hours that running restaurants had on my parents, I also realised I had no desire to 'open-a da ristorante'.

I wanted to be a game ranger.

I think that even then I had a glimmering of understanding that being a game ranger had its rewards in quality of life. I began to believe then, as I do today, that a great motivator in a career as a conservationist is the feeling of satisfaction that comes with knowing that in some small way, each day, you are making a difference, you are contributing to environmental conservation. Ultimately, you hope that through your efforts, you'll leave the world one day in better shape than when you arrived. The responsibility as custodian of a precious wilderness can be weighty at times, but I find it fits nicely and is comfortable to carry, like the feel of a well-designed backpack with you on a beautiful hiking trail. I could not verbalise those thoughts when I was 15, but though immature in their formation, they were there.

Remember my 'Big Game Country' close to home? Well, though somewhat smaller nowadays, it enjoys formal status and is known as the 'Klipriviersberg Nature Reserve'. I'm pleased to say that even though some 35 years have passed, it is still one of the most naturally beautiful areas around Johannesburg.

Overlooking this stretch of wilderness near the suburb of Linmeyer, lived a man who was my mentor when I was a young eager beaver. The last time we spoke, which was a number of years ago now, I was glad to hear he is still living there. Desmond Prout-Jones was an honorary nature conservation officer at the time and is credited for his extensive work on large birds of prey, particularly the African fish eagle, on which he has published two books. His passion for wildlife was infectious, which of course rubbed off on me. He was one of very few people in the country at the time permitted to capture and ring wild raptors, and it was a privilege to have been allowed to go along with him when he did. We spent a lot of time together ringing various raptors, in and around Johannesburg. I will never forget those trips; they were some of the most wonderful learning experiences for me, particularly with regard to raptor identification and their conservation. I owe a lot to his patience and guidance, for which I am ever grateful.

Desmond took me under his wing, so to speak, and recognising my commitment to pursuing a career in nature conservation, wrote my very first reference.

Seven years after my Aunt Joan wrote my first apparently abortive application, I re-applied to Mala Mala. By then I had worked as a ranger at Thornybush Game Reserve, and had hunted professionally for Magna Fauna Safaris on Letaba Ranch under the legendary Steve Kruger. The telephone conversation in response to my written application went like this.

'Hello Mario, this is Tim Farrell from Mala Mala head office. How are you?'

'Well, thank you, and yourself?' I replied.

'Fine, thanks. Mario, I just want to let you know that I have your application here and want you to understand that it is against our policy to employ rangers who have worked on other reserves. We choose to mould our staff around to our way of doing things and so prefer to start with raw material, so to speak.'

My heart dropped.

'However, seeing as your application to work with us when you were 15 years old is still on record ... when can you come in for an interview?'

Mala Mala. I spent over two of my happiest working years at this world-famous destination, gaining valuable experience dealing with people from all corners of the globe. Rubbing shoulders with the rich and famous was a far cry from what the media hype leads you to believe. Mala Mala humbles all but the most arrogant, and out in the bush the social playing fields were levelled, bringing out the best in people, whoever they were.

I have often been asked how Mala Mala compared to some of the other reserves that I went on to visit or manage. Everybody was curious to find out what it was that made this game reserve so particularly special. In my opinion, it is simply this: Mala

Mala is the closest you will come to experiencing what I imagine Hemingway's Africa to have been like. There's nothing pseudo about Mala Mala.

Mala Mala does not pander to political correctness in its décor or its style of operation. Nor is there any embarrassment, real or posed, for the colonial African influence, or the fact that Princess Alice shot her first lion there in the 'old days'. Mala Mala is as close to the real African experience as you will get in a two-night experience. They have managed to create a perfect balance between rugged comfort and luxury, slap bang in a natural, wild environment. Visitors to Mala Mala almost invariably empathised with the formula and loved it.

Having said all this, I realise it has been a long time since I worked there, so some of my fond recollections may be tainted with nostalgia. I have no doubt, due to market pressures, that some things may have changed a little. But, what won't change is that Mala Mala will always remain the yardstick or barometer by which all others are measured. Forget the chocolates on your pillow, invisible staff, gleaming overpowered 4x4s or the superficial trappings of so many of the modern wannabe lodges that use cosmetics like these to cover their blemishes. Mala Mala has never needed any make up. She's just one of those uniquely natural real beauties.

FOOTNOTE

I never did see a leopard in the Klipriviersberg area, but not too far away in the outlying smallholdings near Krugersdorp, reliable sightings of these big cats were confirmed. Within sight of the smoky haze of Johannesburg, the Magaliesberg still boasts healthy leopard numbers. In the village of Kosmos near Hartbeespoort Dam, residents reliably report sightings of leopards in the surrounding hills and, yes, on occasion in their back gardens!

Overseeing the recent helicopter-led game capture operation and actually living that cover illustration I had seen in the classroom all those years ago, I was suddenly aware that the images and emotions evoked by it were still as sharp and poignant as ever. I realise now how little things have changed, except my taste in 4x4 vehicles. Apologies to the Land Rover 90 SWB 'Rag Top'.

Elephants ... Their Future and Our Future

OCTOBER 2008 ... ONGOING!

The problem with the elephant problem is that we have not yet come up with the elephant question, never mind the elephant answer. At best, we can offer some constructive suggestions, at worst we can confuse ourselves with a multiplicity of answers to an array of questions to which we are not totally committed.

The question closest to the core of the problem, and the one most often asked among scientists and laymen alike is: 'What motivates elephant to completely destroy so many mature productive trees, some of which are hundreds of years old?'

For example, in our area elephant appear to focus on, or show a preference for, two species in particular. Marula *Sclerocarya birrea* and knobthorn *Acacia nigrescens* are prime targets, though the damage and destruction are not strictly limited to a select number of tree species. But what on earth drives elephant to destroy vegetation that could potentially provide them with food in the future, if less wastefully utilised? Another factor is that there appears to be a seasonal influence on their choice. In fact, the drier it gets the less discerning their taste; they will eat almost anything green. Anything green, that is, except the shepherd's tree *Boscia albitrunca*, arguably one of the most palatable browse trees in our semi-arid bushveld, which appears to be relatively under-utilised or damaged by elephant. When you next get a chance, pick a leaf or two, chew them and you will see what I'm getting at. The taste is not unlike spinach and there's no trace of bitterness so it is acceptable even to our fussy palates. Yet the pachyderm palate is not pleased by it, for elephant don't appear to utilise this excellent fodder tree.

This fastidious display of selective feeding is not confined to our reserve. The virtually identical lack of interest in the shepherd's tree is found among the elephant in the Tuli Block of Botswana, which bears physical testimony to this phenomenon.

Elephant have inhabited an enormous tract of land known as the Tuli Circle for many years. Detailed and accurate reports of their presence there go as far back as the 1870s when FC Selous hunted them for their ivory in that area. His meticulous records, to which I have referred elsewhere, indicate that the number of elephant there in those days was far lower than we find today. Anyway, back to the trees ... having spent four years in that area and based on my observations in that time and place, I feel I can compare the elephant situation there to what is happening here. Who knows, there may be something significant to learn from this comparative exercise.

When I left Tuli in 1983 there were only two decent-sized knobthorns left standing in a shallow depression at the bottom of the Tuli Lodge airstrip, and I doubt very much that they are still there today. It would be safe to assume, then, that elephant were responsible for the eradication of knobthorn and marula trees in the Tuli Block. I am also prepared to wager that not a single baobab tree with a trunk of less than one metre in diameter survives there today. Conversely, the area is recognised for its ubiquitous shepherd's trees, with both the *albitrunca* and *foetida* species being common, the former more so.

In total contrast, there isn't a single mopane tree or shrub in Tuli that doesn't bear scars as evidence of elephant utilisation, and the same applies to the cluster leaf *Terminalia prunioides*. Yet both species appear to be extremely resilient and coppice well in response to persistent elephant feeding pressure. In fact, were it not for the predominance of this woody component making up the bulk of the vegetation type, the elephant would have either migrated or starved to death by now. The same cannot be said for the red bushwillow *Combretum apiculatum*, marula and *Commiphora* species which make up a large percentage of the woody vegetation component here on Olifants; they're just not as hardy. I have a great deal of faith in the nutritional and resilient properties of mopane *Colophospermum mopane*, and I have no doubt that this single species is the arboreal lifeline in the vegetation that allows Tuli to support its relatively high population of elephant.

We will not be able to mirror this ability here on Olifants, given our predominant vegetation type.

Having now focused on mopane and its beneficial contribution, let me expand by sharing a further observation with you. It also takes me back to the Tuli area and I believe it will also help to create a better understanding of the value of mopane as a source of winter browse, which has significant relevance to this discussion and the hypothesis I am presenting.

It was nearing the end of the dry season and I was tasked with supervising the building of rock gabions for anti-soil erosion work near the Pitsani Valley. Just to illustrate that it's not only in the corporate world that bosses want results yesterday, I was under instruction to ensure the work was completed before the onset of the rainy season. So we were all under pressure and my guys were working hard. They say an army marches on its stomach; believe me, so do men labouring in temperatures hovering around 40° C.

To supplement their maize ration with meat, the men asked me to shoot an impala for them, which I did. About 40 minutes later they were skinning and butchering the animal in the shade of a nearby croton tree. As always, I am interested in the physical condition of any animal shot, in particular those shot for human consumption. Looking at the carcass of this impala ram, I was absolutely amazed at the quantity of fat around the kidneys, and also the criss-cross weave of fat on the rumen, shaped much like the protective foam mesh you find on papaya packaging to prevent bruising. I asked the chap doing the butchering to please open its rumen, as this amount of fat was an unusual find on game at this time of year. It was already late into the dry season, and with apparently so little vegetation on the veld, I was curious to see what this animal had been eating to maintain this level of condition. The rumen was duly slit open and its contents revealed. I'm guessing you guessed right already. The rumen was stuffed full of masticated mopane leaves. Scratching around revealed an insignificant amount of grass material and other unidentifiable vegetation. Mopane leaves constituted approximately 90 per cent of the impala's rumen content.

As an aside to this revelation, as midday approached so did lunchtime, and I became peckish. With the nearest Wimpy about 300 kilometres away, I had to think of something else. A shovel was selected and scrubbed spotlessly clean using river sand and water, thus providing me with a frying pan. Some of the impala fat taken from the kidneys was placed onto the shovel which was then laid on top of a bed of hot coals that had been taken from the main fire. Soon the fat had melted and began to sizzle. The liver was cut into thin strips, lightly salted and fried in the hot fat. Once done, it was eaten with maize meal which had already been cooked in an enormous communal cast iron pot on the main fire. In Afrikaans, they say *'honger is die beste kos'*, well, hunger may be the best food, but this was better than the best and to this day I prepare impala liver no other way.

But, I digress.

Based on observation and what I hope is rational conjecture, my hypothesis is simple. The predominant tree species that characterise the Balule area, particularly our own Olifants game reserve, cannot and will not withstand the unrelenting feeding pressure from the present number of elephant, let alone the potential growth of this population.

I also believe our predominant soil type, which is the foundation that characterises an ecosystem, will not succeed to or support a grassland ecosystem. So, when the trees go, scrubland and not grassland (*à la* Tsavo) will replace the landscape we know today. Areas that have high numbers of elephant, and which are mainly composed of mopane woodland, or have deeper soils, higher rainfall and a slightly milder climate, could very well climax into grassland savannah. The biodiversity of our reserve, however, will continue to be adversely affected, until only a few hardy species are able to eke out an existence.

We live a lifespan that ecologically, relative to time as we understand it, is the blinking of an eye. We understand that succession cycles in an ecosystem may take hundreds or even thousands of years to go full circle. Further, we have no right to interfere with natural processes, even though out of necessity, and cognisant of the consequences, we do. Enough of us watch National Geographic to have had this well and truly drummed into us, but, and here is the big BUT, the underlying geology of an area is pretty much cast in stone, so to speak.

It is primarily the characteristics of the soil which ultimately dictate what ecosystem it will support. Nothing the elephant do to the habitat now, or ever, will change the substrate to support a beneficially alternative ecosystem on Olifants. The potential is in the soil and ignoring this fundamental fact will result in irreversible damage to this reserve.

Maybe the resultant 'rockscape' type ecosystem won't take that much getting used to. Maybe we could modify those 'palm tree' suburban cell phone masts to resemble the beautiful trees that characterise the lowveld as we know it. Maybe we just have to interfere with nature one way or the other, as while elephants may have positive effects on some aspects of the African ecosystem over time, if we leave the elephants to their own devices in our Olifants 'postage stamp', the shaping of the ecosystem will not be positive. Our substrate just won't allow it.

So here we are, interfering as little as possible and documenting the downward spiral. But we ARE doing what we can to protect our future. For example, for three years we have been 'wire mesh wrapping' 1 000 marula and knobthorn trees as an initial experiment to protect them against ring-barking by elephant. Not one tree so treated has been ring-barked to date.

But, just as you think you have one answer to one question, another emerges from the paradoxical pachyderm. None of our 1 000 experimental 'wired and wrapped' trees have been ringbarked. BUT a dozen or so of the medium-to-small trees have been pushed over by testosterone-loaded elephant bulls. None of these trees were fed on at all.

Why?

Next question, please ...

Gerrit Scheepers

JUNE 2009

Let me introduce veterinarian Dr Gerrit Scheepers. He features regularly in this book. He and I go back a long way. It must be around a quarter of a century or so and not only is he one of the finest wildlife vets I have ever worked with, but he is also a close friend and fishing buddy. In the latter context, I have noticed he has a remarkably wide arm span when describing his achievements, whilst in his areas of specialisation, his modesty is legend.

When my wife Meagan and I moved down to the Lowveld from Botswana, we were obliged by veterinary law to vaccinate any dogs being brought into South Africa. This was particularly important, as we were arriving to take up a post in the Timbavati Private Nature Reserve. Even Meagan's utterly beloved and remarkably diminutive lapdog Squealer, who was no bigger than a lion's furball but had an infinite capacity for unconditional love, would need to be jabbed. My best buddy, Shilo, spent his life with me in the bush, so it was critical that apart from the routine jabs, he be vaccinated against rabies. This horrible disease raises its ugly head from time to time in this area, and any dog which may come into contact with wild animals is at high risk.

I contacted the nearest vet we could find and it happened to be Gerrit, in Phalaborwa. He had recently qualified and had established a small clinic in partnership with another veterinarian, Dr Sampie Ras. After some small talk, we chatted a little about relevant matters and, well, then maybe more than a little about the common interest we discovered, namely fishing. It turned out that Gerrit spent as much time as possible in his rubber duck in pursuit of big fish, preferably beyond the breakers off the Mozambique coast near Vilanculos.

In between exaggerations of how big the fish were that he'd caught on his last trip (using that remarkable fisherman's arm span of his) and while avoiding poking our eyes out with his brandished syringe, he attended to the dogs with the necessary vaccinations and soon, we were on our way back to the reserve.

Squealer was in the dog box, as he had tried to bite Gerrit. In this little mutt's case, this meant muzzling, a far from easy job. The back end was remarkably similar to the front end, unless the tail was wagging, which it most certainly wasn't at that time. The other longitudinal identification was teeth, which we waited to emerge from somewhere deep within the tangle of fur and which we used to locate the head and the target for the muzzle. It's strange; while we related to Gerrit from our very first meeting, Squealer never did.

Meagan and I became so absorbed in our work at Timbavati that time just flew by unnoticed. Almost two years elapsed since our dogs were vaccinated and their jabs were now overdue. I phoned Phalaborwa Animal Clinic to make an appointment, hoping but not expecting that Gerrit was still there. We hadn't heard from him for a couple of years, so I was a little surprised when he answered the phone. When we had met initially, he struck me as a dynamic and ambitious veterinarian, someone who may have found small town life inhibiting, and I didn't expect him to still be in Phalaborwa. I cordially asked how he was, and before I could get the subject onto things piscatorial, his answer gave things an entirely different and unexpected perspective.

'I'm fine now,' he said. 'I'm in remission, there's no sign of any more cancer.'

'I had no idea,' I truthfully mumbled in reply.

'Don't worry,' he said. 'Now tell me, how is Shilo?'

So, there we had a man, 25 years old, who had just been through two years of hell with cancer, but he didn't want to know how I was, he wanted to know about my dog, and remembered him by name. That knocked my socks off. If anyone had any idea then how much Shilo meant to me, it was Gerrit. If anyone can understand now what an impression that made on me then, they'd understand why there remains a very special bond between him and me. This is the same Gerrit who will feature in my tales of a porcupine-quilled lion, a buffaloes' gentleman's club, snare removal from elephant and zebra and so many unsung songs of this magic land.

Gerrit, I salute you.

There's No Substitute for Enthusiasm

NOVEMBER 2004 –

ABOUT SIX MONTHS BEFORE THE KLASERIE FENCE CAME DOWN

One of the most significant conservation initiatives undertaken by Olifants River Game Reserve was the successful introduction and subsequent establishment of white rhino in Balule. Originally, Olifants shareholders had no plans of expanding this project beyond our own boundaries, but from an initial group of five rhino we now have well over 30 individuals on the reserve. This number has been boosted on occasion when a few freeloaders come in from the surrounding area to Olifants' winter 'soup kitchen'. The supplementary feed, in the form of lucerne, was supplied when we were still fenced off from the greater system, and in those days, it would take less than a week from the day the first bales were distributed to the rhino all arriving to feed. As the fence hadn't been removed, their foraging area was limited.

The numbers of rhino grew to the point where they were unable to sustain themselves on the natural vegetation in the dry months, and were therefore totally reliant on this feeding programme. It soon became necessary to capture and translocate some of them to outside game reserves and other regions within Balule, in order to reduce the costs of feeding and minimise the pressure that their increasing numbers were placing on the veld. The latter would be of little concern later when the system opened, but at that time, we took advantage of being able to select by ground-level observation which rhino to move for translocation within Balule. In a larger, open system, the process of having to select from free-roaming rhino would have involved extensive aerial observation and equally extensive financial considerations!

Once the removal of the Klaserie fence was imminent, we knew we had limited time left in which to capture and move a group of rhino before they dispersed into the greater system. The total rhino population in Balule at the time was confined to the Olifants region. A suggestion was tabled to do an internal translocation to speed up natural distribution and spread them around within Balule, in areas identified as being suitable.

Of course, every region wanted to have rhino, but not all applicants boasted enough of the specific habitat type that we felt would accommodate white rhino, and as there was no time to employ consultants to do specialist studies, we went ahead on gut feel and experience.

We looked at a number of options and visited the regions that were keen to adopt rhino. Unfortunately, most of the Balule reserve consists of arid bushveld, with shallow orthic soils characterising the substrate. Only about 60 per cent of the Balule area is able to produce the quantity and quality of grass suitable for white rhino, and much of this is marginal. What we really needed was an area as close as possible to the right habitat, this being established by comparing the area on Olifants, where they were at the time, to where they would be released. That was all we had to go on. It was going to be interesting to monitor this aspect once the rhino were released as they would either show us just how far off the mark we were, or how well we had understood their needs and habitat preference. Most importantly at this stage, though, we needed to pen the rhino for a while prior to releasing them. There were no bomas or pens in the areas suitable for rhino, and we didn't have the time to build one, so we had to come up with an alternative workable solution.

As I was chiefly responsible for determining which and how many rhino were to be moved, I needed to be reasonably sure that all the necessary, practical logistics to effect the operation were in place. I also had to ensure that the move be done with the minimum risk of stress or injury to these precious animals.

First in the queue of keen recipients was the young warden of the York region of Balule. He was so persistent and enthusiastic that you would have thought the rhino were to be his personal acquisitions. Rian Ahlers was not only there with passion and commitment, but had already come up with an unconventional yet practical alternative to house the rhino on York while they settled down. He proposed using some old ostrich pens that he would reinforce with three strands of electrified wire. These dilapidated pens looked like something that wouldn't hold a determined turkey escapee, let alone an ostrich. So, in terms of the accepted design standards for pens able to hold animals as powerful as white rhino, they left much to be desired. But these facilities were all there was; it was them or nothing, so we shifted the emphasis from fortification and strength to space and comfort. If we could create an environment in which the rhino felt happy, they would not try to break out, and thus there was an outside chance we could pull it off. The one consolation was that this region appeared to be suitable habitat for white rhino, and that if they did break out prematurely, they could feel right at home and stay in the area anyhow.

Rian went to work immediately, and within a week he was ready to receive his new guests. He had converted the pens into a welcoming environment complete with mud wallow and drinking trough and had extended the enclosure to include two shady acacia trees, where the mud wallow was sited. The mud was brought in by tractor and trailer from miles away, but proved to be well worth the effort. Shade cloth was placed on the 'busy' side where curious onlookers might gather, this to give the rhino a measure of privacy and reduce stress. Now all that remained was to identify which rhinos to capture. My main concern was compatibility, as it was essential that these animals got along well with each other, particularly as they'd be tested under relatively unnatural, confined conditions.

Fortunately, we were feeding nearly 30 rhino on Olifants at the time – one group at Rhino Pan and the other at Hide Dam. This would make selection and capture so much easier and less demanding; at the same time, reduced capture-stress followed by compatibility once in the pens would ensure a high probability that the rhino would settle down quickly. So we settled down to study the rhino and their interaction with each other in their natural state. Rian and his fiancée, Melodie Bates, were actively involved in the preliminary monitoring and then with the capture and translocation a few days later.

We decided on a group of three young rhinos who were conspicuous by their closeness. They would arrive to feed together and eat without aggressive interaction, and during the heat of the day, the three of them would lie up together in the shade.

Although the sex ratio wasn't ideal, comprising two bulls and a cow, in all other respects we could not have made a better selection. This was proved when they were placed in the ostrich pens together, where they appeared to draw comfort from each other in this strange new 'cage'. Fortunately these rhino were also familiar with those thin wires that 'bit' you if you touched them, as the electrified Klaserie fence was right in the middle of their old home range. So, unless they were extremely unhappy and made a concerted effort to break out, I was reasonably confident that Rian's meticulous preparation of the enclosure should be enough hold them.

Rian slept at the pens in the back of his pick-up truck, which Melodie didn't mind, knowing how much the success of this project meant to him, and that he wanted to monitor the rhino until they were completely settled. Within a week they had got so used to him that he was able to stand in the pens and spread their feed, while they patiently waited a few metres away. A week after that he was able to touch the one bull, an incredible experience. The mud wallow proved to be just what the doctor ordered, as well. They loved it, and spent a lot of their time wallowing in it. After several weeks, the rhino were apparently well settled, so much so that as soon as the grass had grown enough from the first rains, Rian felt confident enough to release them, which he duly did.

The three rhino were passively released by simply cutting the wire enclosure of the ostrich pens. That same night they moved out, making their way back to Olifants, where they spent the next couple of days sussing things out. After having a good look around the Palm Loop area, they came onto Warthog Pan, where they drank. From there they made their way across the railroad, back to where they remembered being fed, only to find we had stopped feeding a month before.

Compared to the York region, there wasn't much around this neck of the woods, so they programmed their inborn direction finders, turned around, and headed straight back to York, to where an anxious Rian was waiting with open arms.

To upgrade the ostrich pens had cost R7 000; the translocation and capture costs amounted to R30 000 and the feed was another R5 000. So, for a total outlay of R42 000, three rhino valued then at over half a million rand were successfully introduced to another region of Balule. The credit for this success can be attributed almost entirely to an enthusiastic young warden and his passion for white rhino. Rian demonstrated that not everything needs to be done by the book; that there are times when old-fashioned enthusiasm wins through. In fact, the young rangers I have employed throughout my career can be placed in two categories: the academics and the enthusiasts, rarely a mixture of both. Enthusiasm, I can honestly say, more often than not, won and produced the goods.

Recent sightings in the York region indicate that up to seven rhino have been recorded by game viewing operators in the area. It appears that not only are they happy with our assessment of what we thought was good white rhino country, they have gone and communicated this to other white rhino.

All they needed was to be brought there and shown the place, nature did the rest.

How 'Tau Kopje' Got its Name

JULY 1998

What's in a name? Why do we name certain locations or features in the bush? Well, before GPS co-ordinates, they were all we had as reference points to get around or to calculate relative positions. Also, I suspect that this naming syndrome was and is a perfect excuse to use an exotic or onomatopoeic name that has a traditional or African ring to it. Despite the significance of most place names whose origins were born of association, or were appropriately pertinent at the time, the passion inevitably wanes. Over time, they merely become points of reference, without too much thought as to why that name was given in the first place. Others, however, will linger in the significance of their meaning just that little bit longer. Then there are those places whose names will never fade.

One name in particular that comes to mind, and is indelibly etched in the minds of nearly every South African, is a small town known as 'Tweebuffelsfontein'. This name is the shortened version of the original 'Twee-buffels-met-een-skoot-mors-dood-geskiet-fontein', which is Afrikaans for 'Two buffaloes shot stone dead with one shot Fountain'.

The reason this name will be remembered and talked about is not only because of its unusual length, but also because of the feat it commemorates.

Imagine a bullet from an old single-shot muzzle-loading gun being responsible for this legendary achievement. The projectile was in all likelihood a home-moulded lead ball, a little bigger than a marble, driven by black powder at a muzzle velocity of around 350 metres per second. In terms of ballistics and modern standards, this is so slow you could almost watch its trajectory, and so inferior that you would not be legally permitted (without back-up) to hunt buffalo with such weaponry. The projectiles of modern hunting rifles are more accurate, better constructed, and leave the muzzle at more than twice the velocity and energy than that of a muzzle loader.

Even so, duplicating this feat today, using the most modern hunting weapon, would be extremely difficult, so, two buffalo killed instantly with one lead ball was indeed hunting's equivalent of David and Goliath!

Returning to naming matters closer to home, when neighbouring landowners and Olifants shareholders, Miles and Jetje Japhet, acquired the adjacent farm 'Klipheuwel', they created a beautiful reserve which they called 'Dinidza', the Shona word for Pel's fishing owl. These magnificent birds are specialised hunters whose habitat requirements are quite specific, and although a relatively common sight on Dinidza and on the Balule section of Olifants River, they are uncommon elsewhere. So it is an appropriate name, fitting in every respect.

The property has a generous river frontage of some three-and-a-half kilometres, with a wide floodplain and associated riparian vegetation. As a counterpoint, most of the area inland comprises hilly bushveld, consisting of Commiphora woodland, studded with intriguing outcrops of granite or soapstone boulders. The diverse topography is rugged, featuring numerous hidden valleys and incredibly interesting nooks and crannies with unique vegetation. Needless to say, Dinidza is anything but monotonous to explore. Over time, some of its more prominent or interesting features were given names, usually inspired by endemic animals or birds, or as was the case in the following instance, by association. The most significant and most popular lookout-cum-viewpoint on this reserve is undoubtedly 'Tau Kopje', and this is how it got its name.

'Tau' is Tswana for lion and 'Kopje' is old Afrikaans for small hill. Neither language is used much on Dinidza, and the naming had less to do with the criteria of suitability, location or language but more to do with incidental association.

Jetje wanted an elevated view of a lovely waterhole named 'Nyosi Pan' and the surrounding open plain. The discreet, non-intrusive viewpoint she envisaged could only be facilitated by building a short road to access the crest of a nearby hill. I was asked to take a look at their proposal for the location of the road and to advise if it would be possible to construct it for them. As this simple track would be used so infrequently as to have little or no negative impact on the surrounding ecology, I agreed.

Bear with me while I digress for a moment to tell you about the naming of this waterhole as well. 'Nyosi' means bees or honey in Tsonga, the language spoken by the local Shangaan people. The pan was christened when a resident hive of notorious African honey bees left us in no doubt as to who owned the spot. The swarm had established a hive in the hollow of a large knobthorn tree that grew on the edge of this pan. We accidentally disturbed it when the 17 tonne CAT 966 front-end loader we were using to deepen the waterhole accidentally bumped the tree. To the bees, the bump must have been right off their equivalent of a Richter scale and the disruption to the hive's integrity must have been severe. Retaliation was instantaneous! The massive machine was set upon by the plucky insects, which were so determined with their attack that the operator had to have a net placed over the cab in order to get any work done henceforth. Since then I have noticed substantial traces of dried mud on the trunk of this knobthorn tree, indicating that the odd elephant had tried to use it as a rubbing post. I can only imagine that these unfortunate pachyderms were just as aggressively attacked as we were, and were then obliged to look for another back-scratcher somewhere else.

Although making a road to the point overlooking the pan would be a relatively simple job, I told Jetje that I wouldn't be able to do it immediately, as I had promised to run a half marathon representing the Hoedspruit Running Club on the weekend. My alternative as a resident member of this local community might have been a suitable contribution of an impala carcass or a handful of game drives as prizes. Participation in the run was the least complicated option, I thought.

This 'Wildsfees' fair is an annual wildlife festival centred on game auctions, game farming, tourism and related industries in and around this part of the lowveld. For the small community of Hoedspruit, it is also an excellent opportunity to promote other traditional wares and local skills. It's the time to see who has the best-designed braai grid, who has distilled the most potent 'mampoer' or who is the kudu poo-spitting champion, all that sort of thing.

The fact is, though, there's serious content and intent over and above having fun, and that is the community's focus on the marketing of live game and the promotion of eco-tourism. Having promised to support the local running club, there was no way I could let them down. So, bearing in mind my athletic commitments of the next day, I decided I would go out and mark out the planned road on Dinidza. It wouldn't take too long at all, I reasoned, and getting it done now would mean my chaps could do the bulk of the clearing while I was away doing my community duty.

Following well-worn game paths, I made my way through some fairly open bush, and kept driving until I reached the base of the hill. Parking the vehicle in a spot of shade, I took off my windbreaker and threw it over my rifle, which was leaning, barrel down against the passenger seat. Then I pulled the backrest forward and grabbed my panga, which is always kept behind the seat and slowly moved up to where the proposed road would begin and started up the hill.

Using the panga, I began cutting smaller shrubs and bushes. This task went quite quickly, and as the road being marked wasn't going to be more than 100 metres in length when complete, it wasn't long before I approached the crest of the little hill. Here it opened up, and taking in the view, I could see exactly what Miles and Jetje envisaged. The site was spectacular, offering a commanding view over a relatively large open plain. Yet, despite the position's prominence, it would create minimal, if any, disturbance to the game below as they approached from all directions to slake their thirst or wallow in the cooling mud on the periphery of Nyosi Pan. It also didn't matter from which direction the wind came; the elevation was enough to ensure any scent would be carried over the heads of the game.

There were only a couple of thorny saplings left to remove, and as I cut one of them, its hooked thorns somehow got snagged in my sock. I bent over and wiggled the offending sapling about until I managed to disentangle it. Then, gingerly holding the stem between two fingers, I straightened up sharply and turned to throw it over my shoulder and out of the way.

As I did this, the 'Meaning of Life' took a sharp right turn.

No more than a couple of metres away, totally unexpected, a lioness that had been crouching behind me got up out of the grass that had completely concealed her approach. Startled, she grunted with a guttural growl that seemed to come from the root of her tail, and then she bolted away downhill, collecting a second lioness on the way down. Their departure was followed closely by some choice expletives and my panga, which clattered harmlessly on the rocks behind them. Incredible, I thought, they must have been stalking me for quite a while. I wondered how long they had been watching me. I hadn't a clue. What was chilling was the fact that they could have pounced on me at any time.

Fortunately for me, the lions got just as big a fright as I did and I was so relieved when they ran away, that I didn't want to lose the advantage, so I maintained the false bravado, keeping up the momentum of my attack and the volume of my rhetoric. I kept my eyes on them, shouting the universally effective and as yet unchallenged, 'Voetsek', as well as various unprintables while going down the hill in a side-stepping gait. Dry-mouthed with fear by now, my tongue was reluctant to detach itself from the roof of my mouth, and I felt a need to hurl things other than invective at the fleeing felines.

Every now and then I would attempt to pick up a rock but the preponderance of aptly named soap stones made it a pointless exercise, probably compounded by the perspiration that coursed across the palms of my hands. I was clearly trying to do too much.

Eyes on the lions and off the ground, too much speed, going

sideways down a steep slope on rough terrain ... I was an acci-
dent about to happen, it was inevitable.

I felt my ankle give way as I sprained it! I twisted it so badly that
I actually I heard it go, not quite a snap, more a slower crunching kind of crack, like a wet sapling breaking, and I felt the heat
and pain instantly. The best of it was that I had deprived the
lions of their breakfast. The worst of it was I knew my run in the
Hoedspruit Wildsfees half marathon was over.

Driving home, I was preoccupied with the creation of a cred-
ible excuse to give the organisers of the marathon as there was
not a hope in hell that they would believe me if I told them
the truth. After strapping up the ankle and downing a couple of
Voltaren, I took my children back to 'Tau Kopje' hoping we could
find the lions, but when we got there, there was no sign of them,
my evidence had departed. The next morning I informed a po-
lite, but disbelieving, race organiser of why I couldn't do my bit.
He tried hard to conceal his unwillingness to accept my excuse,
but his disappointment was poorly disguised by his expressions
of concern. In a small community like ours, everybody knows
everybody else's business, and to this day I swear I still get that
'look ' that says 'what a bullsh*t excuse!'

As to the christening, well, I think the name that Miles and
Jetje gave this viewpoint is as appropriate as it is brief. 'Tau Kopje'
sounds a lot better than 'Ankle Sprain Hill' or 'Two lions with
one panga and many dirty swear words chased away Hill'.

In the same vein, for some reason they haven't renamed the
Hoedspruit Wildfees half marathon, though I did hear a rumour
that 'Tall Story Challenge' had been suggested.

'The Gentlemen's Club' ... A Lesson in Loyalty

DECEMBER 2003

Older buffalo bulls are known to form lasting relationships in small bachelor groups of three or more individuals, usually fewer than ten. The largest bachelor herd on the reserve at the moment has 18 members but this is exceptional. These old buffalo are often referred to as 'dagga boys' (mud boys) because of their penchant for rolling in mud wallows. The mud adheres to their sparse coats in a crusty layer, cracking and flaking off in the sun as the day progresses, or when it gets rubbed off against a suitable rock or stump, invariably taking a load of unwanted, encrusted parasites along with it.

Seven old buffalo bulls are fed at Warthog Pan every day. These elderly gents used to number nine individuals, but as is expected of a senior gentlemen's club, the membership inevitably requires replenishment due to the ravages of old age. If that had been the reason for the two missing bachelors, we would have been happy to allow nature to take its course. The remaining seven old timers could then have been left to chew the cud, while they dreamed of green pastures and cool mud wallows and on occasion when the main breeding herd moved through, they could cast a lustful gaze at the beautiful young heifers. Isn't that what is expected of old bachelors the world over? In this instance, though, we were obliged to intervene, because man had a hand in the demise of the two old buffalo. This meant that remedial intervention was necessary to help prevent further unnatural fatalities.

It has become something of a phenomenon that the railway

63

line's verges remain relatively well grassed far into the dry season. In certain areas, green tufts are present throughout the year, probably due to condensation from the crushed granite supporting the tracks. This, in combination with minute amounts of phosphoric acid spillage, has a positive effect on the vegetation in the immediate area.

These old bachelor bulls knew on which side of the line the grass was greener, so to speak, so enjoyed ambling up and down between the tracks and the verge. Feeding mostly at night, they grazed, oblivious to the danger. Their dark non-reflective bodies made them nigh-on invisible to the drivers, until it was too late.

In January 2003, one of the buffalo in this group was hit by a train and knocked head over heels down a steep embankment. Although he moved off and remained mobile for a number of days, his movements became progressively more laboured and slower. After humanely dispatching the old bull, a post mortem was carried out to reveal a damaged shoulder and a ruptured spleen. This particular incident is described in more detail later in the chapter titled 'Not just another buffalo story'.

Two months later, a second bull from the same group was hit. Thankfully, he died instantly, but one of his companions was not so lucky. The bloody stump of his horn was found on the road not far from where the dead buffalo lay. This meant that a second buffalo had been hit and we had to find him to ascertain the extent of the damage. We soon located the spot where the injured bull must have stood shocked and dazed while he collected himself, followed his tracks and found him four hours later. He appeared healthy in all respects except he was minus one horn and as a result had a large wound area that was now susceptible to blowfly infestation. In view of the fact that his limbs and general attitude appeared normal, we gave him the benefit of the doubt and left nature to heal the wound.

For the next three weeks I monitored his movements, being especially watchful for any sign of maggot infestation. Blowfly maggots have the ability to migrate into the sinus passages and eventually into the brain. Signs to watch for would include sneezing and head shaking, with a combination of these two confirming sinus infestation. That would mean having to destroy the animal. Fortunately, no symptoms were noted, so again nature was left to continue doing her best. Eventually the old buffalo moved out of our area and I adopted the 'no news is good news' approach.

A couple of months later, while I was up in a helicopter looking for a suitable buffalo bull to remove as part of our capture programme, I saw him once again, this time in the company of two other bulls. A neat round growth about the size of half a grapefruit had sealed off the jagged break. The best surgeons in the world could not have made a tidier repair and I remember thinking how fantastic nature's healing mechanisms were. After hovering for a few seconds, I decided to leave these old bulls in peace and signalled to the pilot to pull out, so we flew off to try and locate another bull.

Having experienced such a violent, painful ordeal, one would assume that the last place this old bull would venture was the railway line. Surely he would associate it with the trauma and avoid it. But, as the days got shorter and cooler and the grass in the veld got drier and less palatable, the old gents would cruise their old beat along the railway line. Grazing intently, without so much as lifting their heads as you drove by, they made me worry. This display of nonchalance and the thought of having to retrieve more carcasses off the tracks prompted me to start a supplementary feeding plan at Warthog Pan. It's something I'm loath to do, but with supplementary feed I could keep them from going up and down the tracks in search of grazing. Although trying to stop them from crossing over from one side of the line to the other has been impossible, at least it is a lot safer and the results have been positive.

Despite nature's repair work, the growth on the jagged edge of the old bull's broken horn grew noticeably bigger by the day. Red-billed oxpeckers pecked away at this 'giant tick' relentlessly. Each daily onslaught would open a wound that bled freely, the blood being eagerly sought and consumed by these birds. At night, the buffalo's healing mechanism, fed with a rich supply of blood, would repair the damage by growing another thin skin of tissue, effectively increasing the size of the growth each day. The next morning the oxpeckers would re-open a wound and start it all over again. This continued until within the space of a few weeks, the growth was nearly as big as a ten pin bowling ball.

The irritation and consequent continual attempts at chasing away the oxpeckers by shaking his head meant the buffalo bull was unable to function normally and over a few weeks he began losing condition.

Nature had been given a fair chance, but this animal's predicament was clearly the result of an unnatural injury caused by man, and so man was obliged to intervene to put right the wrong.

After deciding on intervention, a quick phone call to the reserve's trusted vet, my friend Gerrit, had him wading across the Olifants River within an hour. We prepared the necessary darts as we knew the approximate location and this would speed things up. Arriving at the scene, we drove to within 20 metres of the bull and darted him. Approximately eight minutes later he went down, but his companions were too curious for comfort and needed to be moved away. We used the vehicle to effect this by gently nudging them off to a safe distance. Their reluctance to leave him was obvious and they took quite a bit of nudging before they were far enough away to allow us to work on the downed bull in relative safety.

Once immobilised, the removal of the growth began. This was done by cutting through the horn using a flexible saw. This tool looks more like a garrotte than a saw, but does the job efficiently. I managed to cut the growth off in about five minutes, though it was a long five minutes. The more horn I cut through the more the blood flow increased, so I knew I had to do this as quickly as possible. Gerrit commented that he had never seen so many blood vessels in a de-horning operation, and that this could be as a result of the body's healing mechanism providing a generous supply of blood to the affected area. The buffalo was losing so much blood, that the loss could be measured in pints per minute and I was very concerned. But, as always, our intrepid vet had a plan which was to prove an unorthodox yet effective procedure to stem the flow. If ever there was an example of necessity being the mother of all invention or *"n boer maak 'n plan'*, this was it.

We were lucky that a couple of shareholders were on hand to help. By positioning their vehicle as a barrier and keeping an eye on the buffalo's two overly curious companions, the vet and I could focus on stemming the flow of blood. At Gerrit's request, a box of matches was produced. The matches were sharpened and used to plug the more than 30 veins.

When the last match was pushed into place and the bleeding all but stopped, I couldn't help noticing that I was shaking a little, for I did not believe the buffalo would make it after losing so much blood and I had begun to question my decision to intervene. Any way, I went through the motions helping the preparation to bring the buffalo around, all the while, cursing myself for meddlin' and fiddlin' and fixin' things that ain't broke. After applying the Stockholm tar and gauze to seal the cut temporarily, long-acting antibiotics and anti-inflammatory drugs were injected. All well and good, but it did little to ease my apprehension.

I lifted a large vein in the buffalo's ear which allowed Gerrit to slip the needle in easily. I watched dry-mouthed as the antidote to the immobilising drug was administered. I honestly did not expect this old buffalo to survive, let alone to get up and walk away. But, despite being obviously weakened by the loss of blood, the buffalo made a determined effort to get to his feet. Drawing on the reserves of power that justifiably gives the Cape buffalo its legendary reputation for toughness, he stood up. In fact, I have seen healthy camels make more of an issue getting up.

Once on his feet, he slowly made his way to the other buffalo, who were still feeding, then walked past and headed for the waterhole. Sensing something was not right, his two old comrades joined him, looking back at us and snorting. The look which they gave Gerrit and myself and our surgical support team could have been interpreted as 'what the hell have you done to him?' One of the buffalo then proceeded to lick the Stockholm tar that had spilled over onto the patient's ear and down his cheek. If you have ever smelled Stockholm tar, never mind tasted it, you will know that this was an act that demonstrated extreme concern and re-defined the bonds of genuine friendship. The temptation to say 'ag shame' was resisted in the face of professional composure.

I was to be further humbled by what took place over the next few days. At the next feed, the 'patient' and his two companions were missing. As there was absolutely nothing to eat out in the bush I expected them to appear the following morning. They didn't. When they had still not arrived by the third day, I was resigned to the possibility that they may have moved out of the area. Imagine my surprise, then, when on the morning of the fourth day a rather skinny, somewhat skittish but otherwise healthy, one-horned buffalo and two buddies came to the feed at Warthog Pan.

So strong is the bond between these old gentlemen that not even four days of hunger caused them to desert their friend. What is so uncanny is that it appears that they knew he would be vulnerable to predation and could see he needed comfort and support. They ignored the lure of delicious lucerne they knew would be at Warthog Pan and stuck by him until they could return to the feeding area together. Initially wary of me when they returned, it appears that all is forgiven and back to normal now. I no longer get that glare that says 'I have forgiven but I haven't forgotten' – or, as the author Robert Ruark so aptly describes, 'buffalo look at you like you owe them money'.

There are many hard-core conservationists who believe emphatically that nature should be allowed to take its course, irrespective of the circumstance, and I respect their view. I believe, however, that if the problem is as a direct or indirect result of human activity or influence, we are then obliged to exercise discretion and try to remedy the problem. There are not many true conservationists I know who can watch coldly as a noble animal dies slowly of starvation. This is especially true if its natural migration route has been cut off or hampered by the intervention of man-made barriers, or the habitat so manipulated by man as to be the prime cause or one of the causes of its predicament. I believe that nearly everywhere wildlife occurs, it will be affected by man to some degree or other, so it's a question of compassion and discretion.

Waterholes and Fire ... a Practical Perspective

We are repeatedly reminded by the eco-purists that even a bird bath in the bush constitutes an artificial watering point. Besides the elephant culling issue and the declining wildebeest numbers in the lowveld, nothing gets a conversation amongst ecologists and local conservationists going more than the debate on waterholes.

Man-made waterholes providing a constant source of drinking water for wild animals in the lowveld is thought to be the root cause of numerous ecological problems facing managers today. Among the more noticeable negative effects has been the declining roan and sable antelope populations in the Kruger National Park and the rapidly dwindling wildebeest numbers in adjacent private reserves. Mainly, these alarming statistics have been attributed to the supply of permanent water which then promotes the proliferation of water-dependent species like impala, buffalo and elephant. They, in turn, are deemed responsible for the retrogressive heterogeneity of the surrounding vegetation. Essentially, through their feeding habits, these animals create conditions that are unable to support the diversity of vegetation necessary for the survival of certain other species. The details of the various ecological inter-dependencies are too complicated to go into here, but we can be assured from what little research has been done, that the closing of artificial water points will improve habitat biodiversity.

There can be no doubt that in a pristine ecosystem where only seasonal drinking points were previously available, artificially supplied permanent water will have a detrimental effect, and depending on the size and number of waterholes, the effect may or may not be immediately evident. Suffice it to say, any manipulation by man of a completely natural functioning or pristine ecosystem will invariably prove to be ecologically unsound to some degree. So, yes, I support the move to reduce or close waterholes. My standpoint on this issue is, however, conditional.

If all artificial waterholes are to be closed and we revert to the natural pans and rivers to supply the water needs for our wildlife, then the system needs to have self-sustaining populations of game. These animals must be able to move and migrate unhindered, as and when climatic conditions dictate, in order to source their requirements necessary for survival. Unfortunately, there are very few areas left in Africa where these criteria can be met and, more specifically, there are no privately owned game reserves in South Africa that qualify. In the words of RN Porter, who compiled an ecological report for the Timbavati in 1964: 'No game reserve in the world is an ecological unit or embraces a complete system.' That was nearly 45 years ago and I am still inclined to agree with him today.

The establishment of the Association of Private Nature Reserves (APNR) and the subsequent opening up of the private reserves to be included in the Greater Kruger Park can be described as an 'ecological milestone and a step closer to minimal management'. Olifants is now part of Balule, which subscribes to the APNR Management Plan that lays down the guidelines for ecological management in an area of 165 000 hectares. As impressive as this figure is, and even if you add a further two million hectares of the Kruger's area, we're still a tiny part of a vast ecosystem that existed in Southern Africa at the turn of the century. In the context of where we now fit into the picture, it is clear that Olifants is not an ecosystem in its own right. Therefore we are obliged to artificially manage the reserve in order to maintain as near as possible a natural balance between all the component factors of the environment, not the least being ever-controversial water management.

Does this mean we just close water points and monitor the

effects? That could be an option in an area that is large enough, relatively speaking, as was done in the area of Kruger where the roan and sable antelope populations are in rapid decline. The scientists there closed all the artificial water points, hoping to discourage some of the water-dependent herbivores, which would also reduce the competition for fodder and in turn, limit those predators dependent on them.

It was thought that if these results could be achieved, the prevailing conditions would then skew the environment in favour of the threatened roan and sable. This concerted effort did have a limited measure of success in this regard. The closing of the water points resulted in conditions which promoted a habitat more favourable to help turn these declining populations around. Unfortunately, despite this, Kruger's roan and sable numbers continue to decline at a rapid rate. It was clear that abundant artificially supplied surface water was not entirely to blame; there were bigger influencing factors.

In a less radical and relatively simple experiment, a 2 000 hectare block was securely fenced off from the surrounding bushveld. The main aim was to keep the larger predators out. Sable and roan antelope were then placed inside the area. A fair sprinkling of other plains game was inadvertently caught up when the fence went up and they also made this enclosure their home. The result has been steadily climbing numbers all round, particularly the sable and roan. Hello! The lack of predation MUST be a major factor. What has also been of interest is how this exclusion area, which was also inaccessible to elephant, stands out in terms of vegetation production, tree canopy density and herbaceous cover. In winter the contrast is most dramatic. Aerial photos taken of this enclosure and the surrounding area reveal what looks like a green postage stamp stuck in the middle of a brown envelope.

What was thought to be ecologically correct 25 or 30 years ago is now outdated; this is scientific progress and we accept it. The concern has to be that there is still way too much 'chucking and chancing' even amongst the so-called boffins. How much trial and error can a natural system tolerate? And to what extent are we able to reverse the damage done to an ecosystem by what we thought was the right thing to do at the time, but has since been proved wrong? Nobody knows.

An excellent example of this was a couple of years ago when Air Force fighters were used to blow a dam wall to smithereens in a world famous national park. The pilots got good practice and the ecologists were ecstatic, whooping with joy as the concrete crumbled and the river system was restored to its former state. The ecologists who built that dam all those years ago would have refused to believe you if, at the dam opening ceremony, you told them that in 30 years' time this beautiful dam they had just built would be blown away by ecologists currently in nappies ... and that this would be done in the interests of conservation! All I can say is, thank goodness nature is as resilient and forgiving as it is!

A highly respected ecologist was recently commissioned to compile an independent ecological management plan for one of the regions in Balule. His waterhole strategy was, in my opinion, a tad on the radical side. He recommended that water points in the lowveld should be placed at 30-kilometre intervals. Try to visualise the whole area from the railway gate in the south to the Olifants train bridge in the north without any waterholes. The only water available would be the Olifants River itself. The hardest to swallow was that the region that commissioned this report was only 3 200 hectares in extent. You would need a reserve area of at least ten times that size to qualify, as per his recommendation, for even one water point!

Before man's manipulation of the lowveld, the Olifants River was nature's winter waterhole in our area for hundreds or thousands of years, so why not take advantage of this and emulate nature, as was being suggested by the respected consultant ecologist? Realistically speaking, given that Adam and Eve 'have left the building' and the system is no longer pristine, implementing this radical policy would require massive sacrifices and a rather strong stomach.

Imagine the carnage on the railway line with herds of game crossing twice each day to and from water. Eventually, fences would need to be re-erected just to keep the game off the tracks. Those animals utilising the riverine area would soon denude all the available vegetation in the proximity of the river and they would then be forced to move back across the railway line to feed. Elephant would concentrate on the trees and shrubs on the river in winter, no problem with that, it's perfectly natural. But, then, so is the ever-increasing wasteland of Chobe!

In ten years' time, given the rate of increase in the elephant numbers on the reserve, this would eventually result in the only prominent features on the Olifants River flood plain being share-holders' lodges and the odd leadwood tree. Due to the lack of vegetation, game would move away en masse for months at a time, much as they did hundreds of years ago, only this time they would encounter national highways, fences, farmland and other unnatural barriers. Then and there, they would die attempting to cross them, or end up piled against the fence, like the eland and wildebeest did in their thousands when the Kuki fence was erected in Botswana.

The veterinary fence that was erected on the Kruger National Park's western boundary in the 1960s also took its toll, account-ing for thousands of dead animals, mainly wildebeest. Before the removal of the fence between the Kalahari National Park and Botswana's Central Kalahari, thousands of animals perished try-ing to migrate in search of water. So, despite the huge conserva-tion drive to remove fences and create Transfrontier Parks, there are still many thousands of kilometres of these barriers still in existence.

If we give due consideration and logical thought to the condi-tions necessary for adopting an '*au naturel*' approach, it becomes increasingly apparent that we must be realistic about a possible reduction in or even closure of waterholes on our reserve. Which waterhole? When? For how long? All questions and all undoubt-edly wildly varying answers will need to be carefully considered. Also, I believe that the modern approach to water provision on privately owned land needs to be tempered with moderation, which, until we know the answers, would be preferable to a radi-cal approach either way.

The management of a private reserve requires the mainte-nance of an interdependent balance between the ecological well-being of the reserve and the enjoyment of the members/owners. Without this symbiosis, neither will be happy and as in any healthy longer-term relationship, there needs to be a certain degree of compromise and sacrifice. 'Appropriate' and 'adaptable' are another two words that come to mind.

Until we have specific and researched answers to all aspects of the waterhole issue, we can, in my opinion, distribute our water points at an optimum spread of one per 1 000 hectares. Each waterhole needs to be large enough to water at least 100 LSU (Large Stock Units) at a time, with bird baths and conventional cattle troughs not featuring in the equation at all. This use of LSU as a statistical measure will be examined further in later chapters.

With specific reference to the larger open system's private nature reserves, the following are three leading ecologists' viewpoints which may be taken as unofficial waterhole management/ distribution guidelines. What I find particularly interesting is that despite nearly 30 years separating one of these reports, the recommendations are pretty much six of one and half a dozen of the other.

A management report submitted 30 years ago for the Sabi Sand Game Reserve recommended, as a rule of thumb, that water points not be closer than three to four kilometres to one another, and one water point to serve an area of between 900 and 1 600 hectares. The Balule management plan compiled by the Agricultural Research Council (ARC) stipulates that a distance of three kilometres between waterholes be regarded as an absolute minimum. An unofficial guesstimate for an area such as the Timbavati is one water point per thousand hectares. This opinion was given by a well-respected ecologist at a meeting with landowners of Timbavati, where they met to discuss this very issue. Currently Olifants has seven water points that almost fit the criteria as recommended and they are spread quite evenly over the area. At this stage we are pretty close, with one per 900 hectares. But ... Shhhhh! Don't mention the river.

I have long held the belief that the even distribution of ample water points in a closed system is the more logical management option; in other words, saturation as opposed to isolation. This has tended to be a safe position to hold for fear of being branded a conservation Neanderthal and being relegated to their beetle-browed dead-end branch on the tree of evolution. Happily, and without scientific backing, I am now 'coming out' on this issue. There is now overwhelming evidence to suggest that one of the prime factors contributing to ideal conditions for the spread of disease amongst wildlife populations, is exacerbated by unnaturally concentrating animals in a small area, and that is exactly what isolated waterholes do. They also concentrate larger numbers of game when they're at their most vulnerable physically, when their resistance is lowest, namely in the winter months. Therefore it is no coincidence that we find the majority of anthrax cases manifesting in the dry months. Conversely, when the rains arrive and there is an abundance of surface water, the game spreads out, their physical condition improves and the disease disappears.

Evenly spreading a population over a number of waterholes means that the concentration of faeces, urine and saliva is relatively diluted. This also minimises the spread of other parasites which may further contribute to animals' already poor condition, due to lowered nutritional levels of the winter vegetation. Fewer hooves stirring up the surrounding soil in which the anthrax resides, means less airborne spores, thereby reducing the risk of infection through inhalation.

Besides the obvious influence that water distribution has on the spread of diseases, the saturation theory has other merits worthy of consideration. I believe that an area saturated with well-planned and evenly distributed water points is a better veld management technique in a closed system, than the rotational grazing method. In my opinion the latter practice is better suited to animal husbandry. This technique isolates the water points, forcing game to concentrate on a particular area, which can have long-term detrimental effects, with possibly irreversible damage.

The basis of the saturation theory is that animals won't travel any further than they have to, to obtain water. An even distribution of water points should therefore result in an even distribution of animals. This even spread of game then applies an even amount of pressure over a larger area.

Spreading a given biomass, or number of animals, over a large area should reduce the damaging effect that the same biomass would have had if it was concentrated on a smaller area. This all presupposes, of course, the all-important qualification – that the biomass does not exceed the carrying capacity of the total area. This is critical to the whole concept of saturation.

Evenly spreading a number of waterholes over a given area will reduce the distance an animal has to move to obtain water, therefore it expends less energy. By reducing its energy requirements, the animal utilises proportionately less fuel and maintains better physical condition over a longer period of time, given the same energy intake. This further reduces demand on the veld.

In large game reserves that have isolated waterholes, like Etosha Pan, for example, the wagon wheel effect is clear to see. This feature is made up of well-worn game paths, caused by the relentless hooves of thousands of animals travelling great distances, focusing into the waterhole and then radiating out again. These paths can develop into dongas on sloping areas, resulting in serious soil erosion. Most of the larger reserves are able to absorb this level of utilisation and resulting consequences, but smaller closed systems cannot sustain this pattern of usage.

The key issue to which I alluded is, then, not so much waterhole management as it is animal biomass management. And, 'that's my report and I'm sticking to it!'

Controlled water points are a definitive management tool if used wisely, but I suspect, as with fire management, the tendency is to overdo things a little because the short-term results can be quite spectacular. Before-and-after photos produce dramatic evidence and speak volumes in a presentation portfolio, but I am of the opinion that the long-term effects of an intensive regular burning programme may negatively affect the animal species diversity. This observation applies for the most part to invertebrates, small mammals, reptiles and birds, and to a lesser degree the vegetation, particularly the woody component.

'Locores' meetings are always interesting and varied. In essence they are informal gatherings of ecologists, local landowners and managers to discuss issues of common interest relating to conservation. The venue for the meeting to which I am now drawing your attention was a successful rare antelope breeder's game farm, which specialises in roan, sable and tsessebe antelope. Nearly all this farmer's emphasis is placed on managing the farm's vegetation with these antelope and their specific needs in mind. Besides an extensive ongoing bush-clearing programme, it requires a burning regime that would be far too radical to apply in an open system such as ours. It was, nevertheless, an absolute model of a farm in terms of grass production. I have to admit to being really envious because, relatively speaking, Olifants was sparsely covered, and our grass species composition is rather shy on perennials. Anyhow, I wasn't really comparing apples with apples, so back to the point, which is to do with one of the effects of fire, or rather, too much fire.

We took a short break at midday, lolling around in their lush grass which appeared to have largish patches of bare earth between the tussocks. There was virtually no dead material, old grass, leaves or that sort of stuff, and what struck me as strange to the point of being disturbing was the lack of insects or signs of insects. When you stuck your face down at creepy crawly level, it was quiet and sterile. That's what worried me then, as it still does now.

Before the pyromaniacs amongst you advocate regular burning, as man has had a positive influence on the creation and maintenance of savanna habitat by doing just that, we need to remember that the use of fire by man is a relatively modern discovery. In terms of man's intentional influence on the ecology, it is a recently discovered management tool. Unconscious of the ecological ramifications, and with only survival in mind, primitive man used fire to make hunting easier for himself, inadvertently creating conditions that favoured grassland rather than woodland. Later, this practice was applied in similar fashion to provide green pasture for his domesticated animals.

Unfortunately we have no reliable records to tell us what the area looked like before this regular manipulation by man and his fires. Nor do we have accurate data on the frequency of natural fires at that time. In all probability, these fires would have been irregular and burned in natural mosaic patterns, following seep lines, river courses and ridges. I believe this would be preferable to neatly cut fire breaks, which facilitate neatly burned blocks and covering tightly defined areas as prescribed by modern fire management techniques. Almost always, these are burned along property boundaries irrespective of what diverse ecosystems the fence or break traverses. This can't be good.

In all fairness, fires are classified in terms of their intensity and alternating the intensity and frequency of a burn is fundamental to fire management. So you will hear of the use of a hot burn, a cold burn or even a wet burn in terms of achieving the desired results. Well, desired by their practitioners, that is.

These questions must have raised enough concern to cause scientists to revisit burning policies in the National Parks. Kruger National Park's fire ecologists have been experimenting with allowing natural fires to burn themselves out. Although some of these fires do tend to cover large areas, they're at least following natural firebreak lines dictated by the characteristics of the terrain. The infrequency of these fires will allow the natural cycles of some organisms to complete the process necessary for survival that otherwise may have been interrupted or destroyed by regular fires initiated under a rigorous fire management programme.

Observations During Drought

OCTOBER 2008

October is often referred to as 'suicide month' in the South African bush and it's not difficult to see why. I refer to IR Tannehill, an American meteorologist, who wrote, 'Drought is unique among spells of weather, it creeps upon us gradually, almost mysteriously, but its consequences are a terrible reality. Drought is one of the best examples of our helplessness before the broad-scale phenomena of nature.' Although this was written more than 60 years ago, it could have been written yesterday.

Having lived through a few severe droughts in my time doesn't make it any easier to accept the present state of affairs. It remains difficult to imagine that this relentless drought will break, that the test will soon be over, and the prevailing hazy grey landscape will change dramatically. In a matter of days following the first good rains, the bush will transform itself from what once resembled a worn-out old witch's broom to lush green growth, vibrant with the promise of life. This process of extreme desiccation followed by good rainfall is essentially an ecological necessity in this environment and contributes in its own way to what makes Olifants the sought-after slice of paradise it is. Knowing this helps us get through this depressing phase and keeps many of us confidently optimistic.

Olifants Game Reserve is blessed with an abundance of big game, but often in the scramble to chalk up the Big Five, the smaller animals don't get the attention they deserve, in particular the smaller antelope species, of which we have four, namely the klipspringer, the common duiker, Sharpe's grysbok and the steenbok. I have never seen a red duiker here and strongly suspect that the 'red duiker' that gave the drive to Grootdraai its name was a quick glimpse of a young bushbuck doe. So I am sticking to four until proven otherwise.

The prevailing drought has resulted in extremely sparse vegetation, which has now exposed the smaller, normally more easily concealed antelope mentioned above. These little guys don't hang around long, which can make positive identification difficult. Knowing a little about the habitat type each prefers, however, will at least narrow down the possibilities somewhat. Let's deal with the most confusing of these, namely Sharpe's grysbok and the steenbok.

The similarities in their appearance are confusing. Both are a light rusty red, weigh approximately the same and in both species, only the male carries small pointed horns. How then do you tell them apart, when all you get most of the time is a quick glimpse? The most reliable rule of thumb clue lies in habitat association. Each of these two antelope occupies a specialised niche in the environment. So specific are their respective requirements that their home ranges hardly, if ever, overlap. To this end, it would be safe to bet that if a small reddish antelope is seen in the hilly, rocky terrain of Grootdraai, ten-to-one, it's a Sharpe's grysbok. Olifants North, similarly, would have more Sharpe's grysbok than steenbok.

A little red antelope seen in the sandy open country on the east of the old main access road would, ten-to-one, be a steenbok, and if you see a little red antelope drinking water, hundred-to-one it would NOT be a steenbok. Later, as you get good at this and manage to get your binoculars trained on them, you will also notice that the grysbok has marginally shorter legs and white flecks in its fur, as if it had been lightly dusted with coconut icing.

Drought conditions, and the subsequent response to resource stress, bring out the survival instincts in all wild animals. How each adapts and copes is key to their survival. As an example of this, let us focus on the often-overlooked steenbok. These little antelope are completely at home in an arid environment and besides the common duiker are probably the most widespread antelope species in Southern Africa. In the Kalahari Desert they draw all their water requirements from the vegetation they eat and those we come across on Olifants rarely utilise waterholes. I have never seen a steenbok drinking water in the 35 years I've been in the bush.

Knowing this, I was intrigued to find a pair of steenbok at Hide Dam. Eventually, after frequent sightings, I began to wonder if, due to the prevailing drought, all the available vegetation was so dry that even they needed to supplement their moisture intake.

Closer observation, however, revealed that they were eating a water herb *Ludwigia stolonifera* that was growing in the shallow water at the edge of the dam. In Elsa Pooley's *Wild Flowers of KwaZulu Natal*, she states that this plant is visited by ants. I'd love her to see what other species also 'visit' this plant in severe drought conditions! The water level of this dam is maintained by pumping water from the Olifants River by means of a four-kilometre underground pipeline and the pump mechanism employed would prohibit even the smallest seed from slipping past the tight fitting rotor and stator. I suspect, therefore, the seeds of this plant were 'flown in', more than likely on the legs of the wading birds that this body of water attracts.

OK, so steenbok are able to utilise vegetation that they normally don't eat and to which they have had no previous exposure. They are not unique, many animals do just that. This could be put down to either opportunism or good fortune or an example of their resourcefulness, or as I suspect, a little of everything. Intriguing as this was, it was another aspect of this little antelope's adaptability that interested me. I was fascinated by the fact that these two delicate little antelope, each a mere mouthful to a predator, were cruising the shallow edges of the dam, nibbling away, fully aware but apparently unconcerned that only a few metres away lay a large crocodile.

Despite a larder of carcasses stashed around the dam, this reptile appeared to be insatiable, taking every opportunity to secure more food. I guess this may be due to the same instinctive response that other predators, such as caracal and leopard, have demonstrated when they raid domestic stock pens. By responding instinctively and taking advantage of the easy pickings, they're branded wanton killers because of the wasteful slaughter they inflict. The economic losses incurred can be substantial and so they are maligned and relentlessly persecuted by stock farmers.

On the other hand, nobody brands the crocodile at Hide Dam a wasteful killer, despite its stash of two impala and a warthog. No, we rather admire its automatic and unconscious instinct to save for a rainy day. This croc has virtually doubled in size in the last few years, giving us an indication of just how successful this predator is. I also believe it has the advantage of being able to lie comfortably and unchallenged in the centre of a dry season game magnet.

Given the probability that in their respective natural environments, steenbok and crocodiles would probably never cross paths as they occupy totally diverse habitats, how then do the steenbok avoid being taken? How do they know the safe flight distance from a predator they have never seen before? I may be assuming a lot here, but to see the confidence with which these little guys cruise the edge of the dam makes you realise there is clearly more to them than meets the eye. The next time you see one, spend some time admiring these little survivors, they deserve more than a quick glance.

Moving up a few notches on the scale of antelope I admire and respect, kudu have always occupied a special place in my heart; they're proud without being arrogant; they melt away in front of you without making a rude exit; they are large yet maintain an unobtrusively low profile; and they're like good house guests who live with you, but also allow you your space. So it goes without saying that nothing pains me more than to see such magnificent animals reduced to skin and bone. These majestic 'grey ghosts' of Africa, although extremely versatile, are not immune to drought, and as we've observed lately, have been utilising a wide range of vegetation to get by. Among the known variety of browse they select are the aggressive, invasive, alien and thought to be noxious cocklebur and then the indigenous, but not endemic, *Aloe marlothi*, and the local aloes which are eaten to destruction. The desiccated, dried-out leaves of the large-leafed rock fig *Ficus abutifolia* are picked up off the ground and eaten with apparent enjoyment. Three enormous kudu bulls had become quite used to my running routine over a period of weeks and as time passed, so their required flight distance decreased. One afternoon, they allowed me so close I could hear them crunching the dry fig leaves. It sounded as though someone had just offered the Pringles around.

I almost hesitate to report that since writing this, the lions have killed the biggest one of the three kudu behind the laundry near my office. Realistically, I must admit that this was probably due to him being older and slower than the other two.

This variation of diet can be understood to be an adaptive response to the drought. The question is, though, if they enjoy bitter dry vegetation, why don't they eat the prickly pear cacti which, although classed as exotic and invasive vegetation, are relatively juicy and sweet? It is well documented that farmers in the Karoo have, in times of drought, fed their livestock on prickly pear leaves, and I know that a particular species of this plant is used to make tequila – which, I am told, has positive effects on humans. I suspect there may be a link between gut parasite loads, which we know tend to proliferate when an organism is under stress, and the relatively high intake of bitter and/or unpalatable vegetation at this time of the year. Could this be a conscious response for medicinal purposes? Or do these kudu know something we don't?

If you come across a thin lion at the moment, it won't be due to malnutrition, it is either sick or injured. There is just so much available to eat due to the weakened condition of many prey animals. Warthog, for example, which are usually tucked away in the relative safety of a cosy old aardvark burrow at sunset, have become crepuscular and are now often found feeding late into the evening. Their poor night vision and being out when most predators are active, is a deadly combination. It doesn't come as any surprise, then, that the game census figures of September 2008 indicate a substantial drop in the warthog population, nearly 60 per cent down on last year's numbers. On the other hand, they respond quite dramatically in good rainfall years, when their numbers can triple!

Initially, predators are not adversely affected during leaner periods; on the contrary, they make hay while the sun shines, taking advantage of higher than normal concentrations of prey on the seep lines and the riverine floodplain. Prey animals are also relatively easy to catch as they're totally focused on finding enough to eat and therefore not as alert.

Then, as if this was not enough, as the season gets progressively drier, the energy value of available vegetation drops, resulting in physically weakened animals becoming more vulnerable to predation. But the big wheel turns, and as I've said, the prey species numbers crash in a drought and then when the rains arrive, the survivors spread themselves over a relatively big area.

The larger predators, particularly lion, now find it more difficult to secure enough food. Prides will set out to hunt, leaving young cubs behind, then when a kill is made, often after covering many kilometres, it is usually completely consumed, and nothing gets back to the cubs. This also adversely affects many of the sub-adults that are denied access to kills by the hierarchy of the pecking order. These inexperienced youngsters are then forced to move off and search for food on their own. This often takes them out of the reserve from where they hardly ever return.

A lioness nursing young cubs will apparently pass up larger prey species in preference to smaller prey which are hunted during the day – often uncharacteristically, in the heat of the day. Do they know the cubs are vulnerable to other predators and so adapt their hunting techniques, or is it that they cannot risk injury because they are the sole providers? One thing is for certain, there is no shortage of prey on the riverine habitat in the dry season, and so hunting forays do not take her far from her cubs and are usually brief. Hunting success in terms of their kills-to-attempts ratio also appears to be relatively higher, enthralling many privileged shareholders who sit on the decks of their lodges and witness these kills.

In drought conditions, animals will utilise whatever they can find wherever they can find it, in an effort to maximise their forage intake. They will frequent unfamiliar habitat or places that are mostly man-made and which under normal circumstances would be avoided. The railway line is a good example of something unnatural that instinctively animals don't like. This is demonstrated by young animals that need considerable coaxing and encouragement to get them to walk across it. I've seen giraffe and kudu cows moving back across the tracks to feed juveniles who won't cross despite their hunger for milk. For weeks, the youngsters refuse to follow their mothers across the granite chips upon which the sleepers are laid. Not only do I think the shiny metal tracks put them off, I'm convinced the coarse gravel stone bed is too loose and insecure for these 'tenderfeet'. Until their hooves harden and they become accustomed to the tracks, all their instincts tell them this is not a natural part of their new world.

Another reason wildlife use this hazardous man-made habitat, particularly in the dry season, has to do with finding enough food in times of scarcity. At the end of a reasonably good season most of the grass matures and then dries out, with the only green grass to be found being that growing in low-lying areas or seeplines. The railway line, on the other hand, in the same conditions, will always have some green grass throughout the winter months irrespective of topography. The sharp granite chips that make up the rail bed undergo a level of expansion and contraction that creates an ideal medium for condensation. The retention of moisture is facilitated in this mini rock pile. To add to this, every so often there is a little phosphoric acid spillage from the trains and this combination becomes ideal plant food. This 'nourishment' may be the reason why vegetative production along this otherwise ugly, unnatural blight on our reserve's landscape is relatively good. The negative impact is that due to resource stress brought on by the prevailing dry conditions, animals, particularly the browsers, are attracted to this 'danger zone'.

The danger to our wildlife from both the trains and heavy vehicles using this route is evident by the number of deaths we record in the dry months. To this end, every growing season, we employ a team of men to remove all palatable browse along the line, particularly in the cuttings. This vegetation control is necessarily confined to the section of the railway within our reserve's boundaries. In a single week prior to me 'getting the hump' and placing more speed humps on a section of the rail road, we lost a sad list of two steenbok, two squirrels, two hornbills, a honey badger and an impala to speeding trucks. This was on the short section between the Sable Dam and Warthog Pan turn-offs. Only those animals seen or physically collected are recorded. Realistically, this figure could be much higher if we consider those that get away injured to die later, or those that have been scavenged by predators and we don't find.

So, when you admire or curse these 'tank traps' as one of our shareholders refers to them (or 'mumps' – Mario's bumps – as my editor calls them), know that they're not there for decorative purposes. If I could put 'mumps' on the railway tracks themselves to slow the trains down, I would do that as well.

Baboons have responded to these adverse conditions with one aim, and that is survival, plain and simple. As part of their strategy, they have broken up into smaller, more effective foraging units ranging from single adult males to groups of large males numbering three to six individuals. Only the strongest females are seen with a dominant male. These groups seldom number more than 10 to 15, this being drastically down from the normal troop size of 40 to 60. Other signs of stress are that adult females are not coming into oestrus, pregnant females are not lactating, and mothers hang on to new-born babies who have died from starvation for a day or so before they drop them.

I have recently recorded cases of infanticide and cannibalism. In one instance, a baby already past the 'black hair phase' was the victim. A case of cannibalism was reported from a neighbouring property where the carcass of a dead baboon was stolen before it could be incinerated and was then eaten. In all the instances the perpetrators were large adult males. On another occasion, we found a number of dead baboons in one location at one time, which raised some concern as we suspected a virus might be responsible. We needed veterinary certification of our suspicions, but as Gerrit was bobbing about on a rubber duck in the Indian Ocean, the state vet was called in to carry out the autopsies. His examination revealed the cause of death to be starvation, a direct result of resource stress.

I suspect the reason baboons have taken so much strain this particular winter is more than likely the convergence of a number of inter-related factors:

- the 1996 flood washed away a large percentage of riverine fruit trees and shrubs and recovery has been slow
- the pylons for 'our' power lines have created roosting areas that are safe from predation, this in turn leading to an increase in numbers
- supplementary winter feeding of at least two troops by a local rehabilitation centre has artificially maintained and promoted more numbers than the habitat can naturally sustain
- the unfavourable rainfall pattern last summer resulted in low vegetative productivity
- resource competition for fruit and fruit trees by elephant, whose feeding habits have resulted in the large-scale destruction of marula and knobthorn trees, both of which are important food sources for baboons
- the change of their legal status from vermin to animals that require a permit before they can be hunted or captured, has contributed to an increase in their numbers
- an increase in human activity in the area (builders, etc), which resulted in more waste being produced. This in turn provides more opportunity for baboons to scavenge dumps and garbage disposal units.

As you can see from the list above, which is far from exhaustive, our reserve presents its baboon scenario in a contradictory fashion. We have created a favourable environment which encourages a proliferation of their numbers which nature then ruthlessly culls.

Of all the herbivores on the reserve, wildebeest and zebra appear to be the least affected by the drought, particularly wildebeest, which have not only increased by 25 per cent this year, they all appear to be in good condition. I also suspect this unusually high increase can be attributed partially to us having benefited from some recruitment from the neighbouring Klaserie reserve. At the same time, who has ever seen a thin zebra? It seems they die before becoming emaciated. As desperate as things may seem to be, the reality is that not only are these dry spells regular occurrences, but they are a necessary process governing our ecosystem.

When you see a wild leopard feeding on a freshly killed impala a few metres away, you are privileged ... privy to one of Africa's most rewarding scenes. The antithesis of the drab, drought-stricken, apparently lifeless bush framing the scene, the leopard is vibrantly beautiful, alert and in the prime of its life – as was its prey until its final moments. It is difficult to understand how an animal so well-designed, so perfectly proportioned and in such superb condition could be the product of the surrounding bush, which to the naïve eye appears dead and unproductive. What you are seeing is the tip of the production pyramid, the top of the food chain.

It is this seemingly barren habitat that moulds the building blocks, making up the base of the pyramid, which itself is the product of millions of years of exposure and adaptation to adverse climatic conditions. Much like the dry spell we are experiencing now. The diversity of life that can be sustained by a system such as ours has proved to be rich enough to culminate in such rewarding sightings, over and over again. Many recent visitors who did not let the late winter appearance of the bush depress them, were rewarded with leopard viewing at Big Dam that would be hard to beat anywhere.

I end this chapter with a poem written by my daughter Eleana when she was 13. In her own way, she captures the essence of drought and its effects. Of course I am proud of her, she is my daughter. At the same time, I am humbled by her insight into the phenomenon of drought, something few people of her age, living in a First World environment, are exposed to, and who are possibly the poorer for it.

Drought

Disaster, death and worst of all – fear,
This is how we know that the end is near.
Animals suffer and starve from it,
We hate it with all our heart – we don't like it a bit.

People concerned try and sort it out,
This painful, pitiful, merciless drought.
Of course we know that there is nothing we can do
Rain comes when it wants to, but then its drops are so few.

So we ask ourselves the question 'Why?'
And gaze towards the cloudless sky.
The plants turn grey and shrink to the ground
There is no hope any where to be found.

All we can do is hope and pray
That rain will come soon some day,
The grass will be green again –
And the flowers will bloom
Let's hope this all happens – very, very soon...

Global Warming and Rainfall Patterns

FEBRUARY 2007 ... REVISITED 2009

We now know that global warming is neither a Greenie scare tactic nor an unproven theory. Rather, it is a scientific fact that the globe is getting warmer and the world's climate is changing as a result of greenhouse gas emissions. When the mercury shot up to 45°C in December, evaporating what little moisture there was, withering the new growth of grass and turning it from green to blue grey, exacerbated by the total absence of rain in that critical month – well, I was convinced.

In my world this was a sure sign, the beginning of the end in this rain-driven environment. As the northern lowveld is already hot and semi-arid, the change in these two important limiting factors, namely more heat and less rain, would undoubtedly have a negative effect on the ecosystem. Although I was understandably depressed, before reaching for a double dose of Prozac and looking at retirement homes in Greenland, I was reminded of Christmas 1982, while working in Botswana's Tuli Block.

The day was spent up to our chins in the lukewarm, but nonetheless relatively cool water of a concrete reservoir as the ambient temperature was hovering around 47°C in the shade! The cicadas appeared to be the only creatures unaffected by the oppressive heat; it was almost as if, the hotter it got, the more intense their staccato song. It would be interesting to know at what ambient temperature they stop 'zizzing'. Nothing else except them dared expend a single kilojoule of energy – even the emerald spotted wood doves were conspicuously quiet. A number of small birds of various species congregated on the concrete stoep floor of the main house, obviously the coolest spot they could find. I recall that the fork-tailed drongos and white helmet shrikes appeared to be particularly susceptible to the heat as many of them actually died. An African goshawk squatted on its long legs, undignified, open-beaked and wide-eyed, surrounded by dozens of panting and dying birds. Clearly focused on staying alive, it showed absolutely no interest in the other birds and they in turn were too stressed to care or move away.

Using chunks of ice taken from the deep freeze, we cooled the water in the nearby bird-bath and those birds that had the energy to drink did so. A garden sprayer was turned on; it proved to be a life saver for many of the birds when they moved into the fine spray, and competed for space as they fluffed and shook their feathers in an attempt to absorb the cooling moisture. So, yes, there have been some hot days in the past and summer temperatures in the mid-forties are not a recent phenomenon. Anthropological evidence of early hominids in East Africa's Olduvai gorge suggests that they lived in a hot climate and perspired a lot, millions of years ago. How do they reach these intimate conclusions from a few fossil fragments? How do they determine that they once belonged to a sweaty creature, or is this perhaps a hypothesis based on evidence of what the climate was like at the time, particularly the ambient temperatures? What a fantastic avenue of science anthropology is … I find the piecing together of our origins fascinating, and have no doubt that I would have pursued this as a career, had I not gone into nature conservation.

Knowing that it was as hot, if not hotter, years ago, should allow us to believe that maybe we are not becoming less tolerant of the heat per se, but rather that we are becoming less tolerant of the effect of direct sunlight on our skin. It definitely feels harsher and is becoming progressively more so – and there is no doubt that ozone depletion is the culprit here, something early man did not have to put up with.

When I visited Italy in the height of their summer, even though the ambient temperatures were in the low thirties, you could walk around all day in the sun provided you were adequately hydrated. The sun's intensity was never intolerable, nor for that matter did I ever feel sunburned, as I do in similar conditions in South Africa.

This contributes to my belief that the intensity of the sun varies quite dramatically, depending where you are on the planet. For example, the Chilean town of Punta Arenas on the southern tip of South America is apparently drenched in UV, so definitely not the place for 'gingers'.

Opening our rainfall record book to write up the miserably few millimetres of rain that followed December's heat, I came across the rainfall figures for the reserve from 1986 to 2008, which I studied with interest.

On the face of it, there's nothing abnormal in the figures and nothing jumps out at you to suggest that, here on Olifants, our rainfall allocation from on high has been adversely affected over the years. We have accurately recorded 22 consecutive years of rainfall, and the variance is a mere 3 mm! There is, obviously, no evidence of a gradual descent into the abyss. Those sceptics among us who believe that this is enough to muffle the alarm bells and who wish to bury their heads in the sand will, in light of the following, hopefully change their minds. It is now 2009, 22 years later, and our rainfall for last season was 402 mm, which is slightly above average. The 2009 season's figures sit at 585 mm as I write, so we're getting more rain than before, not less.

Why then are we concerned? Whilst a cursory glance at the chart is cause for optimism, it does not tell the whole story. In our case, our specific veld conditions are deteriorating despite the quantity of rain received. It's the quality, not the quantity, that's the problem.

Our rainfall pattern within each period recorded is erratic. Let me concoct a couple of extreme examples to demonstrate the point. If we received 3 mm of rain every day for a year, we would have received three times our annual average, but nothing would grow. Conversely, if we received a metre of rain in a day, Olifants would be an eroded wasteland once the floodwater had subsided. Our actual quality of rainfall isn't as bad as either of those scenarios, but there are some similarities in effect.

Spacing of rainfalls, how far apart the falls occur, the timing of the rainfalls both in terms of time of day and position within a season, and quantity of rain received in a measured period of time, all combine to become the key to our decline or otherwise – and, of course, the 'wild card' is global warming, which is impossible to quantify on such a microcosmic scale as Olifants.

It is not how much you eat but rather what you eat and when you eat that helps you maintain good health. So too is the health of our rain-driven ecosystem dependent on quality rather than quantity. We are now beginning to understand the characteristics of rainfall in relation to vegetative growth. It is becoming increasingly apparent that the cumulative amount of rainfall recorded for a particular period is not as significant as the effectiveness of the falls. The question is, then, what influence has global warming had on the quality of the rain as opposed to the quantity? What we're finding is noticeable variations in summer rainfall patterns and the nature of the rainfalls. They have become more erratic and inconsistent, resulting in less benefit to the vegetation and subsequently lower productivity.

Examples of negative effects include lack of timeous follow-up rains. As a result, seeds germinate only to have the young shoots burned off. Another example is the erosion of topsoil and the destruction of seed beds as a result of heavy falls early in the season. We tend to focus primarily on summer rainfall patterns, while relatively little is known about the effects of winter rainfall. Statistically these dry season figures for the lowveld have shown the most dramatic drop. Some authorities suspect there is a significant link between winter rainfall and the decline of sable and roan antelope in the Kruger Park.

You must be wondering why I am expressing some reservations about what I am saying. You might even detect a hint of contradiction. Well, neither applies, really, I'd just prefer to try and put things in the perspective of reality rather than in some convenient hypothetical model. We recognise that ecology is not an exact science, so we cannot rely on statistics alone. We also know that in order for a system to tick over, a complete and complex set of conditions is necessary, and that's mostly beyond our control.

I believe we need to accept that some things are just bigger than us at this point in time. Even though the numbers and statistics of those factors in play appear normal, there are abnormalities in function, but not yet abnormal enough or so out of control that we need to ring the doomsday bells. I do not unreservedly support the belief that we are teetering on a knife edge of environmental tolerances at this stage.

Having said that, I'd prefer we erred on the side of caution rather than complacency and adopt 'a stitch in time saves nine' attitude. There is already some light at the end of this tunnel, too, in that the biggest culprits contributing to global warming are the very countries with the expertise and ability to do something about it before it's too late (as Al Gore is trying to do something about it, whether you agree or disagree with the smoke and mirrors he employs).

Pragmatically speaking, there is comfort in the fact that organisms have responded and adapted to various environmental stimuli since life began. Some make it, others don't; it's Darwin's theory being put to the test again. After all, man had nothing to do with the onset of the Ice Age, the erupting of Krakatoa, or the extinction of the dinosaurs.

The optimist in me believes that in the event of this region getting progressively hotter and drier to some as yet undefined peak, the vast majority of Olifants' fauna and flora will adapt and cope. As compensation, there are actually many species which will thrive in those conditions.

The bottom line is that we can draw on the recorded history of our rainfall to paint a positive picture of the quantity of rainfall we can expect. At the same time, we cannot draw on those figures to interpolate anything to do with the quality of the rainfall. As an example of this, come with me to 1995/1996, and my son's third birthday and the best rainfall season in 22 years.

My son Dino was three years old when he felt the first raindrop on his face! I can still see him on the concrete pathway to our back door, looking up at the source of the drops, only to have another pelt him in the eye. Holding his hands out, palms upward, with an occasional sideways and upward sneak peek, he giggled

Olifants River Game Reserve rainfall 1986–2009

Year	Total mm
1986–1987	343
1987–1988	442
1988–1989	318
1989–1990	464
1990–1991	393
1991–1992	135
1992–1993	395
1993–1994	257
1994–1995	403
1995–1996	718
1996–1997	398
1997–1998	229
1998–1999	424
1999–2000	660
2001–2002	428
2002–2003	155
2003–2004	408
2004–2005	329
2005–2006	531
2006–2007	465
2007–2008	402

Over the years the lowest rainfall was 135 mm in 1991/1992 and the highest 718 mm in 1995/1996.

with pleasure at the new experience. Although it does rain here sometimes, this was his first encounter with this phenomenon, and little did we know then, that he would see a lot more later on in the season. In fact, 1996 would be the highest rainfall recorded for 22 years. But, it was not just the quantity, it was the quality that made such a difference. The reserve had good rains to begin with; in a little over two months, nearly 400 mm of rain had fallen, 25 per cent more than was recorded for the previous 12 months, and the total for the year was well over 700 mm, nearly twice our annual average. In the Olifants River catchment area it rained enough to produce the heaviest flooding in 60 years.

This rain-driven ecosystem wasted no time responding. Within a week the bush began the transformation from apparently life-less grey stubble to the new spring green, or first green, *'prima vera'* as the Italians say. Regular, well-spaced follow-up rains kept the new flush of life moist and nurtured and it wasn't long before the vegetation took on a more mature, verdant, green hue. Even to those of us living here and able to monitor the change from day to day, the vegetation appeared to erupt rather than grow. Species of mostly alien plants whose seeds had been lying dormant for the right rainfall conditions to germinate did so.

Amongst others these included thatching grass *Hyperina* sp., lantana, black jacks and khakibos, but fortunately for us growth was restricted to isolated pockets, mainly where we had brought in feed for the rhino, along the supply road, transport routes and the river floodplain. That was the only time I had ever seen blackjacks or khakibos in such profusion, until 2008/2009 when an unusually wet season resulted in a similar eruption of these weeds.

Driven by the desperate drought conditions of the previous winter, elephant had pushed down, ring-barked and uprooted trees in search of moisture and nutrition. What at the time appeared to be senseless destruction for little or no return is now providing seed reservoirs for the vegetation component of which our reserve is so critically short.

The perennial grasses, buffalo grass *Pannicum maximum* and finger grass *Digitaria sp.* are typical examples. These grasses can be identified by their heavily laden inflorescence competing for sunlight in dense thickets, or standing proud of the thorny, twisted branches that were once the crowns of tall trees. These tangled shrouds now form micro-environments that provide protection from grazing pressure and create the conditions conducive to propagating healthy seed beds for the future seasons' growth.

In contrast, the rate of recovery on the cleared areas is understandably slower. The effect of heavy grazing pressure, combined with severe drought conditions, means that these exposed areas will need a succession of growth to aid the recovery process and therefore will take more time to recover. At present, the vegetation on these open areas consists primarily of pioneer plants, mainly recovery weeds, herbs, and forbs, interspersed with annual grasses of low to medium palatability. These under-utilised plants, most of which are unpalatable, are left to allow their root systems to perform the necessary function of binding the soil. This effectively helps control soil erosion, while mulch forms from uneaten vegetation and also serves to trap seeds, which prepares the way for the next stage of vegetative growth. Basic conditions for recovery on these areas are now greatly improved.

The most recent vegetation analysis, done by the Agricultural Research Council (ARC), indicates that Balule has the lowest yield of vegetation per hectare, when compared to the other reserves in the association. However, this conclusion is qualified by the fact that, relatively speaking, Balule is carrying the largest biomass of plains game. Furthermore, the ratio of plains game species is more representative and proportionately better balanced on this reserve than anywhere else in the APNR. So it is clear that you cannot have your cake and eat it. With an average of just over 400 mm of rain per year, the reserve is presently carrying too much game to allow for a noticeable recovery of the vegetation in the short term.

In the long term, if we are to see the vegetation improve, we have to make some serious, far-reaching decisions pertaining to water provision and animal biomass management. No decisions, no improvement!

We just can't rely on natural progression, particularly in the light of the relatively unquantified effects of global warming on our environment. As humans, we can use brain power (and science) to cope, but many organisms out there cannot employ that mechanism for survival, no matter that Darwin said survival of the fittest and strongest would be the defining law of the jungle.

Riding the Crest?

MAY 2006

I came across a well-known investment broker's newsletter the other day, not quite the sort of reading material I usually digest. However, in amongst the projections, performance graphs, and tables of mathematical hieroglyphics, the sort of stuff that only Deloitte and Touche and the boffins of the accounting world can decipher, I found an interesting article written in lay terms which alluded to certain similarities that I could relate to.

The discussion centred on the steady rise in our local markets and the factors thought to be responsible for the recent positive trend. What I found most interesting were those factors that were expected to have a negative effect. For example, the AIDS pandemic, our increasing crime rate, the influx of illegal immigrants, local power demand exceeding supply, the Zimbabwe issue, local land claims and the Zuma trial, to mention just a few. All negative factors? Well, yes, but all of which appeared to have little or no effect as local and foreign investors still pour money into the market with confidence.

Investment analysts appear reluctant to make long-term projections, and clients are understandably insecure, asking their brokers questions like 'how long before things go pear-shaped?', 'how long before the inevitable levelling-off or drop?', and 'how best can I prepare for it?' Even the layman knows this positive trend cannot continue indefinitely.

What has this got to do with Olifants? Well ...

I find myself asking the same question an insecure investor might ask: 'When is the bubble going to burst?' Continuous feedback from members is that the game viewing is better than they can remember. Those who keep records say there has been a steady increase in the quantity and quality of game each time they visit, and this in spite of the following factors which should have produced a bear market in terms of game viewing … but didn't.

We know that the removal of the Klaserie fence was an ecological and conservation milestone, but the relatively low numbers of plains game in Klaserie at the time meant that there was more grazing available across the border. We all thought that our drought-stressed game would realise this and migrate, thereby effectively diluting the numbers on our reserve. Except for a couple of rhino, this doesn't appear to have happened.

We know that years of drought which led to desperately dry conditions and the lack of vegetation should have taken their toll. Again, this doesn't appear to have happened. We also know that the increase in train traffic could scare game away from the railway line which bisects our reserve. Except for the occasional inevitable casualty, this doesn't appear to have happened. In fact, dare I say it, you can almost always anticipate a good game drive along the railway line service road.

We know that Easter is normally the busiest time of the year, with more shareholders making use of the reserve than at any other time. This means more vehicles cruising around on drives, supposedly disturbing game and causing them to retreat into the thickets. Once again, this doesn't appear to have happened. (In 2009, nature's Easter present to us was a rash of leopard sightings and the return of wild dog to Olifants.)

No matter how many expected negatives I produce, the negative effects seem virtually non-existent. This season's unusually high rainfall has resulted in tall grass growth, as well as dense shrub and tree foliage, all of which effectively screens game from view, yet even this appears to have had little effect, as reports of good general game viewing continue to be recorded in the game sightings register. The abundant rainfall also meant that all the natural waterholes, pans and wallows that are hidden from view are holding water. The riverbeds and drainage lines are so saturated, that digging down a few centimetres produces sweet clear water. Why would animals trek to known waterholes with curious onlookers around, when they could drink unobserved and far from the madding crowd? Again, this did not affect the viewing negatively as expected. The artificial water points were as productive as ever.

I must reiterate that seeing the Big Five is not a scientifically accepted criterion for rating an area's ecological productivity, nor is it everybody's measure of a good game viewing experience, though it remains a recognised yardstick in the bush. In a sense, the Big Five give an impression, or rough gauge, of the 'natural-ness' or 'wildness' of an area, particularly if they're endemic and free-roaming. Some of our shareholders are getting even cheekier, having chalked up the Magnificent Seven. For the uninitiated, that's the Big Five plus wild dog and cheetah!

At the risk of sounding like a cautious investment advisor, I suggest that you 'hedge' your expectations and spread your view-ing portfolio to include a spread from the many other fascinating aspects of Olifants. Don't expect a Big Five return each time you invest in a game drive, because if you do, like the stock market, there are going to be times of little or no return, and in spite of my limited knowledge of things fiscal, I can make that prediction with a fair amount of certainty.

Even for those of us whose wealth is measured in African sun-sets, the Olifants stock market will always offer something of value, and just like the JSE, the harder you work on your invest-ment, the more you'll get out of it.

'Til Death Us Do Part ...

Besides the day-to-day running of Olifants River Game Reserve, as warden of the surrounding Balule private nature reserve, I am obliged to take care of conservation-related matters beyond Olifants' boundaries. In some instances I am requested to respond to calls beyond Balule's jurisdiction as well, although landowners within the Olifants region of Balule who need assistance are almost always given priority.

Early one morning, I received a call from one of our neighbours saying he had come across an injured buffalo. He said it appeared to have a slight limp and thought it may have a snare on its back leg. As he was unable to confirm this for sure, he requested my help in checking it out, and then to advise him on what recommended course of action to take. I agreed and told him I'd be along as soon as I could, but I wasn't too quick to assume the worst, knowing the man well, and also knowing from previous dealings that he can be an alarmist at times. He also has a penchant for embellishing a story with more than a coat of varnish when he needs to, particularly when it comes to injured or apparently abandoned young animals. Nevertheless, a report of a wounded buffalo is never to be taken lightly.

I gathered what equipment I thought I might need, got into the Land Cruiser and drove off to meet him. I also took the opportunity to phone the authorities at the Department of Environmental Affairs and Tourism (DEAT) informing them of the possibly injured buffalo, and that I was on my way to investigate. Essentially, in my position as warden, this situation now became my responsibility. On-the-ground action like this means that judgment calls and decisions often have to be made on the spur of the moment, and this courtesy call unofficially negated the delay that red tape formality could otherwise cause.

I arrived at the scene some 30 minutes later and as it was starting to get warm, the buffalo had moved out of view into the thick bush. Besides my neighbour, there were a number of keen and concerned observers perched on the back of a 2x4 pick-up.

I suggested that everyone climb on to the Land Cruiser as we should try to approach the buffalo by vehicle, as given the terrain we needed to negotiate, the 4x4 was a better option. We then proceeded, albeit at snail's pace, to keep track of the buffalo's spoor while moving through the thick bush. It was difficult going – then, not surprisingly, 100 metres or so from the road, we got a puncture. In order to save time, I asked the young ranger in charge of the group to change the tyre and keep an eye on the guests while my neighbour and I followed the buffalo on foot.

The tracks were relatively easy to follow now that we were on foot. It had rained a few days earlier and the buffalo's hooves left discernible imprints in the soft ground. We tracked through some really thick stuff for about 200 metres or so then it began to open up a little. A few metres later we reached a small clearing, about the size of a couple of tennis courts. These natural open areas are characterised by sodic soils with high clay content, and besides the odd tamboti tree, magic guarri bush and stunted turpentine grass, not much grows on them.

This particular clearing had a small rain-filled wallow on the far fringe, surrounded by guarri bush which formed a secluded thicket … an ideal place for the buffalo to lie up and nurse an aching wound, I thought. Typical of mid-morning conditions in the lowveld, the breeze was erratic and began to swirl, shifting our scent directly towards the thicket and wallow. I thought it would be pointless to spook the buffalo, only to have it thunder off without giving us a glimpse of its injury, so I suggested we do a wide circle of the bush surrounding the wallow and approach from upwind.

Motioning for my neighbour to move in behind me, as we

would now be moving through the perimeter of thick bush, we slowly began to circle the clearing. Moments later I heard a rasping snort in the bush, about 20 metres in front of me. The sound was not unlike what you get when you place your teeth on your bottom lip and exhale sharply. Normally, after the snort, you hear the usual hoof beats and cracking of twigs and branches as these massive animals run through the bush away from you, but not this time. This buffalo burst out of the thicket directly in front of me, about 15 metres away. It was shrouded by a small flock of chirping red-billed oxpeckers which were clearly upset as their host abruptly shook them off and charged me.

In a situation where a hunter wounds a buffalo and is following its tracks, there is always an expectation that these dreadnoughts will suddenly, without warning, charge, invariably from a well chosen area of concealment. You can normally rely on the fact that, even when wounded and pursued, the majority of buffalo will try every trick in the book to get away from their pursuers rather than confront them. Having said this, once a buffalo does make up its mind to charge, only one thing will stop it ... its death or yours.

I was reasonably sure that this buffalo had not been wounded by a hunter, nor had it been harassed by anyone in a capture attempt, but the sheer resolve and determination of its charge left me in no doubt that it was intent on getting me. Incredibly, I managed to remain focused; no doubt my previous experience with buffalo in similar situations helped hone my instinctive reactions.

I remember thinking clearly and methodically as I raised the rifle to my shoulder, flicking the safety off in the same motion, feeling the knurled metal of its tiny lever on my thumb as I slid it forward. I recall distinctly the moment the front sight of the rifle settled on the chest area of the charging buffalo. At a range of approximately five metres, with its head held high in typical charging attitude, I was able to place a shot in the relatively pale and hairless crease, where its powerful neck met its body. At the impact of the 410 grain slug, a pencil-thick stream of blood spurted straight out of the bullet's entry wound. Later, we determined that a major artery had been severed somewhere along the bullet's path into the chest area of the buffalo.

Despite this mortal wound, the buffalo's momentum and determination carried it straight into me. With a flick of its horns, I was thrown sideways into a grove of knobthorn trees also known as 'wait-a-bit' trees because of their vicious hooked thorns. These thorns will physically hold you back, making you wait a bit until you've unhooked them from flesh or clothing. I soon found out how aptly named this tree is.

Knobthorn leaves also happen to be highly nutritious and these particular specimens were thick and stunted from relentless browsing by kudu and giraffe. This was definitely not the ideal place to land head first, as while the going in was no problem, the coming out was to prove more than a little painful. I can assure you that these observations were added long after the event. I was too busy at the time to document matters of ecological relevance.

How I was able to be thrown without being gored was later ascertained when we studied my tattered shorts. The horn had hooked on and ripped my left pocket, then, missing my groin by a couple of millimetres, slid under my leather belt. The combined resistance and strength of the belt against the powerful thrust of the buffalo was enough to get my nearly 80 kg airborne for a few metres.

On the ground now, with my head and shoulders firmly wedged in the thorn bush, I tried to part-pull, part-rip, my head and face out of the thorny tangle. I knew that despite the damage these vicious thorns could inflict, it was nothing compared to what a buffalo's horns could do. I particularly didn't want my rear end exposed to them, so I flipped over onto my back with my knees bent up to my chest to protect my torso. I desperately kicked out at the buffalo's head and face, but I might as well have been kicking a leadwood stump for all the effect I had. I remember thinking that if I could grab hold of, and hang on to, those sweeping horns, I may have a better chance. Otherwise, if this animal didn't die first, this was how I was going to die.

As the side-to-side sweeping motion of its horns slowed down,

I managed to grab hold of one of them and could feel the power of the thrusts ebbing. The consequences of blood loss and tissue damage from my bullet were taking their toll and the buffalo was dying. Despite this, I was still yelling for my neighbour to shoot it, shoot it, because even a half-hearted thrust from those horns could disembowel a man. Up until this point, no other shot had been fired, and the delay felt like ages when split seconds could make all the difference.

Later, when I asked him why he had taken so long to shoot, he said his rifle had misfired and that he had to eject the dud cartridge before he could chamber the next round. In due course, a thorough search revealed nothing and we never did find the 'dud' round he supposedly ejected.

The buffalo, intent on killing me and still feebly trying to hook my body, was now side-on to my neighbour. Its forequarters had now collapsed and it was on its front knees dying, its chin virtually in my lap. This now afforded him an easy coup de grâce side shot to its heart. A couple of shots later, only one of which actually found its target, it gave a short bellow as its hindquarters gave way, almost pinning my legs under its head and chest. I didn't need any help in squirming out from under it, and in a second was on my feet. The first thing I did was to pick up my rifle and give it a quick once over. It was covered in blood and except for a few small scratches, it seemed to be okay.

The people who had followed the young ranger to the scene gathered around me staring open-mouthed at my blood-soaked clothes. I must have looked a sight, even though most of the blood belonged to the buffalo. I remember being offered condolences, prayers and the dregs of some lukewarm Coke in one of those two-litre plastic bottles. Under normal circumstances I don't drink Coke, let alone warm Coke, and the little that was left in the bottom of the bottle had me thinking that it was probably mixed with backwash. It's funny the things you think about at a time like that, but even then, I declined and took the offer of a bottle of water instead. After drinking a little, I washed the blood from my binoculars and my rifle. Blood is extremely corrosive so I needed to wipe it off the metal as quickly as possible. Again, in retrospect, it's funny the things you think about ...

At this point someone asked me if I had seen the hole in my leg and I honestly hadn't. I had absolutely no idea that I had been gored; the cuts from the thorns on my face and head were burning and getting most of my endorphins' attention at this stage. I remember craning my neck around, looking down at the back of my thigh and seeing the gash, bloodless and rimmed with fat, and this grossed me out a little!

How could I possibly have fat there, I thought, I jog nearly every day! Later, at the doctor's consulting rooms in Hoedspruit, I was told that the horn had penetrated deeply, almost to the back of my knee. Luckily for me, it had gone between the muscle sheaths without rupturing them, and had missed my hamstring, hence the virtually bloodless wound. The same could not be said for the rest of the cuts, they bled profusely and together with the blood spatter from the bleeding buffalo, I really looked a lot worse than I actually was. It made for quite a dramatic picture though!

What was the most painful recollection of the whole incident? Without question, it had to be the intramuscular injection of 'Rossofin'. Apparently this potent antibiotic is normally administered intravenously. In my case it was 'sit-down-on-the-bed-before-you-pass-out' painful! Also painful was the fact that I couldn't make our friends Mark and Andie Rodwell's wedding that day. So, while I lay on the couch at home languishing in pain and self-pity, Meagan and the kids went and had a ball. Come to think of it, I wouldn't have been much good on the dance floor, anyway.

The reason I now carry two spare wheels on my Land Cruiser is as a result of the lesson learned from this incident. Not only did I get a puncture a few metres in, but after the incident, on my way out, I got a second! This was enough proof that radial ply tyres may look good and ride nicely, but they are absolutely useless in the bush. There was no way around this predicament, my vehicle had to be rescued, I couldn't leave it there and this meant having to radio my wife Meagan. In not much detail, I had to explain the situation regarding the vehicle and calmly continue in a 'by the way' sort of way, so she wouldn't worry, to ask her to let our doctor in Hoedspruit know I was coming in for a few stitches in the next hour or so. I then proceeded to give her some directions on how to find us, this meaning she would have to concentrate and hopefully wouldn't ask too many questions.

Apparently the directions I gave were not that good, the result being that she and one of our drivers got a little lost, and in so doing came upon the remnants of a buffalo calf that had been killed and eaten by lions the night before.

This happened a mere 50 metres from where the buffalo had first been seen, and could explain why the buffalo was on her own, had lion claw marks on her body and was so belligerent. She had obviously spent some time during the previous evening trying to protect her calf against the lions. This harrowing experience was later made worse, at the sight of two men following her on foot, probably the last straw.

I believe that essentially this was an unnecessary call. There was certainly nothing wrong with any of this animal's legs, and where the suspected snare came into the initial observation, I don't know. This buffalo should have been given the benefit of the doubt and left alone to get over the loss of her calf. If we had to track down and harass every buffalo in a bad mood or nursing a wound or displaying a limp, we would face near tragic predicaments like this one more frequently. My only reservation is that should a dangerous animal be noted displaying abnormal behaviour in an area anywhere near walking trails, the manager or warden is obliged, in the interest of safety, to conduct an investigation. The assessment of the degree of injury and subsequent action required should always be ascertained by a competent professional, or failing this, at least get a second objective opinion. If in doubt, leave things be.

I'd love to know how many of you reading this actually placed your teeth on your bottom lip and exhaled sharply, just to hear what that snort sounded like.

Maybe you will forever remember the sound.

I will never forget it.

Shilo

1981–1995

They say a man has only one dog in his lifetime. This is the story about mine.

Shilo was born in 1981 at the Pont Drift border post, on the southern bank of the great, grey, green, greasy and now, due to soil erosion, gritty Limpopo River, which forms the border between South Africa and the north eastern corner of Botswana. He was the shyest of the five puppies that I was there to choose from, and I can still remember how reluctant he was to come out of the 44 gallon drum that served as his mother's kennel. It had been his home for the six weeks he'd been in this world and he wasn't ready to leave the comfort of his mother's side. As Spartan as this was, he had her protection and love, he felt safe and secure. This was all he knew until I entered his life and he entered mine. And so it was, since that day I reached in to touch him and he licked my hand, we were never apart for longer than a few days at a stretch.

I was living alone at that stage of my life and therefore could devote a lot of time to him. This closeness developed to the point where commands were hardly necessary, simple gestures and tone were enough to communicate. As time went by, it became increasingly apparent that I was completely mistaken with my first impression of him. What I initially thought to be timidity and shyness was, in fact, a combination of sensitivity and intelligence. He was able to pick up on the most subtle nuances to the point that later, Meagan and I would have to spell certain words if there was something we didn't want him to react to.

109

His ability to respond to hand signals probably saved his life one day. We were on the Transkei Wild Coast at the time, fishing on the incoming tide at the mouth of the Mkambati lagoon and the shad were biting well. We were totally preoccupied with the task at hand and so no one noticed when Shilo ran off chasing after one of the local bitches who happened to be on heat. When we realised what was happening, he was already crossing the lagoon after her.

The only way I could call him back over the noise of the sea was to get his attention and wave my arm beckoning for him to return. Thanks to his obedience, he responded immediately. This must have saved his life, for another 15 minutes and the back wash current would have swept him out to sea.

The African bush is filled with dangers for dogs, so Shilo went everywhere with me, it being too dangerous for a young pup to be left alone at camp. This emphasised the immediate need for discipline and training, neither of which was a problem. He responded enthusiastically to training and learned quickly, which I was really pleased about. An untrained dog is particularly vulnerable and curious puppies are at most risk. To any dog, however, the most serious threats come from warthogs and baboons. Nothing tests a dog's resolve and discipline quite like an arrogant baboon. Aggressive and over-protective dogs in particular, are easily lured out of their safety zone and then torn to pieces by these well-armed primates who are masters at gang fighting.

Another test is the cheekiness of warthog piglets scampering around and playing on the lawn. This provokes even the most restrained dog to chase them, but unfortunately Mother Pig with her razor-sharp lower tusks is usually only a belly-ripping swipe away. Baboons and warthogs were part of his first real world lessons, and undoubtedly amongst the most important for him to learn. Shilo took to these instructions very well, and was soon taught not to chase anything unless given the command 'teksit'. There were times I could swear he was co-operating just to see how happy it made me. As luck would have it, we were moving bricks from a brick pile and came across a nest of young snakes. I recognised them immediately as egg-eaters. These little snakes resemble night adders, but because they're absolutely harmless and don't have a tooth in their mouths, they strike repeatedly at the least provocation to make themselves appear dangerous. As a result, they turned out to be the most perfect props for teaching Shilo that snakes were to be avoided. This was one occasion when he was encouraged to bark.

Shilo was built leaner than a Labrador but heavier than a Doberman, his deep chest and relatively narrow waist predisposing him to speed. He really loved to run, so much so, that unless you reined him in, he would run the pads off his feet on the rough roads in the Tuli Block, which were littered with quartz, and this would put him out of action for a few days while they healed.

As an aside, I understand that timber wolves have thicker pads than any domestic breed. Apparently, during the Angola/Namibia border conflict era, the military canine unit was looking into the possibility of cross-breeding dogs with wolves, in order to obtain a breed with hard-wearing pads. This would have enabled this unit to track terrorists over rough terrain for longer periods. Shilo could have done with some of those calloused and hard-wearing 'wolf pads'. At one stage I contemplated importing or making those booties they put on Huskies' paws for those gruelling sled races in Canada and Alaska, but it turned out that these shoes could only be used in snow and ice, not on sand or gravel. Anyhow, I believe the toes and claws of dogs play a crucial role when turning or needing to gain purchase on dry ground, particularly at speed. With his feet covered, Shilo would have been seriously handicapped, so we abandoned the booty idea.

Shilo's first journey to the big city, the first time he placed his pads on paved roads, was in Johannesburg. What I saw him do on that trip convinced me that he and I were destined to be together, for life. A good friend of mine, South African 250cc motocross champion, Tyrone Stevenson, invited me to watch him race while I was in town. I told him I would love to, but had a dog I couldn't leave on its own. I explained that my dog had never been to a city before and was totally street unwise.

'No problem. I'm sure he'd love Sasha,' Tyrone said.

'Who's Sasha?' I asked.

'She's my dog, a cross Doberman Rottweiler', he answered.

When they met the next morning, it was love at first sight. Sasha was slightly bigger than Shilo, but both dogs were about the same age and appeared to have similar energy levels.

Despite this ideal match, I was a little apprehensive, as this would be the first time I would be leaving Shilo on his own with an attractive lady in unfamiliar surroundings. But, the high walls and secure gate gave me a measure of assurance; I was sure that he'd be safely confined and enjoy himself at the same time.

We returned late that afternoon, in high spirits, for it had been a successful day at the track for Tyrone, and Meagan and I were looking forward to a hot bath, eager to soak away the day's dust and grime that is part and parcel of motocross. I must admit to being quite keen to see if Shilo had missed me, as much as I had missed him. I imagined him waiting at the gate for me, but when we arrived at the house, only Sasha was there to greet us.

My heart sank. Despite an extensive search, Shilo was nowhere to be found. The maid then informed us that when she came to work and opened the gate, Shilo took the gap and slipped past her out into the road, and there was nothing she could do. This meant he was now exposed to busy road traffic to which he was totally unaccustomed and with no familiar smells or landmarks to guide him who knew where he could end up. I began to paint a really negative picture in my mind. Meagan and I decided to drive around the area, which we did for what seemed like hours, questioning everybody we could and calling his name repeatedly. When it became too dark to see anymore, we decided to call it quits and head on back to my father's house, which was about six kilometres from Tyrone's.

Dejected, expecting the worst, we drove in silence through the two busy intersections where I half expected to find Shilo's lifeless body. Thankfully there was nothing. I was going through the mental process of preparing for the prospect of never seeing my dog again and I was behaving like a zombie, just going through the motions. Then, nearing the turn-off to my father's house, I caught sight of a familiar shape in the headlights as they swung in an arc round the corner.

I couldn't believe my eyes initially, but it was no mere illusion, it was Shilo! Nose to the ground and only 200 metres away from my father's house!

'Shilo!' I called, not quite as loudly as I would have liked. Either I was choked emotionally or some motocross dust must have been lodged in my throat, but it was loud enough for him to hear, and in a flash he was on the front seat between Meagan and me, licking my face, something he was not normally encouraged to do. He also smiled a lot when he was happy or embarrassed, which made him sneeze, so it was lick-smile-sneeze, lick-smile-sneeze, all the way home to my father's house.

So what is so extraordinary about this? Countless domestic dogs throughout history have been known to run home from hundreds of miles away. Be this as it may, Shilo's situation was rather different as all the odds were stacked against him.

He had never set foot on the ground between Tyrone's house and my father's, nor had he ever walked on a tar road, or seen so many people and cars, except from the inside of my vehicle. He had come straight out of the Botswana bush to Johannesburg's concrete jungle in the back of a vehicle. What scent he was following when we found him, and how had he negotiated two busy intersections without mishap, I will never know. All I do know is that this was but one of many instances which made me realise that Shilo was a dog in a million, and that I was privileged to share part of my life with him.

Being a cross Doberman Pinscher/black Labrador, meant firstly he wasn't the ideal colour for the hot bushveld environment, and secondly, he had a light layer of underfur inherited from his Labrador genes, which assists with insulation in cold weather. Strangely enough, this proved to be no problem in the heat either, as this under-fur also trapped and held water, so once wet, the 'radiator effect' lasted a long time, proving to be an effective means of combating the heat. Having been born and bred in the bush, Shilo showed a remarkable degree of tolerance for the bushveld heat although he appeared to be more comfortable in the freezing wetlands of the southern Drakensberg or eastern Free State.

At one stage I considered dyeing his coat a lighter colour for the summer months, but never got around to doing it. In any event, this cosmetic solution was never really necessary.

Shilo's own characteristics soon proved to be the attributes that allowed him the ability to work in the heat of the bush and earn a legendary reputation as one of the finest retrievers around, and also in temperatures well below freezing.

Besides running, he loved to swim, and thought nothing of swimming in icy cold water. Often the pans and dams had two or three metres of thinnish overnight ice around the edges, which he would have to crack through before swimming out to retrieve waterfowl. With ambient temperatures sometimes as low as minus ten, which caused the steam to rise off his wet body, he would remain completely focused on the horizon and the next flight of duck. These were his finest hours. His retrieving skill went beyond the retrieval of waterfowl, sticks and balls. One afternoon at Motswari camp in the Timbavati, he jumped into the swimming pool, grabbed a young girl by the arm and pulled her to the safety of the shallow end. It wasn't much shallower than the rest of the pool but did have a set of stainless steel rung-type steps. The only way Shilo could get out of this particular pool was if you helped him by grabbing the nape of his neck as he got close to the edge, then he would push himself against the resistance of your hand and clamber out. Worried that he may have hurt the girl, Meagan questioned her friend who then confirmed that the young girl was having difficulty in the deep water and splashing excessively. This, I suspect, is what triggered his instinctive response to retrieve. We had purposely never taught Shilo to grab or retrieve people in water rescue scenarios, for fear he may exert too much holding pressure and puncture their skin. We could never lose sight of the fact that while he was able to employ the soft mouth pressure essential for retrieving wild fowl and attributed to the Labrador in him, he was still 50 per cent Doberman.

Shilo very seldom barked, so when he did, we knew that there was usually a problem. This was another necessary discipline in the tourism/game lodge environment. You couldn't have a yapping dog around while guests are trying to enjoy the sounds of the African bush.

As it happens, this is also one of the biggest problems with dogs in urban areas, and yet it was one of the easiest things to teach him not to do. I had Shilo sleep with me in my bed from day one, until many years later when he took to sleeping next to the bed. When he was a little pup many of the night noises were strange to him, so every time he heard something out side he yipped. When he did, I'd utter an urgent 'uh! uh!', dog speak for 'no! no!' Then, if unable to suppress the urge to keep quiet, he would growl. When he growled, I praised him. Initially the growl would break into a yip, but, with praise, he was soon able to control this. So, Shilo became a growler not a barker.

Sixteen years ago, when Meagan and I went to interview for the position at Olifants, Shilo came along as well, of course. As I mentioned earlier, he was my shadow and where I went, he went. It really was a case of 'love me, love my dog'. The back of my truck was customised for his comfort while travelling and for when he had to spend the night in the vehicle – when, for example, a B&B didn't allow dogs. In these instances I used to leave a Fisher Price baby monitor in the back with him.

Knowing that the Olifant's interview could last for an indeterminate length of time, I had to make him as comfy as possible. So, in the courtyard-cum-parking lot of Dimension Data, I found a shady spot to park and let him out to do his ablutions on a nearby patch of lawn studded with lovely trees. Once this function was complete, it was back into the truck and onto his mattress. Sliding both the side windows of the canopy open, I then filled his water bowl, turned the 12V Hella turbo fan on to medium, and closed the door. I never locked the canopy door when he was in the back.

Unbeknown to us, we were being watched the whole time from one of the upper floors. On termination of the interview, I was asked directly, 'and what about the dog?' My answer was simply that my dog was old, bush-wise and well-trained, and if I were to go to Olifants, so would Shilo.

Time passed and age was catching up on Shilo.

Slowly, his quality of life was deteriorating, to the point that in his 14th year he could hardly walk without discomfort, and this condition became progressively worse. I knew the day I had dreaded all these years would soon dawn, and when it did, I phoned Gerrit. About 30 minutes later, his Cessna 172 touched down on the airstrip. Without elaboration, we drove in virtual silence to the house, this wasn't the time for usual small talk and both of us knew that. As usual, Shilo had heard my vehicle and was waiting for me at the door, smiling so hard he sneezed repeatedly. His tail wagged with increased vigour when he saw Gerrit. He may have thought we were going wildfowling together again, something we hadn't done for a long time. His mind was now occupied with excited anticipation of what he lived for.

When Gerrit ruffled the skin on the back of his neck, as he usually did when they met, Shilo didn't notice that this time, a tranquilliser was gently injected into the loose folds by those same hands, nor had he noticed that Meagan had taken Eleana and Dino for a walk up the road past the water tanks. Soon after, in the basket next to my bed, where he always slept, I held his head in my lap while the final 'sleeping' drug was administered. Moments later, the canine love of my life for so many years slipped quietly away in my arms.

Shilo lies buried under a shady knobthorn tree at the bottom of our garden on Olifants. There could never be enough space on a headstone for a fitting epitaph to his memory, so I chiselled a granite sliver to clearly mark his grave. It reads, simply, 'Shilo'.

With a Little Human Help, 'Hang-lip' Gets a New Lease on Life

JUNE 2008

I don't like giving names to wild animals. I believe there is a risk that name association creates a too personal, almost domesticated impression of the creature in question. Wild animals are living free and are not pets. Emotional attachment can, and often does, cloud your judgement if and when you need to make an objective decision in their management.

That may sound harsh, for in our reserve's history, we have had many names tagged onto many wild animals. In the 1990s, there was Tripod the hyaena, so-named after his three-legged configuration. There was Pumba, the grumpy old warthog who got even grumpier when deprived of his human friends and their highly disapproved-of feeding routine. There was a pair of civets called Windscreen Wiper and Babe, who would watch their human neighbours from just outside the circle of light created by a braai fire. I am sure there were, and are, many other names for reasons of affection or convenience.

In my case, exceptions are made to my judgemental position on a temporary basis when needing to identify a particular group or individual, as, for example, during certain research projects. Further to that, I accept that over time certain individuals can grow on you, especially if you're seeing them virtually every day. Then, the natural progression is to give them names. It's inevitable – and no more so than in the case of what are arguably the most popular animals on the reserve … lions.

So lions will get named and that's that!

Neil Hulett, one of the longer-standing shareholders of the reserve, and whose name is synonymous with Olifants, was out with his wife Morag on a routine morning drive when they came across the resident pride of lion at Hide Dam.

Neil noticed a number of broken porcupine quills protruding from the chest of one of the two dominant male lions of the pride. It happened to be the older of the two, known as Hang-lip because his lower lip, although completely healed, hung open all the time. Male lions often carry scars from fights and I suspect his torn lip was a result of an old injury sustained in a territorial dispute with rival males.

However, the predicament in which he now found himself didn't appear to be one he would recover from without help. The lion had obviously tangled with one of our large prickly rodents recently and apparently didn't get off too lightly. Yes, a porcupine is a rodent ... and in this case, a few of the rodent's quills appeared to have been broken off by the lion's repeated attempts to remove them. The result was that remaining portions of quill shafts had become deeply embedded. There was no way this lion was going to be able to remove the quills himself. He also appeared to have lost a considerable amount of weight and was in obvious pain and discomfort.

It is not unusual for a lion that tackles a porcupine to get 'quilled'. Even the most skilled porcupine killer gets 'quilled' now and again. It is an occupational hazard with which wild lions have had to contend since they discovered porcupines are delicious. In most instances they're able to remove the quills themselves. Nobody knows what happened to the porcupine in this case, but it was obvious the encounter was not one-sided, whether or not the porcupine became a meal.

Hang-lip, now past his prime, was starting to show his age and had not been in the best of health lately. Over the years, Neil has spent an enormous amount of time observing the lions on the reserve and has built up a special relationship with them, many of which he has watched grow from tiny cubs. Taking pity on the plight of his old friend, he radioed in to ask me if there was anything that could be done to improve his lot. Having bred and raised cheetah on his farm in KwaZulu-Natal, Neil was no stranger to big cats. He understands more than most the 'tough love' attitude that is often necessary, particularly with regard to self-sustaining wild predator populations.

The life of most large predators in the wild, particularly lions, is not an easy one, and the majority of them never reach maturity. The battle-scarred veteran of the Olifants pride was now in trouble and Neil could see this. Given Neil's experience, I was able to make the call on his observation alone. This was around 05.30 so there was plenty of time to arrange things. A few minutes later, I phoned my long-time friend and local veterinarian, Gerrit Scheepers, who is based in Phalaborwa.

Brushing aside my apology for waking him so early, he mumbled something about 'have some good coffee ready when I arrive' and, 'it's never too early to save an animal's life'. He then grabbed the necessary darting and medical kit he always keeps in a 90 per cent state of readiness, drove the short distance to the airport and scrambled his light plane. Less than an hour later, the familiar silhouette of his Cessna 172 appeared in the early morning sky and then, dropping the little plane with practised purpose, he touched down on our runway.

Within minutes, we were on our way to Hide Dam and the lions, some ten minutes' drive away. While waiting for Gerrit's arrival, I had acquired the carcasses of a couple of large impala rams which would be used to distract the rest of the pride, keeping them occupied while we worked on Hang-lip. This is not as easy as it sounds, these were wild lions that had never been 'baited' before. Hang-lip was successfully isolated from the rest of the pride, which enabled Gerrit to dart him without any hindrance from the other pride members. Once the drug had taken effect and the lion was tranquillised, we moved in and immediately started to work on removing the quills. Two were very deeply embedded and required the judicious use of my 'Leatherman' to extract them. What fantastic tools these are, I use mine all the time and am completely lost without it. Please excuse the commercial (unpaid!).

The wounds had begun to go septic and we were now certain the lion could never have removed the quill fragments himself.

Long-acting antibiotics were then administered and a few of his other war wounds were also treated while we had the opportunity. Hang-lip was not in good physical condition, so he was given a vitamin booster injection which would also help bolster his immune system and facilitate the healing process.

While this was all going on, a handful of shareholders who were in the vicinity at the time became actively involved. Everyone assisted by strategically parking their vehicles as a barrier between the lion we were working on and the rest of the pride, which was occupied with feeding on the impala carcasses. The sound of contented lions feeding was interrupted only occasionally by loud guttural growls, as one or two greedily tried to get a bigger piece of the action and were cuffed back into line.

We didn't really consider cosmetic surgery in the form of a 'lip lift'. At his stage of life we thought it unnecessary as his appeal to the females of his species had little to do with his physical beauty. Seriously, though, there are actually very clear limits as to the extent we are able to interfere with nature in an open system such as that of which Olifants is now an integral part. So, no matter how compassionate the motivation, even the quill removal was a marginal call and a little 'nipping and tucking' would have been taking the concession way outside acceptable limits.

Zoletil, the immobilising drug of choice, has no antidote so needs to be processed through the animal's liver, taking up to five hours. We kept tabs on the lion until he had recovered completely from the tranquilliser, bearing in mind that even large predators are particularly vulnerable while in a groggy state. The unnatural movements and staggering gait can trigger an aggressive and opportunistic response from other lions, or cause the animal to fall awkwardly and injure itself.

From the time of the radio call from Neil that morning to Gerrit's plane taking off back to Phalaborwa, less than three hours elapsed. Some of this time was spent making the lion comfortable while he slowly recovered. Strong black coffee and homemade rusks were sampled while we all shared some good-natured chat. There is always a moment for reflection and great sense of relief when an operation like this goes smoothly and once we knew we had given a magnificent old monarch a helping hand, it was that much more rewarding.

The next day, Hang-lip had reason to really drop his lip! Four younger males moved into the area looking for a brawl. Although we were monitoring the situation, truth be told, our two dominant males were getting a little long in the tooth and we weren't sure how much longer they could defend their territory. Whatever the outcome might be, though, it would be better than a slow death from starvation and septicaemia.

Over a year has passed since this incident and both these lions are still very much in the picture as pride males. Recently, however, in response to pressure from two new males from the east, 'Hang Lip' and his pride crossed the river onto Olifants North and appear to have taken up permanent residence there. Discretion being the better part of valour proved to be the right option, because a little while later, a further three males moved in, increasing the coalition to a formidable five lions.

So, Hang-lip retained his pride, in more ways than one.

Elephants Don't Like Joggers

AUGUST 2004

The influx of elephant into our reserve meant that we needed to be extra vigilant due to the associated dangers. The most significant policy change was that shareholders were no longer allowed to walk on the reserve – and this included the former wilderness area originally designated for this purpose. This has since been made into one of the most beautiful drives on Olifants, known as Pel's Loop.

As far as a 'day in the life of a ranger' goes, it has been a relatively uneventful period, punctuated with meetings and other routine but necessary tasks. This gave me the chance to dig into the archives to come up with a story that will hopefully convey a relevant message against becoming complacent with our new and ever-increasing resident elephant population. I would rather sound like a stuck record on the walking issue, than have to record a sticky end.

In a previous newsletter, I had listed a number of tips for viewing elephant, which mainly focused on how best to approach them, and how to take evasive action if necessary when viewing from a vehicle. What to do to avoid them or how to take evasive action when meeting elephant on foot was not covered. The following story may provide a practical hint or two.

About a year ago, the numbers of elephant on the reserve were less than half of what they are now. Despite this more comfortable and relatively low density, there was always the chance of unexpectedly bumping into them, which though not usually a problem, could on occasion become one. One afternoon I was on the return leg from a fairly long but interesting run on neighbour-ing Dinidza. I always enjoyed following the hippo path along the beautiful riverine section. On my way back, I decided to go home via the Hide Dam pump on the riverbank near the clubhouse. The pump had been playing up for a while and I wanted to check on it.

Approaching the beehive-shaped stone cairn that protects one of the air valves on the main pipeline, I could hear the faint hiss of air pressure escaping.

'Great,' I thought. 'It's working.' And on I ran.

As I headed up the floodplain loop road approaching a familiar sjambok pod tree I run past almost every day, I heard the shrill trumpeting of an elephant behind me. Looking back over my shoulder in the direction of the river, I saw a young elephant bull about 100 metres away, standing facing me, his trunk up and ears out. Having picked up my scent, he was making it obvious he wasn't happy with the sweaty human odour that filled his trunk. He was shaking his head and trunk vigorously as if trying to get rid of the smell – not that I could blame him: after a ten-kilometre run in the bushveld heat, I could barely tolerate my own odour.

I judged the distance from where I was to where he was stand-ing as being greater than the distance to the relative safety of the tree line. This meant there was a good chance I would make it, if I cut the corner in the road and sprinted across the flood plain. So, I decided to go for it. At this point the little troublemaker that had sighted me and cried wolf was joined by eight other elephant which seemed to materialise out of nowhere. Encouraged by their support, and seeing my rear end disappearing away from him at a rate of knots no doubt helped boost his confidence to lead the charge.

Having made it safely across the open floodplain to the trees, I selected a tall slender leadwood. 'Selected' in this instance could be more accurately interpreted as 'the nearest tree I could find'! The branch jutting out that I needed to grab onto in order to haul myself up into the tree required a little jump on my part. This was asking a lot of a pair of legs that had just done a fair run topped off with an adrenalin-charged sprint. The first feeble attempt showed I was about six inches short, reminiscent of those nightmares when you need to run, but cannot lift your legs. Another shrill trumpet, now getting too close for comfort, was all the encouragement my adrenal gland needed, and the six-inch deficit suddenly evaporated.

I hauled myself up into the tree, then wriggled upwards to the topmost branches where I quietly hugged the trunk and pretended I was part of the environment.

With blue shorts, white running shoes, cream T-shirt, pink legs and arms, well, I must have blended right in, or they mistook me for a giant lilac-breasted roller, because at that point, without slowing down, two elephant ran past right underneath me, one on either side of the tree. I can vividly recall every detail of the cracked pattern of the skin on their backs and remember how this contrasted with the relative smoothness of the tops of their heads.

I also remember thinking that I must get high enough to stay out of reach of their trunks. Looking back now at that tree, it is hardly what I would describe as a representative of the species, as by giving it a good shove, I'm sure a determined elephant would have been able to push it down. Despite this, instinctively climbing the tree was the only option at the time, and, in hindsight, appears to have been the right option in any event. The height gained allowed my scent to be carried away above the elephant, this being doubly fortunate because it was blowing in their direction. Furthermore, I suspect, like many other wild animals, they're just not inclined to look up, especially to locate human beings. Keeping still and pressing up against the main trunk, despite my 'camouflage', also helped, I'm sure.

A hundred metres or so past me, they slowed down and stopped, standing dead quiet, trunks in the air sniffing for a trace of the elusive smelly man. A couple of minutes later they appeared to settle down completely and a few of them started feeding.

Colleagues Ron and Cindy Hopkins, having heard the trumpeting from their house, which overlooks the floodplain, decided to take their guests out to view the elephant. They had no idea the elephant were chasing me. Ron drove slowly along the road in the direction of the trumpeting, and slowly approached my position. I could see him and the other occupants peering into the bush at eye level looking for signs of the elephant.

'Oi!' I shouted.

Although they heard me, they didn't see me until the second 'Oi!' and the frantic waving of a white sock.

No, I am not suggesting that a white sock is a *de rigueur* part of one's bush kit, it's just that I always carried one, it being used to wipe the sweat off my forehead when I'm running. This eventually caught their attention and it didn't take Ranger Ron in his rugged Rover too long to effect the rescue. We then drove up the road to where the elephant were milling around. In total contrast to the pandemonium earlier, they appeared totally relaxed when approached and viewed from the vehicle.

Things have changed since then, and I have had to adapt my route in order to minimise the danger that the increased elephant numbers pose. The circuit I run now is repetitive and relatively boring, but at least I have now identified a few easy-to-climb, sturdy trees, at reasonably regular strategic intervals.

The new rule is simple ... 'You must be able to climb before you can run!'

White Lions

1983 – 1993

When Chris McBride 'discovered' white lions on his property, it prompted him to write *The White Lions of Timbavati*. This not only put the Timbavati Private Nature Reserve on the map, it also exposed to the world what many believed to be a unique, previously unrecorded phenomenon. People are generally fascinated with lions, so when white ones were discovered in the wild, it stimulated far more attention than would have a white blesbuck, for example. Also I suspect that this was deemed more sensational or newsworthy by the media, who perpetuated the awareness and perceived plight of these lions.

The white lions of the Timbavati stole the limelight and fears were raised about the future of these lions in the wild. In turn, this captured even wider public interest and soon they became the focus of attention in conservation circles. For a while, they were accorded the same priority status as if a new species had been discovered.

Every now and again, it appears that nature will 'test the water' by throwing out a wild card to see how it copes. This pale, almost white colour is not exclusive to lions, the same mutation occurs in numerous other mammal species. White lions are not albinos, they're the consequence of what is known as a 'chinchilla mutation' occurring as a result of a recessive gene. It appears that among wild lions in particular, the occurrence of this mutation is confined to Southern Africa, more specifically the Timbavati area. White lions have also been popping up in the Tshokwane area of the Kruger National Park for years. In their case, nobody made a fuss about them, or tried to capitalise on the 'freak show'. Ironically, the hype concerning the threat to their survival in the wild, and the motivation for the conservation of white lions, has been of more benefit to man and his greed than to the lions themselves.

During the nearly ten years I spent in the Timbavati, I was fortunate enough to have spent days on end in the company of these famous lions in the wild. By recording the observations made on a particular white lion within the pride, I was able to compile some interesting material culminating in an unpublished paper.

This was submitted as one of my projects when I studied Nature Conservation through correspondence. Although I received a satisfying pass, the contents of this paper are too detailed (and too 'dry') for inclusion here, but some points may be pertinent to the ongoing controversy surrounding these animals. So, I invite you to join me while we take a brief look at some aspects of this fascinating animal's life.

The white lioness I studied was born under a thick overhang of wild date palms *Phoenix reclinata* on the banks of the Sohebele River in 1982, and to the best of my knowledge there were no other white lions in the Timbavati at the time. The rest of the pride, including her sister, were all 'normal' tawny-coloured lions, as were the two recessive gene-carrying pride males known as Rex and Adonis, who were both beautiful, black-maned males. Two years later, a white male cub was born to the same pride, and again, both his brother and sister were 'normal'. As is often the case with young male lions, they were nudged out of the reserve when they were a little over two years old. They were never seen again. Rumours and speculation all pointed to them having been shot by bow hunters from overseas.

A couple of years later, Rex and Adonis were shot on the farm 'Goedehoop' (Good Hope) situated north of Motswari in the Umbabat Nature Reserve. The event was catalytic in the fragmentation of the white pride. This property proved to be anything but 'Good Hope' for the two males, as to add insult to injury, the following morning we found Adonis at 'Moenie Jag' crossing on the Sohebele River. This crossing got its name from an old signboard that dated back to the early fifties which used to read 'Moenie jag nie asseblief' (Please don't hunt). How ironic!

The cowardly man or men responsible for wounding Adonis lacked the courage to follow him and finish what they had started. They also failed to report the incident to anyone. Sadly, it didn't end there, as I will now explain.

The rangers from Motswari were always on the lookout for lion spoor. It wasn't unusual for them to find fresh spoor and follow it until the lions were located. The guests loved this and the rangers thrived on the challenge. This time, however, when the fresh tracks of a large male were found, all was not as it seemed – there was something wrong. It was apparent from the drag marks and associated blood spatter that these tracks were made by an animal that was seriously injured. Our immediate thoughts were that a territorial dispute had ensued resulting in an injury from fighting between males. A short while later a low guttural growl emanated from a thick stand of wild date palm that grew in the middle of the sandy dry river bed, indicating we had located the injured lion.

When the lion got up to move away across the open sand, we could see it was Adonis and he was dragging his back leg. He was immobilised soon after. Upon closer examination we found that his hip had been shattered by a bullet from a .375 Magnum and that the slug was deeply embedded in his leg. The prognosis was dreadful, there was nothing that could be done … and so the white-gene-carrying pride male was euthanased.

In November 1985, the white lion and her sister, now well into their third year, came into oestrus simultaneously. For almost two weeks they were observed on the farm Sumatra, mating with two new males who had recently moved in from the Kruger National Park. Interestingly, most of the courtship took place less than half a kilometre from where the two sisters were born nearly three years previously. Three-and-a-half months later, seven tawny cubs were born, three to the white lioness and four to her tawny sister. A month later six cubs were observed, one having died of an unknown cause. All six remaining cubs survived to adulthood.

One day I saw something rather unusual, which was thought to be inconsistent with the behaviour of these social animals. The white lion and her sister had killed a large giraffe cow, clearly more than they and their four-month-old cubs could utilise, yet when the pride called from approximately 500 metres away, neither lioness answered. The pride moved on, blissfully unaware of all that meat so close by.

By the next day, however, they had found the kill as the wind must have changed and drifted the scent onto them, or they might have been vulture watching. I suspect that the two females kept quiet the previous day because they were instinctively concerned about the safety of their cubs, and didn't want to expose them to the risks associated with a feeding frenzy. Not too long after this, these same cubs would be catalytic in an incredible display of lion behaviour never recorded before. In defiance of all we understand about lions, I was to witness what could only be described as a unique phenomenon.

If I was asked today what the chances were of a wild lion pride accepting an orphaned wild lion cub from another area, my answer would be, 'no chance'. It's not like bringing home a new puppy and introducing it to the other dogs. Wild predators, particularly lions, have established social structures and will not tolerate outsiders and interlopers. Therefore, orphaned lions are placed in zoos or similar protective sanctuaries for the rest of their days, or they are put down, and that's that; there is no alternative as far as I'm concerned. With regard to small cubs, the same rule applies: if they were not immediately torn to pieces, they would be ostracised and then die a slow death by starvation. Either way, placing an orphan lion cub among strange lions is a death sentence. Over the years I had seen too many stray lions dealt with this way to believe there was any other possible outcome. So, when the warden of the Timbavati asked if he could dump a young lion on my doorstep, my reply was initially negative. Of course, as he began giving me details on this particular lion, and that every alternative except a bullet had been exhausted, I weakened, thinking there may be a glimmer of hope, albeit a glimmer of minuscule proportions.

The orphan cub was a female approximately five months of age, and came from an area close to the Sabi Sand Game Reserve. Her mother and two sibling brothers had been destroyed by the problem animal branch of the Nature Conservation Department for killing cattle in the Bushbuck ridge area. Somehow the official didn't have the heart to put the little female down and so was pleading with us to see if she could be released in the reserve.

This request came at the time when the white lion's and her sister's cubs were about four months old. The rangers had been out earlier that morning and reported that they had found the lions. So we knew the whereabouts of the two lionesses and their cubs at the time. Lying in shade out of the midday sun, they would probably lie up in that area for most of the day waiting for things to cool down towards evening. The situation and timing could not have been better. The venue for the release would be a nearby waterhole on the bank of the Machaton River, where I suspected the lions would drink that evening.

The warden and his team arrived in two vehicles, the carcass of a zebra on one, and in a cage on the back of a second vehicle was the frightened little lion cub. We secured the carcass to a tree on the edge of the waterhole, covered it with magic guarri branches and then removed the cage from the back of the other vehicle. Everybody now backed right away, leaving only the warden to open the cage. The cub needed no encouragement when the door was opened; she ran straight out, passed the carcass and hurried on down the embankment into the soft sand and relative seclusion of the river bed. And that's where we left her as we all hastily drove away. I remember feeling so sorry for this tiny, lonely animal, left to fend for herself in this seriously tough neighbourhood. It felt cruel, and yes, I did feel guilty for not resisting this 'chuck it and chance it' release ... I was playing roulette with a life.

Returning about three hours later, I was hoping to find that at least she had eaten some of the zebra, but through my binoculars I could see none of the small branches had been moved and the bait was untouched.

It was now getting late; the sun slipped away behind the

Drakensberg Mountains and, as it did, the temperature cooled measurably and the wind dropped completely. Except for the raucous calls of a couple of crested spurfowl as they settled in to roost for the night, the atmosphere was thick with an oppressive stillness. Although I was perched in a hide some 40-odd metres away, the ripe smell of the carcass hung heavy in the air. I remember thinking that if I could smell it, so would the lions. After setting up a spotlight, I poured a cup of tea from my small stainless steel flask and settled down to wait.

I am always amazed at how quietly these relatively large animals can move through the bush at a normal walking pace. This time was no exception, and even though I knew the lions were coming, they are built for stealth and I heard nothing until the rustle of the guarri bush I'd used to cover the carcass as it was being removed. The guttural growls and snarls that followed meant they had begun to feed on the carcass. Allowing them a few minutes to settle down, I turned on the light which revealed that except for the two big males, the whole pride was there. The crunching and the munching as all of them fed was only interrupted by the occasional growl or grunt when one of the cubs forgot its place in the pecking order, even though there was more than enough for all of them.

I watched the interaction between the feeding lions for a while, then gave them a break from the spotlight, not that it seemed to disturb them in the slightest. I couldn't help feeling sorry for that lonely, frightened lion cub somewhere out there in a strange and hostile territory without the reassuring comfort of its mother. The picture being painted in my mind was not pretty; in fact it was downright depressing, until I reached for the spotlight and turned it on again.

No words can describe what I saw next, or the emotion I felt when I did, but it was the sort of stuff fairy tales are made of.

Unfortunately, because this happened in the dark and in a relatively short space of time, I am unable to provide a sequential blow-by-blow report as to how it happened. All I can say with certainty is that when I turned the spotlight back on, the number of lions in the pride feeding on the zebra carcass had grown by one! The impossible had happened and this orphan cub had joined the pride without hesitation or any sign of diffidence from the others! The big test was still to come: would this little waif be accepted by the pride males? We were to be astounded yet again, when a couple of days later the big males were seen with the rest of the pride including the new little cub. We were considering rewriting everything known about the social behaviour of lions, but realised this was unique, a one-off exception to the rule.

The new lion was easy to distinguish from the rest of her pride mates and adopted siblings; she was a darker shade of tawny, almost a teddy bear ginger. As she grew older, we also noticed that her face was slightly shorter, more 'puggy' than the adult females of the white pride, which had an unmistakable 'pink panther' look about them. The white lioness and her sister were apparently completely blind to these differences, and treated the cub as if she were one of their own.

Broad-based conjecture about this incredible phenomenon is that this adoption resulted from the totality of a complex and coincidental set of circumstances that would be virtually impossible to replicate in the wild. Firstly, the cub was about the same age and size as the adoptive pride's cubs. Secondly, it was a wild lion that was used to competing with siblings for food and so slotted into the feeding ritual without arousing suspicion. Thirdly, the overpowering smell of the carcass and fatty nature of the meat would have imparted the same rancid smell to all the lions feeding on it, thereby completely disguising any strange or foreign scent. Fourthly, when lions are focused on feeding, very little distracts them, and it was this crucial timing when the cub made her approach that played the biggest role – though this timing was purely coincidental and fortuitous. Fifthly, the pride's big males were not present at the time. If they had been, they would most certainly have dominated the carcass, leaving the rest of the pride waiting around for their turn. Not being engrossed with feeding, and with not much else to do except wait for the males to eat their fill, it's difficult to imagine any scenario other than that they would have noticed the newcomer making an approach, and then, almost certainly, they would have attacked and killed her.

Ironically this pug-faced lioness grew up to have cubs of her own and became one of the dominant females of the white pride. One day, about four years after her adoption, she and two other females attacked and almost killed two young male lions that had inadvertently strayed into the white pride's territory. The white lioness had now proved she was a good mother, but the question on everyone's lips was, how was she coping with her white coat handicap when hunting? Popular speculation was that her tawny sister was doing the majority of the hunting, but this hypothesis was soon to be dispelled.

One afternoon I found the tawny lioness near death. She had been attacked by two strange males who had moved into the white pride's territory unchallenged. The pride's territorial males were at one of the landowner's camps, where they had already been for a while. Here they would wait patiently, as they had been doing every day that week, for meat in the form of a giraffe which had been shot, suspended in a large leadwood tree known as 'die aasboom' (the bait tree), and then lowered by block and tackle each evening for the amusement of the landowners. They would watch the lions feeding and once it was felt the lions had eaten enough, the carcass would be winched up and out of reach until the next evening, when the same, slightly smellier ritual, was repeated.

Without the support and protection of the pride males, the lioness had no chance. She was so badly mauled by the new males that the warden, who I'd called in to dart her and ascertain the extent of her injuries, could do nothing but euthanase her. The white lioness must have realised that there was no contest, and so, unable to defend her sister, again put her cubs first and got out of harm's way. We were to realise later that this would not be the only casualty of 'die aasboom' and its destructive effect on the white lion pride.

Now a single mother, the white lioness once more demonstrated her independence and mettle when she successfully raised a second litter of cubs, all of which were tawny. What was particularly important was that during the first six weeks after the cubs were born, this lioness was doing virtually all the hunting herself. Not only was she a totally self-reliant provider, but on occasion, would inadvertently provide for the pride as well. When larger prey was killed, she would eat her fill, and then when she went back to nurse her cubs, the rest of the pride would finish it.

The controversy of camouflage as an essential adaptation raged on, despite this lioness punching big holes through this speculative theory. Among scientists and laymen alike, it was thought that a white predator would be unable to conceal itself or blend in with its surroundings. The ability to launch an attack or undertake a stealthy approach to within striking range was thought to be essential for the survival of a predator such as a lion.

Therefore, it was concluded that a white lion's hunting success ratio would be severely compromised by its contrasting colouration. My study, although by no means conclusive, found this to be unsubstantiated.

One hunt in particular busted this myth good and proper, in my book, anyway. In broad daylight, I watched her stalk and kill a huge waterbuck bull, in spite of her white coat being in stark contrast to the dark green foliage of the surrounding mopane scrub. Her success seemed to have more to do with technique and maintaining a low profile, than relying on blending into her surroundings. It was also clearly evident from the healthy condition of her cubs that despite her colour, the white lioness was not only an excellent hunter and provider; she was also a highly functional, perfectly normal member of a wild lion pride. As time passed and she went on to raise more cubs it became increasingly evident that the colour of this lioness's coat was no handicap. If there were drawbacks, they were easily compensated for with skill.

Initial fears that white lions would not survive in the wild on the basis of their colour handicap was the prime motivation for their capture and removal from the wilds of the Timbavati to the protective custody of zoos, without being given a chance to prove themselves. This interference, born of well-meaning concern, created awareness and huge media interest making white lions world-famous for all the wrong reasons. They were being treated as if they were an endangered and threatened species; their popularity soared; the demand for white lions as tourist magnets sky-rocketed. On the darker side, exorbitant amounts of money were being offered by trophy hunters who were after something unique. This increased demand meant that somewhere, somehow, somebody would find a way to exploit them.

In 1990, Alois Adlekopfer, a good friend of mine, who manages the farm Hermansberg in the Southern Timbavati, phoned me one evening to say he had just seen a white lion. My initial reaction was one of doubt, as there had been many mistaken sightings of what people thought were white lions but invariably turned out to be nothing more than a lighter than usual tawny lion.

It was an easy mistake to make, especially when viewing in isolation at night, in the beam of an extremely powerful spotlight. He went on to say it was a young male, no more than twelve months old, and that it was on a zebra kill with another four tawny lions. Up until that point in time, except for the well-known lioness I was studying, no one had reported seeing another white lion in the Timbavati, nor were there any rumours of one. Furthermore, the territorial boundary of the white pride I was monitoring on a regular basis lay some 25 kilometres to the north, so it was highly unlikely that she could have covered this distance overnight. The most important factor was that the description I had been given didn't match that of the white lioness – and it was from a most reliable source. It meant there was definitely a second white lion in the Timbavati! This was further substantiated when we saw a photograph taken of the lion alongside the contrasting four tawny lions. As exciting as this was, we were not to know at the time that the sighting of the young white lion was the last time he'd be seen in the Timbavati. As suddenly as he'd been sighted, he disappeared.

Eighteen months later, one of the finest trackers I ever had the privilege to work with, Phinias Sibuyi, returned from leave with some news that was to shock me to the core. Phinias had been with me for nearly seven years at that stage, and his knowledge and understanding of lions – the white pride in particular – was outstanding. Without his tracking skill and sixth sense, I would have missed a lot of information that was gained about these lions. What he told me confirmed a suspicion that had been niggling at me since the sudden disappearance of that young white lion. He said that the taxi driver was going really slowly, picking his way along the badly rutted gravel road, so he was able to get a good long look at what he was convinced was a white lion inside the fenced area of a neighbouring property. There was enough time to point it out to the other occupants in the vehicle, who all saw it clearly. He estimated the lion to be about three years old. In those days, the road to Acornhoek went right through the Southern Timbavati and alongside this farm. To cut a long story short, this was the beginning of one of those so-called 'Lion Breeding Projects' where white lions were bred for commercial purposes.

They were 'canned lions', hunted for huge sums of money, or sold to other breeders for the same purpose – ultimately, either way, legal in those days. Many of the white lions from this station were so inbred they were cross-eyed or squint, no doubt as a result of indiscriminate breeding due to greed and ignorance. I am convinced that all the genetic material was sourced from that one male! I can only leave to your imagination the question of how that white lion ended up on that property on the inside of a double line of electric fences.

In 1992, another white lion was born in the Northern Timbavati, a female called Ntombi. She was born near the Shlaralumi River on the farm Java, not too far from where the white lioness and her sister were born. As a member of a large stable pride, with a strong coalition of pride males, there appeared to be little that could threaten this new little girl. Well, that's what we thought.

Despite vehement protest against lion baiting, it remained a common practice among those landowners terminally afflicted with '*Myne* syndrome'. As outlined before, they attracted the white pride onto their properties for staged viewing pleasure. They would use the carcasses of large animals, usually giraffe, and on occasion even donkeys. This grossly selfish act effectively denied anyone else in the reserve the pleasure and privilege of viewing those lions for weeks on end. While this was frustrating enough, the ecological ramifications were huge, and in the case of Ntombi, it proved to be as tragic for her as it had for her aunt a couple of years earlier. For weeks, the pride would hang around the carcasses provided for them, so they had no need to hunt. Worst of all, the pride males did not go out defending and marking their territory, which again led to new males moving in unopposed, taking over what was essentially vacant territory in the eyes of 'lion law'. The inevitable cub infanticide carried out by the new males did not discriminate on the basis of colour, and Ntombi was killed along with the rest of the cubs in the pride.

In spite of these unnatural disruptions, the white lioness went on to successfully raise a third litter of cubs, all of them tawny. She was now eleven years old and still going strong. As with any pride in Africa's wild systems, there are constant changes and territorial shake-ups and shifts, and the white lion's pride was no different.

Eventually she moved into an area where regular monitoring was proving difficult, and weeks would go by without a sighting of her. It was while on these extended forays that she was caught in a wire snare probably set by the construction workers of a newly developed shareblock to the north of the Timbavati. Thanks to modern technology and advances in veterinary medicines, the snare was removed and she made a full recovery. 'Whitey' was just over twelve years old when I saw her for the last time, and I have no idea how much longer she lived, but I suspect it wasn't for much more than a few months. Nevertheless, with many tawny lions failing to achieve half that age, this was a fair innings for a white lion that was never expected to survive in the wild.

The passing of the white lioness left a huge void in the area. Many of us who had known her would have done anything to have her back. Some felt strongly enough to want to replace her with another white lion from one or other breeding project. There was even talk of trying to reintroduce the white gene by bringing in from Pretoria Zoo a particular white lion called Naas, after you-know-who, and mating him with wild lions. An elaborate holding facility was constructed to facilitate this project. Complete with a feeding and monitoring system that would ensure there was no association or contact between man and lion, it was state-of-the-art. Unfortunately, although the facility was used on occasion to house lions for treatment of injuries until they recovered, the 'White Lion Gene Project' never materialised.

Essentially I am against the reintroduction of captive-bred white lions into the wild. My main concern is regarding the quality of the genetic material that would be introduced into a naturally healthy system. Another is that it is tough enough for seasoned brawlers out there, and any captive-bred lions, particularly males, would not be 'streetwise'. In my opinion, if you introduced captive-bred lions, white or tawny, into the Timbavati, you would be sentencing them to certain death. In any event, I personally prefer tawny coats and black manes on lions in the African savannah bushveld and feel that chinchilla coats are better suited to polar bears.

The Timbavati's lion gene pool already contains the recessive gene responsible for producing white lions, of this there is no doubt. The birth of two white lions at Ingwelala in 2006 is proof of this. The cubs were seen on the farm Buffelsbed, adjacent to Goedehoop; both properties are now part of Ingwelala and are in good hands.

This gene is endemic to the lion population of that area, and I am convinced that in the future, more white lions will be born there. This will happen without our interference, notwithstanding the damage man has already inflicted in this regard. In conclusion, I do not believe a white lion to be more important or special than a normal lion, nor is it any less capable of surviving in the wild than a regular tawny lion. Furthermore, if those white lions that were removed and placed in zoos all those years ago, had been given the opportunity to prove themselves as Whitey did, there would probably be more white lions in the Timbavati today.

When it happens, perhaps we will come up with a better name than 'Whitey'.

Some more news ...

In June 2009, I received a phone call from Howard Walker, a good friend who is one of a fortunate few to own land in the Timbavati Nature Reserve. His portion happens to be a beautiful slice of bushveld which includes a generous stretch of the Klaserie River, about 1 kilometre before it flows into the southern boundary of the neighbouring Klaserie Nature Reserve, and about 40 kilometres as the crow flies south of its confluence with the Olifants River. Twenty-five years ago, his portion of the reserve had not yet been incorporated into the Timbavati – much of the Acacia bushveld along the Klaserie River floodplain had been cleared and was under irrigation in those days. Some of the finest crops in the region were grown on these rich soils and I remember that the Wiggel family who had farmed that area since the Year Dot, won the national champion tomato growers' award one year in the mid-eighties. Even then, despite the agricultural activity, it was always good game country.

Just across the road, Howard's portion, having been opened to the rest of the greater open system for over 20 years, boasts some of the richest diversity of wildlife in the Timbavati. He would often phone and tell me how happy he and his family were with their farm. The calls were usually a non-stop recounting of the wonderful variety of animals he'd seen out in the bush, and, of late, how the building of their new camp was progressing. I always welcomed these chats as they were also a good opportunity to find out how things were on the Lunsklip River near Dullstroom, in the heart of trout country where Howard lived. But I could tell from his tone of voice that this wasn't going to be one of those calls – all was not well. Howard wanted my opinion or explanation of what he described as extremely disturbing and unusual lion behaviour he had witnessed the previous evening.

He told me that he was woken by the guttural growls of lion, which as it turned out, had killed a large buffalo bull about 50 metres from his camp. Lions regularly kill buffalo in the Timbavati, so this was a sight Howard had seen before. Nevertheless, he decided to brave the cold, drive out and have a look. He arrived to find a pride of lions comprising two large males and four females panting a little from the huge effort, about to start feeding on the buffalo. Howard said he then noticed that a third large male was off to one side feeding on something else about 30 metres away. Intrigued, he drove to within 10 metres of the lion and in the beam of the vehicle's headlights could now clearly see what it was eating. What he saw was so gruesome it shocked him. The lion was feeding on another lion, but not just any lion, it was a six-month-old white lion cub! The cub was being devoured from the rear, so the head and shoulders were clearly visible in the photographs that he took and sent to me.

Of course there were rumours and speculation as always with the appearance of white lions, as to where this cub, apparently one of two white lions, originated, and who their mother was, but nothing is certain, and it remains a mystery. Howard's camp attendant admitted that he had heard of two white lions in the area but hadn't seen them himself.

It is apparent that for the last six months, two white lions had been roaming the southern Timbavati without fuss and media hype, and they were born from the same wild genetic material that produced the white lions that McBride wrote about more than a quarter of a century before! This gene, largely endemic to the Timbavati, is evidently spreading, albeit very slowly, as more area is included in the greater system. My suspicions are that there are possibly two recessive gene pools in the Timbavati, one in the extreme north including the Umbabat region and the one that gave rise to these two cubs 35 kilometres to the south.

As tragic as this is incident is, it is comforting for those campaigners of white lions to know that the gene carriers are still alive and well and more white lions will occur in the wild without human interference, when and where nature decrees.

Why this healthy cub was eaten, compounded by the fact that these cubs almost certainly belonged to one of the four females that helped kill the buffalo is impossible to guess. Furthermore, this behaviour couldn't have been motivated by hunger, as there was a whole buffalo to feed on only a few metres away. This act of infanticide and cannibalism goes in the face of 'normal' lion behaviour that I have come to know.

In my opinion it was a one-off experience. I have witnessed numerous cubs killed by males, but I have never seen one killed *and then eaten*, nor can I find any reference to this phenomenon, although it could well be recorded and documented somewhere.

Could what Howard witnessed that night on the northern bank of the Klaserie River have something to do with the young cub's colour contrast? Could that have sparked an instinctive reaction amidst the chaos and confusion of the buffalo kill? I doubt it.

On the other hand, could this lion simply be the Jeffrey Dahmer of the species taking advantage of the situation? That's what I suspect.

Some More on Lions, and a Word or Two on Trophy Hunting

OCTOBER 2007

The African lion is probably the most well known and thoroughly researched large carnivore in the world. Volumes of scientific papers have been written documenting the ecology of lions. Man has always stood in awe of these magnificent animals. Empires have adopted the lion as a symbol of all-encompassing power and dominance, and so it is understandable that enormous amounts of time and energy have been spent and still are being spent, trying to find out what makes lions tick.

The social life of lions makes for very interesting study and is well publicised. It seems that more has been documented on this aspect of lion ecology than any other and yet there is so much we don't know about these big cats. Just when it was thought we had lion behaviour predictable enough to become complacent about it, new facts are emerging that show there is still a lot of work to do. Recent research reveals more complex dynamics within their ecology than was previously known or even hypothesised. We now know we cannot generalise; lions are highly adaptable creatures and characteristics of their behaviour differ greatly from region to region, from pride to pride and from individual to individual.

This was highlighted at a recent workshop on lion held at the Timbavati and hosted by renowned wildlife ecologist and lion expert Dr Petri Viljoen. Petri has published numerous papers and recorded an incredible amount of information on wild lion behaviour from many regions in Africa. He has compiled thousands of hours of research data which is now available at the click of a mouse.

142

I couldn't help noticing the enthusiasm with which he related his knowledge to us, especially when he explained why there was a need for ongoing research on wild free-roaming lions. It appeared that this need was a relief to him, as if he had been given a valid excuse to continue studying the animals with which he so empathises.

Petri's approach is tempered with a realistic maturity that is so refreshing. He is long past the egotistical, romantic allure associated with studying large carnivores, particularly lions, in remote areas of 'Darkest Africa'. He's been there, done that and has a wardrobe full of T-shirts. He is clearly concerned with bigger issues facing the long-term survival of wild lions and is convinced that the practical and effective conservation of wild lions in modern-day Africa is reliant on continual research.

In many remote parts of Africa, the pressure on wildlife resources in terms of sustainable patterns of consumption is increasing. In fact, the survival of many of these areas often depends on the benefits derived by the surrounding communities. This takes the form of employment opportunities and related spin-offs associated with or derived from tourism. Depending on the location, logistical practicality and seasonal climatic restrictions, an area could be more suited to photographic safaris or trophy hunting safaris. The latter are less dependent on infrastructure and more adaptable than conventional lodges dealing with photographic safari clientele. Trophy hunting, as we know, is becoming increasingly unpopular and fraught with controversy. While the demand remains a reality, though, every effort should be made to ensure that any hunting that does occur does so with the least possible negative impact on the ecosystem and with minimum disruption of wild lion populations. This is where science comes in ...

Although not a hunter, Petri's expertise has been called upon by nature conservation authorities and reputable hunting concessionaires alike, specifically to determine what lions, if any, could be hunted in an area, and what criteria were necessary to ensure sustainability. Exhaustive studies and consultation followed and recommendations were made, both proving practical to implement and sustain. These studies have taken place in specific regions and dealt with lions resident in those particular areas.

With canned lion hunting in the process of being outlawed, pressure on the trophy hunting of wild lions will increase. Fortunately, no permits will be issued until specialist studies are done to determine the effects of hunting on the wild lion populations in hunting concessions. Just imagine how difficult it must be to remain objective while one scientifically calculates what lion or which category of lions, are more expendable than others.

What is becoming increasingly apparent is that management techniques need to keep abreast of the most up-to-date research. By way of example, he referred to a particular study done recently to determine the effects on the lion status in an area where dominant males in prides were prematurely removed – in other words, when pride males were hunted while still in their prime. This openly challenged conventional thinking and the present hunting protocol, which states that only six-year-old and older lions are eligible, and, in addition, it must be determined that such eligible lions must have no affiliation with a pride or coalition.

These rules were set in place based on research findings at the time. It was concluded that if only lions fitting these criteria were removed, they would, ecologically, be the least disruptive to the population.

The findings from the latest research referred to by Petri, however, indicated that the removal of pride males in their prime had little or no negative effect on the lion population in the study area. This radical conclusion is logically explained by the fact that the vacuum was quickly filled by males patrolling the periphery of territories. In addition, these were usually young, enthusiastic and strong lions which quickly boosted numbers as is known to happen in a natural pride takeover when older males are ousted. An increase in lion numbers does not necessarily mean an unhealthy over-population as wild lion populations are self-regulating, but rather that there will be more lions in the system, from which nature can select the fittest.

There appears to be a point where pride male turnover or rate of turnover could be clinically optimal, though in a natural situation, this would be difficult to determine.

What this study revealed is that unlike other large social predators, like hyaena and wild dogs for example, lions are not only able to tolerate unnatural disruptions in their social structure from time to time, but dare we say it, actually appear to thrive on it.

The latest research methods and technology available are giving scientists tools that are unlocking so much about lion behaviour that was previously either inaccessible or simply unknown. We are now gaining a deeper insight into and better understanding of lions, which, notwithstanding the trophy hunting industry around us, bodes well for wild lion conservation in the future.

Mamba ... a True Sssssssssstory

MARCH 2004

Very few people are happy to share their living space with a black mamba. In fact, very few people are happy to tolerate any snake of any description anywhere near them. As a result, I'm called out from time to time to remove these reptiles from in and around our lodges.

Lawrence Clark, one of the shareholders of the reserve, takes some of my suggestions seriously, certainly as far as what to do when you have an unwanted snake on your deck. The other day, on an otherwise quiet and lazy afternoon, the peace was interrupted by the harsh crackle of the radio. The ensuing conversation is not that unusual, particularly in the summer months.

'Mario, Mario come in,' crackled the radio.

'Go ahead,' I replied.

'Hi, this is Lawrence, I have a large black mamba on my deck.'

'Keep it in sight until I get there,' I said (this reply is part of my standard procedure). I continued, 'I'll be about 10 to 15 minutes, it is most important you make every effort to keep the snake in sight, please.'

On arrival, I found Lawrence with camera in hand gazing into the area of thatch covering the deck where he had last seen the snake. I immediately thought he had taken his eyes off the snake, so now we would have to scratch around to find it again, a prospect which filled me with dread. Mambas don't hang around if they know you have seen them, and they are escape artists of note. But, and it's a big 'but', if they cannot escape or feel threatened, then you have a potentially dangerous situation on your hands. The worst thing you can do to someone who has to remove a dangerous snake for you, is to point into some dark storeroom filled with boxes and junk and say, 'I last saw it go in there, and then I ran back into the house.'

In Lawrence's situation, it was different. Mambas are notoriously quick and sneaky especially if they know you're after them. Being outside meant it could go when and where it wanted to, and this one had simply slithered out of sight under his nose.

As our search proceeded, while peering over the edge of the deck, Lawrence caught sight of the mamba's tail disappearing under a large log. Efforts to relocate it were in vain. I showed Lawrence a hole in the rock wall under the deck where John Chiburre, the lodge guard, had previously seen a mamba on his routine daily patrol. I commented to Lawrence about it being amazing to think a snake can be so territorial and that it was quite possible this was the same snake. Bearing in mind that idle chatter always helps when you're nervous, we continued discussing the enigmatic qualities of this legendary species when suddenly, Lawrence spotted it again. This time, his sharp eye picked up a movement as the snake moved out of its hidey hole and now it was moving down towards us.

It was a relatively large mamba, probably some two and a half metres long, and was moving slowly and purposefully as though it wasn't aware of us. This gave me the opportunity to position myself and intercept it with my snake stick. It stopped momentarily, testing the air with its black tongue, long enough, however, to allow me to clamp it firmly a few centimetres behind the head.

It didn't expect this and was instantaneously enraged. The mamba writhed and twisted, wrapping itself around the stick, its black mouth agape. Incidentally, this pitch black mouth is the feature that gives this species its name, rather than its body and underbelly, which are coloured light grey and grey-green respectively.

Venom oozed as it bit repeatedly on the closed-cell foam that I had glued on the metal so as to not hurt the snakes when they are clamped. I find the snake sticks I make myself are far more suitable than the overpriced tongs from the USA as mine have been custom-built to handle snakes firmly but gently and also are a little longer. Length is important as it means you distance yourself a little more from the fangs and the venom they carry.

Some of the larger mambas I have caught were so powerful that they were able to twist themselves free of this type of clamp in its prototype form. I have since modified my sticks to the point that they are now able to hold even the largest mambas or cobras firmly ... not that the design of the snake stick should ever encourage complacency.

Even expert snake handlers get bitten. I don't know of a single professional herpetologist who hasn't been bitten. 'Handling' is the operative word and is the key to the frequency of snakebite incidents. I am the first to admit that I don't readily touch or handle snakes and have no extraordinary passion for these reptiles, beyond recognising the necessary role they play in an ecosystem. I have a healthy respect and admiration for dangerous snakes, but have no immediate desire to take this relationship to the next level. Touching a dangerous snake with my hands is something of a last resort. As far as I'm concerned, if I'm not able to handle a snake with one snake stick, the next stage is to use two snake sticks, not my hands.

Recently, on a neighbouring reserve, a 23-year-old ranger gallantly removed a snouted cobra from a curio shop in a game lodge. He was comfortable around snakes and frequently handled them when demonstrating to tourists, so he confidently caught the snake by the tail and took it out to release it into the bush. As he swung the cobra outward, it twisted its body and managed to get a glancing bite on his wrist. Feeling threatened, the snake's fangs must have been oozing venom, so even a scratch would have injected a lethal dose. This, combined with the time lapse in treatment, meant the poor guy had no chance. He died in the hospital doorway, less than 40 minutes after being bitten! As a matter of note, both black mambas and snouted cobras are capable of injecting nearly ten times the lethal dose of venom with a single bite, and multiple strikes, particularly from black mambas, are not uncommon.

Holding Lawrence's black mamba firmly in the snake stick, I could study its potent beauty closely, while it literally chewed on the foam that lined the aluminium of the grip. Eventually the lining glistened, soggy with enough venom to kill a dozen people.

I then walked down to the river bank to release it a good distance away from the lodge. Initially I thought of letting it go in the thick riverine vegetation but changed my mind and decided I'd rather release it in the river itself. Although the river was swollen from recent good rains upcountry, it was not a raging floodwater, but flowing steadily and smoothly. Knowing that snakes

149

are excellent swimmers, I assumed that the flow would carry the mamba downstream until it found some flotsam, or managed to swim to the bank, which hopefully would be some way off down river. So I tossed it in.

I then drove home quite pleased with myself and also pleased to see there was still enough time left to go on a run. It was quite humid that afternoon so I took it easy, returning to base shortly before sunset. I remember drinking what seemed like a gallon or so of Oros and ice cold water before taking a cold shower and beginning to cool down. Then it was time for supper.

The radio crackled and disturbed the peace of the evening.

'Mario, Mario come in,' went the caller.

'Go ahead,' I replied.

'It's Lawrence again,' he said, then paused. 'I just wanted to let you know, our friend is back again, but don't worry to come out again, I'll just live with him!'

At the time, I wondered how to interpret this. Had Lawrence lost complete faith in my ability to rid his space of a deadly snake? Or did he realise the mamba's homing instinct and territorial imperative was so strong that in order to guarantee it would not return, I would have had to kill it.

Having got to know Lawrence and his conservation ethic, I now know it was the latter.

A Close Call at Hide Dam

JANUARY 2006

The first effective rains of the 2006 season unleashed a deluge of 110 mm in less than three hours. The relatively bare and fragile substrate could do little to contain or absorb this volume in such a short space of time, with predictable consequences. Frankly, the reserve could have used half this amount to more beneficial effect, had it fallen at a more moderate rate. The difference between quantity and quality of rain again raised its contradictory head.

Having not seen rain like this in years and knowing that heavy falls are often localised and patchy, Meagan and I were eager to see how widespread the rainfall pattern was. We climbed into the Land Cruiser and headed along the usual route that would take us through Palm Loop, up over the railway line and into the main part of the reserve.

On approaching the Palm Loop crossing, our headlights fell on a sight not easily forgotten. The river had broken its banks and the floodwater had swollen the stream to about 30 metres wide and well over two-and-a-half metres deep. In 13 years I had never seen Palm Loop carrying so much water, but it was not the volume of water or rate of flow that concerned me, but the colour of the water. Normally, within a few hours of heavy rainfall, the clarity of this river's water resembles that of good homemade ginger beer, which then fines off within a day or so, running gin clear. The chocolate brown water we were seeing tumbling across the headlights in mini tsunami-like bulges, could mean only one thing.

'Hide Dam's wall is gone!' I blurted to Meagan.

The knot in my stomach would only untie itself if I could see for myself one way or the other just what had happened. I had to get to the dam quickly, but I'd have to go the long way round. How frustrating this was, the dam was only two kilometres away on the road that the waterway now blocked; the alternative route would mean a detour of at least ten kilometres.

Worse, while I mentally reviewed the reserve and its network of roads, there was only one option and, given the present conditions, there was no guarantee that we would get there. We had to try, and the Land Cruiser did what was expected of it, churning easily through the washaways, ruts and muddy sections. Eventually, we made our way to where I knew there was a narrower crossing of the Palm Loop River, which is near its catchment area and source in the Klaserie. The gamble paid off, as by the time we got there it was only about half a metre deep and receding.

Approaching Hide Dam from the north-east, I stopped the vehicle, took out the powerful spotlight I keep behind my seat, and plugged it in. The cacophony of thousands of frogs all competing for call space was almost deafening, but it was good to hear them, as frogs meant water. Apprehensively I shone the light on the tail end of the dam ... it was full. I breathed a sigh of relief, because I knew this picture would not be possible if the wall had been breached and washed away.

Moving slowly along the road, we approached the edge of the spillway, switched off, and climbed out of the 4x4. The roar from the water tumbling over the jagged rocks that make up the base of the spillway was deafening. As awe-inspiring as the sight and sound of so much water was, my mind recalled the words of Lyle Thole, a founding shareholder and our tame consultant engineer who understands the mechanics and power of water better than most. Years ago, when we widened the throat of the spillway by 100 per cent, which I thought was ample, I remember him saying that he would have been more comfortable if it was even wider!

Relieved that the spillway appeared to be doing its job, even if only just, Meagan and I sat a while taking it all in. I remember wondering where all the different frogs came from – Hide Dam was at least five kilometres from the Olifants River and there wasn't a wetland or vlei anywhere on the reserve. On our way back I stopped in at the airstrip vehicle park and went over to read the rain gauge we kept there. Incredibly, the gauge read a mere 40 mm, while a couple of kilometres away over 110 mm had fallen. This rain gauge has since been trampled to pieces by elephant so they probably weren't too impressed with the reading either.

At first light the next morning, I drove around and came in from Jackal Plains on the eastern side of the dam. Approaching the parking area behind the hide enabled me to ascertain the source of the dark brown water seen in Palm Loop the previous evening. The debris left by the water told the whole story. The storm had released so much water in such a short time, that a wave of water too large for the spillway to cope with had topped the dam wall itself. We estimated that the wave would have been something over half a metre high when it went over the wall. It then subsided so quickly that the erosive power had only enough time to gouge out the back slope of the wall, before it dissipated to the volume and level that the spillway was able to cope with. Had the wall not been so well-compacted during its construction it would not have held.

The wall needed extensive repair. The hide itself, which was not accessible at the time due to the damaged wall, we planned to demolish and rebuild, once repairs to the wall had been completed. A second spillway or an enlargement to the existing one was also considered. Three months later all the repairs envisaged to the wall were carried out and a second smaller spillway was cut.

The storm's 'epicentre', for want of a better word, appears to have been the area, roughly triangulated, between Hide Dam, the four power lines and Nyosi Pan on Dinidza. This translates into an area of approximately twelve square kilometres. Most of the roads downslope of this region were washed away completely. As a result, landowners couldn't get into town until our heavy machinery effected repairs to the main access road a few days later.

Many of Olifants' lodges had their retaining walls silted up and overtopped. We prioritised what had to be done and where, then got stuck in, concentrating on clearing the silt. The office and admin block was flooded to a depth of 200 millimetres. Due to the water reticulation behind the lodges, we could not use the grader to cut mitre drains for fear of cutting into the main water supply pipelines. In some cases, laborious, time-consuming berms or humps were built to divert any possible future floodwater, which have since proved extremely effective.

Dinidza's Nyosi Pan, a beautiful waterhole about the size of a large swimming pool, was completely silted up and flattened so smoothly that if you didn't know what had been there before, you'd be forgiven for thinking someone was preparing a volleyball pitch. Situated in a valley, it lay in the path of channelled floodwater which was too powerful to be contained. The hand of man played a major role in the reconstitution of this pan, involving enlarging and extensive rebuilding. The rich silt loads brought down by the floodwater have been employed to create a mini-wetland with a substantial reedbed and a perimeter of nutsedge. Nyosi Pan's appeals are now well-established and natural, with a little helping hand ...

Thousands of small fish, mostly tilapia *Oreochromis mossambicus* that were washed out of Hide Dam, were found trapped in rapidly drying pools below the dam. The larger fish, some of which were pan size, were netted and eaten by the staff. Others were relocated and established in Double Dam and Big Dam. Saddle-bill storks, black storks, hamerkops and kingfishers made short work of the remainder we left for them. All the fish, including a sawtooth catfish or barbel *Clarius garipinus* of over ten kilograms, which was found in a pool a kilometre downstream, were descendants of a few specimens of each species represented when we stocked Hide Dam six years ago. Some of the smaller *Barbus* species have also done surprisingly well. This is important as these fish play a vital role in the control of mosquitoes by consuming the larvae of this deadly pest. Tilapia are eaten by the barbel, which are in turn eagerly taken by crocodile.

Giant bullfrogs *Pyxicephalus adspersus*, the first I'd ever seen in the bush, seemed to have erupted out of nowhere. There were thousands of them in and around the dam, but where they came from is still a mystery. Hide Dam is in the middle of the reserve's driest area, and there are no wetlands or natural water for miles. I know this threatened species can lie buried in the soil for a year or so waiting for the right storm conditions to trigger emergence. Could it be that they had lain buried in the soil near the dam for some twelve years? As suddenly and as mysteriously as they'd appeared they were gone, and a mere week later there wasn't a bullfrog to be found. The only evidence they left were millions of tadpoles, but we have never seen their parents since.

In the Marula's Shade

AUGUST 2004

The late Rodney Kapelus, a former shareholder of Olifants, was one of the more familiar and regular intra-African migrants to the reserve. Each year he eagerly anticipated his winter migration up from the rich feeding grounds of Plettenberg Bay's Keurbooms River estuary to the banks of the Olifants River. Here he would soak up sun-drenched days relaxing in the tranquillity, while re-charging his batteries and putting on enough condition for the return flight a few months later.

This season, however, was a little different, and not as peaceful as he'd hoped. Rodney found he had to share his space with mil-lions of red-billed queleas. Each evening, for over a month, these incredible little birds roosted in the larger riverine trees in front of the lodges on Olifants. They would concentrate in such numbers and in such a small area that in the morning the trees and the area underneath their crowns would be blanketed in white from their droppings. At times, the smell became overpowering and quite impossible to live with. It was a bit like having the aroma of an in-tensive poultry farm in your back garden, and that wasn't the only problem. Their collective chirping would coagulate into a din that could drive the most enthusiastic twitcher to enlist the services of those inexplicably trigger-happy Italian bird hunters on the open-ing day of their 'If it flies, it dies' season. This cacophony turned out to be the least of Rodney's worries, however, as something far more surreal was to make this year's migration even more memo-rable and besides, the queleas were considerably concentrating their roosting activities at the lodge next door.

Many of you may have read Herman Charles Bosman's classic 'In the Withaak's Shade', which takes place in the old Western Transvaal area, on the edge of the Kalahari Desert. This area has given rise to some of the most interesting characters of yore, notably J Barnard or 'Bvekenya' as he was better known, whose exploits as a hunter and adventurer are legendary, and, of course, Groot Marico's most famous storyteller, Oom Schalk Lourens.

One day, Oom Schalk was out looking for some strayed cattle. At about midday it occurred to him that they might be under the withaak trees, because of the softness of the grass. And since cattle were large enough to be seen from a recumbent position, he lay on his back under a tree, with his hat tilted over his face, from where he noticed that the tip of his boot looked just like Abjaterskop, a familiar peak in the local mountain range. His reverie was interrupted by the appearance of a strange spotted cloud on top of the mountain, which turned out to belong to a leopard sniffing his boots. Paralysed with terror, Oom Schalk was unable to stop the leopard from progressing embarrassingly to his trousers, which were old and torn. He decided that the next time he lay under the withaak tree looking for cattle, he would wear his best black 'Nagmaal' hat ...

Back on Olifants, on a similar quiet lazy afternoon, Rodney also felt like a snooze and lay down, not on the grass as Oom Schalk did, but in a reclining deck chair on the edge of his deck. Drenched in dappled shade from a large false marula tree, this area of the deck was effectively shielded from the midday sun. Shaded and relatively cool, it must have produced the same effect on Rodney as the withaak did when Oom Schalk lay in its shade. So, understandably, it wasn't too long before he too dozed off.

It didn't seem as if he had been asleep more than a few moments when he was woken by an ever-so-gentle, but insistent, tugging on his foot. Lifting his head up just enough to see what or who had the audacity to disturb his siesta, Rodney found himself looking straight into what appeared to be the side of a moving grey mountain.

As he emerged from his doze and began to focus, the rumpled

forehead of a large elephant bull loomed in front of him. The curious pachyderm was nudging and sniffing at his foot with the tip of his trunk!

Needless to say, once the reality that this was no dream dawned on him, he spoke rather firmly to the elephant. Apparently the expletives he used to articulate his feelings had the desired effect. The startled jumbo, unaccustomed to such abusive language, moved quickly away.

Confirmation of the position of the elephant in relation to the deck chair was plain to see by the tracks it left behind in the soft sand in front of the deck. According to the spoor, it was clear the elephant had spent quite some time milling about, before actually reaching out to touch Rodney's foot with its trunk.

What was it that prompted this tactile curiosity from the elephant? Could he determine Rodney was asleep, or was he trying to find out if he was alive? Maybe Rodney's feet smelt interesting, or he'd stepped in something the elephant liked. Who knows?

I remain convinced, however, that while Rodney's experience shares a few common threads with Oom Schalk's tale, it is less likely to be an exaggerated account; it is too new, too recent. There is a certain licence given to exaggeration that legends allow and thrive on, but they need the key ingredient of time. The more time that passes, the more imaginative and colourfully embellished the recollection becomes. More important to the establishment of the truth of this tale, though, is that we know Rodney Kapelus, as opposed to Oom Schalk, was not partial to the midday consumption of *witblits*.

Management of Game Populations

We know that ecology is not an exact science and that no game reserve encompasses a complete, self-regulating ecosystem. Depending on what the objectives and vision of a reserve are, policies may be determined which will necessitate some degree of intervention by the hand of man. This means implementation of agreed policies through active management from time to time. This is usually justifiable in situations where growing game populations begin to adversely affect their own habitat in a confined area, and where we then make use of all the scientific information available to balance things a little.

Prior to the removal of fences, some serious management decisions had to be made each year on Olifants. This process mainly dealt with game removals in the form of live capture and translocation. Up to 50 buffalo, 60 zebra and as many as four rhino were being captured and sold in severe winters. This may sound like a lot of animals, but if we take the buffalo population as an example, study of the actual results indicates a conservative rather than radical approach. When I arrived in 1993, the buffalo population stood at 65 and at the time of our inclusion as full members of APNR twelve years later, the number was nearly 300. In this twelve-year period, we had captured and sold more than 150 buffalo, with predation, natural deaths, hunting and train deaths accounting for quite a few more. Despite all manner of intervention by man, the population grew by nearly 15 per cent per annum. However, the same cannot be said of wildebeest numbers.

159

Prior to the removal of the internal fences in Balule, the wildebeest population in the Olifants west region stood at nearly 800. Today, as I write, that number is down to fewer than 200. Fence removals, which allowed predators into an area that they formerly found difficult to access, combined with a bad management decision to capture and remove 85 wildebeest, pushed the wildebeest population off the knife edge and into a spiral of decline.

Giraffe have been removed in the past, albeit in relatively low numbers, but I have never been an advocate for the removal of browsers from our reserve, particularly giraffe.

Our stipulation with regard to removals from Olifants was always that the animals captured represented as closely as possible a natural breeding group. As a result, we would often risk lower financial return rather than place any stress on the existing population structure. We have always adopted a conservative approach. For example, when taking off buffalo, buyers only wanted breeding heifers and trophy quality bulls. In the case of rhino, only cows and adult bulls were wanted. However, we insisted on only removing a rational mix in order to prevent structural imbalances in the herds. It may have cost us money, but the result of our fastidious selection policy over the years meant that when we approached the APNR for membership, we did so with a healthy representation of the larger species of herbivores. We were proud of it and others envied it.

Since the removal of the Klaserie fence and the adoption of the APNR management plan, this intensive hands-on manipulation is no longer necessary. Population control of large mammals such as elephant, if implemented, would be a collective management decision made at APNR level. A small percentage of certain big game is taken off in the form of commercial hunting and trophy hunting. This provides income for the running of certain APNR reserves that are unable to generate the necessary funds from levies alone.

It is important to understand and accept that we're not an isolated farm, game farm or reserve. Olifants River Game Reserve is now an integral part of the Balule Nature Reserve, which is a member of the larger APNR, which in turn is open to the Kruger

National Park and Transfrontier Park. It's all quite a mouthful, I know, but in order to appreciate how we fit into the bigger picture – more importantly, the extent to which we actively manage the reserve in relation to this affiliation – the following background lays the foundations. As a reserve integral to and integrated with the Greater Kruger Park, we no longer decide unilaterally how many of this or how many of that we're going to capture, sell or shoot.

Supplementary feeding of rhino, or any free-roaming animal, without scientifically motivating this through the approved channels and protocols, is also no longer accepted. Intervention to this degree, in what is an essentially open system, would be frowned upon. The bottom line is that the bigger the area, the less we need to interfere. At the same time, the bigger the area, the less autonomy we can exercise. With regard to our general veld conditions or vegetation biomass on the other hand, it seems we have a little catching up to do, before we let go of the handlebars and say, 'Look, Ma, no hands.'

The aim of the following is to give the reader a very basic idea of how one can use the carrying capacity figures for a known veld type to determine the optimum number of herbivores to stock a reserve. For example, we will be looking at the larger herbivores (biomass) that the Balule PNR should carry. Remembering that ecology is not an exact science, these guidelines are there to eliminate as much of the guesswork and conjecture as possible, and to try and establish a yardstick that can be applied or adapted, to different scenarios.

The opinions in, and the compilation of the following, are not entirely the result of a focused scientific study; they are more of a composite, gleaned from numerous ecological reports, past and present. It also takes into account observations, recollections and opinions of landowners, farmers and local residents. There's a lot to be learned this way – just as if you want to know where to find the biggest trout in a stretch of river, don't go to the library, the mayor, or the chairman of the local fishing club, find the resident young rascal who fishes surreptitiously, with a home-made rod and worms: he will show you.

What are we doing? There is no intention to bring back the past, or to dwell on the good old days, they're gone. We need to take stock of the present and look to the future, with an unblinkered, open mind and holistic approach.

It doesn't take a professor of ecology to see that our area (Balule) is in relatively poor shape in terms of vegetation production. Some areas are better than others, but the overall picture is not pretty.

Successful game farmers have proved that in drought years, the most effective and practical remedial action is to reduce the number of animals. These reductions are usually made to the point where the population remains viable, while drastically reducing their impact on the vegetation.

There are 55 vegetation monitoring plots in Balule. This is where the dedicated chaps who spend weeks at a time with their noses to the ground come into their own. The data compiled by the Agricultural Research Council's technicians provides essential information, indicating how much fodder is available on the reserve. This is expressed as vegetation biomass and in the past has been measured at a high of over one ton per hectare (anywhere up to 2 000 kg) but at present measures a scant 350 kg per hectare, and has been as low as 190 kg in very dry years. For comparative purposes on the other extreme and to give you some idea of standing crop vegetation biomass for other areas, the Kruger National Park has areas of high average annual rainfall that yield nearly 4 000 kg per hectare. While a high percentage of this is moribund, the message is clear enough and supports the suggestion that we have some catching up to do.

The one advantage of a smaller closed system is that it is possible to exercise a higher degree of control. In the greater Balule area, which is regarded as 'open', we now need to factor in and consider numerous other factors, not the least being large predators and their effect on the herbivore population.

The landowners, irrespective of the particular way in which they choose to enjoy or utilise their property in the reserve, need to be considered wherever possible, within the broader context of the reserve's management plan. The mere fact that everybody's fences are down, and the reserve is becoming more representative of a natural open system, indicates that there is a common like-minded desire amongst the landowners to look at the bigger picture. This takes much of the risk of miscalculation out of the routine, as was shown with the wildebeest population decline in Klaserie. More importantly, many of the more sensitive and difficult decisions could be left to Mother Nature, but we need to be aware of exactly what we are doing and of the risks when we adopt a laissez-faire approach. It has a way of coming back to bite you, witness the elephant problem we have now.

Balule PNR in itself comprises a landscape with varied habitat types, some of which are favoured by certain species in preference to others. Therefore, care must be taken not to extrapolate figures to cover all the properties on a pro-rata basis. An example of this is waterbuck, which show that they are habitat-specific to some degree. It is a well-known fact that they have a marked preference for the areas north of the Olifants River. Game counts over the last 16 years indicate the ratio is as high as a three-to-one count in favour of the northern section. On the other hand, white rhino don't like this 'waterbuck habitat' and have never used the Olifants River, the flood plain or adjacent Commiphora woodland, since their introduction 18 years ago. Technically, waterbuck and white rhino are grazers that utilise different levels, and could theoretically complement each other's feeding preferences.

It is interesting to note that according to Rowland Ward's book of world records, we have the biggest waterbuck in the world, right here in our reserve!

Ecosystems are dynamic, and as has been shown, there are subtle considerations within each that need to be understood and taken into account. The paradigms are constantly shifting in response to various influencing factors; they are not always clear-cut and calculable. Therefore, we often rely on the fact that nature is forgiving and constantly trying to heal any wounds, and this also helps us to round off any sharp edges.

Our system is chiefly rain-driven, so there are going to be years when one may very well see 'wheat fields' of grass and not too much game, and we will question the need to hunt, capture or cull a single animal. Then, within a few short months, things can decline to the point where even those hardened supporters of 'leave it to nature' will be tempted to intervene. Resorting to supplementary feeding of general game in a relatively large system such as the Balule would be impractical and economically unsustainable.

There should be no need to intervene to this extent, nor should the veld be littered with carcasses during an average winter season. What this may well indicate is that the area is going through an unusually dry year, or is over-stocked or poorly managed. Somehow we must strive for a balance, but I do believe that if you have introduced animals into a habitat which is marginal for them, as with the white rhino, then there is a management obligation to feed them in extremely dry periods, or alternatively, capture and translocate some of them.

The following calculations are based on the numbers of the larger herbivores, and are represented in LSU (Large Stock Units). Simply put, an LSU is a cow-sized herbivore. There is an acceptable number of LSU that a reserve may carry comfortably under ideal conditions, and this is shown in relation to what we are actually carrying at the moment. It gives you some idea of the challenges we face.

A conservative estimate of one LSU per 13 hectares has been the basis for my calculation. Figures have been rounded off and where necessary, I've used my own judgement based on the last 16 years on this reserve. The first two tables published give you the opportunity for two totally different interpretations, one based on a calculated hypothesis, the other on recorded, measured statistics. The first table is a rough guideline as to what would be the ideal scenario, the 'optimum stocking rate' of our area. Please do not consider these figures as graven-in-stone, rather take the table as an indication of how a middle-aged man going to gym would regard achieving the same physical shape and characteristics as Arnold Schwarzenegger. The objective is certainly possible, but it is practically improbable.

Well, for most of us, anyhow.

Balule Private Nature Reserve: Area size 35 000 hectares

Optimum stocking rates of larger herbivores				
Species count	**Feeding class**	**Recommended**		**Highest**
		Low	High	
		(2400 LSU)	(3150 LSU)	
Elephant	Mixed	60	90	482
Rhino	Bulk	16	20	30
Hippo	Bulk	50	60	110
Buffalo	Bulk	250	300	398
Zebra	Bulk	600	650	806
Waterbuck	Selective	600	650	806
Wildebeest	Short grass	600	700	691
Impala	Mixed	3300	3800	4445
Warthog	Short grass	350	400	401
Giraffe	Browse	400	450	480
Kudu	Browse	400	500	548

The next table is more specific, being a game census over the last ten years. The measured, recorded figures provide clear indications where we as managers need to focus our efforts in order to try and achieve the best balance possible. The key word here is 'trend'. It is of little use responding with a knee-jerk reaction to a sudden spike in the figures year-on-year. Before decisions that may have far-reaching consequences are made, a study of the trends over time needs to be evaluated.

The longer the period you have data for, the more informed your decision will be and the better the end results. Olifants is blessed with an excellent level of statistical input, gathered over time by a remarkably consistent group of 'counters', for want of a better term.

Balule game census figures for the last ten years, given in two-year intervals

Species	1998–1999	2000–2001	2002–2003	2004–2005 Fence down	2006–2007	2008
Impala	4445	3694	3713	3276	4398	3904
Waterbuck	683	806	522	388	519	490
Wildebeest	691	580	533	335	217	262
Giraffe	480	358	477	325	268	234
Zebra	828	607	652	448	450	447
Kudu	420	548	361	428	487	441
Warthog	254	401	286	315	400	170
Bushbuck	33	34	44	27	67	36
Buffalo	192	272	168	235	391	390
White Rhino	17	17	27	14	30	28
Elephant	0	25	88	304	401	141
Hippo	82	70	42	73	56	112

Finally, on this statistical game drive, you may be interested to note the current (as at mid-2009) estimated head count of six 'favourites'.

Balule Private Nature Reserve: Area size 35 000 hectares

Estimated number of large predators	
Lion	45–50
Leopard	30–35
Cheetah	<12
Wild Dog	0–6
Crocodile	>50
Hyaena	25–30

Back to My Roots ... Turning 50!

16 JUNE 2006

It was a beautiful, midwinter afternoon in the bush. It also happened to be my fiftieth birthday. Approaching sundowner time, we gazed over Sunset Plains where we had gathered and watched the red winter sun sink behind the Drakensberg Mountains silhouetted in the distance. A herd of zebra, their tails constantly swishing more out of habit than chasing away flies, grazed contentedly, unperturbed by our presence a mere 50 metres away. Beyond them, a number of wildebeest and a huge herd of impala were moving onto the plain for the evening. Amidst this dramatically beautiful setting, the modest ceremony became all the more poignant for my being surrounded by many of the shareholders of Olifants, who were there to share this milestone in my life. Following a brief toast and birthday wish, I was presented with an envelope. Opening it, I read a brief message, 'This is to be used for a trip of a lifetime.' The message and the generous cheque which accompanied it couldn't have been clearer or meant more sincerely. So I will tell you about 'The Trip' and let you decide whether or not I fulfilled the instruction as stipulated.

I am a keen fly-fisherman. My friend and the doyen of trout fishing in this country, Dr Tom Sutcliffe, had something to say about this affliction. In one of his books, *Hunting Trout*, he dedicates a chapter to our exploits with the long rod on the Eastern Cape streams, wherein he writes that I am 'terminally besotted' with fly-fishing. So it should come as no surprise that I now confess to having been oft times preoccupied with delusions of piscatorial grandeur and thus having a hard time focusing on reality.

167

Mental pictures of catching trout and salmon as long as your arm occupied my mind more than I should admit. I could see myself posing for photos with a backdrop of snow-capped mountains in Alaska, New Zealand or Patagonia. I could already feel the frigid air on my face and the pleasant ache in my fingers from the icy water, as I gently released a magnificent fish back into some remote river. The message and the cheque were about to make all these dreams a reality.

But this was not to be.

I still have no idea what prompted my sudden last-minute rethink. Something deeper-seated than rods, lines and hooks was calling. Up until a few weeks prior to taking the trip, I'd had no serious thoughts on the subject, but, once the thought emerged, there was no doubt this trip would not be a holiday of fun and fish, but would rather be a mission of meaning and purpose. I was unexpectedly overcome by a desire to find my roots, which had previously been on my 'something to do before I die' list and now was an urgent priority. I wanted to go to Italy and find where my father was born and locate the odd relative or two, while I was in the neighbourhood. Nothing else mattered, so the world's trout and salmon were safe to swim another day.

My father was a young man of 20 when the Germans wrenched him away from his family in Italy to fight in the Second World War. He told me that he hid under a bridge near his home to try and evade them, but they eventually found him and bundled him off to war. A year later, after having spent nearly all that time on the front line in the Sahara Desert, he was captured by the Allied forces near Sidi Barrani in North Africa. From there he was sent to the Zonderwater prisoner of war camp in South Africa, where he remained for the duration of the war. When the war ended he was released, but instead of returning to Italy immediately, he decided to earn a little money first so he wouldn't arrive home empty-handed.

Make no mistake, all Italians can cook, so despite not being able to speak a word of English, he found a job as a chef in Johannesburg which turned out far better than he could have hoped for. Those around him quickly realised that he was good at what he did and soon he was head-hunted by the Langham Hotel in Johannesburg. Once settled in his new job, earning relatively good money and able to send some of it home, it was inevitable that he would end up staying a while longer. My father and mother then met and were soon married. They bought a house in Johannesburg, started a fairly large family and never looked back. He purchased a small farm near Vereeniging, which was more a part-time hobby than anything else.

Although he was not really a farmer at heart, he had 'green fingers' and loved to grow vegetables. He also dabbled a little in livestock and used to supply veal to his friends in the Italian community of Orange Grove. At that time, though highly sought after by Italians, veal was not readily available in this country. I suspect this interaction enabled him to establish and maintain a rewarding camaraderie with his expatriate Italian friends. He was content; he had a family; he had a new home ... South Africa.

My father's memories of Italy before the war were of poverty and struggle, a daily grind to make ends meet. Being the eldest of four brothers and having lost his father when he was a young boy made it really tough on him. Caught up in the responsibilities of his new home, his work and his family, he never went back to Italy until a few years before he died, which was something he regretted. More than 55 years had passed since the Germans found him hiding under a bridge, so the reunion with his family was extremely emotional. Although he had kept in contact with them over the years, seeing them and touching them again was truly memorable for him. The country he saw when he returned was not the Italy he remembered prior to and during the war. It was now a prosperous, leading, First World country whose people were happy and comfortable. Everyone he knew had done well for themselves and he was once more proud to be Italian.

When my father passed away a few years ago, my family cleared up his personal effects and discovered that, unfortunately, only photographs with the odd name scribbled on the back were kept. All records of addresses, letters and contact numbers were lost, probably due to the fact that none of us could speak or understand Italian. From the outset, it was obvious that Meagan and I had very little to go on apart from a wad of photographs and the one and only official document we salvaged, my father's birth certificate. That faded, fragile piece of paper gave us hope and with a few names and some photos of people we had never met, we started the search. Meagan and the Internet became very good friends. Her research located a number of Cesares in the province of Campania, near the town of Benevento.

Although a common first name, Cesare is not a common surname in Italy, despite its famous lineage typified by Giulio Cesare, the Italian spelling of Julius Caesar. It turned out that a relatively large percentage of Cesares live in the province of Campania, particularly in and around Santa Agata dei Goti (Saint Agatha of the Goths). This beautiful historic town 190 kilometres south of Rome and 110 kilometres east of Naples dates back to 300 AD and, more importantly to us, according to the birth certificate, is where my father was born.

Despite contacting a number of Cesares with the help of an old family friend in Johannesburg, who could 'parlo Italiano', none of them knew of my father or any of the family names we mentioned from the photos. However, Francesca Cesare, a young schoolgirl living in Santa Agata dei Goti, despite not being related, took the trouble to try and help us, after we had convinced her that she wasn't on some candid camera-type telephone show. Catching a bus, she went to their local municipal offices, which were over 10 kilometres away, and with her mother's help, managed to come up with a couple of names they thought might be distant relatives of ours. It appeared that most of them lived in Laiano, a nearby village close to the small town of Frasso Telesino. With this scant lead we changed our plans and began to follow our noses.

We flew from Johannesburg to London and then connected to Naples. Meagan and I were blessed with perfect weather and we excitedly absorbed the views as we flew over France and Switzerland. Somehow, as we crossed the Alps into Italy, everything felt quite different to me with the knowledge that we were now flying over my father's country. This was the land of my roots and I desperately wanted to place my feet on its soil and smell the air. I couldn't wait for the plane to land despite the awesome view of Mt Vesuvius with still enough light to give life to the warm late afternoon colours splashed across the calm and oily-smooth waters of the Mediterranean. It was as if the pilot had read my mind and, banking steeply, we circled the bay once more, landing in Naples just as the sun was setting. After a taxi ride from the airport to the hotel that would make our minibus taxi drivers look like little old ladies driving to church on Sunday morning, we booked in.

The next morning we awoke really early and started packing, but my impatience was all for naught. It was Sunday and all the main roads in downtown Naples were closed for a war veterans' military parade. All the provincial regiments in Italy had gathered in spectacular regimental regalia, and led by marching bands, were parading through the city that morning. When we asked a taxi driver to get us to the station at 10 am, his initial response was that it was impossible, but he must have seen how disappointed we were, because then he shook his head, took a deep breath and said, 'OK, we try!' And try we did, using every short cut he knew and even the wrong side of the road on occasion, but there was just no way out of the maze of barriers, crowds of spectators and cordoned-off streets. Eventually he pulled up at a couple of police cars, walked over to the attendant policemen and started a hand-waving conversation that only the Italians and the deaf have perfected. We later learned that he must have said something like, 'If you don't help me get my fare to the station, you will get a horse's head on your pillow tonight!' Barriers were moved and with the siren wailing and blue lights flashing, we were escorted all the way to the railway station by the police! Naples has to be the epitome of organised chaos.

Fantastico, Madonna mia!

We bought two tickets to Benevento, boarded and settled down for the ride, my first on a European train. It was surprisingly fast and relaxing compared with other transport options in Naples and took us through the really poor suburbs of the city, right through the middle of what must have been Sophia Loren's 'Back Streets of Naples'. In less than 20 minutes, we left the urban sprawl behind and were hurtling through beautiful Italian countryside while I couldn't stop jiggling with anticipation. I knew that within a couple of hours we'd be right in the heart of Campania province, my father's home turf.

Benevento is a relatively small city about the size of Pietermaritzburg, and although off the beaten tourist track, it is steeped in history, as evidenced by some of the ancient architecture, which pre-dates Rome. Not knowing the prospects for finding accommodation, we booked into the first decent hotel we found, called Hotel Grande Italiano, where we were the only guests.

That afternoon was spent sightseeing, walking around the relatively quiet city, which was reminiscent of when as young children, after Sunday lunch, we played on the streets of Johannesburg where my father used to have a restaurant. I was experiencing the Italian lifestyle on the piazza for the first time and marvelling at the architecture as we went. We stumbled onto an old amphitheatre, older than anything we later saw in Rome, tucked away in the middle of the suburbs, and though it was closed, we were allowed to look around.

Sitting down to dinner back at the Hotel, Meagan and I discussed strategy. I was all ready to head into the hills the next morning with my backpack full of photos, and do some door-to-door hunting for long-lost relations, but Meagan suggested that we first try the Carabinieri (Italy's military police). Years ago in conversation with my father, he had proudly mentioned that one of my cousins was a member of the Carabinieri, and she thought this would be a better starting point.

The next morning we took a taxi to the headquarters of Benevento's Carabinieri. Wheeling our baggage behind us, we walked up to the reception area, and armed with an Italian/English dictionary, asked about our cousin whom we thought worked for their organisation. The chap at the front desk was very patient with us, checked on his computer and made a couple of phone calls. Nothing, nobody knew a thing. Disappointed, we turned to leave, but as we did so, a tall man in civilian clothes and with an imposing air about him, approached us and inquired as to what the problem was. The man at the front desk rattled off something in Italian. The tall man then turned to us, introduced himself and said in broken English, 'Leave your luggage here and follow me.' Two floors up the stairs and we were in his office where we learned he was Capitano Massimiliano Bollis, the commanding officer of the region. Within five minutes a translator and their best undercover detective were in the office with us.

Through the interpreter we managed to explain who we were looking for and why. With that, the undercover guy quietly left the office. Fifteen minutes later he returned with an original file dug up out of the archives, containing details of my father's military records, and a document listing my father's family history back to 1887.

Copies were then made and given to me and we started with the search for my cousin who was supposed to be in the Carabinieri. We found him. We had made a simple mistake, trying to trace him using the Christian name Michele, instead of Vincenzo. We were given telephone numbers and told to take the train to Caserta, from where it was only a short bus ride to Laiano. We thanked them profusely, caught a taxi to the station and bought two tickets to Caserta.

It would be over an hour before the train departed, so Meagan and I walked down the road to a small trattoria for some coffee. We were sipping away when, in typical Italian fashion, a car stopped practically in the middle of the road and our friendly plainclothes undercover man got out and walked up to us. Going down on his haunches to be on our eye level, he explained in broken but perfectly comprehensible English that my cousin had phoned and would pick us up at their headquarters in 45 minutes. Then he added that while we had some time in hand waiting for my cousin, he would love to show us a little more of Benevento. We were really happy with his offer and thoroughly enjoyed his guided tour of the city of which he was so proud. Just before returning to the Carabinieri HQ, he turned to us again and said, 'I hope you don't mind, but we have called the press to cover your story!'

Meagan and I looked at each other and replied, 'Not at all.'

When in Rome...

At the HQ we found a journalist, a cameraman and a number of high-ranking Carabinieri officers. Not only was the beautiful young reporter dressed like she had just stepped off a catwalk, but she spoke perfect English as well. We were just getting acquainted, when in walked my cousin Giulio and his wife Lucia. You would have sworn we'd known each other for years from the emotional greeting we shared. The cameras clicked, the chatter was recorded and the next day we were on the local TV. Apparently the story featured in three newspapers, although we only saw the one. Meagan and I were beginning to understand how important 'La Famiglia' is in Italian culture; it's unlikely, as Meagan cynically joked, that it was just a slow press day.

Giulio is the spitting image of my brother Dino, only a little heavier, and it soon became apparent why. He simply loves his food. In the coming days we were to find out about another Italian passion ... food! By that I mean, not just any food but, simply, the best food in the world.

It turned out that I have a big family in Italy, and most of them live within a radius of 30 kilometres, so Meagan and I spent much of our time being hosted by each in turn. During a rare quiet moment, I indicated to Giulio, whose English wasn't too bad as he had spent nearly a year in Jersey, USA, that my mission would be totally fulfilled if I could find the house my father was born in, or even where it once stood.

'No problem,' he said. 'I know where it is, we will go there tomorrow.'

The following day we drove up into the mountains towards Santa Agata dei Goti and Laiano, and as we climbed up the twisting mountain road, the temperature dropped noticeably. About half way up, we stopped at a roadside fountain for a drink of the sweetest water you have ever tasted. The source of this icy cold mountain spring was way up in the Apennines and is one of many like it, hundreds of years old and still used every day.

A little while later we drove past groves of olive trees that seemed to be growing out of a sea of poppies, some of the trees being so old and gnarled I'm sure they could have produced the olives my father ate. Slowing down, we eased our way through a herd of goats in the middle of a small village. Meagan insisted on taking a photo of the goat herder, who thought she was a little dippy.

'This was your father's village,' Giulio said, his Alfa Romeo's low-profile tyres rumbling over the cobblestone roads. A couple of minutes later we pulled up outside a relatively modern look-ing house.

'And this is where he was born,' he added. Goosebumps sent a tingling itch all over me as I tried to collect my thoughts.

Parking the car, we noticed three men in the driveway of the house. One of them was on his knees holding a small dog on its back, while another gently dusted its belly with flea powder. As we approached them, the men stood up and released the dog, which scampered away, shaking a lot of the powder off in a trail-ing cloud as it went. Giulio did the introductions and we shook hands, flea powder and all. He explained why we were there and asked if we could take photos.

'Of course,' they replied. 'Come in, we will show you a section of the original house that we still use as a wood store and barn.'

I could hardly contain myself. I was standing where my father stood and looking at the same mountains he did. This was seri-ous lump-in-throat stuff and it was so much more than I ever expected. We took a few more photos of the humble, yet solidly built remnants of the stone and timber house that was once his home. Some time later, after some rather poignant comments, we thanked the owner once more and slowly began to make our way back to the car. We hadn't gone far, when one of the three men called us back.

'There is someone who would like to speak to you,' he said, motioning to the main implement store. From behind one of the big Fiat tractors, a little old man approached us. He looked at least 90 years old and was dressed in a jacket and tie topped with a trilby. Leaning lightly on a walking stick, he hobbled straight up to me. I'll never forget his striking blue eyes, unusual in the south of Italy, which were reflecting the broad smile on his weather-beaten wrinkled face. Placing the cane's crook on his forearm, he took my hand and held it with both of his, then looked straight at me with his now watery blue eyes and said something that brought tears to mine. He told me that he and my father had played together as small boys and that they were best friends ...

We had one more thing to do and that was to visit Francesca and her mother in Santa Agata. I am so glad we did, as Meagan and I were quite overwhelmed by the kindness they showed us. Here were people we never knew, except through a long-distance phone call, and they were openly emotional and genuinely happy for us.

We had the best coffee you have ever tasted served in their best china, but I had to decline the offer of grappa, one of the proudly Italian products I just cannot learn to like! We presented Francesca with a simple but beautiful Pondo bead necklace as a token of our gratitude. With an emotional wrench, it was time to travel on.

There is just so much pasta one can eat and just so much home-made vino one can drink. To add to the challenge, we were handicapped to start with; Meagan loves pasta but her colon doesn't, and I love vino but my head doesn't. So, I ate her excess pasta, putting on 1 000 kilograms in a week, and she was permanently blotto! After my 120th espresso one day, I tried to dilute the next one by sneaking a little hot water and milk into it, but Giulio caught me red-handed, looked at me and said, 'What-a you drink-a now is-a coffee baby!' By the time we had learned how to say, 'No thanks, I've had enough' without offending anyone, it was time to leave.

The next stage of our journey took us north, where we would meet up with Mauro and his beautiful wife Deborah, two Italians whom I had met when they were on holiday in South Africa a few years previously. Despite having only spent a couple of days teaching them the basics of trout fishing in the highland streams of Mpumalanga, we kept in touch. It was not easy to lose touch with someone who insists on posting you a couple of kilograms of Parmesan cheese every few months.

'Why,' I asked, 'do you keep sending the cheese?'

'Ah no want-a you must-a forget-a me,' Mauro said, and I never did.

It was really good to see them again, and they appeared as excited to show us their part of Italy, as we were to see it. They set aside their busy lives, drove all the way down from their studio in Munich, picked us up in Florence and took us on the most wonderful road trip you could imagine. We were exposed to the Italy few tourists ever see and for a few days we lived the life Italians live. We visited their friends in Pisa who owned a restaurant, and after an enormous lunch, drove up the west coast to more friends in Comogli and Portofino, where we stayed the night.

The following day we headed north to their family who live in the beautiful town of Trento where Deborah grew up and attended university. The town was littered with cycling paraphernalia, and even though we'd missed the Giro di Italia cyclists by an hour or two, the atmosphere was still charged with the aftermath of this truly Italian sport. Finally, we wound our way up into the Alps, to the ski resort village of Madonna de Campiglio, situated almost on the Austrian border, where yet more friends opened up their picture postcard hotel just for us despite it being out of season and nowhere else being open.

Words to describe the setting fail me, it was so beautiful and more, much more. I even managed to spot some wild trout in a fast-flowing alpine river close by, and a herd of deer, as they sunned themselves on the hillside just outside town. The next day we bade a fond farewell to Mauro and Deborah who motored on through the Alps back to Germany.

Wildlife in Italy, 'she's not-a beeg,' so I was really happy to have seen some deer. I didn't get to see the European brown bear, which has been re-introduced into the surrounding forest, but it was good to know they were there, and that the locals were really proud of this conservation effort.

The owner of the hotel was a keen hunter, one of the most ethical I've come across. He clearly loved the outdoors and was keen to take us into the Alps, as far as one could drive, that is. We went off the beaten track into the wilder parts in his Land Cruiser, while his daughter, who spoke English, translated for us.

Even though it was not the right time of year for snow, it snowed just enough to lay down a white blanket of welcome for us. The day we left, they gave us a vacuum-packed Italian ham and a bottle of grappa. The grappa? I've been rude enough already, but the ham, Mama Mia, delizioso! After two fantastic days we boarded a bus driven by Robert de Niro's twin brother and we were bound for Milan. There was only one other passenger on the bus besides Meagan and I, an elderly lady who bent 'Robert's' ear for the entire four hours it took to get to Milan. What was she talking about? You guessed it ... food!

When I got home, I contacted all my South African relatives; I couldn't wait to put them in the picture. I told them we were all guilty of not taking my father seriously enough and that while the language barrier may have been partially to blame, it was a weak excuse. Italy, I said, has a heritage of culture and history second to none, from which we can all be truly proud to have descended. Best of all, there was still time to go and experience it, be a part of it.

My only regret is that my dad isn't around to see how much we appreciate what he gave us. But...

'Well, Papa, maybe there's still time to open that restaurant.'

Fence Gone ... Game Gone?

NOVEMBER 2007

Everyone was keen to see what effects the removal of the Klaserie fence had on our game numbers, so I compiled the following table and a brief analysis of the situation. The numbers show we're on a winning streak. It is fascinating to see what the game census results have revealed over the years. For instance, who could ever have predicted the rapid increase in elephant numbers from seven to nearly 500 in only 14 years! It is now difficult to believe that about six or seven years ago, a few well-meaning shareholders were thinking about actually introducing elephant to Olifants because we hardly ever saw them on the reserve!

Theoretically speaking, the removal of the fence in 2005 gave game the freedom to travel from Olifants River Game Reserve to the Indian Ocean without being hampered by a fence. It was a fantastic dream, indeed, but what was the reality?

It has been more than two years since the Klaserie fence was removed. This is enough time, we feel, for the effects on game distribution in the re-created open system within the Association of Private Nature Reserves (APNR) to be revealed. More specifically, we can now see what happened within the Balule Nature Reserve itself.

Although there have been perceptible changes, they're subtle enough to elicit debate as to whether these would have occurred had the fence remained. In short, there is nothing unexpected or surprising to report. This may indicate that the time frame allowed for observation and analysis is too narrow, or conditions in Balule are not as markedly out of synch with the rest of the

Larger herbivore numbers before and after the fence removal

Species	Before: 2004–2005	After: 2006–2007
Impala	3276	4398
Waterbuck	388	519
Wildebeest	335	217
Giraffe	325	268
Zebra	448	450
Kudu	428	487
Warthog	315	400
Bushbuck	27	67
Buffalo	235	391
White Rhino	14	30
Elephant	304	401
Hippo	73	56

APNR open system as originally suspected.

As we have seen from the neighbouring Klaserie Nature Reserve's game census figures (not tabled), there is an increase in their numbers where ours have decreased, though proportionately we still have more general or 'plains game'. A percentage can be attributed to increased predation on our side. At this stage, I suspect, however, that the losses are largely due to natural dilution in a larger open system, rather than a looming predator/prey problem. The overall balance ratio between species, except elephant and wildebeest, appears to be comparatively healthy in Balule.

I feel that we can finally put to bed the fears we had of masses of our game migrating to greener pastures. Our balanced numbers and our species mix is the best among the four reserves. But the situation is not as rosy as it seems. Our live animal biomass per hectare has increased dramatically, way beyond the reserve's carrying capacity, and yet most of the species making up the herbivore biomass are on the decline. How is this possible? The answer is that the bulk of this biomass is made up of huge numbers of elephant. The bottom line is simply that the biodiversity of our reserve is being negatively affected in the short term.

Elephant numbers have increased in one year by nearly 25 per cent, not that this increase can be attributed solely to the removal of the fence. Elephant were moving into Balule in large numbers prior to the fences coming down. At the time of its removal there were already 251 of them in the reserve. This upward trend has its root cause beyond our boundaries, because although the removal of the fence did encourage the breeding herds to move more freely, they had found ways around the fence long before it was removed. Frustratingly, it's still a wait-and-see approach that we're obliged to adopt. Until a national policy decision on elephant population management is taken, we can expect them in greater numbers as the pressure for space and food increases in the reserves around us.

Surprise, surprise! Lion numbers are up! Although each and every lion cannot be counted from the helicopter due to their excellent camouflage at this time of the year, the figures over the last seven years indicate a consistent upward trend of the actual numbers seen from the air. This does not bode well for the wildebeest population, whose numbers are rapidly declining. Zebra, another popular prey animal, are also beginning to show the effect of increased predation on their numbers. Kudu are slightly up, but these 'grey ghosts' of Africa are notoriously wary and difficult to hunt, so should always hold their own, as the census figures reveal.

Hyaena numbers appear to be showing a positive upward trend and greater numbers are being recorded at kills. On a giraffe carcass deserted by lions on Lisbon recently, nine adult hyaenas were seen.

Despite the effect of the wild dog pack on their numbers, impala bred so well last season that their numbers have remained virtually unchanged. Buffalo numbers are showing a steady increase. We suspect some 70-odd may have crossed the river into the state-owned property and the wetland area created by the Palabora Mining Company's tailings dams. Hippo numbers appear stable. Giraffe numbers are down, though this may not be evident when going on a game drive, because they're larger and relatively easy to see. Of concern is that fewer than usual juvenile and sub-adult giraffe were counted this year. This may be indicative of an increase in predation on this tier of the population.

The most encouraging outcome of the census was the number of white rhino counted. There can be no doubt that they feel at home on Olifants. Census figures indicate that they were marginally up on the previous year's count. The number of baby rhino seen by shareholders recently attests to the fact that the cows are happy to have their calves in their old familiar range. I've also noticed a few optimistic rhino near Sable Dam still waiting in the vain hope that we may start our feeding programme again. When they hear the Land Cruiser approaching, they move closer, that's proof enough of their wishful thinking! Despite the relatively poor veld conditions, all the rhino we've seen are in excellent condition, which indicates they're able to range over a wider area and source quality natural feed now that the fences are down.

The increased number of baboon troops is a concern although this phenomenon is not fence-related at all. These primates, specifically the larger males, regularly catch, kill and eat the young of antelope such as bushbuck, grey duiker, Sharpe's grysbok, and klipspringer. With the number of large male baboons having the potential to take out one or two young antelope per year now estimated to be over 100 individuals, this translates to a possible loss of nearly 200 antelope. At this rate, baboons may very well qualify as predators in their own right. A baby nyala was rescued from the clutches of a large male baboon the other day, bringing to three the known number rescued from baboons since I've been at Olifants. This clearly demonstrates that even the young of larger antelope are not safe. With the nyala population numbering as few as they do, I acted against our policy of allowing nature to take its course and made a judgement call. I believe there are times when science needs to take a back seat, and in view of the fact that so many of these primates are artificially encouraged in the region north of our reserve, I felt it was justified.

The game viewing for which Olifants has become well known

has continued to live up to expectations. The acid test is usually when the reserve's shareholders give feedback on the game viewing, and again, all reports indicate a positive trend. Some days were better than others, but even the worst days were good.

Despite a record number of visitors over the Easter period there was *lebensraum* for everybody, including the wildlife, and psychologically it felt less claustrophobic and the game viewing was far better than expected. The myth that more vehicles and subsequent viewing pressure equals less game seen was well and truly 'busted'... I believe the attitude and approach of members towards their reserve is largely responsible for the prevailing vibe of Olifants.

Even those of us not given to wearing kaftans and sandals would have to agree that Olifants is blessed with 'good karma'.

Tree Huggers ... We Have Them, Too!

BASED ON A NEWSLETTER FROM FEBRUARY 2005

It was about mid-morning when I received a call to say a large elephant bull was steadily making his way from Idube Dam towards the office. In those days, shareholders nearly always called in the odd jumbo sighting, whilst nowadays it's such an everyday event no one bothers any more. This jumbo continued walking along the road until he reached the flood plain on the banks of the Olifants River. He then cut across the clearing and made his way straight to a small wallow that had formed from recent rains. There, he proceeded to give himself a mud bath, a luxury which only took a few minutes. Turning on his crinkly and calloused heels, he resumed walking along the road and made his way to the office, moving purposefully through the car park area and up the road heading towards the Palm Loop. So far, nothing unusual about all this, but what happened next and why it happened, only another elephant will understand ... maybe!

With apparent single-mindedness, he made his way directly to Serengeti Plain, an open grass plain of some ten hectares on which stood two prominent umbrella thorn acacias. (At a stretch of the imagination, this clearing resembles a miniature version of its Tanzanian namesake.) Later we back-tracked his route and confirmed that he had neither deviated from this route nor stopped to feed. Moving onto the plain, he ignored the smaller of the two umbrella thorn trees and made a beeline for the bigger one. At that time, both of these trees were clearly visible on Google Earth, which gives you some scale to these events.

Cautiously, he tested the rocks that we had packed around the base of the tree specifically to discourage elephant from damaging it or pushing it over. This elephant showed no respect for our labours and was obviously determined to prove a point. Using his front feet, he began manipulating the rocks. The soft soil soon yielded and the stones toppled over like dominoes, while others were slid aside to accommodate his feet and his angle of attack.

In fact, pushing over the tree didn't take a lot of effort: having exposed some of the root, he broke off a carrot-sized piece, which he chewed and then spat out. That done, he again turned on those crinkly calloused heels and left as unceremoniously as he had arrived. As always in this sort of situation, I felt completely helpless and resigned myself to the fact that nature should be allowed to take its course. But, shortly thereafter, I realised this was not to be.

Bad news travels fast and it wasn't long before a deputation of concerned shareholders visited the office enquiring as to what I proposed to do about their precious tree. My ecologically motivated viewpoint, punctuated with the longest biological terminology I could muster, did not convince them at all. Initially, they showed a measure of restraint, quietly mumbling their obvious discontent amongst themselves. But as more of them got to hear about the tree, they began to take on the characteristics of a mob, and when they began rolling up their sleeves to demonstrate they meant business, I could see I was dealing with extremists. These were 'tree huggers', a hitherto unsuspected social stratum of Olifants that defined the meaning of fanaticism.

The insides of their arms were now exposed and they were chafed, as were their cheeks, sure signs of people who spend large amounts of time hugging trees, particularly the rough-barked African species. Australian tree huggers are less inclined to this affliction, as their eucalyptus trees have a smooth-textured bark, and so do not cause the abrasions associated with other trees. Nevertheless, their tree-hugging status is still easily identified by the claw marks on the outside of their thighs and arms made by male koalas, who mistake them for female koalas in the breeding season.

Making my way nervously through the picket line of chanting protestors, I calmed them down by promising to try and save the tree. A few hours later, with the help of my bemused labour force and a CAT 966 front-end loader, the tree was re-positioned and supported in place with carefully selected wooden props. Fortunately, the wet conditions meant that the roots were quite pliable so they didn't break off.

New topsoil was placed over the one tender fractured root, and a handful of fertiliser was thrown in for good measure. To speed things up a bit the site was watered to facilitate the healing process. I am pleased to report that the tree has survived its ordeal and is on its way to a full recovery. When we are satisfied with its progress, the life support system in the form of a rubber-clad cable and timber props will be removed.

In the greater scheme of things, this tree-rescuing effort, though noble and well-meaning, was actually quite ridiculous. Thinking of Grzimek and Michael's book *Serengeti Shall Not Die,* I wondered what they would make of our attempt years later and 3 000 kilometres to the south, where their prophecy would be immortalised on Olifants' own Serengeti.

Not long after the tree incident, I noticed Idube Dam's water level was dropping, which it shouldn't. The large ball valve system that feeds this water point is designed to deliver water almost as fast as it is consumed, so something was clearly wrong with the mechanism. On closer inspection, I found that the same elephant bull had managed to lift the specially designed recessed steel cover protecting the ball valve chamber, and had removed the ball and valve by simply breaking it off. He then apparently tried to play soccer with the copper ball, which I eventually found crumpled, discarded, and resembling what the tree huggers would have done to me had I not complied with their demands to save their precious tree. The elephant had done all this in the hour or so prior to making his way to Serengeti. What is so incredible is that he had managed to lift this ball valve chamber's lid. It was designed with two small metal 'ears' that would only allow two human fingers to grasp them and lift the lid. How on earth this animal managed the task is beyond me, and yet, it is just another demonstration of the dexterity of an elephant's trunk.

On a more serious note, key tree species and certain vulnerable specimens of the more common representatives of this reserve's habitat type are being singled out for protection against ring-barking and subsequent destruction by elephant. These trees include those providing shade and ambience around our lodges as well as those providing nesting support for white-backed vultures, Pel's fishing owls, ground hornbills and myriad other vulnerable bird species which are dependent on them primarily as nest supports.

As an experiment, we have selected approximately 1 000 trees which have had large-diameter chicken wire wrapped loosely around their trunks. The reason for using large-diameter mesh is to prevent tree agamas and other small wildlife from becoming trapped when they scale the trunks. The loose fit of the wire allows for tree growth to the point that by the time the trunks reach a girth where the wire may become too tight, it would have rusted away long ago.

Unsightly as this process may seem on initial inspection, the wire soon becomes quite difficult to see against the grey-brown bark. Additionally, those trees used as back scratchers by the elephants acquire a layer of mud which actually plasters the wire against the bark, rendering it nigh-on invisible. Furthermore, the galvanising on the wire is scoured off by this abrasive action, which dulls it and accelerates the slow but sure rusting process.

This project was started over four years ago at the suggestion of Doctors Michelle and Steve Henley, who are based in the Timbavati Nature Reserve, through the Save the Elephant Foundation, in conjunction with the APNR. This team has been conducting research in the area for nearly ten years now.

So far, the results of our wire-wrapping experiment have been most encouraging. Only a couple of dozen of the smaller and medium-sized trees, mostly knobthorn and marula trees, have been pushed over by bull elephants. But, it has been interesting to note that hardly any of these trees were fed on. Nor has any attempt been made to remove the mesh. It appears that the trees were pushed over for the sheer hell of it, or as testosterone-charged displays of strength. What we have observed is that the breeding herds which are chiefly responsible for ring-barking trees have, as yet, made no attempt to get through the wire mesh or remove it to get to the bark.

What we have also learned is that there is more chance of protecting a larger diameter tree than a smaller one. Logically, if a tree is more difficult for an elephant bull to push over, it will further benefit from mesh protection. It is abundantly clear, though, that this entire experiment will not be of any long-term ecological significance, due to the gap that will be created by the absence of younger trees that are necessary for recruitment and succession in an ecosystem, which incidentally is a huge concern among conservationists today, and is the subject of an on-going PhD study by Georgette Lagendijk.

This radical measure will not provide long-term protection of trees against elephant damage, nor is it in any way intended to be a solution to the problem. All we are doing is buying ourselves and our trees a little time until elephant population management encompasses the protection of the reserve's biodiversity.

That, in turn, will keep the tree huggers happy.

The Dynamism of Lions on Olifants

JULY 2006

The Greater Olifants Reserve covers roughly 180 square kilometres. This is the area in which our lions move relatively unrestricted and makes up approximately 70 per cent of an average pride's territory for this habitat/veld type. Although we cannot single out one factor above all others that determines how large a territory will be, I'm sure that of numerous options, the availability, number and density of prey must be at or near the top of the list. These requirements are prevalent on Olifants, largely due to the man-made clearings and the evenly distributed permanent water points on the reserve. Within this spread are 'hot spots', usually relatively small patches where plains game tend to congregate, and the lions are quick to capitalise on them. If one were to ask where on Olifants lion are most likely to be seen or have been reported most often, the unhesitating answer would be the Warthog Pan/Palm Loop area. The reasons for this are, among others, large open areas, concentrated prey species and three permanent water points within two kilometres of each other.

Airstrips in particular have been found to be favoured by lion for hunting. These long, narrow open stretches, fringed by an apron of grass and surrounded by thick bush, allow excellent approach cover. This, in turn, may contribute to more kills than would otherwise have been possible. In the Klaserie Private Nature Reserve, landing strips are thought to be a major contributing factor to the heavy predation on wildebeest. It is not so much that lion show a preference for wildebeest, it's more a question of knowing that they are likely to find this prey with predictable regularity on these open areas. Airstrips are invariably built on high ground. Therefore thermal inversion makes these areas warmer in the evenings – and open areas that are warm at night are popular resting areas for prey species.

When two or three groups of lions are seen in different parts of the reserve, they are often thought of as being different prides or belonging to different prides. The term 'different prides' is too strong a definition, as I believe they are sub-groups of a major core pride that has split into more effective hunting units. Although not closely knit, the sub-groups appear to tolerate each other's presence, drawing the line at kills, which they don't appear to share. This was evident when the previous pride, known as 'the Klaserie Gang' was eliminated by so-called cattle farmers. The fragmented Rusermi sub-groups seized the opportunity, the smaller units combined, and together formed a cohesive pride. They then moved into the vacant territory and claimed it for themselves.

At present, the total known lion population on Olifants is 23, made up of 13 in the 'Rusermi pride', seven in the 'Venice pride' and two males and one female seen in the Madrid/Venice area. It would take a more serious population study to include nomadic lion movement, so these are 'resident' figures.

A recent visit to a reserve in the Jejane Conservancy, immediately to the south of us, revealed that there is now a known population of seven lions in that area, three of which are pregnant. Olifants West, the old Balule, now boasts lion sightings on a regular basis, which was not the case before the fence between our railway gate and the old carports was removed; even hyaena were scarce in that region at the time.

The gap created by the removal of this small section of fence actually funnelled game movement as well as being uncomfortably close to a neighbouring reserve's lion breeding enclosure. These captive-bred lions, whose calls attracted 'our wild lions' through this narrow opening in the fence, were also a major problem. Members of the old Olifants pride moved through this bottleneck, probably nudged by a territorial shift and the resultant pressure from the Klaserie Gang which was moving ever closer to the southern cut line.

We know that roughly 70 per cent of our lion territory consists of a formal nature reserve at its core surrounded by a zone that is a relatively well-protected conservancy area, tapering off rapidly the further one goes outward. The boundary lines of a lion pride do not necessarily follow reserve perimeter cut lines or other man-made demarcation.

This means that the periphery of these areas will include some territorial overlapping consisting of either totally hostile territory and/or areas where we have no control over what happens to them. This is not unique to Olifants, and this scenario is commonplace on the boundaries of even the most pristine and remote game reserves in Africa. Losses due to hunting, poaching, farmers protecting livestock, diseases from domestic dogs and cats and other man-induced mortalities appear to be on the rise. These are just some of the hurdles that lions in Africa are faced with today, on top of many others with which they have had to deal since man and lion first began using the same turf.

When lions leave an area of relative safety, they usually do so under pressure from other lions. In fact, if they were not able to get away, they would more than likely be killed by those 'enemy' lions. Under normal conditions, these losses to neighbouring areas are hurdles that natural self-sustaining lion populations overcome and adjust to very quickly.

In our reserve, young lions, particularly young males, are pushed out by the larger dominant pride males, or by new challenging males who enter our region from the surrounding reserves. Young lionesses also move onto the reserve from time to time in search of mates, or accompanying their young brothers who are fleeing from territorial males. More often than not, it is as young male lions approach two years of age that they meet resistance from the resident pride males. In response, they move to the extreme edges of the territory that they're familiar with, although this stay is usually short-lived.

With hostile lions close on their heels, and driven by hunger, they invariably continue onwards into new territory and enter farmland, where they meet another kind of hostility, which is often just as deadly. On the other hand, females, especially those in oestrus, tend to find it relatively easy to 'melt' into an area, and they appear to be more easily absorbed. There is also the constant reality that our resident lions will one day be pushed out by younger, fitter interlopers who are always patrolling the periphery waiting for the right time to move in.

This has happened in the past and will happen again. Although we actively try to limit man's negative effects on the lions in our reserve whenever and wherever we are able, we do not make a habit of interfering with the intra-specific interaction or conflict that occurs naturally between lions. The following illustrates the folly of man's interference in these matters.

One evening we were sitting around the boma fire at a shareholder's lodge discussing the meal we were about to enjoy. Our host was adamant that he knew less than I did about flame-grilling and said that it would be my fault if he ruined the meat. His psychological ploy – to get me to grill the meat while he supervised proceedings over the rim of his glass of Chivas Regal – was never put to the test. All conversation was suspended when I received a call from one of the regional rangers. A call at this time of the day usually meant some urgent matter had cropped up, and indeed it had.

He had immobilised a three-year-old male lion that was under pressure from the two dominant males in that area, as in his efforts to get away from them, he had been desperately trying to break out of the reserve onto the main road. The question was, could we try to relocate him by releasing him in a known low-lion-density area in the extreme north-east of the reserve?

'What have we got to lose?' I answered. 'It's better than having him breaking out where he has been wanting to for the last week, and then getting run over on the road, or getting shot by a hostile farmer.'

I saw our host toss back the remnants of his whisky in a wasteful gulp, then move across from the fireplace to ask me if he could come along. I pretended not to have noticed the disappearance of the Chivas Regal as though his accompanying me was a foregone conclusion, as I was always glad of his company. Three uncomfortable, cold and bumpy hours later, about 25 kilometres from where the lion was darted, we arrived at his new 'safe house' and, without ceremony, laid him down in some soft grass and released him.

The following afternoon, less than 18 hours later, he was back, attempting to break out along the same fence line where he had been darted the previous evening! Back-tracking this lion, we found that he swam across the Olifants River and walked straight back. As if heading on a built-in compass bearing and without deviation, he didn't stop until reaching familiar territory again.

Expecting to see the same lions and basic pride structure remain intact, year in and year out, is unrealistic and could lead to disappointment. Lions are dynamic creatures, and although pride stability is a key to survival, changes in pride composition and the number of individuals is a natural progression. These mechanisms of change are sometimes dramatic, often violent and apparently cruel, but are necessary for the long-term survival of the species. Even when these changes are initiated by the hand of man, the ability of a pride to bounce back is no less efficient, as indeed the lions on Olifants continually demonstrate. This resilience is a demonstration of their degree of adaptability as a species, but also relies to some degree on the specific character traits of individuals.

Simply put, I believe that like people, lions have personalities that can influence their survival potential. Within any given lion population you will find it comprises individuals with specific traits and temperaments; there will be good mothers and not-so-good mothers, good hunters and poor hunters, and so on.

The question is, then, how do our lion come through these gauntlets and still remain strong enough in numbers to be effective survival units? I think the answer may lie in the cub survival rate. In numerous other relatively wild and unmanaged areas, cub mortality is very high. In Savuti, for example, on average one in seven cubs will make it to adulthood. If we compare these figures with the last eight years' statistics in the Olifants area, where the cub survival rate has been nearly 100 per cent, it is clear that this factor becomes more significant, deserving more focus. Even in captive breeding situations, a 100 per cent cub survival rate is the exception rather than the rule.

I suspect our exceptional cub survival rate has a lot to do with the excellent hunting opportunities that the Warthog Pan/Palm Loop area facilitates. It comes as no surprise, then, that many of the lions born on Olifants are born in the shade of the beautiful *Phoenix reclinata* palms that form thickets and give rise to the name 'Palm Loop'. The most favoured section appears to be the section from Ian's Pan to the Palm Loop sub-station.

As explained in 'Observations during drought' the proximity of the lions' den in relation to where the lionesses hunt means they don't have to leave the cubs for too long while procuring food and water. The rocky crevices and thick vegetation, particularly the palm fronds that curve in arches over the sandy river bed, offer excellent concealment, shade and protection. Low hyaena numbers in the area mean that predation is a relatively minor risk. Based on records prior to train speed reduction, it appears the train was a limiting factor on lion numbers. Both adults and cubs were vulnerable, as the track runs right through this prime breeding and nursing area. This is less of a hazard now, due to the speed restriction on all trains moving through the reserve.

Two of our shareholders had just returned from an overland safari to Botswana and mentioned the legendary Kalahari lions they had seen on their trip. They revealed an interesting fact about these desert-dwelling felines. The cub survival rate in the Kalahari Gemsbok Park is apparently lowest of all in that only one in ten reaches twelve months of age. Talk about a tough childhood!

The ripple effect of being part of an open, free-range system means that young lions from the neighbouring Klaserie Reserve will continue to enter our area to test the water, a natural process in lion ecology and essential in ensuring only the fittest pass on their genes. If young male lions meet strong resistance from resident lions, they tend to continue through, into areas outside the reserve. Although relatively safe from the ruthless pride males, the young lions now find themselves in direct conflict with farmers, and sadly, the outcome is usually a foregone conclusion.

In larger natural systems, some of the ousted lions form a coalition and later return, stronger and with the advantage of youth, often turning the tables in their favour. The largest coalition I've known is seven males, but apparently there is one in the Timbavati of eleven or twelve males – formidable but unsustainable.

In the worst case scenario of losing all our lions simultaneously it would not be long before the vacuum would be filled by lions from the Klaserie/Kruger area. I suspect there are lions lurking on our periphery, ready to colonise vacant territory at the first opportunity.

Kudu and Bushpig Country

We had just finished supper and were busy deciding what to watch on TV. My son Dino had the advantage. Firstly, the remote was in his hand; secondly, as he was home only on weekends from boarding school, he had the emotional edge ... and Meagan and I gave in too easily. As it turned out, it didn't matter, because moments later I received a call from my colleague Ron, saying he didn't think I would believe it, but outside his house he had a full-grown bushpig eating out of his hand; it was so tame, it was allowing him to scratch it behind the ears, and ... wait for it ... the pig was wearing a plaster cast on its right back leg! I immediately suspected that this was a plot to get me around to his house for a couple of celebratory ales, as not long had passed since the Springboks beat the Wallabies and Ron was in a justifiably prolonged mood of celebration. There's no victory that brings us more pleasure than one against the Aussies, and this is not confined to rugby and cricket; it is every bit as sweet for me when Casey Stoner kneels before the Two Wheel King, Valentino Rossi.

Giving him credit for an original ploy, and that he had chosen an animal very few people get to see in their lives, let alone scratch behind the ears, I decided to go down and have a look-see anyway. Dino agreed this was worth giving up the remote for and went along with me. This would be the first bushpig he had ever seen and probably the last one he'd ever be photographed hugging.

We arrived to find that Ron had not concocted the tale at all. There was a real, live bushpig complete with a plaster cast on a hind leg and it was being fed a sweet potato by his wife Cindy whilst being stroked lovingly. A few phone calls later and we'd established that the pig belonged to one of the neighbouring plot owners across the river, who had recently had the local vet set its broken leg. Why the animal had decided to burrow out of its enclosure and walk some three kilometres with a broken leg is still a mystery. The ever-grateful owners came across the following morning and retrieved their beloved pig.

Bushpigs are not common in this neck of the woods; our game census figures over the last 16 years indicate that they're only just able to hold their own in this semi-arid environment. Our best estimates put their numbers at between eight and twelve, so they are a rare sight on the reserve. This is in total contrast to areas where higher rainfall, agriculture and the lack of large predators combine to act as magnets for these pigs, where they have become a major problem. A farm manager who was responsible for about 600 hectares of maize in the Pilgrims Rest area shot 53 crop-raiding bushpigs in a year. Although this sounds like a lot of bacon, apparently this was no more than an average-to-good year: he maintained it was a relatively small measure of success in his relentless war against these wily animals. In the context of the numbers estimated to live in that area, 53 pigs was probably less than ten per cent of the population.

As we are talking about bushpigs, I can now introduce you to a relatively unknown piece of country where they thrive. It's an area many of us drive right through on the way down to the reserve, without too much thought, which is exactly what I did until recently.

Not too long ago, I had the pleasure of spending some quality time with a good friend of mine, Mark Jevon, who was then the manager of a sizeable stretch of land belonging to one of the largest companies in the country, situated in a triangle roughly between Pilgrims Rest, Bourke's Luck Potholes and Ohrigstad. It is a magnificent piece of country that includes a 28 kilometre stretch of the stunningly beautiful Blyde River, which cuts through the rich alluvial floodplain surrounded by mountains on either side.

The lower slopes, which are covered in bushveld, soon give way to montane grassland and isolated shrubs as the altitude reaches 1 500 metres. The transition is quite dramatic and these highlands feature Drakensberg vegetation that we normally associate with the Natal Midlands. Mark promised to take me backpacking into an area so remote that it is only accessible on foot. It is real pioneer country where Sir Percy Fitzpatrick, of legendary 'Jock of the Bushveld' fame, rode and hunted over 100 years ago, and where gold prospectors and pilgrims made a fortune or lost everything. We would be heading into places where we'd see wildlife that had probably never seen man before.

'Incredible,' I thought. 'It's 2006, not 1906; this sounds too good to be true.' But, knowing Mark, any doubts I may have had were quickly converted to optimistic expectation. So, filled with anticipation, we prepared our backpacks. My former scoutmaster would have been really proud of me.

I had never been into these mountains before, and was really looking forward to catching a glimpse of the wildlife, particularly of their legendary kudu bulls. These magnificent antelope share these remote hills and valleys with a number of other interesting animals. The larger mammals included mountain reedbuck, leopard, brown hyaena, aardwolf, grey rhebuck, eland, caracal, black-backed jackal, bushbuck, common duiker, oribi, baboons, bushpigs and a small herd of wild horses descended from gold prospectors' horses deserted a century ago. Speaking to one of the local community elders in the Bourke's Luck area, he told me that when he was a child there were still a few rock hyraxes to be found in the hills but now there were none.

I asked him if they used to hunt them and he replied that indeed they did, but with very limited success. He recalled that when he was a youth, his father had already noticed a steady decline of these creatures, and he was convinced they had simply moved away to another area. I doubt that over-hunting was the cause of the hyrax's demise. I suspect that a virus, possibly carried in by the early prospectors and the plethora of domestic stock they brought with them, may have been responsible for the steady decline of this species in that area.

The inaccessibility and steep, rugged terrain meant that few, if any, people have made the effort to explore the area in recent times. This was apparent from the narrow game paths that were made exclusively by the endemic wildlife, so it was quite evident from what Mark had said earlier, that some of the local wildlife had never seen a human being.

The bird life was rich and varied, ranging from numerous open grassland species to thick forest dwellers. We also spotted a good number of small- to medium-sized raptors, including a pair of peregrine falcons, which we watched for a while. What masters of the air – it was no wonder, I thought, that every falconer I know covets these magnificent birds.

There wasn't a sign of recent human activity. There were no footpaths, roads or erosion dongas from abuse by domestic stock. Occasionally we'd come across overgrown and weathered shale piles, alongside shallow indentations or tunnels, indicating where somebody's hopeful digging for gold took place in the late 1800s. Regardless of Mother Nature's determined reclamation efforts, ruins of some of the more solidly built stone dwellings still stand as silent monuments to man's one-time presence. If you know what to look for when scratching around among the old ruins, evidence of the day-to-day mining activities and the methods used is clearly evident from the rusted bits and pieces of worn-out hand tools they left behind. Much more lies buried around these sites, and a metal detector would no doubt unearth all manner of interesting things. As desperately curious as I am, however, I found myself torn between leaving these things be and digging deeper for answers.

Evidently, baboons are the main culprits when it comes to the destruction of the old dry stone wall dwellings. In their search for scorpions and other insects, they will inadvertently demolish the stonework, often exposing hidden nooks and crannies and revealing interesting artefacts. Mark told me he once found an old kettle filled with Martini Henry bullets this way. One cannot but wonder if the owner struck it rich and just didn't bother to return, or perhaps he suffered some mishap, and was unable to go back for his bullets – but if so, why didn't he tell someone where they were? We'll never know, but the more we scratched around, particularly among the ruins of these old dwellings, the more poignant the relics we uncovered. Almost everything we found was a tangible reminder that the life of a gold prospector must have been extremely hard, at best a 'bare necessities' existence.

Some islands of evergreen bush that rose up out of the grass-covered slopes with dense thickets of prominent trees, usually large wild fig, milkberry or jackalberry, were used as cemeteries. Stone mounds marked most of the graves, as the headstones or wooden crosses that may have been placed there were long gone. We noticed that these cool and peaceful groves also made good resting places for living creatures.

Horn scrapings and scattered piles of droppings deposited by kudu and bushbuck indicated that these animals spent a considerable amount of time confidently concealed in the seclusion of these shady refuges. After a quick brew and a rusk, we decided to get going, as we still had a long way to go before we reached our overnight campsite.

The variety of habitat types we moved through ranged from acacia thornveld dotted with a variety of aloes, and stunted bush willows in the lower areas, to temperate grass-covered hillsides higher up. As we began climbing, we noticed more typical mountain vegetation like bushman's tea, mountain syringas, proteas and kiepersols as well as the odd patch of bracken, which began to dominate the landscape. In the protected valleys and north-facing lees, beautiful dense mini-forests, with a wide variety of indigenous evergreen trees, completed the patchwork mosaic that comprised the mountain landscape. The trees making up these thickets, to mention but a few of the most prominent species, are milkwoods, wild olives, ashes, boerbeans, coral trees and wild figs.

The steeply sloping hillsides led us down to valleys characterised by dense forest growth that completely shrouded the small streams that flowed through, which at that time of year still boasted a modest flow of gin-clear, cool water. The tree canopy was so dense that you were able to hear the water tumbling over the boulder-strewn stream beds long before you saw it. Dappled sunlight squeezed through the crown here and there, and trees competing for light grew straight and tall in an effort to reach a place in the sun.

Magnificent specimens of yellowwood, stinkwood and iron-wood trees were still to be found here. On the verges and side slopes, enormous wild strangler fig trees grew amidst vines, creepers and other dense undergrowth, which made the going difficult in places. At times we were forced to crawl on our hands and knees, which was particularly difficult because our backpacks kept on hanging up. It was then that we decided to take the relatively easier route, the stream bed itself. Boulder-hopping on slime-free rocks was a lot easier than wrestling with vines and roots and as a result we made good progress up the valley. The gurgling water and quiet footfalls of our rubber-soled hiking boots on the rocks allowed us to move as quietly as shadows.

From the amount of fresh tracks and droppings on the banks of the stream, it was evident that animals were utilising the water course regularly and it appeared that they were dependent on it. During winter, I suspect this may be their only source of drinking water, as the next water to be found would probably be over the mountain in the next valley. Except for the birds and the gurgle of the stream, it was quiet. We had been making good progress when Mark, who had moved a few metres ahead of me, stopped, and waited for me to catch up.

'Feel this,' he said, holding out his closed fist, which he then opened. The kudu droppings I felt in his hand were still warm!

I looked around, knowing that they couldn't be far, but even though I strained my eyes searching the shadows, I didn't see any sign of them, and so with renewed concentration, we continued. Hardly had we hopped over a couple of boulders when just ten metres in front of us, three huge grey ghosts exploded into life. Small branches and twigs snapped as they broke cover and clambered up the steep bank, disappearing as quickly as they had appeared, leaving me with an indelible image of their enormous lyre-shaped horns thrown back over their rumps as they scythed through the bush. I couldn't believe it ... we'd just been up close and personal with some of the legendary kudu bulls of that region.

I eventually managed to close my mouth, but was still shaking from the adrenalin. We slid the load off our backs and sat down on the smooth water-worn dolerite boulders, chatting excitedly, knowing we had been privy to an extraordinary experience. After a long, cool drink from the stream, and somewhat calmer, we shouldered our backpacks again and carried on upstream.

Kudu are widespread and relatively common in South Africa, but for a free-ranging kudu bull to reach the size that some of them do in these mountains, requires good genes and exceptional survival skills. The enigmatic qualities and highly elusive nature which earned them their reputation have no doubt resulted from an adaptive response to running the gauntlet of relentless hunting over the years. These attributes have been honed to such a degree that, in this context, they cannot be compared to their game reserve and flatland cousins.

These 'highland kudu' are in a league of their own, and this region can justifiably claim to produce some of the most magnificent and wary kudu in Africa.

Back to bushpigs ... besides the black-backed jackal, baboons and to a lesser degree, caracal, there is one other species that continues to give farmers 'the finger', and that is the bushpig. Like the kudu in the mountains around Lydenburg, they have been hunted relentlessly, the one difference being that unlike the kudu, bushpig was declared a problem animal or vermin. Until recently they could be shot on sight and hunted using any means possible and there was no closed season on bushpigs. Their response? They became more wily and reclusive, and I am convinced that this is now inherent in their genetic code.

Bushpigs in this region are almost exclusively nocturnal, they retreat to the thickest cover they can find to lie up in during the day and are usually in position before sunrise. They lie in a circle, snouts outward, so that nothing and no one gets close unannounced. It is common knowledge among hunters in the area that to try and stalk bushpig on foot in this environment is an exercise in futility. So when my friend and I walked into a sounder of three bushpigs, not 20 minutes after seeing the kudu, even though we had the advantage of the stream completely muffling our approach, we just couldn't believe our luck.

Later that afternoon we managed to find a patch of relatively level ground where we put up the tent. Gathering enough wood for the night, we then lit a fire and started to get the food on the go. To have plenty of wood at hand is essential, as the nights up in these mountains can get very cold. That night, however, it rained on and off right through to dawn, and being in a good tent with good food and comfortable clothes made all the difference. Lying snug in my sleeping bag with the rain pelting down on the flysheet, sipping a hot mug of percolated coffee, I couldn't help thinking about those early prospectors and the hardship they must have endured. Nevertheless, I didn't allow either these pensive moments, or the rain trying its damnedest, to put a dampener on such a wonderful day. The next morning was cool and overcast, but Mark was confident it would burn off by mid-morning. After a quick breakfast, we packed up and carried on up the valley, as there was still quite a way to go.

I soon realised we'd need to turn back short of the dense forest at the base of the mountain. I was disappointed at this, even though Mark assured me that the trees there were not much bigger than those we had already seen. I'd heard that the cycads and tree ferns that grew there were spectacular, and due to their inaccessibility, huge specimens still clung to the steep slopes in defiance of man's attempts at removal. Thousands of these ancient plants elsewhere have not been so fortunate and many are still being dug out and illegally removed from the more accessible areas of the Drakensberg.

During our descent, we were filled with anticipation each time we approached an interesting-looking thicket. But the word was out, every spiral-horned grey ghost in the valley knew we were there, leaving us with only yesterday's memories of them. There was no time to revisit the old ruins either. As we climbed out of the valley, the mountain slope opened up, affording us a commanding but distant view of the Ohrigstad/Lydenburg road. Through my binoculars I could see cars making their way along the thin black ribbon that snaked through green valleys whose slopes were peppered with the rusty autumn colours of mountain syringas. Were they heading for the lowveld ... Olifants perhaps? I couldn't help wondering if the cars' occupants even suspected what a wildlife paradise and rich history lay largely undisturbed in these hills and valleys. Perhaps our big game experiences could start in these mountains, as did Martin Botha's of lodge 81, who saw a leopard in his headlights near Ohrigstad recently.

Although the two days I'd spent in that remote valley were filled with so much, I wanted more. Sensing my mood, Mark promised to organise a longer trip including our wives. What a great idea, I thought, there would be so much more to be had sharing this with Meagan ... but, sadly, time flew and before we could get around to doing a second trip, Mark had left the area and moved down to his farm near the Kei River mouth in the Eastern Cape.

When next you're en route to Olifants, knowing there are secrets hidden in these valleys, perhaps you will give them more than a casual glance, and perhaps the kudu will be giving you more than a casual glance, too. After all, their continued safety and natural happiness is largely dependent on man's willingness to leave well alone.

A Stressful Time of Year

BASED ON AN OCTOBER 2002 NEWSLETTER

Have you ever witnessed the social interplay between wild dog pups and their sitter? When the rest of the pack leaves the den to go hunting, it is usually the alpha female that is saddled with the unenviable task of puppy sitting. The pups appear to have inexhaustible energy and are also mischievous by nature. This, combined with their natural curiosity, causes them to constantly wander off and explore. It is at these times that they are extremely vulnerable to predation and I suspect that were it not for the puppy sitters, we would probably not see any wild dogs at all.

The task of running around constantly chasing these happy wanderers back to the safe perimeter of the den is not an easy one. The little reprobates are hell-bent on going where they shouldn't. I often wonder if border collies are such fantastic sheep herders because they have the same coded-in desire to keep pups (and sheep) in the safety of a den? Not only do wild dog pups wander off endlessly, they bite playfully at the sitter's hocks and being almost always hungry, jump up and nip painfully at her nose and mouth, demanding food. Those puppy teeth may be small, but they are as sharp as needles, just like a genet's. I'm sure you will agree this can test even the strongest resolve.

Wild dog pups are not the only creatures that need herding for their own protection. The following shows that desperate times call for desperate measures.

Every year, from August to October, the natural order is stress. The last couple of months leading up to early November rains and hopefully the start of the rainy season, are always the most stressful for our animals and their custodians. As the grass gets de-nuded under the relentless mouths and hooves of the herbivore biomass, the bulk grazers, particularly buffalo, will wander great distances in search of food regardless and unaware of the dangers that moving off the reserve poses. This search for 'greener grass' exposes them to the dangers of poachers' snares and unscrupu-lous hunters who concentrate their efforts in the area north of the river, a favourite winter feeding ground for our resident herd of buffalo.

Another scourge that threatens our wild buffalo herds and ul-timately our responsibility to contain foot-and-mouth disease, are the fly-by-night buffalo breeding projects that have popped up all over the lowveld. A few of these projects illegally 'recruit' wild buffalo, absorbing them into their breeding programmes. The animals they can't use, like adult bulls, are hunted by trophy hunters, and the younger bulls are used for meat. One such breed-ing project on our boundary was suspected of supplementing its numbers in this way. In one season, a herd of over 40 buffalo just disappeared. This herd had a particular cow with unique horns. She was subsequently seen and photographed on the other side of the fence inside this buffalo breeder's property. This proved beyond doubt that this practice was not only rife, but that it was carried out with blatant and total disregard for veterinary law, let alone civil law, and was tantamount to rustling!

In another instance, a breeder to the north of our reserve laid his fence down and when 35 buffalo walked into his prop-erty, lifted the fence up again behind them, as simple as that. Thankfully, new laws and stricter control measures have since been implemented, all but eliminating the possibility of acquir-ing more buffalo than their project permit allows.

The urge to cross the river is hunger-driven, as are most migra-tions of game, and our buffalo are determined to go where they shouldn't. So we take enormous risks trying to get them back when they cross. Watching the game guards running up and down the river bank, trying to chase the buffalo back when they behave just like naughty wild dog pups, trying to dodge around them and go where they know the grass is greener, reminds one of the situation the pup sitter often has to cope with. Unlike the pup sitter, however, which would have taken an unruly pup firmly by the scruff of the neck and deposited it safely back at the den, our guards cannot resort to scruff-of-the-neck treatment with the notoriously dangerous and uncooperative Cape buffalo.

To cut a long story short, all but two buffalo were safely encouraged back to the reserve and as a result of the good rains in the Blyde River catchment area, the Olifants River has risen sufficiently to discourage any buffalo from crossing back over again, so for the time being our buffalo sitters can take it easy. Well, until the river drops again, of course.

Later we found that there are buffalo that will swim a dangerously swollen river to get where they want to go.

The reality is that we did our best, but the other reality is that an animal driven by hunger is determined and our well-meaning efforts were ineffective, particularly as the season became progressively drier. Ultimately, we had to make an offer they couldn't refuse! Prior to the removal of the Klaserie fence, we spent hundreds of thousands of rands on supplementary winter feed to discourage the buffalo from wandering off across the river. I'm pleased to say that the cost we incurred and the logistical difficulties we handled were well worth it. The excellent configuration of the buffalo herd today owes much to the commitment of Balule Nature Reserve generally and the shareholders of Olifants River Game Reserve specifically due to their initiation of this project.

In the next chapter, I deal in more detail with this issue and the events that led to a sustainable solution.

Lion Update

BASED ON AN OCTOBER 2000 NEWSLETTER

There is no doubt that the most sought-after animals on the reserve are lions. Understandably then, due to the ever-changing demographics of the population, continual updates on the status of the reserve's lions are a welcome addition to the newsletters. But there are times when the news is not so welcome.

Until recently, the Greater Olifants region had a relatively stable population of approximately 28 resident lions, which basically consisted of two core prides, one of which was more centrally located within the reserve and was therefore regarded as the resident pride, and a second pride that ranged over a wider territory which occasionally overlapped on the periphery of the resident pride's range. Nomadic lion movement and interlopers increased this figure to over 30 on occasion.

The resident pride was known as the 'Klaserie Gang' or 'Klaserie Pride'. Associated with this pride were the two dominant males that recently moved in from the Klaserie, and had already made their presence felt in no uncertain way. Reports from our anti-poaching patrol unit indicated that the previous pride male who was ousted in the recent shake-up was moving in the quieter north-eastern region of the reserve accompanied by two loyal females. There didn't appear to be a concerted effort by the two new males to chase him any further; they seemed confident that he no longer posed a threat and they tolerated his presence on the periphery of their newly won territory.

The second pride, known as the 'Rusermi Pride', broke up and formed two loosely connected groups. One consisted of three young males and the former two dominant females of the pride, one of whom still had three cubs in tow. The other group comprised two younger females, presumably the sisters of the three young Rusermi pride males. They have been seen on occasion with their three young brothers on Olifants North, but it appears they may feel safer across the river.

These two sub-groups hunted as individual units and were comfortable with each other's presence, albeit at a distance. When they occasionally did meet, the greetings were never hostile, mainly due to the fact that even though each group did their own thing, essentially they were members of the same pride. In a lion's world, everything revolves around territory, which as we all know is often defended to the death; it is as if nothing else matters.

Just how strong this territorial imperative is, was clearly demonstrated one morning when one of the shareholders who was watching the three young males from the former Rusermi pride, called me in. He was concerned about one of the males who had porcupine quills embedded deeply in his armpit area and asked me to have a look at him. By the time I'd made my way from the office to lodge 10 and lifted my binoculars a couple of times to get a closer look at the lions, the two new Klaserie males were already on the scene and were aggressively chasing the three younger males.

These two males had made their way clear across the reserve to locate and target the young lions. Their determination was further evident from reports received from members all along the river who watched as the lions systematically and single-mindedly drew the 'battle lines', walking right past their lodges in broad daylight. The lions showed no fear of the curious on-lookers as they marked territory and roared repeatedly, making sure the three interlopers knew that they had over-stepped the boundaries of tolerance and would be severely dealt with if they were ever caught on the wrong side of the river.

A female and her three almost fully grown cubs, whose territory includes Wild Dog Pan and Nature's Valley, sometimes travel down onto the river floodplain at the point where the Mohlabetsi River flows into the Olifants River. This group appears to be rather secretive and so is not often seen. They appear to be predominantly resident on Venice, and according to the warden in that area, who comes across her occasionally, she never responds when hearing other lions calling. Instead she and her cubs make a hasty retreat in the opposite direction.

Another lone lioness with which I became intrigued was one whose pug marks I had often seen on top of my running shoe tracks from the previous day's run; it was like we knew each other but had never met. At four o'clock one morning, on my way to drop off the kids in Hoedspruit, I finally managed to get a visual of her. This enigmatic lioness turned out to be a relatively small yet beautifully proportioned animal, I would guess that she had not yet had cubs, and judged her to be about three-and-a-half to four years of age.

Her favoured area included the Dinidza river road along to the clubhouse and past Idube Pan, into the Pel's Loop area and then back again, pretty much covering half of my old running route. I say 'old' because since the riverine area has become so popular with the elephant breeding herds, I have had to do a territorial shift of my own and find a safer route to run, so my lady friend and I don't share the same path anymore. Funny, I really miss her presence.

Not long after this, Jetje Japhet told me that a lioness with three tiny cubs was seen under the deck of their house on Dinidza. At least she wasn't alone any more, I thought.

Besides having to compete for territory with other lions, lions often come into direct competition with man for space, mostly with negative consequences. Bad news travels fast, and we were understandably shocked to hear that our resident pride of lions crossed the Olifants River into hostile territory and were shot. Except for three sub-adults, the Klaserie pride was completely wiped out by one of the so-called cattle farmers leasing the state-owned farms.

This property, of some 2 500 hectares, and which is leased

from the government for R2 000 per annum (no misprint), is designated for 'cattle farming', so he claims to be 'defending his livelihood' when shooting large predators which he claims deprive him of an income. Prior to this, a number of our shareholders concerned about the situation wanted to engage the problem proactively, to the extent that they committed themselves in writing to compensate for any cattle killed by 'our lions'.

The only stipulation was that our game scouts were to verify that the lions responsible for any death of cattle were indeed lions that emanated from our reserve. This was conveyed to the lessee, who ignored the offer and went ahead with his lion culling programme anyway. Legally, there was nothing that could be done, until the antiquated laws governing this activity were reviewed.

They say, 'The big wheel turns.' In the next chapter, which unashamedly focuses on 'revenge' in its title, you will see how.

Shortly before the pride crossed over into the area where the lions were shot, we darted one of the young males in order to treat an old wound to his hind leg. Zoletil, the drug used to immobilise lions, has no antidote, and once darted, an animal can take up to six hours to recover from its effect. This is a dangerous period for an animal in this condition to be left without being monitored, but this turn of events and the characteristic limitations on the drug were instrumental in saving his life, as it turned out. Once the Zoletil had worked through his system, he picked up the trail and got to the point where vocal contact could have located the rest of the pride. Unbeknown to him, the rest of his pride were being systematically destroyed at this point; I believe the males were shot first, then the females and finally all but two of the five-month-old cubs. When he called, there was no response from his family; nor would there ever be. The remaining two cubs which had managed to escape being shot died of starvation two weeks later.

He may have thought they had gone back into the Klaserie Nature Reserve, because a couple of weeks later I saw him again inside that reserve on the other side of the fence, which was still up at that stage. This time, however, he was seen in the company of another young male and a darker coloured sub-adult female. Shortly after this, the trio moved back, crawling under the fence and onto the Olifants area, where they filled some of the vacuum left by the Klaserie pride.

It took a while before the soft dust on the roads revealed the unmistakable signs of lions on our reserve again. The emptiness without their presence was depressing, but the vacuum was slowly filling, and it wasn't to be long before a pride established itself again.

Typical of a vacant territory, prospective inhabitants begin to crawl out of the woodwork and stake their claim.

Since the slaughter of our pride across the river, besides the three that crawled in from next door, the following lions have been reported on the reserve.

- One large male mating with two adult females – this trio often seen on the railway line road from the steel train bridge over the Mohlabetse river to the Sable Dam turn-off. They appear to spend most of their time in the south.
- A group of sub-adults comprising two young males and three females is seen in the Olifants area on a fairly regular basis.
- A single female with three-month-old cubs is in the Palm Loop area, not too far from the wild sage thicket

Understandably, the demise of our lions was an extremely bitter pill to swallow. We had become accustomed to seeing them on the reserve; we almost became reliant on them. While our emotions were clouded with anger and frustration at the helplessness of the situation, there was a faint lining of silver on this cloud. In particular, we knew that in an open system such as ours, this vacuum would be filled sooner or later, and the absence of lions would only be temporary.

The absence of the pride was not entirely negative. Some good did come of the tragedy, notwithstanding the opportunism of the other predators in the absence of lion, but the collective impact of other predators on the wildebeest and giraffe was relatively small. Although there was no means of showing it at the time, the evidence is now plain – when last did the Warthog Pan wildebeest herd raise a single calf beyond the juvenile brown colour? Well, they now have four youngsters sporting adult coats. Other herds boast up to five calves, young giraffe can be seen everywhere, and the waterbuck are regular visitors on the flood-plain again.

Cheetah will spend extended periods in a relatively small area when there are no lions in the vicinity to threaten them, and particularly when there is sufficient prey to hunt. This was evi-dent in the recent temporary absence of the lions, when a group of cheetah confidently took a number of young wildebeest, as well as making a sizeable dent in the impala numbers. Cheetah do not appear to have as much of an impact on the wildebeest calves in this area as lions do; they tend to focus mainly on impala. The exception was one individual, a large male cheetah that accounted for two calves in a week! Despite this toll, we nev-er recorded him taking any calves older than the brown stage, so it appeared that if they could grow to that point of development, their chances of survival were substantially increased.

Hyaena took full advantage of the situation – but then, don't they always? A fully grown wildebeest of the Warthog Pan herd was killed by these underrated predators at the bottom of the airstrip. It was unfortunately an adult cow with a youngster, so its unweaned calf stood around waiting for the inevitable, its fate sealed.

I believe that the threat to our lions from the hostile territory to the north will continue until cattle are removed from the area across the river. In the latter half of winter, when the Olifants River levels are very low, the cattle wade onto the sand banks in the middle and at times cross onto our side. We have chased them back across the river a number of times. On one occasion they were a mere one kilometre from the office! This is too much temptation for any lion to resist, so they give chase, and at half the speed and twice as tender as anything the lions are accus-tomed to hunting, the result is usually a foregone conclusion.

There are wheels being set in motion to try and get the lease of the farms north of the river in friendlier hands. The authorities have been made aware of the situation and will be seeking more justification from the lessee for killing the lions, and making sure he understands that he also needs to construct protection kraals for the cattle at night.

It would take a vehement protest and commitment from us to eventually get the cattle removed and veterinary exemption status for this area officially declared. Ironically, the lion issue would not be catalytic in this decision; it would be the Cape buffalo and its associated veterinary and economic implications.

The Olifants River has always been regarded by the Department of Environmental Affairs and Tourism as a natural boundary for wildlife. This may have had some merit in the early days but since then more than half a dozen dams have been constructed upriver, which facilitates thousands of megalitres of water being extracted daily for agriculture.

Today, this perennial river would cease to flow in winter if it were not for the release of water from the Blyde Dam to supply its primary user, the mine in Phalaborwa. So, many years ago, prior to the rape of this river, it may indeed have held enough water through the dry months to either prevent or limit the crossing of wildlife from one side to the other. This situation has now changed completely, but the veterinary and conservation laws have not. The reserve supplied irrefutable photographic evidence of buffalo's total disregard for the river as a boundary or barrier, which helped convince the authorities of the predicament.

The background to the veterinary risk is contained in the area's history. Foskor Mine, the state-owned farms north of our reserve and some of the farms along the Selati River all farmed cattle. Disease-carrying buffalo grazed on the same veld as the cattle and drank from the same water points. This inevitably led to physical contact between the wild and domestic animals which greatly increased the risk of a foot-and-mouth outbreak. With this in mind, some reactions from our officialdom may seem initially to be soundly based on historical facts.

We heard through the bush telegraph one day that the Veterinary Department was planning to destroy a herd of 70 buffalo that had crossed the river into 'cattle country'. This unilateral decision couldn't go unchallenged, even though I knew how seriously the department viewed the potential foot-and-mouth disease risk this posed. I believed their decision was a knee-jerk reaction without thought for a long-term solution.

I could not stand by while our buffalo were routinely slaughtered whenever they crossed the river to feed during the winter months, something they had been doing for years, long before I arrived here 16 years ago.

I sent a letter to the Minister, and got the media involved. The authorities then convened a series of meetings co-ordinated by the Department of Environment and Tourism (DEAT) as well as the various interested and affected parties, including the farmers, Balule Nature Reserve, the mines and the state veterinarian based in the Kruger National Park. Our objection as conservationists was not to the culling of 70 buffalo per se, with there being well over 400 buffalo on the reserve, but that the removal of these buffalo would merely create a vacuum that other buffalo would fill. This would perpetuate the need to destroy more of these animals ad infinitum, and the authorities would still not be any closer to solving the foot-and-mouth problem.

Pulling a trigger is to some minds how problems like these are sorted out, but all this does is treat the symptom without addressing the cause, so we just couldn't allow this 'open season' attitude to manifest itself without some attempt at a long-term solution.

It is amazing what power the media wield. They succeed where all others fail, particularly when it comes to getting bureaucrats to 'pull finger'. Four high-level meetings and less than ten months later, the following transpired:

- Foskor, one of the two big mining companies concerned, erected a veterinary approved fence along the relevant boundaries at a cost of close to R400 000. (Hats off to those guys.)
- None of the herd of 70 buffalo had to be shot.
- The Department of Land Affairs will erect a boundary fence on the relevant state-owned land (still to happen).
- Olifants River Game Reserve has electrified the Grietjie boundary with state-owned land.
- The elephant and buffalo on the northern side of the fence

were chased into our reserve, totalling six buffalo and five elephant. Any remaining after this were destroyed, so in reality only three stubborn old buffalo had to be shot in the Selati River.

- Olifants, Foskor and Palabora Mining Company have undertaken to do regular patrols on the boundary fences.
- A process is underway to register the state-owned properties as 'buffalo country'.
- And now for the really good news ... all the cattle have been removed!

Don't you just love it when a plan comes together?

Vendetta ...

BASED ON A MAY 2004 NEWSLETTER

Many Olifants shareholders will remember the anger and frustration they felt when they received the news report confirming that eleven of our lions had been shot. The lessee of the neighbouring state-owned land and his associates systematically killed these lions with the official backing of the Department of Environmental Affairs in Phalaborwa. In his motivation for the destruction permit, the lions were listed as being a threat to his livelihood. If only the authorities had taken the trouble to look at the seven emaciated cows that constituted this man's supposed livelihood, a permit would not have been issued and instead, the Animal Anti-Cruelty League would have been notified. The poor cattle were in such pitiful condition that death by any means would have been an act of mercy. They were obviously kept on this property for one purpose and one purpose alone, to be used as an excuse to hunt predators that could be deemed a threat. In terms of the Act's definition of stock-killing predators, everything was legal and above-board. So, you can imagine the sense of utter helplessness and failure I felt at having my hands tied by an outdated law. This law, which is still enforced, and which governs the relationship between stock farmers and predators, was devised by farmers, for farmers. It is filled with loopholes so big you could drive a high-suspension Land Cruiser through them with ease.

We had made many attempts over time to resolve the impasse with our neighbour, ranging from offers of compensation for proven losses caused by our lions right up to a suggestion we build, at our expense, a predator-proof cattle kraal for him. But his obstinate resistance made it obvious he had only one agenda, and the fact that the law protected him suited him down to the ground. Little did he know that, ultimately, the law would be used with great determination against him.

Happily, I am now able to report that there's truth in the sayings, 'What goes around comes around' and 'The big wheel turns.'

Law enforcement in its many forms is dependent on informers to some extent. Our 'bush telegraph' is no exception. So, it came to pass that information gathered from various informal sources that constantly monitor 'things' in our area revealed that an illegal hunt for a leopard on this same farm was being planned. Subsequent investigation by our anti-poaching team over the next few days confirmed this information was correct. The hunting locale was found and there was no doubt as to the intent of the set-up, complete with a well-prepared blind from where the hunters would shoot. An impala carcass being used as bait had already been secured with wire high up in an apple leaf tree, so they were specifically targeting a leopard.

Preparations for the apprehension of the would-be hunters were made. Photographs for later use as evidence were taken of the impala carcass bait. The blind from where the hunters would shoot was also photographed in relation to the bait. The relevant authorities both national and local were informed and involved. Together with our anti-poaching team, wardens from the north of Balule and an official from the local Department of Environmental Affairs, the sting was planned and implemented.

The following week we observed that the remnants of the old bait had been removed and a fresh carcass put up. The blind was made more comfortable with a mattress and they had also fitted a spotlight, complete with a dimmer switch and a battery. This ingenious device allowed the bait area to be slowly flooded with light so that no matter how wary the leopard, it would become a clear target in the rifle sight without suspecting a thing. To round things off, a bottle of Dimple Haig was tucked away in the corner of the blind, no doubt for anticipated celebrations. We knew this was our cue and that they would be sitting up for the leopard that night.

Late that afternoon, the vehicle was heard approaching. It was still far in the distance, it being forever amazing how far sound can travel in the bush. Then they came to a halt about 300 metres away, more or less. Not long after this, the two hunters quietly approached the blind, crawled in and, in eager anticipation, settled down to monitor their bait, blissfully unaware that another three pairs of eyes were simultaneously watching their every move.

With the onset of darkness, we needed to get closer, so until it got dark, all communications were by silent text messages only. The official accompanying us was convinced there was now enough evidence to show intent and we didn't need to wait for them to actually shoot a leopard. Initially, we had considered and accepted this sacrifice of a leopard, and as difficult as that decision was to make, it was an indication of how desperately we wanted to nail these bastards.

At a given signal, the team quietly approached the blind. The hunters had no idea we were there until the voice of authority boomed out from behind the hide. After the greeting, the two men in the blind were asked to explain the purpose of their activities. One of the men was well known to the officer, so it must have been much more frightening when out of the darkness he was addressed by his first name. This courteous demand was so intrusive, however, that even the nightjars shut up for a while. How those poor so-called 'hunters' must have felt! I use the word 'poor', because they both ended up quite a bit poorer a few months later.

Stammering a little, the two men said they were 'waiting for poachers'. When shown and asked about the carcass in the tree, they changed their story, now stating they were baiting for hyaena, which were killing their cattle. Despite the official pointing out that it would be impossible for any hyaena to access a bait four metres from the ground in a tree, they stuck to their story. On the way to the police station they turned to one of the regional wardens, Marius Fuls, who was chiefly responsible for coordinating the arrest.

'How can you want to arrest one of your own people? You are

also an Afrikaner!' one of them said to him in Afrikaans.

'I know,' replied Marius. 'But that doesn't make me a criminal, which is what you are!'

As it turned out, one of the men was the unofficial, unsigned lessee of the farm and the other was a friend who later admitted to having shot four of the eleven lions two years previously. The men were taken to Phalaborwa police station and three charges were laid against them.

Prior to this, they asked sheepishly if they could change out of their camouflage outfits. Short of the black SWAT team war paint on their faces, they looked like two turkey hunters straight out of ESPN's outdoor huntin', shootin', fishin' show. Suppressing the urge to parade them through the middle of town in their ridiculous outfits, we relented.

The two men were found guilty and convicted of illegal hunting. Their rifle was confiscated and a hefty fine imposed, and they now have a criminal record. With the new firearms regulations now in place, this effectively means they will probably never qualify for a rifle licence ever again. That is really going to hurt. To separate a Boer from his 'roer' is, next to divorce, probably the most traumatic separation he has to face.

To put this in context, if this had taken place in the south of my father's homeland, where getting even is an accepted part of their culture, the lion killer would have lost much more than his rifle; he'd be sleeping with the fishes, wearing a pair of newly cast, custom-fitted, cement shoes.

Do I believe in the concept of 'vendetta'? No, not really, but the unmistakably sweet taste I savoured may have had more than a little to do with the good few litres of hot Italian blood in my veins.

Jogging in the Bush

BASED ON A MARCH 2000 NEWSLETTER

Jogging, among many other forms of vigorous activity, has been proven to have a positive effect on longevity, and in moderation is accepted as a healthy form of exercise. This was not always so. In his book, *The Lore of Running*, Dr Tim Noakes wrote that years ago, a writer concerned with the hazards of jogging suggested that US Congress enact legislation requiring a warning to be displayed on all running shoes, shorts and books. The suggested text was:

WARNING

Excessive jogging may lead to quasirandemous wanderitis.

I wonder what the label would need to read were we to require its display here, warning against the health hazards of running on Olifants. There are many hazards, dangers and surprises in store for the unwary. For the purpose of this story, though, I have narrowed things down to what most of us regard as *the* danger at the moment.

WARNING

Jogging on Olifants can lead to confrontations with lions.

Yes, running or jogging into a pride of lion is undoubtedly the perceived Number One hazard. [Note: In a few years' time, as elephant numbers grew, this changed and they became *the* animals to try and avoid on a run.] The effect on the health and longevity

221

of the runner in an encounter with either lion or elephant would vary, and I am sure would be entirely dependent on the circumstances. In the majority of encounters with members of the Big Five, excluding black rhino, of which I have no experience, the sudden appearance of a jogger would be enough to send them running off. In contrast, plains game could become quite used to seeing a runner and would often continue feeding as you ran past, though if you changed your tempo or stopped, they'd also move off. By and large, we consider the safety level of an activity in relative terms. For instance, it is a proven fact that it's safer to fly than it is to drive, a statistic based on the comparative numbers of fatalities per kilometre travelled.

If the same formula were used to calculate the risks and determine the danger level of jogging on Olifants, then, I guess one encounter with lion per 20 000 running kilometres has got to be considered low risk.

The following encounter could have been avoided had I been able to consult one of my early warning systems, namely John Chiburre, the Grootdraai security guard who, I might add, hasn't let me down in ten years. John not only gives me a daily situation report on the lodges, he also informs me of any interesting game movement, particularly lion and elephant. The combination of John being off sick for a while, my change of running route and the statistical 20 000 trouble-free kilometres behind me conspired to deliver the inevitable and into play came The Law of Averages, Murphy's Law, call it what you will.

It had been a long day, most of which was spent locked in wage negotiations with our labour union, whose officials arrived four hours late, without so much as an apology. I am new to these tactics, but have since been led to understand that this is a pre-negotiation ploy and is quite normal. Incredible! Deciding against overdosing myself with blood pressure pills or Valium, I thought I would resort to the one sure-fire way of relieving the resultant stress and frustration – and that was to go on a run.

Breaking away from my usual circular route around the flood plain and along the river bank, following the well-worn hippo path to the Japhets' camp on Dinidza, I decided to kill two birds with one stone and check on some work that was being done at one of the lodges, stupidly neglecting to tell anyone of my change of route. On my return, approaching the home straight, as it were, I began opening my stride a little, anticipating the ice-cold Oros and cool shower that I knew was only minutes away.

Nearing the turn-off to lodge 1, the landscape began to change from relatively dense Commiphora woodland to the more open and denuded floodplain habitat, so typical along the Olifants River. I ran past a large herd of immaculate impala which practically live on this grassless plain, and then nearly tripped over a family of warthogs with bad road manners. Up ahead, a couple of curious giraffe stopped browsing on a large sweet-thorn acacia, and looked down at me from under those just-curled eyelashes of theirs, not quite able to figure out what I was up to.

It always amazes me how close they allow you to run past them, at times so close that they will cheekily lift a back leg, as if to warn you they will kick out if you come any closer.

With the stress and frustration progressively dissipating with each footfall, I began to feel my spirits lifting and I revelled in the sense of well-being and in the privilege of being able to run in such beautiful surrounds. But, all was not as peaceful as it seemed. Ahead of me a flock of guineafowl uttered their shrill alarm call from the tops of a couple of dead leadwood trees on which they were perched. I slowed down and became more alert, as I knew that from their vantage point they could easily see a predator that I couldn't. I ruled out an airborne threat immediately, as the guineafowl themselves were too exposed. It had to be either a black-backed jackal or a leopard, I thought, glancing left then right in the hope of catching a glimpse of whatever it was that was upsetting them.

Alerted by movement some 30 metres further down the road in front of me, but probably not registering as quickly as I would have liked, I came to a sudden, intentional stop. I focused warily on the unmistakable tawny forms of lions. I could clearly see four of them. They were all startled at my sudden appearance and abrupt stop; two of them beat a hasty retreat up towards the old

Mica mine road, and the other two skedaddled across the flood-plain down to the river.

I remained motionless, waiting for their curiosity to overcome their initial fear, and for them to move back onto the road. If that had transpired, I would have climbed a tree that I had already picked out for this purpose. To hell with the guineafowl, I thought, they will have to make space for me. When the lions did not return (admittedly I didn't wait too long), I surmised that they had got quite a fright and had continued moving in the direction they were headed, and if so, this would effectively cut me off from any detour route back home.

Realising my predicament, I walked down to the river opposite Umfubu Lodge and tried to raise one of our neighbours across the river, to ask them to phone Meagan and ask her to come and pick me up. No one was home. From there, I jogged back the way I had come with furtive glances over my shoulder every now and then.

I was feeling quite confident that I was not being followed, but I was getting really tired by now and I knew I had at least another four kilometres to go before reaching one of the lodges, or a vehicle parked there which may have a radio which I could use to call Meagan for help. Starting with the closest, lodge 49, I found no one at home and a vehicle with no radio. Same story with lodge 46, also no radio in the vehicle. The Hulett's vehicle was a banker, I thought, but actually, also no radio! Reaching the top of the hill, there was one last lodge to check. Success! Getting there, though there was no one at home, there was a radio in the vehicle but no microphone. Eventually I found the microphone in the glove compartment, connected it and switched on. You guessed it, no power. Opening the bonnet, I found the battery power switch, turned on and called Meagan. Before I could tell her what had happened and where I was, she pre-empted my explanation, saying she was already on her way, and that the neighbours I had tried to raise earlier saw everything from their house and phoned her. (Big Brother is always watching.)

On the way back to the area where I'd first bumped into the lions, we found not four, but five lions disembowelling a zebra they had killed, exactly where I had encountered them on the road. They must have only just made the kill when I happened on them earlier. The carcass, being slightly off the road in some thick bush, was well hidden and so was not visible from where I'd stopped on foot. Had I known they had a kill, I would have taken a detour via the old Mica mine road knowing they wouldn't move far from their successful kill. At no time, however, did I feel the situation was desperate or dangerous, and would gladly have exchanged the lion interlude for a recent encounter with an unusually large black mamba that reared up at me while I was running on a small bush track with a well-grown 'middelman-netjie'. I still shudder when thinking about it, but that's a mamba story, and this is a lion story.

Finally, if you absolutely have to go jogging in the bush, make sure someone knows your route and timing before you start and don't make last-minute changes. If you spot anything that could develop into a threat, turn round and go back the way you came. Know where the bigger trees are; pick one that you're confident you can climb. You're safer up a tree than behind a bush.

Something of Value

'You know you are insufferably spoilt when you come home from a day on the river disappointed with a three-and-a-half-pound wild trout.' These words are taken from the pen of Dr Tom Sutcliffe, talented author, artist and the doyen of trout fishing in South Africa. He refers to an afternoon spent fishing on one of the many mountain streams in the Eastern Cape, where peering into a pool below a low-water bridge, he spotted an enormous trout, estimated to weigh at least five pounds. I know the spot well and had the privilege of fishing this very pool, with the master himself, a couple of years before. Mustering all the skill acquired in a lifetime's pursuit of trout, Tom succeeded after some time in landing a magnificent specimen, a wild trout weighing three-and-a-half pounds, a leviathan by South African river standards. The five-pound fish spotted earlier evaded capture.

What has all this about fishing, particularly fly fishing for trout, got to do with a Big Five game reserve? Well, no, this is not going to be followed by an article on the merits of fly fishing for buffalo with grass-fly imitations or how to tie an Eragrostis streamer, but there are many and relevant parallels.

Tom's message has as much relevance to a Big Five game reserve as it does to a trout stream. Essentially, his message poses two questions. 'Are you allowing complacency and unrealistic expectations to rob you of real value? Are you rushing through the reserve missing out on the less noticeable, but equally interesting creatures this area has to offer?'

Whether we're talking about tortoises or trout, animals everywhere interact with their environment in much the same way. They are governed by the same basic ecological principles. As trout respond to favourable environmental conditions by increasing production, which in turn results in good fishing, so will our game respond to their own set of paradigms, providing the variety and diversity that creates the conditions for good game viewing. Ecosystems are cyclic and dynamic in function; no two days are going to be the same.

Therefore, over time, you will experience times of plenty and times of not-so-plenty. You will even learn to love the days of near-as-dammit-nothing.

It is well known that the general game on Olifants, particularly on and in our open clearings, can provide good viewing on many occasions. An example of this is the sighting recently of nearly 100 zebra, about 30 wildebeest, 17 giraffe, over 150 impala, eight warthogs, a troop of baboons, seven kudu and two black-backed jackal, all seen at one time on Wart Hog Pan clearing! This is spectacular value by any standards, although I am not sure it's a record.

Despite good general game viewing, if some of the Big Five aren't seen on a game drive, you will hear the odd tongue-in-cheek comment like 'It's a desert out there, we had no luck today, plenty of general game around, but we haven't seen any lion, elephant or leopard.'

As a counterpoint, to introduce comparative reality and practicality into the equation, when I worked as a young ranger at Mala Mala game reserve in the late seventies, to see three of the Big Five in a day comprising two game drives was considered good. The ultimate goal was to deliver to your guests the chance to see the Big Five in a two-night visit, for which they were awarded a certificate to prove they had achieved the epitome of an African big game safari experience. How expectations and values have changed since then!

Commercial pressure and competition means that everyone is now chasing the Big Five as a *de rigueur* minimum – with the addition of wild dog and cheetah as the cherry on the top of a Big Seven Cocktail. There's every likelihood that soon black rhino will replace their white cousins on the big five podium. While I agree this does make for memorable viewing, it should not be the standard by which you rate your experience, because the operative word here is 'enjoying', not 'chasing'.

I wasn't nicknamed Mario Andretti in my impatient youth for nothing, so I speak from experience when I say, I really do believe you miss a lot by racing around to get the big ones. I know I did – been there, done that, spent too much time rushing hither and thither to see what was under my nose.

Here is a small piece of advice I would like to pass on. Slow down, take time to enjoy the myriad creatures that the reserve has to offer. Taking birds as an example, there are over 342 species of birds recorded on Olifants. That's not to mention the enjoyment to be had from simply taking in the richness of the flora, never mind the fauna. This area is also rich in geology, a relatively unknown dimension of the reserve waiting patiently to be explored.

If you have the luxury of being able to spend more than a couple of days in the bush, and you don't have unrealistic expectations, your satisfaction and enjoyment are guaranteed.

Even if you have a relatively quiet drive or two, pause a moment and reflect on what you have seen; there is every chance you will return home after a day's game viewing, content and satisfied with a three-and-a-half-pounder rather than being disappointed because you didn't get the five-pounder.

Oh, and never forget that the five-pounder is still there, waiting to be 'caught' another day.

Bring 'em Back Alive ...

BASED ON A SEPTEMBER 1997 NEWSLETTER

In the days when Jim Corbett 'brought 'em back alive', he captured wild animals from India and Africa, crated them and shipped them to zoos all over the world. Due to the methods of capture and the subsequent stress, mortality rates were horrific. However, because the supply of wildlife appeared abundant, even unlimited, and there were no chemical capture options at the time, the dangers and tragedies were an acceptable part of the process, calculated risks that 'came with the territory'. Things have changed. Capture and translocation have become technically advanced sciences and the loss of an animal today is a rare occurrence.

Our dominant rhino bull was reported to be on Umhlametsi, a reserve south of the Balule boundary line. Apparently one of their cows was in oestrus and had lured him and their resident bull into conflict for her favours.

The dispute happened to occur right on the fence line. The contest, with a combined mass of over five tons of rhino smashing repeatedly into the fence, resulted in the support pole snapping like a toothpick. The wire parted to open a gaping hole through which our bull went and then he proceeded to chase the Umhlametsi bull to the far corner of his erstwhile territory. With the competition now safely out of the way, our hero then moved into courtship mode and spent a few happy days in the company of the rhino cow and her young calf.

Although our system is an open one, this occurrence was on our extreme southern boundary, which effectively took the animal out of our area. This meant that unless 'ownership' could be proved, the rhino would be lost to us. Under normal circumstances, unless historical factors had to be considered, I would not have given this crime of passion a second thought. After all, this is a natural process that these animals have always followed and will continue to follow.

Present boundary constraints, however, coupled with the fact that our bull had a 'criminal record' earned by killing a bull from the Klaserie a couple of years ago in a similar territorial dispute, meant we were obliged to take remedial action. We had to remove, or at least make a concerted attempt to remove, our rhino from the neighbouring area to prevent or minimise the possibility of there being the further loss of another valuable animal.

Despite repeated efforts at enticing the rhino with bales of fresh lucerne, he refused to come back through the gap in the fence; he was in love and would not leave his new-found mate and her youngster. I knew the manager of Umhlametsi well, and with his co-operation we were able to look at alternative means of getting our rhino back, alive. Not able to contract a capture company at such short notice, we decided to go ahead with the equipment and manpower available.

Early one cool morning in September, I had our CAT 966C front-end loader move into position on the boundary in the vicinity of the area we knew the rhino to frequent. We then sent our trackers in to physically track down and find our bull, with instructions that when they located him, they were to radio in and gave us his exact position, and then to stay with him.

Meanwhile, in Boy Scout mode, I had packed everything I thought could possibly be needed to move this huge animal, including rope, water, conveyor belting and other paraphernalia. I then proceeded to the airstrip and picked up Dr Gerrit Scheepers, our local veterinarian who had succumbed to my wheedling and flown in from Phalaborwa.

After a few final checks that we really did have everything necessary for the operation, we climbed into the Land Cruiser and drove to our fence line, the border with Umhlametsi.

To keep noise levels down we kept the darting team to an absolute minimum of just the vet, a tracker and myself. It's one thing to track a rhino and get a glimpse of it, but to get into position and correctly place an immobilising dart required a greater degree of stealth – and more feet means more twigs to snap.

It wasn't long before we located our bull resting in the shade, about 20 metres away from the cow and her half-grown calf, both of whom were also in the mood for a siesta. The only movement discernible was the constant flicking and periscope-type twisting movement of their ears, on the alert for any unnatural sound, and in response to the persistent and irritating flies. Despite a careful and stealthy approach, we were caught out by a shift in wind direction which presented them with the faintest whiff of man. That was enough to get them on their feet and moving off at a slow trot into thicker bush.

Which was exactly what we didn't need.

Persisting, we followed them, keeping a low profile by half crouching and half hobbling through the bush. At times we were reduced to leopard crawl. This uncomfortable approach paid off and Gerrit was able to get a dart into the bull, without him knowing where it came from. Nine minutes later, the 3 mg of M99 gently put him down, not two metres from where he was darted.

'Just think,' Gerrit said with a smile. 'We're getting paid to do this.'

I was about to give him one of my dissertations on quantity versus quality and conservationists' remuneration, but decided the time wasn't right. By now the vehicle had arrived, bringing along the water we needed for cooling the rhino as well as the cooler boxes containing refreshment for us humans and the veterinary medicines respectively. I covered the rhino's eyes with a towel after smearing an antibiotic lubricating ointment onto its eyeballs. Some blood pressure muti was injected, the dart removed and an antibiotic sprayed into the needle wound. We also took this opportunity to microchip and ear notch him.

Gerrit was quite taken with the rhino, and said that in all his years of working with rhino, he had never seen such a magnificent specimen. Msimbi, which means 'iron' in Zulu, was clearly the largest-bodied bull rhino he had ever worked on. I felt a sense of pride and was happy that in a relatively short space of time, Msimbi would be physically back home while Gerrit would be winging his way back to where he belonged.

As a matter of interest, where the distance you need to move a white rhino is relatively short, you can 'walk' it from point A to point B. This is done by reversing the effect of the original full knockdown dose of M99 with M50/50 and then administering a new, very much lower and critically judged active dose of M99. In this condition, the rhino will still be groggy, but stable enough to stay on its feet and allow itself to be 'walked'. It's a fine balance to keep the rhino tranquillised enough to allow itself to be manipulated and directed without too much stress, with professional manpower using blindfolds and padded rope leashes to lead the animal gently to its destination. It's surprising just how far you can 'walk' a rhino, but in our case the distance was just too great, so an alternative travel plan was devised.

Forty minutes had ticked by since the rhino went down, and as it was getting hotter, we kept him wet and cool while we waited for the front end loader to arrive. Once there, the loader operator, Phillip Mathebula, skilfully manoeuvred the bucket into position. With the combined efforts of us pushing the rhino over whilst the bucket dug underneath and scooped up some six inches of soil to help cushion him, he was gently cradled in the bucket with rubber matting strategically placed to prevent any risk of chafing. After a few quick checks to see that he was relatively comfortable and secure for his journey back to Olifants, we moved off in the direction of the boundary fence.

It wasn't long before we reached the fence line, and a pair of sturdy side-cutters quickly took care of the wire barrier. Driving through the gap, we then selected a soft, sandy spot in a small riverbed a couple of hundred metres or so into the reserve, and as gently as we could, we laid the rhino down back on his own turf.

Gerrit now administered the antidote, known as Narcan, or M50/50, which, I'm told, is the same stuff they use to neutralise the effects of opiate derivatives like heroin and morphine in human drug addiction. M99, incidentally, is a powerful synthetic morphine, literally hundreds of times more concentrated than the stuff humans use, so strong that a scratch from a dart needle can kill a man. Consequently, whenever Gerrit goes to work on Olifants using M99, the antidote M50/50 is always at the ready in my top shirt pocket and there's always some M50/50 in the fridge down at the office. This extremely powerful substance is classified as a schedule seven drug, therefore you won't find a trace of M99 anywhere except under the strictest professional supervision, for obvious reasons.

While the antidote was weaving its magic, Gerrit whispered something in the rhino's ear, something only he and the rhino will ever know. He does this every time, saying it's his special time with the animal. Within a brief 30 seconds the indignant bull was up on his feet and on his way. He knew exactly where he was and slowly headed back to his old familiar territory. We then repaired the fence, breathed a sigh of relief that all had gone well and headed back along the railway line road. A movement in one of the drainage dips caught my eye, so, slowing down and peering into the dark culvert, we saw three male lions just lying there in the perfect spot to avoid the midday sun.

This sighting rounded things off nicely, a fitting end to a productive morning in anybody's book, including this one. This incident happened nearly ten years ago. According to everything I've read on white rhino, dominant bulls can expect to maintain their position for six to eight years. Maybe the Zulus could recognise his potential when they named him, because he certainly lives up to it. He was the dominant bull when I arrived at Olifants 16 years ago, and apparently he still is! He is living proof that size counts.

Poachers Caught ...

FROM AN OCTOBER 2002 NEWSLETTER

Poachers were giving our field rangers a really hard time. Moving in from Masheshimale near Phalaborwa, these reprobates had less than ten kilometres to cover and they were in the 'pantry', so to speak. On foot, they could cover this distance in a couple of hours, and once back on their home turf they simply melted into the population. Initially they were operating on the extreme limits of our reserve, adopting the favoured hit-and-run tactic, which meant that they would be gone before we could make plans to apprehend them.

Worse, as their confidence grew, so their forays took them deeper into Olifants, an indication of this fact being the evidence of a crude overnight camp that our game guards found. They were getting excessively confident and had become really cheeky, we thought at the time.

Normally, poachers are no strangers to discomfort and discipline, both being key to their success, and they leave virtually no evidence of their passing. They travel very light, carrying only the very bare necessities. This overnight camp indicated to us that complacency may have started to creep in, or, driven by greed, they were starting to take risks. We needed to take advantage of this by giving them a little more rope, until we were ready to pounce on our poachers.

When a large animal the size of a giraffe is snared or they manage to procure more than they can carry, a team comprising mostly women will be brought in to help transport the meat. As many as twelve people have been caught in a single group of poachers, each person carrying approximately 25 kg of meat on their heads in plastic fertiliser bags. With these loads, they're slower, easy to track and their escape routes are more predictable. In more remote and larger conservation areas, poachers usually make a temporary base and air-dry the meat, reducing the weight by more than 60 per cent. However, they don't get the time to do that in our area.

Vultures, and to a lesser degree, short-tailed eagles, are the field ranger's greatest ally in the fight against poachers. The presence of these birds circling over an area invariably indicates predator activity and the whereabouts of a carcass. As a matter of course we routinely follow up on these unpaid 'spotters' to obtain kill statistics for our predator/prey relationship studies. They also help us find any unclaimed carcasses from recent poaching activity, which may be lying rotting in a snare. It was by vulture watching in an area that we suspected was being targeted by poachers that our anti-poaching team was able to home in on a group of them.

This gang had been plaguing us for months, getting more brazen as their self-confidence and greed grew to the point that they began setting more snares than they could monitor. Slowly but surely they began to get ahead of themselves. Consequently, the 'eyes in the sky' found dead animals the poachers had missed or couldn't keep track of. What these birds do for us is to narrow down the area of activity or kill zone, helping us to lay an ambush or to know when to start moving in stealthily.

I was in the process of writing a brief update regarding the poaching situation for an upcoming committee meeting, when I received a call from an obviously excited Jabulaan, the head of our anti-poaching unit. 'We have caught the poachers who have been giving us problems on Seekooigat,' he exclaimed.

I listened with mixed emotions, relieved, yet frustrated, as I knew what little effect arresting them would have on the overall poaching situation. The amount of valuable anti-poaching time wasted in the courtroom as one hearing gets remanded to the next, was frustrating and even infuriating. Nevertheless, I couldn't lose sight of this achievement. It was the culmination of months of dedicated hard work by the team and had paid off in a solid arrest. We needed to follow through, no matter what frustrations lay in store. What Jabulaan told me next, however, made the blood drain from my face and gave me a sickening feeling in the pit of my stomach.

'We shot one of them,' he said.

My reaction was one of fear of the consequences of this action, no matter its justification.

Nowadays, the authorities view shooting a person, any person, criminal or otherwise, in an extremely serious light and the first docket they open is one of murder. Plus, it had been shown on several occasions that most magistrates see poachers as just trying to make a living and that their rights are as important as everyone else's.

Fortunately, Jabulaan's dramatic outburst wasn't the whole story. He went on to tell me that in order to stop the poachers, who, after eight warning shots still wouldn't stop running away, he shot at their legs and that one of the poachers had been hit. Dry-mouthed, I asked if the man was seriously injured. 'No,' he said. 'I'm sure he is fine, because we used the shotgun and not a rifle.' Apparently a few SSG buckshot pellets had hit him in the lower legs and thigh, causing painful flesh wounds only, but this was enough of a shock for him to know our game guards meant for him to stop when they said so. Nonetheless, our team having to use firearms in an anti-poaching operation put a different complexion on the entire situation.

This incident highlights the seriousness of the matter and is not to be taken lightly. This sort of action is forced upon private anti-poaching units because the provincial authorities are financially strapped, slow to react and less than committed to prosecute. The increasingly brazen audacity of the poachers is a concomitant reflection of the ineffectual enforcement of present legislation and the leniency of punishment meted out to offenders. Most poachers are back in business within days of being released, or worse, immediately after paying the paltry fines usually imposed. In this case, the police and the courts were most co-operative with us as the gunshot victim was also guilty of a number of conventional crimes and had eluded justice for some time. However, that positive reaction was not the norm.

It is this very frustrating situation that makes us resort to one of two approaches.

The first approach seems indigestible, but it's an option given the pressures that exist, that you just allow anarchy in the bush to reign and 'turn a blind eye' to the carnage involved other than employing a 'mop up' routine.

This means relentlessly following the poachers hoping to pick up and remove each snare shortly after they lay them and thereby avoid the involvement of confrontation and arrest. The second approach involves taking the bull by the horns, making an authoritative stand and protecting that which has the right to protection. I believe our game guards did the right thing under the circumstances and they acted within the law. For once it was not important whether these poachers were convicted or not. I knew that the word would now spread amongst the poaching community – leave the game on Olifants alone, their game guards mean business!

Whatever time this buys us, it is more than we would have bought if we'd passively mopped up behind the swine who wreak so much death and destruction on our wildlife. Best of all, though, is that the many animals that would have died a miserable death in wire snares will be spared for now.

As in the aftermath of a guerrilla war when the removal of mines becomes an urgent priority, so we also need to sweep the area for snares after the culprits have been caught. On occasion, when caught, poachers may indicate the location of their snares, but more often than not they're reluctant to admit to anything that proves their guilt or involvement. It is vital that the area be thoroughly swept, as even inactive snares can be effective. Most of the snares removed from the lower legs of animals are often old and could have been lying in the bush for years, waiting for the right shift or bump to set them just proud enough of the ground to ensnare the foot or hoof or trunk of some unfortunate animal.

At the time of making these notes, I wrote: 'The wounded suspect is recovering well in the Phalaborwa hospital ... we're all praying for his speedy recovery and sincerely hope he is not in too much pain ... the other is in police custody awaiting trial ... our anti-poaching team is back on the beat ...'

Disregarding the cynicism evident in those notes, the reality of the ever-present threat to our wildlife from human lowlife in the form of poachers is something that keeps us forever vigilant.

The captured poachers on that occasion did eventually admit that there were other poaching groups active in our area. We were fairly sure that the captured group would spread the tale that not only had they been shot at by our reserve's guards but one of their number had actually been shot. The fact that he lived to tell the tale was a huge bonus, in a way.

We had showed our intent with our shooters' response. It proved that we were determined to protect our animals, and if anyone was caught harming them, they would be shot. I can be certain that this was the message the gunshot survivor spread, because since the shooting over eight years ago, there has been no serious poaching activity south of the Olifants River on our reserve.

Our response was 'bang on'.

The 2000 Floods ... 46 Years Early!

BASED ON NEWSLETTERS WRITTEN IN 1996 AND 2000

We learned a lot from the 1996 floods. If nothing else we learned that the strength of the floodwater was 'awesome'.

The word 'awesome' seems to be used a lot these days, especially amongst the younger crowd, but I guess I shouldn't complain as it's a lot better than the old Rhodesian habit of describing everything as 'super'. Now, I learn that 'these are awesome shades' and 'we had an awesome time at the mall.' The word 'awesome', applied correctly should, I believe, be left to describe phenomena of some considerable awe. I mean things of the magnitude of colossal, uncontrollable and overwhelming. This would include the eruption of Krakatoa or, closer to home, the Olifants River in full flood. 'Super' doesn't quite cut it.

Awesome floods are categorised as 'one in 50 year' or 'one in 100 year' floods, which describes the proportions in relative terms to normal spate flow, rain-swollen river or summer flooding. This is also supposed to allow you to make plans, by knowing when the water will put pay to them. Four years after a 'one in 50 year' flood, you think, what the hell, we're too old to be still alive when the next flood happens, so let's enjoy the river and build right on the edge. The minute you finish building, another 'one in 50 year' flood whacks you, 46 years early!

Life's just not fair, is it? The only vaguely beneficial aspect of the second flood was that because it came around again so soon, you were better prepared, as the procedures learned in coping with the previous flood were still fresh in your mind.

If Meagan and I we were ever to start our own business, it would

239

be in competition with Stuttafords Van Lines or Elliot's. Our 1996 and 2000 experience of unpacking and re-packing furniture has got to have surpassed, or at least to have equalled theirs by now.

What we found the second time around though, was that our staff knew what was expected of them, which was half the battle won. Systematically and in half the time, the most vulnerable lodges were identified and cleared in preparation for flooding. There is no teacher like experience, and we were fast becoming professionals!

As expected and as usual, one of the very first lodges built on the reserve took the brunt of the 2000 floodwater, but its solid foundation stood up well to the aquatic attack and it did not fare as badly as it did in the 1996 flood. One of the owners was visiting the area at the time and decided to come and inspect the damage for himself.

Seeing there was not much anybody could do, he opted for the 'if you can't beat them, join them' approach and without fuss removed a flimsy kayak from his vehicle and unceremoniously slid off the deck into the raging Olifants River. Off he paddled, downstream to Dinidza. He did have the courtesy to ask me if I would like to join him.

'I have a spare canoe,' he said.

'I have to be on standby, er, and I have to watch for hippos …' I reluctantly declined.

Truth be told, I was plain scared of competing for space on the water in an elongated aluminium coffin in which I had never sat before, never mind paddled. Huge trees came barrelling down the river like a flotilla of invading Vikings and I had visions of getting caught up in those massive tangles of twisted roots. These living anchors had once held enormous trees secure until that first, insidious finger of water broke through, slowly eroding the soil and washing it away. Then would come the time the roots could no longer support the tree's weight, or resist the battering-ram effect of other drifting logs, and the entire tree would join the maelstrom.

It was only when I was disconnecting a gas bottle at one of the lodges, standing waist deep in water, that I realised there was no 'safe' area in or around this raging river. Suddenly a two metre crocodile thrashed past me, bringing it home that not only was the floodwater itself dangerous, but so was the calmer water on the edge.

Hippos and crocs congregated there to avoid the turbulence and chaos of mid-river. Snakes and insects piled on top of the flotsam in the calmer eddies in an effort to keep from being swept away.

Many of the lodges damaged by the floodwater in 1996 were rebuilt after the flood. However, once the water had receded, it seemed that the fear of it happening again and conservatism in planning also receded. Only a few lodges were re-built above the 50-year flood line, with many just being repositioned slightly and with minor compromises being made to allow for the possibility of further floods. No one, it seemed, ever expected to have to do it all again in a few years' time. But we are not the only ones in the world with short memories. The same phenomenon occurred in the flood-ravaged southern states of the USA, where residents of towns which were completely wiped out by tornadoes just went and built the same plywood shacks with the same shingle roofs on the same foundations! The same happens time and again on the floodplains and in the river deltas of Mozambique.

One of the first radio calls we received on that fateful 13 February 2000, when the river was at its highest, was from one of the shareholders upstream to say that he had just seen a deck go past his lodge on the river. He asked if we thought it could be one of ours. We advised him that it was indeed one of ours, being the ill-fated small lookout deck from another lodge about two kilometres upstream. Shortly after that, the Civil Defence Unit from Hoedspruit called to say that the Olifants River was expected to flow through at up to 2 000 cubic metres per second. It's difficult to imagine that ... it's the equivalent of about 25 average-sized swimming pools going past you every second!

Although the damage was minimal in comparison to the floods of 1996, the raging river and the volume of water was, nevertheless, an equally frightening experience. The feeling of helplessness was overwhelming when confronted with the phenomenal power of flood water. Truly 'awesome'. And it was not just humans who felt the effect one way or the other

A troop of terrified baboon whose 'alarm clocks' didn't go off was marooned by the rising flood water. The troop found itself stranded on a new island in the middle of a new river. They must have gone to roost the previous evening only to wake and find a raging flood all around them. It was a pitiful sight; beyond any help, they were forced to sit the ordeal out. Fortunately, the trees on the small island were covered in ripe figs so the troop managed to survive until the water level subsided a couple of days later, allowing them to wade across to the main bank.

A python of some three-and-a-half metres in length was seen fleeing the flood water. One of the shareholders saw a hippo carcass floating downstream. No incidents involving crocodiles were reported this time around. A couple of smaller wooden decks, fridges and dead domestic livestock from way upstream were also spotted in the river en route to the Indian Ocean.

Rummaging through some old maps and photos the other day, I came across an aerial photo taken of the Olifants River area in 1944. The scale of the photo is identical to a more recent one of the reserve taken in 1990. It wasn't until I put the two together for comparison that I noticed how relatively depleted the riverine vegetation of the earlier photo was some 46 years earlier. This clearly indicates that the Olifants River is subject to regular flooding, and its riparian vegetation is subjected to periodic 'thinning out'.

Re-reading this in 2009 makes me realise just how extraordinary having two floods in four years must be in the scheme of things. It was an exceptional occurrence that is definitely not sustainable in ecological terms.

But please don't push your luck and plan riverside deck extensions.

Mother Nature's watching!

Today's Special ... Free Leopards!

EXCERPT FROM A NEWSLETTER OF APRIL 2002

It is all very well to capture problem animals. This prevents them from being destroyed by the farmers or the communities that have suffered stock losses or threats to the safety of their people; however, besides the physical problems associated with the capture and subsequent care of these predators, the procedure is fraught with logistical and administrative hurdles. The biggest problem, according to Rob Harrison White, who champions an effective Problem Predator Relocation effort, is finding suitable alternative homes for them. For example, there are only a few areas available which are suitable for leopard rehabilitation and Rob will not release an animal, particularly these large predators, unless he is convinced that they have at the very least a 50/50 chance of surviving.

In response to an appeal from Rob, Olifants River Game Reserve offered to take two 'free' leopards. The first, a particularly large male weighing 78 kg, was released near Sable Dam in October 2001. The second, a slightly smaller leopard, was released at Double Dam in December of the same year. During this process, an Italian biologist doing research on a small population of leopard in the mountains of the Middle East got to hear of our efforts and contacted me. Included in his list of queries was verification of the size of leopards in our area and he was fascinated to hear that exceptional male leopards in South Africa's lowveld can exceed 80 kg, with the average male around 65 kg. The average weight of male leopards in his study area was 35 kg, with the largest weighing in at just 40 kg.

The second leopard released was fitted with a radio collar in an effort to monitor his movements. This was a pioneer project, and as no data were available on what happens to relocated problem predators, specifically those released in areas where other leopards occurred naturally, we were able to obtain a permit for this release without too much difficulty.

Releasing a previously wild but currently captive leopard is not quite as straightforward as you would imagine. There follows a classic example of what can happen when the release is undertaken by someone who doesn't understand the ways of leopard, in particular a wild leopard being released from captivity. Incidentally, this was all caught on camera a few years ago and stars a couple of Kenyan wildlife officials, who clearly lacked the necessary respect for these extremely dangerous animals.

The two officials thought they would simplify the release protocol by taking a short-cut and doing without the established routine. They drove to a designated point of release with a caged leopard on the back of their vehicle. The cage was not covered and was then opened by the manual expediency of releasing the latch of the rearward-facing door, allowing it to swing open. This would allow the leopard to simply jump out, straight onto the ground and into the bush. I have to assume that's what these chaps thought would happen.

In reality, once the cage door was opened, the rather large official then climbed back into the vehicle with a surprising turn of speed and shut the door. Then ... nothing, nothing happened at all. The leopard did not immediately bolt out to freedom as they expected; it did absolutely nothing. As the seconds ticked by there was still no response from the terrified animal which was now cowering at the back of the cage. This was taking far too long for the large man, who appeared anxious to get the job done. Wait for it. He got out of the vehicle, took a stout stick and proceeded to prod the leopard through the bars of the cage. Although obviously impatient, he remained cautious, I'll give him that, because he did keep one hand on the door of the cab while doing his leopard-prodding act, didn't he?

Now snarling and thoroughly angered by this abuse, the leopard burst out of the 1.8 metre cage in a yellow blur, and then, to the envy of every scrum half in the world, twisted in mid-air before it landed on the ground, almost facing the way it had come. Now it only had another three metres or so to cover before reaching the cab door. All in all, the leopard had moved nearly six metres before the large man had made the one metre slide into the cab, and then he only just managed to pull the door shut in the animal's face. But it wasn't over yet, far from it.

The large man obviously had no respect for game handling and release protocol, so had left the window open. This was all the space the leopard needed to dive in and viciously attack the screaming man inside the cab, and it was able to do this with most of its body still hanging outside the vehicle. Had the leopard's back feet managed to find a point of purchase, instead of the slippery smooth surface of the outside of the door, I would not be able to begin to describe the carnage that would have ensued.

So, now we know what not to do. Rob Harrison White, who has a deep empathy for these enigmatic big cats and also knows what they're capable of when stressed, did things a little differently when he released the two leopard on Olifants.

These captured and confined predators go through intense trauma, and often become extremely vicious, damaging themselves in fits of rage. Their muzzles, teeth and claws are particularly susceptible to injury while in captivity. More often than not, they cannot be released until they're fit again and this can take up to six weeks, which is a long time to keep a wild animal in a captive situation. In order to minimise stress, three sides of the cage are kept covered almost all the time, only the one side facing away from any activity being left uncovered to ensure air movement.

At the release site, the covered cage is carefully lowered to the ground from the vehicle transporting it. The cage, still completely covered, is placed with the door facing a remote-controlled camera. The camera, which has already been positioned prior to the arrival of the leopard to be released, is mounted on a tripod about five metres away. The door portion of the cover is then removed from the side so that the door is exposed but the leopard has not seen any human activity at any stage. That doesn't mean the leopard doesn't know you're there; the guttural growls leave you in no doubt of that, but the lack of eye contact helps to minimise stress levels.

A nylon rope is then attached to the side-release mechanism of the door, after which the vehicle is driven approximately 50 metres away, paying out the rope in the process.

The release is made by pulling on the rope from inside the cab, with windows wound up three-quarters of the way, while monitoring the leopard's progress on the camera.

Eish! ... It is much better this way.

Prior to releasing the first leopard, the larger male, we were shown some fascinating infra-red footage that Rob had taken of his first night in captivity, which revealed again what incredibly intelligent and crafty animals they are. The holding enclosure into which he was placed is approximately three metres wide, by two metres high, by five metres long, and the sides are completely closed off from any inquisitive spectators. Monitoring takes place through a couple of very small apertures during the day, and at night canvas blinds are lowered to give the animal total seclusion, which helps to minimise stress. When night falls, it is pitch dark in the enclosure, the only intrusion being the infra-red camera. This is the time when the leopard comes into his own. Completely ignoring the haunch of wildebeest put there for him earlier, he begins to test the enclosure.

What I found fascinating was how thorough he was, how methodically he checked the whole perimeter at the base, where the sides meet the floor, a common point of weakness in any enclosure. He then stood up on his back legs with his front paws against the mesh and started walking on tippy-toes around the entire enclosure, testing every centimetre.

Once this was done I thought he would settle down, but no way was he giving up, he was about to test the strength of the structure with his own, by using his strongest point of leverage. By curling his body into the foetal position then lying on his back and pushing up against the mesh with his hind legs, he tested each corner. It was unbelievably efficient and any weakness would have shown up under that strength of pressure. Only after this entire process did he appear to resign himself to his captivity. What an absolute privilege to be able to view footage like that!

Once the collared male was released in December, Mark Wolter and Jonty Aitken, two Olifants shareholders, enthusiastically took the receiver and monitored the leopard's movements for a number of days. When he moved through the fence into the Klaserie Nature Reserve, and we couldn't follow any longer, I gave the transmitter frequency to Colin Rowles, the warden of that reserve, who said he would take it from there, which he did.

He continued to help us monitor the leopard's movements for a couple of weeks, with his co-operation and interest being of great importance. This continuity made all the difference to the value of our project, as otherwise there would have been a big blank in the timeline of the data. Joining the plotted points helped us complete the pattern of his movement, until he left the APNR area. His movements for the first two months after his release are summarised as follows. Three weeks after entering the Klaserie near the trigonometric beacon on Lisbon, the leopard moved back onto Olifants near the Rhino Pan area. I picked up his signal there again a week later. He then continued heading south into Venice, where we were unable to follow the signal any further. The timing couldn't have been better, because we had used the receiver for longer than we were supposed to and reluctantly had to post it back to its owner.

Both leopards came from the North West province, one from Stella and the other from Zeerust. Although Olifants is a leopard paradise, it has its own leopard population, and a new individual in it could theoretically mean the displacement of a resident. Personally, I feel this particular species is relatively unique due to its high degree of adaptability, and therefore if there was a disturbance at all, it would be absolutely minimal. Despite this positive prognosis and the minimal risk of displacing established residents, however, we cannot just continue to release problem predators into our system.

We are working on finding other suitable areas for release programmes. All the same, Rob needs to be commended for his dedication to giving these beautiful predators a new lease on life, or
at the very least, a fighting chance. Although he asks nothing for
this thankless task, depending almost entirely on the goodwill of
veterinarians and donations, I insisted on paying his transport
and accommodation costs.

Time went by and we heard nothing. Nobody reported seeing a
collared leopard in the area, so we assumed it had simply melted
into the population within the APNR somewhere. This was not
so.

Approximately five months after the younger leopard's release,
I received news of a badly injured leopard that had to be put down
in the Acornhoek area. He had got himself caught in a poacher's
snare in an area largely dedicated to stock farming. As it happened, the animal was positively identified as the younger male
we released on Olifants. The fact that it had a collar, even though
it was no longer functioning, was the first clue, but the missing
toes on his left front paw put his identity beyond any doubt. Two
of his toes were amputated after his initial capture in a farmer's
gin trap. We have to assume that this leopard had tested all the
suitable territories from our reserve through the Klaserie and
Timbavati, only to find them occupied by other leopard. This in
itself is an indication of healthy leopard numbers in the private
reserves. He had moved approximately 65 kilometres due south
as the crow flies, from his release site into hostile territory.

After moving through the APNR, the leopard had to have also
moved all the way through the Kapama and Guernsey blocks to
reach its final destination. Obviously, we were saddened by the
untimely and inappropriate death of this particular leopard, but
he had been given a fighting chance, the dice had just not fallen
as well as we had hoped.

The large male leopard released in October 2001 wasn't fitted
with a transmitter, nor did he have any distinguishing features
that could have identified him at a glance. However, given this
leopard's size advantage, I am convinced that he found himself
a niche soon after being released. Subsequent sightings of a skit-

tish male were recorded at Wild Dog Pan not more than two kilometres from the release site.

As a final illustration of the infinite variations of adaptability evidenced in the release of captured leopards, we move to the mining town of Phalaborwa. It is situated on the boundary of the Kruger National Park, so it is not unusual to see leopard in the town's environs from time to time. Unfortunately, some inevitably fall foul of subsistence poachers' snares. A leopard caught in a wire snare on the outskirts of town was tranquillised, the snare removed and the wound treated. She was then taken down to the Timbavati Private Nature Reserve for release, a journey of more than 140 kilometres by road. It was thought that being a healthy adult female she would have a favourable chance at integrating with the resident leopards, or at least be tolerated while she looked around.

A collar was fitted and the monitoring programme began. GPS plottings showed that point to point, the distance from capture site to release site was approximately 60 kilometres. After spending two months in the Timbavati, she decided to go home. Once her mind had been made up, no matter how many fences she had to negotiate one way or the other, she was back in town within a week. Why this leopard couldn't find a place for herself in a large reserve like the Timbavati remains a mystery. The intrigue is further compounded by the fact that one would have thought an adult female would have been a prime candidate for relocation.

I believe that either the call of home was irresistible or, possibly, she was pregnant and wanted to have her cubs in familiar surroundings. Whatever the reason, I suspect we will never really know what drives these enigmatic big cats to survive where they do. Maybe it's simple, and there's no place like home.

Snare Removed from Elephant ... Poachers Removed from Circulation

INSPIRED BY AN OCTOBER 2008 NEWSLETTER

The curse of poaching has resulted in many calls for humanitarian and veterinarian help. In this case, we had been called in to relieve the plight of an elephant that had a steel cable snare on its left front foot. The young bull was estimated to be eight years old and was part of a breeding herd of fourteen elephant. The herd was reluctant to leave him, and their loyalty was unabated even though his attention was on pain relief rather than feeding. They waited patiently while he lingered in the soothing water of the river. The victim was the same elephant we had unsuccessfully tried to locate in the same area a year ago, but as he was smaller then, the snare had not cut in as deeply as it had now. Over time, he grew bigger and the snare slowly cut in deeper. The increasing pressure as the result of blood flow restriction must have been agonising.

The elephant was totally preoccupied with his swollen foot and was obviously in great pain as he rocked and swayed gently to and fro, placing absolutely no weight on the affected foreleg. One minute he would splash cool river water onto it, the next he would try to coat it with mud. Then, when these temporary pain relief measures wore off, he would lie down in the soft sand on the water's edge. Apparently, he was getting some relief from the throbbing pressure, by keeping his heart on the same level as his foot for a while. It was a pathetic sight and human intervention was long overdue.

We used his preoccupation with pain relief as an opportunity to call in a helicopter and our local vet, who had already been placed on standby. Some aircraft regulation glitch in Phalaborwa meant that the helicopter was delayed for an hour while the necessary paperwork was checked. When they did eventually arrive, our vet, Gerrit again, wasted no time in getting the dart into the elephant before it moved into the thick riverine bush and disappeared for another year.

Besides the fact that this operation took place right underneath the four power lines, and there were a number of elephant involved, everything went according to plan and without interruption from the rest of the herd, including the old matriarch known as Joan.

As though a co-operative part of the operation, the herd moved

off to a safe distance from the immobilised elephant, enabling us to remove the snare quickly. At this point, even though tempted to, I'm not going to humanise the situation and say that I'm sure the 'Mommy' elephant knew we were trying to help her son and so didn't bother us as these overprotective mothers often do. Seriously, though, this can be one of the biggest problems when working on a member of a breeding herd, so we were most grateful that it went as smoothly as it did and that we were able to alleviate an animal's suffering.

Among those witnessing the dramatic proceedings was a highly motivated group of conservation students out from Holland, all young women in their late teens and early twenties, who were staying at a camp on one of the neighbouring properties. Thrilled as they obviously were to have been on hand to experience meaningful conservation at work, in stark contrast to the mundane anti-erosion work and exotic plant eradication exercises with which they had been occupied, they were hungry for more of the same. The image of our anti-poaching guys in their neat uniforms, rifles slung over their broad shoulders, prompted them to ask if they could accompany the unit on their next patrol.

Initially, I was hesitant, because these patrols are not to be taken lightly. Anti-poaching is a very serious business ... but I weakened, it being virtually impossible to say no to a beautiful woman. Confronted by six of them? All resistance crumbled. While I relented and condoned their involvement in the upcoming patrol, I did emphasise that it would be no problem as long as the risks and the conditions of this dangerous patrol were fully understood and accepted.

Early the next morning, together with their camp manager and course leader, who took official responsibility for the students' safety, the anti-poaching unit, followed by the students, crossed the Olifants River onto the northern bank. This area is notorious for poaching activity, and, as expected, it wasn't long before fresh signs of poachers were picked up.

Like a pack of bloodhounds the game scouts homed in on the clues, the 'scent', and pursued it with focused determination. The quiet efficiency this team displays when tracking 'hot tracks' has to be seen to be appreciated. The first thing is a perceptible attitude shift in the team. Then you notice a gear shift, a subtle urgency of gait, which tells you they're getting close to their quarry. You can't mistake the signs as the tension mounts, mouths start to lose saliva, and any attempt at speaking fails miserably with your tongue stuck to the roof of your mouth. Then, without warning, the stealth of movement, hushed tones and sign language are abruptly discarded, to be replaced with absolute pandemonium. The apparent chaos that follows is in total contrast to the discipline and order of the previous two hours. Moments later, gun shots are fired, amidst much shouting and yelling and the odd dull thump followed by subsequent groans ...

Try to picture the scene and imagine the faces of these fresh-out-of-Europe young ladies, wide-eyed and open-mouthed, as a poacher is physically apprehended while his accomplice dodges bullets and shotgun pellets to escape. Up to that point, these students may have thought they were being treated to a well-rehearsed bit of play-acting. But those thoughts must have quickly evaporated when they heard some real thumping and saw some real blood, as the reality of what they had witnessed sank in. Tracking, catching and arresting armed poachers is extremely dangerous.

The fact is, they make their living from killing methodically and without feeling, so they wouldn't hesitate to treat human interference with the exact same lack of sentimentality.

When they are caught, they resist. When they resist, they are handled firmly and decisively. The young students seemed to have lost the power of speech, never mind conversation. I would describe them as being in a state of shock as they quietly and quickly made their way back across the river. Once back in the relative safety and comfort of their camp, they were able to reflect on the excitement of the morning, but even so, it was obvious they had had enough for one day, judging from the excited chatter around the camp fire that night. On the other hand, one can only begin to imagine the stories that were taken back home to Holland.

253

I'm sure that tales of taking poachers out of circulation in the African bush would be more interesting than the usual European sidewalk café chit chat, whatever that might be.

The poacher who did not get away and was arrested that day was convicted and sentenced to a fine of R 2 500 or five years' imprisonment. Although his accomplice is still at large, I have a feeling he will be lying low for quite a while. Truth be told, it's actually good anti-poaching PR to have a 'survivor' live to tell the tale and to spread the word among his comrades-in-crime about how he so nearly got caught, having to dodge bullets to make good his escape.

The total cost of removing the snare from the young elephant with which we started this tale, including the previous year's failed attempt, was R22 600, ten times the fine imposed on the poacher we caught. There is no doubt that the poacher's wire snares had killed and maimed far more than just the one elephant we were able to help back to a good chance of a healthy future.

One of the greatest rewards of this life here on Olifants is that our shareholders and so many of our neighbours see the protection of our wildlife and their ways of life as being beyond price. In this instance, by removing a snare from an elephant we improved its circulation while removing the poachers from circulation!

Compassion ... A Game Ranger's Virtue?

DECEMBER 1979

I was working for one of Africa's premier game reserves at the time, and as we were in the bush for most of the day, meal times back at Mala Mala's main camp were always a great time to get together with colleagues, to relax a little and generally shoot the breeze. The staff table had the best position in the dining room, right next to a large window. Our 'looking glass' presented us with an uninterrupted view out over the Sand River, so our meals were often pleasantly interrupted by something interesting happening in the bush beyond.

We were on summer schedule at the time, which meant we went out into the bush at first light, while it was still relatively cool, and we returned for breakfast around mid-morning. Invariably, we were famished by the time we sat down to eat, so there wasn't too much chatter between mouthfuls. I remember that on this particular warm, sunny morning, it was unusually quiet and there wasn't much going on outside.

Suddenly there was a loud thump against the window. A beautiful malachite kingfisher had flown straight into the glass, and it was stunned by the impact. We gently cradled the tiny bird in our cupped hands, and while we watched it slowly recover, the magnificence of its colours could really be appreciated. These delicate creatures are brilliantly clad in some of the finest feathers from nature's wardrobe, so it was understandable that some of those around wanted to capture this beauty on film.

As the bird got a little perkier, it was carefully placed on one of the stems of a purple nut sedge growing near the garden tap, the same plant that this little kingfisher often used as a perch. It looked perfectly normal as it sat there, though it must have still been somewhat dazed as it allowed the photographers to get really close and take some spectacular photographs. The photos must have been good, because one of them went on to win a prestigious award.

Obviously the judges were none the wiser as to how the 'model' was so co-operative. Someone said the photographic technique was a knock-out.

Despite the positive side of the foregoing little tale, in that we were able to capture the beauty of this bird for ever, it actually took the intrigue of wildlife photography out of the equation for me. It was this experience nearly 30 years ago that took away, in my opinion, the skill and challenge of photography and re-placed it with luck and manipulation. This was a very simplistic and naïve view to adopt, I know, but I was very young and im-pressionable at the time. Perhaps unfortunately, though, the end result has been that I have never shown much interest in photo-graphy. On a practical level, I only ever use a camera to provide the back-up to a report or to record something I want to remem-ber. My photo albums are more of a random collection of happy snaps and that sort of thing, not much more. I realise now what a huge pity this has been, because in my life in the bush I have seen things that would have been wonderful to share through the medium of photography. Except for the mental images I have stored, so much is lost for ever.

To this day, that kingfisher 'set-up' still nags at my conscience to the point where, except for David Attenborough and one or two others whose work I admire, I have become quite cynical about the authenticity of some wildlife imagery. I am particularly suspicious about certain material employed in the production of wildlife documentaries. The lengths that some reporters and documentary photographers will go to for fame and awards are quite astonishing. How do you condone a film-maker who films a person walking down a street in Kosovo, when he knows there's every chance the subject will be shot by a sniper within minutes; worse, the photographer knows where the sniper is hidden! This

same lack of ethics in 'getting the shot', no matter the consequences, is sometimes applied to the making of wildlife documentaries. For example, there are documentary film-makers who
will film the slow, agonising death of an elephant being eaten to
death by a pride of lions and then, with a smile, accept an award
for filming something else's pain. Hell! That doesn't take skill; it
takes cold-blooded indifference and the ability to be able to sit
immobile on your backside for long periods of time.

Not to mention that in the good old days of actual film, it was
too damn expensive to leave the camera rolling, while today,
the advent of videotape and then digital recording has removed
the accountant's financial control from the equation, more's the
pity.

'Oh, come on!' I hear you say. 'This is nature in the raw, get
real, tough it out, it happens ...' Yes, I know it happens and I
am the first to concede that the documentary evidence, however
brutal, has value in a historical and scientific sense. But I draw
the line when the subject predators are given the advantage of
an easy kill by the prey being highlighted and then blinded by
powerful spotlights! I also find it difficult to stomach the double
standards evident in the industry. It's no stretch of our imagination to envisage a film-maker getting up late the next morning, by which time, hopefully, our elephant example is dead,
and while delicately sipping coffee and nibbling lightly buttered
toast, to harangue anyone who will listen about the cruelty and
questionable ethics of trophy hunting!

OK, let's get back to the manipulation and the 'set-up'
business which, intrinsically, is the cause of my inability to
accept the authenticity of so much that I see under the banner
of wildlife documentary. I have a particular problem with work
that is presented as authentic real-time footage. A well-known
documentary on the San Bushmen in the Kalahari is an example
of questionable authenticity. The film – which is, incidentally,
one out of a series I really enjoy – tries to capture a hunting scene
where a kudu is supposedly killed by a poisoned arrow. To create
a moment of high drama, the editing process includes a shot of
the arrow being removed from the dead kudu. The problem is

that, in reality, the arrow is being removed from what is clearly a high-velocity bullet wound channel. I've seen enough of these to know what they look like, but the average viewer is being presented with fact when it is pure fiction.

Another example depicts a scene in Savuti, documenting the demise of lion cubs where the cubs are bitten and killed by a black mamba. Again, clever editing brings the drama to poignant life. Unfortunately, the snake filmed leaving the scene of the crime is a snouted cobra.

Again, it's clearly a set-up, resulting in a skilfully directed and edited re-creation of actual and library material being presented as real-time, real-life, factual footage.

The worst case I've seen of poor continuity in a documentary is where a man is filmed going into thick reeds to track a leopard. The weapon he carries into this precarious situation is a lever-action rifle similar to those used in the old Wild West. When the leopard charges him, bursting through the reeds, the now back-pedalling man is clutching a bolt-action rifle. Now, I've heard of gun bearers who can slap a rifle into a hunter's hand quite quickly, but I have yet to meet the man who is quicker than a charging leopard!

I wish they'd just be open about it. Why not tell the audience that an attempt at a realistic recreation has been made as the authentic scene could not be documented for reasons of bad weather, time constraints, lapsed visas, insurrection or the star having a cold? The audience will understand. It's the attempt to hoodwink us with a set-up we can't understand.

Another side of this scenario is their unrestrained use of close-up violence in the belief that this is a necessary endorsement of the realism and authenticity. The more cries of suffering, the louder the crunching of bone, the more blood and tearing of live tissue, the happier some documentary film-makers appear to be. These features, like the parallel usage of footage of human violence and misery, make for the drama that sells, and they know it and capitalise on it. I hate it; it's not what should be focused upon to the exclusion of all else; it's only a part of the process, a small fragment of the whole.

In a situation like the filming of the elephant kill, for example, discretion could have been exercised, and the scenes of prolonged suffering brought to a swifter end. It would have made no difference whatsoever to the outcome of the feature, or to its value as a documentary.

Switching my standpoint to that of a parent, I accept that kids, mine included, will sit through a movie like 'The Texas Chain Saw Massacre', yet skip channels featuring wildlife gore.

Violence can be a part of their entertainment, but it's fiction and not to be taken too seriously. In the case of my kids, living in the bush as they have for a major portion of their lives, they aren't blind to some of the less pleasant realities of that life. My daughter has had to hold a spotlight for me while I shot a hippo suffering from a broken jaw. They both know about taking a hook out of a trout's mouth and shortly thereafter consigning it to the frying pan. They're not vegan pacifists and neither am I. But they are, as are many of their friends, extremely uncomfortable with the excessive volume of blood and gore portrayed in wildlife documentaries, even though they have been exposed to more than a normal share of the harsher side of nature. And this has nothing to do with my concerns about the truth being massaged for cinematographic effect; they just don't like the focus and emphasis on what comes across as cruelty.

My point, in a nutshell, is that I consider the preoccupation with gruesome detail to be a misguided focus and the emphasis on getting the shot, no matter what, a misguided motivation.

Now, how does this relate to our everyday life in the bush? Well, if we followed the lead of some of these documentary filmmakers, we would have to endorse endless suffering as part of nature in the raw. As an alternative, I believe, in situations like the examples quoted, we as game rangers should make a judgement call. We should intervene where and when we can, and to hell with letting nature take its course in such circumstances!

Just as I question the morality of employing endless scenes of suffering in the interests of so-called authenticity in the production of documentaries, I question the morality of taking the supposed high ground and letting wildlife endure unnecessary pain when we could step in and end the suffering. This is particularly applicable in situations where the prolonged agony of an animal appears to serve no other purpose than sensationalism. In my opinion, if documentary filmmakers were as in love with their wildlife subjects as they claim to be, they would temper their activities with more compassion. It appears that on occasion, authenticity is subject to flexible interpretation. All I ask is for the need for compassion to be considered with a similar degree of flexibility.

Again, if David Attenborough can produce the quality documentaries he does without the gore, then perhaps others can take a page out of his book. However, the need for compassion is subject to infinitely variable considerations. We could ask: 'Where does one draw the line?' and the words 'it depends' would have to be in the answer.

It was the Great Soul, Mahatma Gandhi, who said that one can judge a country and its people by the way they treat their animals. I suspect then that the exploitation of needless suffering of animals would most certainly have qualified for his black list.

In the world of nature, in every ecosystem on earth, death is a functioning and necessary process, and as such is an everyday part of our jobs as game rangers. We understand that wild animals are going through suffering to some degree all the time. This is particularly evident in large, ecologically dynamic systems such as ours, and we accept this. What I won't accept is the promotion of a laissez-faire attitude to preventable cruelty when it is evident we cannot adopt a cavalier attitude to the concept of leaving nature to its own devices. We need to exercise reasoned and reasonable judgement and apply it with compassion.

Game rangers do not run around dispatching every animal with a limp and I am not advocating that they do. Nor are they expected to assist lions in killing their prey because they believe the victim could be killed more efficiently with a well-placed bullet. Rangers are called upon to make some tough decisions at times, and acting out of innate compassion, will paradoxically need to destroy a surprising number of injured and suffering animals in the course of their duties. The culling of surplus animals for the purpose of population management is another duty, but is not part of this moral and ethical discussion. While the mechanics of killing become more efficient and routine, it never becomes a pleasure. And game rangers don't get extra points for killing, not ever. The majority of true conservationists I know feel as I do, and would sooner put an animal out of its misery, and have it filmed being eaten dead, rather than leave it to slowly die in agony as it is eaten to death.

And please, don't believe any of the self-serving nonsense about 'in shock ', 'endorphins' and 'painless'; believe me, warm-blooded animals feel pain just like you and I do! They just don't understand it as well as you and I do.

The possibility of raising the eyebrows of proponents of objec-tive scientific management is something of an additional concern to game rangers. This means that not too many rangers will have the courage to voice their opinions, or act on their convictions for fear of professional recrimination. This is notwithstanding

the present unwritten protocol which concedes that any 'man-induced' injury sustained by an animal should be managed by man, either in the form of treatment of the animal where warranted, or the humane destruction of the animal if necessary.

We all know that there is nowhere in the world where the influence of man's hand cannot be felt, so the question is, what is the definition of 'man-induced' and at what point do we interfere?

The overpopulation and unnatural concentration of elephant is the prime reason that lions will resort to treating this cumbersome and dangerous animal as prey. In our reserve, the ratio between the plains game species and the buffalo and elephant populations is relatively well balanced. Lions emanating from the Klaserie, which grew up on buffalo, do not actively hunt them on Olifants, because there is still abundant plains game available. It's logical – why tackle animals that are large, difficult to kill and fight back, when there is easier prey to be had? In the Klaserie, buffalo constitute 52 per cent of known lion kills, while just across the border in our region of Balule, with a similar lion density, this figure drops to less than three per cent. In living memory, not a single elephant has been killed by lion on this reserve, despite the majority of the elephant population constituting cows and calves.

So what's the point of this apparent digression? I believe that in an area where lions are known to routinely kill elephant, you can be reasonably certain that it is because there is very little else for them to hunt.

This massive imbalance could be the result of severe ongoing drought conditions, in which water is being artificially provided, and/or there is large-scale and gross habitat mismanagement. Whatever the reasons, the influence of man can always be held responsible to some degree. Therefore the argument for unconditionally leaving things to nature holds no water, and consequently there is no excuse to turn a blind eye to what is essentially 'man-induced' cruelty. If we injure the environment, we injure some of its inhabitants.

In context with everything I have gone on about, I have a few snippets of personal and pertinent advice for any prospective game ranger.

- Be compassionate but always allow discretion to temper your decisions in this regard.
- Despite wanting to get into the bush and as far away from humanity as possible, learn to communicate with people first, and then if you must, try the Dr Doolittle stuff with animals later.
- As old-fashioned as this may sound, it is important that you learn to shoot, and to shoot well. The better shot you are, the more efficient you become, and the less suffering there will be when you are called upon to put an animal out of its misery. I have come across many instances of campaigners crying 'leave things to nature' and then turning out to be very poor shots, incapable of ending unspeakable agony with a single well-placed bullet. Thus they have no confidence in themselves to do the job that deep down they know should be done; they lack true compassion.

FOOTNOTE

Education, and a nationwide poverty upliftment programme, is being regarded as the most effective long-term solution to alleviate the scourge of man's cruelty to animals. In the meantime, the suffering goes on. This situation includes appalling cruelty to domestic animals in some of the outlying smallholdings, informal settlements and townships in our country.

Apparently the cheapest and most practical tool needed to alleviate the misery of the thousands of creatures that are beyond help is a .22 calibre pistol! This was from the mouth of a young volunteer working for an animal anti-cruelty organisation, when, in general conversation, I happened to ask him what piece of equipment he most needed to ease the suffering he encountered on a daily basis.

The opinions expressed here are my own. They reflect my personal feelings about certain moral and ethical issues concerning the capitalisation upon cruelty, the lack of compassion and/or the portrayal of fiction as fact in certain documentary films. The references to specific incidents is in no way meant as a general statement about all documentaries made by all film-makers. The criticisms are specific; they reflect my personal viewpoint on those specific examples and I make no apologies for that.

Rangers and Rifles

MARCH 2010

Weapons are usually associated with death and destruction ... true. So understandably many people find it difficult to understand the incongruity of how something so devastatingly destructive as a high-powered rifle finds a place in nature conservation management, or indeed that rangers are required to know how to use them.

In the hands of a dedicated conservationist, a weapon is used on occasion to deliver a merciful quick death when called upon to end an animal's suffering. They are also essential culling tools when used to control herbivore populations, particularly in smaller reserves, where habitat management requires a hands-on approach. From a conservation ecology perspective, this is another example of the weapon being used for a constructive purpose as apposed to a destructive one. Lastly, due to the nature of our work in Big Five reserves where we may be confronted by armed poachers and dangerous game from time to time, a weapon for protection in these life-threatening circumstances would be indispensable.

Although the use of firearms is widely accepted as integral to the management of game reserves, I'm hoping that by the end of this discussion, those concerned will better understand that the judicious use of a weapon in skilled hands is an absolute necessity at times. Critical to this understanding is that it is only when a weapon is placed in a conservationist's hands that it can be regarded as a 'tool' of the ranger's trade, so to speak.

There are those fortunate individuals who have a natural ten-

dency or talent for a particular sport; others are born gifted artists. It goes without saying, then, that in the majority of these
situations, procedural application and training is merely a pre-
cursor to inevitable excellence and achievement ... well, it was
never like that for me.

I was captain of my school's first rugby team, and although I
regarded myself as a good scrum half, looking back in objective
hindsight, I have to admit I was probably chosen to captain the
team for other reasons. Perhaps it was my attention to the little
details, or my persistence in getting the technical side of things
right that made me the best I was going to be. I would read about
the world's best players, their techniques, the type of kit they
wore, and how they trained, absorbing as much as I could to
improve my playing. Basically I made up for my lack of natural
talent by working with whatever I could glean from the best. I
combined this with an ability to read a situation and sometimes
make the right decision under pressure. It was probably this that
helped us win the odd game, or what made me a better player,
and at least the coach was happy... It was the same with shooting.

Many good marksmen are born with a predisposition to becoming good shots; not all of them are hunters or interested in
hunting. Sandy Watson stands out in this regard. His parents
emigrated from Scotland to South Africa in 1965, and although
the family settled in suburban Johannesburg, they spent every
spare moment outdoors or crafting things. His father and brother
preferred fishing to shooting and initially Sandy enjoyed the latter, he was a natural with a rifle, a gifted marksman. Anybody
who can shoot red-billed teal on the wing with an air rifle steps
into this arena, in my book anyway. As a young schoolboy he
would provide the family with a regular supply of guineafowl
and francolin, all taken with head shots using his air rifle. These
were roasted on weekends and enjoyed by the whole family, including myself on occasion.

The turning point in his shooting life came later when he
was able to join a few friends on an antelope hunt in the northern Transvaal. One morning, he shot an impala, a head shot of

course, but instead of the expected jubilation that comes when an animal is painlessly killed with a good shot, there was none. The look of shock and disbelief at the destructive power of a soft-nosed bullet was written all over his face: the impala's head wasn't a pretty sight, but then what slaughtered animal is? Sandy didn't say much, he seldom did, but this time he was quieter than usual, then he handed the 30/06 rifle back to his brother and to this day has never hunted again ... not even with his air rifle. Sandy went on to pursue another talent of his and became a graphic artist. His love for the outdoors never diminished: he took up scuba diving and went on to become a scuba diving instructor.

I knew what I wanted to do with my life from an early age, so I prepared myself with the absolute basics from the outset. I immersed myself in the ways of nature wherever I could, and biology became my favourite subject at school. I built a huge aviary which gave me untold enjoyment and taught me so much about certain wild birds and their breeding habits. I also taught myself to shoot. I was not born with a silver bullet in my mouth, but I found that with a lot of practice and the best accessories I could afford, I soon became an above-average shot. Although my marksmanship was nothing approaching proficient, I was comfortable and confident that I could get the job done if need be. However, to this day I still practice to keep my eye in.

Besides a BSA air rifle which I used to sharpen my shooting when I was a youngster, my first 'real' rifle was a 30/06 Springfield which I bought when I was 17 years old.

Irving Stevenson and I were walking the downtown streets of Johannesburg one day when we happened on Laxton's Hunting and Fishing shop at the bottom end of Bree Street. The display in the window drew us in like moths to a lamp. It had obviously been done by someone who knew the outdoors intimately. The scene, complete with twisted logs, dry winter grass and camping equipment amidst a strategically placed plethora of fishing and hunting gear, transported us off the concrete paving underfoot, out of the busy traffic in the street behind and into the wild unknown. Naturally we were lured in to browse, even though I had not planned to buy anything that morning, let alone a rifle – I couldn't afford one anyway.

As if the window display wasn't enough, the man behind the counter grabbed my attention immediately. He was a tall grey-haired man in his late fifties with a neatly kept full beard, a little like Ernest Hemingway, I thought at the time. Although he looked the part standing in front of the rows of firearms on display, he didn't give the impression of wanting to be there. As we approached he thrust a strong hand that had spent too much time in the sun across the counter, and with a smile introduced himself as Manny Laxton.

Cutting through some small talk, we got down to the more interesting stuff and started talking about remote areas of the African interior, hunting and guns. I couldn't keep my eyes off the display of big game and fish trophies, and unlike those one sees in a museum, these appeared to come alive as he spoke. It turned out that Manny was a retired big game hunter, with an enormous amount of experience. There was so much I wanted to ask him, but was too embarrassed; I'd never hunted with a rifle before, let alone ever visited a big game area, and didn't want to make a fool of myself – it was better listening to him anyway. Nevertheless, he casually got around to asking me what I intended hunting and where. Now I was really stuck for an answer: how do I tell him I have no intention of shooting anything anywhere at this stage – I just wanted a rifle, a 'real' rifle of my own. However, it didn't take him long to get my measure; turning to the row of rifles behind him he selected one and carefully handed it to me. 'This is a 30/06, one of the best all-round rifles ever made,' he said. He went on to say it would be suitable for most antelope in South African conditions; in fact, I remember him saying that with the right ammunition you could shoot just about anything with it ... how could I resist?

The brand-new rifle, an Austrian-made 'Voere', cost R249.00, and while there were other more expensive makes on display, Manny had read the situation perfectly: the rifle was a standard sporter without any fancy cosmetics; he could see that what I needed was a reliable and functional weapon. Could he possibly have known that all I had in my pocket was R8? I somehow doubt it - Irving helped out with another R10. Without comment he took the small deposit and filled out an application form, after which he wiped the rifle down with a soft cloth and told me he would store it away for me pending the granting of the licence. Three anxious weeks later I received notification to collect my license at the local police station. I borrowed the balance of the money from my father and collected my rifle from a beaming Manny Laxton. Possibly the fond memories of his first rifle as a young boy brought on the smile as he slid my rifle into the second-hand gun bag, which he threw in for free ... It certainly wasn't for my meagre custom.

Good rifles and shotguns can be bought, but the ability to use them skilfully cannot. I realised I would need to take every opportunity and maximise my advantage in becoming a better marksman. As a young lad I never gave in to peer pressure to try alcohol, even though I must admit there were times when I thought I may be missing out by not joining in and 'letting go' occasionally, but I didn't want to risk it. I'd seen an alcoholic once whose hands shook uncontrollably and I thought, rightly or wrongly, that if I had a beer or two on a regular basis, I'd also start shaking, and this in turn would affect my shooting ability. To this day, even though I love a glass of good wine and the odd draught or two, that's about my limit. However, my motivation for this limited intake has nothing at all to do with shooting, but rather to do with having being plagued with migraine headaches for most of my life – and in my case, alcohol was found to be catalytic in bringing on a migraine.

I spent most of my spare time outdoors camping, fishing, catching snakes, and when I could I'd spend ice-cold winter days wildfowling and pigeon shooting. Wingshooting with a shotgun is not what most people would have you believe; it is extremely difficult to master shooting rapidly moving airborne targets with regularity. A shotgun is a great equaliser, and there is no better arena to sort the men from the boys, or those who believe you cannot miss with a shotgun, than a field of ripe sunflowers on a windy highveld day. Shooting – or rather, trying to shoot – speckled pigeons with the wind up their tails as they fly in to feed has been known to reduce grown men to tears of frustration. A fair shot on their first outing will score no more than five birds per 25 shots fired! ... five's actually quite good.

Shooting a scattergun is excellent practice; it hones your ability to snap shoot at moving targets with a rifle, and this is the most likely scenario a ranger would have to deal with. Hitting the vitals of large animals moving through thick bush is difficult, and it can mean the difference between an injured animal getting away, or in the case of confrontation by a wounded dangerous animal, serious injury or even death. This was so aptly described by the author and big game hunter, Robert Ruark, who wrote that he was not interested in knowing if his white hunter could shoot the eye out of a downwind gnat at 300 yards. He wanted to hunt big game with a man who could hit a charging buffalo at five yards!

The question I'm most often asked in regard to dealing with dangerous game in tight situations is what goes through your mind when you're being charged by a dangerous animal, and what does it feel like to be in that situation? The answer can be as varied as the wide-ranging circumstances that will influence how you feel at the time – for example, the species involved, the individual character of that animal, the terrain and vegetation, and who you have as a backup gun, etc. Speaking for myself, I find there is usually a definite brief moment of calm acceptance that prevails when staring danger in the face ... not fearlessness, please don't confuse the two. As far as I am concerned, there needs to be a healthy measure of apprehension and fear when going into thick bush or reeds after a wounded buffalo or lion, otherwise complacency will get you killed sooner than later. There's nothing that sharpens your senses quite like the fear of knowing that going home to the wife and kids in one piece that day depends largely on making snap decisions, composure under pressure and your ability to use a rifle. You get to understand some of what base jumpers mean when they say you need to have death touch your shoulder to really appreciate being alive. The fear is visceral, it dries the saliva in your mouth, and causes a wobble in the knees; however, unlike base jumpers, I don't choose to put myself in these precarious situations for fun.

Okay, back to the question. What does it feel like to be charged by an enormous animal hell bent on killing you? I would imagine it could be analogous to being chained by your feet to a railway track facing an oncoming train and all you have to stop it within 20 metres is a heavy calibre rifle. The brake system has been modified so that if you hit a football-sized container located on the front of the locomotive, it will stop instantaneously! As fear-provoking as this may sound, there are some mitigating advantages in this hypothesis. Firstly, you will know where it is going to come from. Secondly, the target will be coming at you on an even plane, not bobbing up and down as a living animal would, and thirdly, there is no emotion, no eyes filled with pain, hatred or intent. Of course, if you missed you could dive to one side or the other, either way you will lose both legs – messy, sure, but so is having your body torn limb from limb by some pain-crazed elephant, or being disembowelled by a buffalo. Knowing this, the next question could be, would aspirant hunters who expect professionals to stand there and deal with their botched shots be able to stop the train? Maybe they should have to pass a similar kind of test (even an unchained version) before being issued a permit to hunt dangerous game. I know one thing for sure, if this was instituted, there'd be far fewer wounded buffalo and elephant to deal with, which reminds me …

I will concede, with a little kicking and screaming mind you, that there is a place and there are suitable target species for bow hunting, but I unequivocally draw the line when it comes to hunting thick-skinned herbivores with these relatively under-powered contraptions. In the context of the above discussion, I refer in particular to those bow hunters who insist on maiming thick-skinned dangerous game. These unfortunate beasts are supposedly given a more 'sporting chance' than when they're hunted with a powerful rifle … But please, don't just take my word for it, come along with me on a typical big game bow hunt and I'll let you be the judge.

The outfitter has brought the bow hunter within shooting range of the quarry. At a given signal the archer draws his bow, but this is not the local archery range, where he is able to consistently hit a saucer-sized target at 50 metres; this is the real thing and despite its relatively large size, this is a potentially dangerous living target. Understandably, then, the involuntary flood of adrenalin into the bloodstream makes his hands shake a little more than perhaps they should when the arrow is released. The bow string twangs or doesn't depending on whether it has those fluffy bits attached or not, sending a piece of wood or graphite with a razor blade on the one end and some chicken feathers or plastic on the other, into the unfortunate animal's gut, approximately 10 saucers off target. The outfitter hisses between clenched teeth: 'Hell, if it wasn't for that blade of grass which deflected the arrow, it would have been a safe lung shot.' Another common excuse is: 'Shit, he moved just as you released the arrow!' And yet another: 'The arrow must have hit a bone and been deflected.'

Hours later the ranger or warden in charge of the reserve or district is obliged to take up the spoor, crawl after the unfortunate animal, often for days, and finally put an end to its misery with a rifle bullet. Sometimes there is no report and subsequently no follow-up, as we found the other day on a routine anti-poaching patrol. An elephant had been shot with an arrow as described in the preceding bow hunt scenario. It died a lingering death from septicaemia and gangrene some two weeks after being shot in the gut ... verrry sporting.

Choosing a personal weapon can be a very difficult decision – so much depends on the person's budget, individual taste and of course the purpose for which it is required, the latter being the most important consideration. To add to the dilemma, the 'old days' are gone, new firearms licensing regulations discourage regular 'upgrades' as is common practice with cell phones or computers, for example. Unlike fashion accessories or electronic gadgetry, once you have made your choice, you're pretty much stuck with it until death do you part, or, until you find a really beautiful one that you fall in love with and can't live without ... and this does happen. But the present draconian firearms legislation frowns upon having two firearms of the same calibre owned by one person, so one would have to go.

Some people are completely besotted with weapons. Many are not hunters or rangers, in fact there are collectors who own weapons that are never used – they merely love to own and invest in beautifully made firearms. There are weapons that reflect some of man's most exacting craftsmanship and artistry. Such a hand-made rifle or shotgun by one of the leading British makers will cost about R500 000 today, and depending on the detail of engraving and quality of wood selected, could cost much more. So there just might be a modicum of truth about an advertisement which some lonely ranger was said to have placed in 'The Hitching Post' section of *Farmer's Weekly*, which read. 'Handsome young game ranger seeks wife to share his life with. Must be nature lover, own a weapon and be able to shoot. Please send photo of weapon.'

In the real world, most of the game rangers employed in the National Parks are issued with weapons for the duration of their service. These firearms are carried around the reserve from one situation to another, or just in case of need. It's the classic case of rather have it and not need it than not have it and need it. Essentially these firearms are no more than tools used to get a specific job done. Having said this, however, nowhere are the old adages 'horses for courses' or 'the right tool for the job' more applicable than when a ranger needs to use a rifle for a specific purpose, particularly when it is employed to take a life or save a life. Not surprising, then, that they become reliant on these weapons and get to know how to use them with remarkable skill.

Game rangers have an innate respect for firearms and not surprisingly, many of them take this to the next level and become interested in ballistics, bullet performance and accuracy. All to one end ... to get to know the parameter of the weapon's capability and the purpose for which it was built, and to use this knowledge to be as effective as possible when making that vital shot, be it to cull antelope for rations, put a suffering animal out of its misery quickly or to stop a charging buffalo.

In some private nature reserves guides are required to have their own weapon (I use the singular in reference to those rangers that conduct guided tours and walking trails in big five reserves on a contractual basis). Wardens and conservation managers employed by private nature reserves will invariably make use of a number of company weapons at their disposal; however, many still prefer to use their personal firearms.

When selecting a rifle, do some research first, speak to people who have weapons, professionals if possible. What rifle and which calibre you choose can be quite confusing, despite being given the broader guidelines and criteria: there is such a wide range, with so little to choose between them. The decision can vary considerably, depending on individual skill and personal preference. Once you have made your choice, get to know how to use it well. Getting to grips with the way your rifle fits, how well it points and the all-important confidence that a weapon you're familiar with instils in you is vital. This is where reliance on a personal weapon is preferred, particularly when having to deal with potentially dangerous animals in difficult situations.

In a similar vein, I have a selection of fly rods, each of which is specifically designed for the various conditions and species of fish one may encounter. (This is what I tell Meagan, anyway). In essence, then, this analogy is not too far removed from the preceding discussion – however, I strongly suspect that like me, you may find yourself reaching for a specific weapon or fly rod more often than any other, a favourite if you like, despite the specification not being entirely applicable. You are able to present an artificial fly without a ripple or place the bullet with perfect precision, due to your familiarity and confidence with that rod or rifle ... you get the job done without thinking, in a reflexive way.

To try and discuss the merits of the individual firearms, makes and calibres that are used by game rangers in the course of their duties, and to give a fair appraisal of them all, would be an arduous task to say the least. However, I would like to very briefly share with you what I have learned through practical experience and what I consider to be a very basic battery of suitable weapons. The following recommendations made and opinions expressed are based on personal preference.

Starting from the smallest, moving up to the larger calibres:

- .22 Long rifle. Bolt action. This is used mainly for pest control, small game and birds. Due to the total absence of recoil and cheap ammunition, it is also an excellent training tool for teaching young children basic marksmanship. The other advantage of this little weapon is that it is relatively quiet, and can be made even quieter by using a silencer and subsonic ammunition, where it can be effectively used in very selective culling operations or built-up areas.

- .223 Remington. Bolt action. Although not my favourite, it does an excellent job as a ration rifle when long-range head shots on impala-sized antelope are called for. I have never used a .222 Remington, but feel that it would be equally effective for the same purpose. For this application, choose the most accurate rifle you can buy – one that consistently groups 5 bullets under 25 mm at 100 metres, would be a minimum requirement.

- 30/06 Springfield. Bolt action. This is probably the most versatile medium calibre rifle I've ever used. I also have a lot of respect for the 7 x 64 mm Brenneke and the .270 Winchester for use in general-purpose antelope hunting applications. Remingtons are apparently among the most accurate mass-produced rifles, but don't take my word on this. A controlled feed bolt action is not as important here, so choose any smooth action rifle that feels good in your hands and shoots a respectable grouping. Remember only accurate rifles are interesting rifles, and pretty rifles don't always shoot well.

- .416 Rigby. Controlled-feed Mauser-type bolt action. This is my favourite all-round heavy calibre for dangerous game. The .458 Winchester mag has a good reputation for reliable penetration and stopping power: I have used one on many occasions with good results. It is probably the most widely used large-bore cartridge in Africa today. As an aside, if I were allowed only *one* rifle, I would have to choose a .375 Holland and Holland mag – arguably the best all-round cartridge ever made. However, as with most all-round calibres it comes with compromises, so be aware of its limitations.

- .470 Rigby. In side/side double barrel configuration. A proven charge stopper, one of the best weapons to have as a back-up when the poo hits the fan. Not recommended as a carry-around, general-purpose weapon. They're heavy on the shoulder and in a double barrelled setup, are prohibitively expensive.
- 12 bore shotgun. Preferably a double barrel in over/under barrel configuration. (Not the riot pump specification.)
- For security/anti-poaching purposes the old R1 assault rifle in 7.62 calibre using military rounds is recommended; it can also be used for protection against dangerous game if necessary and has been used for big game culling operations. These weapons are usually carried by anti-poaching and field rangers, but would be virtually impossible to licence under the new laws.

Telescopic sights are essential on all but the heavy calibres and assault rifles. Never skimp here: if the scope costs more than your rifle you're on the right track. The Austrian-made Swarovski and Khales range are the best, with Germany's Zeiss and Schmidt and Bender following closely behind. The optics on these sights are streets ahead of anything from the USA or Japan.

The new laws governing firearm ownership mean that guns are becoming more difficult for the average person to obtain. What is of major concern is that the law doesn't discriminate either: I know of game rangers, game farmers and professional hunters dependent on weapons for their livelihood who are also being hampered by these laws. Any youngster interested in shooting today is so overwhelmed with procedural requirements that it puts them off before they've started.

Given the four-gun limit that legislation imposes, I'd be happy with a .22 long rifle, 30/06 Springfield, .416 Rigby and a 12 bore shotgun.

Jest Jurgen ... and There's More!

Jurgen loved to take the scenic route up to the reserve and would often travel on his own via Polokwane and Magoebaskloof. For security reasons he always carried a big handgun on his hip, except for the short period when he accidentally lost it in the refuse trailer up at the workshop. This happened when he hoisted the bin bag and threw it into the receptacle; the bag must have hooked the exposed hammer on his revolver, which lifted the gun out of its holster and into the bin. A couple of days later it was found when the garbage was being sorted for incineration. Were it not for a sharp-eyed staff member, it would have been incinerated along with all the other trash. How this slightly built man didn't feel the sudden weight loss of a .357 magnum revolver disappearing from his waist beats me.

In the days when the game-viewing vehicles were all parked at the reserve's main entrance gate, shareholders would park their Jo'burg vehicles there, unload all their supplies into their game-viewing 4x4, or merely transfer their pre-loaded Venter trailer from one vehicle to the other. With the trailer and the other paraphernalia loaded, the journey then took you along the winding, bumpy access road and through the wide, soft sandy crossing of the Mohlabetsi River. Once across, you continued through some beautiful Combretum and Marula woodland which took you past Wild Dog Pan, a popular game watering hole. Then you could either turn down to the Madrid lodges or continue on to Spaghetti Junction. This drive was approximately 18 kilometres long and took about 30 minutes, all of it through prime big game country, so it was always a bit of an adventure; in essence, it would be the first game drive of your visit.

Looking forward to a relaxing weekend on the reserve, Jurgen was probably in deep contemplation, thinking where he would go for that afternoon's drive, and what he'd pack in the cooler box for sundowners.

Approaching the sandy river crossing, he slowed down, engaged a lower gear, pushed down the yellow knob to engage four-wheel-drive and then eased the Land Rover into the soft sand. As the vehicle was churning its way through, he saw two men running towards him from the fence line. They were about 30 metres away, approaching fast, waving long knives known as 'pangas' and shouting something Jurgen didn't understand. It must have been a terrifying sight. Although always armed, he told us that he thought better of reaching for his handgun to protect himself and decided to rather try and drive away from them, which fortunately he managed to do. As the Land Rover climbed out of the river bed and up the steep bank on the opposite side, he looked back over his shoulder, and could see that although the two men had long since given up the chase, they were still gesticulating in his direction.

The next morning, a very shaken and worried Jurgen stood in the office and in wide-eyed detail related the story to us, pausing only to lift a shaking hand and take another deep draw on his cigarette. When he had finished telling us about his ordeal, he must have noticed that we were not taking the story as seriously as he might have expected. Eventually I couldn't contain myself any longer. I decided that before I burst out laughing, I'd better tell him what really happened, and then we could laugh about it together, which we did. Despite his Germanic sense of humour instinctively searching for logic, the explanation that followed had him laughing until he had tears in his eyes.

In fact, the two panga-wielding attackers were employees of Olifants who had been clearing the grass and scrub growth along the fence line with our neighbouring reserve, Ukhozi. Being a Saturday meant that it was a half-day, which had been overlooked by the person who was supposed to pick them up, and so they had not been collected. That was when they realised that the vehicle approaching them was a perfect opportunity to get a ride back to headquarters. Jurgen was on his own and had plenty of room in his Land Rover, so they waved their pangas to show they were bona fide workers, and to attract his attention to their plight. In order not to inconvenience Jurgen, the two men thought they would save time by running up to him, knowing that the shareholders were often quite keen to get to their lodge as quickly as possible ...

Can you blame anyone who didn't know these two men for reacting the same way as Jurgen? It makes you think just how something so innocently funny could just as easily have ended in tragedy by Jurgen turning into an armed and dangerous person exercising his right to self-defence, or by the entire tale starring a couple of poachers whose objectives would have been far from innocent. But Jurgen did the right thing and exercised restraint, something we all have to do on various occasions in the bush. Not only is it prudent to exercise restraint when apparently being attacked by panga-wielding poachers, but dangerous animals also need to be given the benefit of the doubt, time and circumstances permitting, of course. As an example ...

Olifants had recently closed its walking trails, and for good reason. The influx of nearly 500 elephant and the burgeoning hippo population meant that walking on the riparian floodplain of the Olifants River, once a popular route, was now too dangerous to contemplate unless you were accompanied by an adequately armed ranger. This possibility prompted one of the shareholders to ask if he and his partner could accompany our anti-poaching ranger on his next patrol. These patrols take place over the entire Olifants region, including privately owned neighbouring properties surrounding our reserve. As a matter of courtesy, permission from the neighbour was obtained for persons other than our bona fide rangers to walk on their property, and this was granted.

The weather that morning was perfect picnic weather for Scotland, overcast and cool with a light drizzle. Despite this dampener on the day, the young couple set out early with our chief ranger, in eager anticipation of a brisk walk along the breathtakingly beautiful floodplain. Following the well-worn hippo path, they walked in virtual silence, the soft sand muffling even the most clumsy footfall.

One of the first animals they saw that morning was the rare Pel's fishing owl. At their approach, the huge bird dropped silently from the thick foliage of a huge grove of Natal mahogany trees. Swooping low, it then settled plainly visible in a sycamore fig tree a little further downstream. 'What a start to the day,' the couple thought. As they continued, a number of waterbuck and even the normally wary bushbuck were startled at the walkers' silent approach, only breaking cover at a heart-stopping few metres ahead of them.

By now used to the odd animal revealing itself at the last moment as they walked, there was a hardly perceptible hesitancy when a louder crashing of vegetation was heard off to the side. Only when this revealed a hippo bull hurtling towards them at full speed was there any reaction. After seeing the tracker throw his rifle down and climb the nearest tree, one of the party simply picked the next best tree and also climbed up it. This left only one option for the remaining walker ... the river! But this was the same river the hippo was heading for. Fortunately, the hippo path followed a fairly gentle gradient into the river, which allowed the hapless walker the opportunity to dive off the steeper edge of the path at a right-angle into the river and avoid the hippo. There really was nowhere else to go!

The startled hippo had no intention of attacking anybody that morning. The short-sighted old bull was merely determined to get back into the water along the path with which it was familiar – only this time there were three strange animals standing in his way. On cool, overcast days hippo often move quite some distance from water, particularly in winter when the grass on the floodplain has been depleted and better feeding is to be had further inland. These nocturnally active animals will often extend their hours of grazing by taking advantage of cool conditions such as this, foraging late into the day. Being caught between a hippo and the water can be an extremely dangerous situation, as effectively you are blocking its route to safety and it will attack if given no alternative.

Did the ranger register this lack of intent in the hippo's tiny pig-like eyes when he dumped the rifle, or did he also just 'pop his clutch' and use 'four-limb-drive' to get the hell out of the way as Jurgen did, and then in hindsight, breathe a sigh of relief, happy not to have used his firearm?

Everybody survived the ordeal unscathed, except for the rifle, which to this day, despite repeated stripping and cleaning, still has a gritty feel about its action.

Tracking – Science or Mysterious Art?

SEPTEMBER 2009

On a cold winter's day, nearly 60 years ago, a young boy by the name of Roy Weatherby was out hunting white-tailed deer somewhere in the North American woods. He was alone but enjoyed the solitude of the back country; it was how he preferred to hunt. To date he had needed nothing more than a basic knowledge of his quarry, the woods they lived in and his skill with a rifle to fill the freezer with venison.

The air was crisp and each breath hung in a vapour cloud before drifting slowly away: windless conditions like this were ideal for hunting. He had been out since first light that morning hoping to spot some deer sunning themselves on the higher slopes. Using the shadows of the tree line along the contour and moving slowly along the narrow valley with patches of open meadow which lay between the high ground on either side, it wasn't long before he came across a small herd of deer browsing on the opposite hillside. Among them was a huge 12-point buck, but at a distance of over 400 metres they were much too far away to risk a shot. Bending over in a low crouch and with deliberate foot placements Roy began to stalk them. In the relatively open sections he was reduced to crawling on his belly at times, but all the while he quietly crept closer. When he had managed to close the distance to less than 100 yards he was now in a more favourable position to take a shot. Steadying himself against a Ponderosa pine tree whose lower branches offered concealment, he released the safety catch on the rifle and peered through the telescopic sight. Despite his pounding heart shifting the point of aim with each beat, he squeezed the trigger as the crosshairs settled on the shoulder of the buck.

The impact of the bullet caused the buck to stumble momentarily, then, appearing to recover, it disappeared along with the others into the forest. This would be the last image Roy would ever have of that deer. Any doubt that it had been hit was soon dispelled by the blood spatter that was found on the ground which trailed off to smaller droplets – and then after a few metres the blood trail seemed to evaporate completely. The young boy was frantic: he tried desperately to locate the deer by using a random, grid-searching technique that continued for hours but which yielded nothing; the buck was never found.

Roy was deeply troubled by this incident, so much so that it led him on a quest for the 'magic bullet' – one that would kill an animal quicker than conventional bullets. He never wanted to wound or lose a deer again, and like so many dedicated hunters was preoccupied with ballistics, focusing primarily on improving bullet performance by increasing their velocity and energy. He dedicated his life to the design of powerful rifle calibres with superior ballistics, and popularised a range of weapons that went on to become the famous Weatherby magnums.

At this point you may be wondering what all this preamble on bullets and ballistics has got to do with tracking. For one, had Roy been able to track down that deer he wounded in the woods all those years ago, he would probably never have developed his famous magnum calibres, or for that matter felt the need to. More to the point, however, I believe that despite his contribution to the hunting world in terms of weaponry, he would have achieved more success as a hunter by learning the basics of the art of tracking. Being able to track your quarry down enables the hunter to curtail unnecessary suffering relatively quickly, something no badly placed shot, irrespective of innovative bullet design, high velocity or energy, is capable of doing.

It is bullet placement and good tracking that is the key to efficient hunting – and of these two criteria, being able to track is the most dependable. This can be illustrated by the fact that the San of the Kalahari use small poison-tipped arrows to deliver their toxin into the game they hunt; the shaft is then designed to fall off while the arrow head remains embedded in the animal. Depending on the body mass of the animal and the rate at which the poison impedes its progress, they will persistently follow its spoor until they find it, then deliver the coup de grâce if necessary. Animals as large as eland and giraffe are successfully hunted this way.

Tracking and the use of expert trackers is as old as mankind itself, but for the majority of us, our modern lifestyle no longer depends on tracking animals for the purpose of hunting them for food. However, the skill is still widely used in the safari industry, law enforcement, forensic science, military, wildlife research and finding lost pets and livestock. Even in this day and age, there are situations where using an expert tracker can still mean the difference between life and death, success or failure, or profit or loss.

One of the countless memorable examples of what a fine tracker can do happened in the Timbavati Nature Reserve nearly 25 years ago, and although this occurred in the heart of Big Five country, this particular story involves a dog, a very special dog.

Shilo loved to run, so much so that he would often yelp with delight when he was let out of the Land Rover to run behind it for a while. When we did this I would always pull ahead of him for fear of him running next to the vehicle where I was afraid he might lose his footing and fall under the back wheels. To avoid this I'd need to pull quite far ahead of him; otherwise if the road surface was good he would turn on the pace and catch up to me when I was compelled to slow down for a bend in the road or to negotiate a sandy drift. This particular day was no different, except that it was a warmer than usual summer's day and the cooling effect of the wind driving in an open Land Rover was deceptive. Relenting to Shilo's cold-wet-nose-against-my-ear-pressure to run, I let him out and drove on ahead.

At this point we were about two kilometres from camp as the crow flies. A few minutes later, climbing the gentle slope that led up to M'bali, I glanced over my shoulder expecting to see the familiar sight of Shilo, ears pinned back in the wind, running up behind me … but there was nothing. I turned the vehicle around and drove back to where I'd last seen him … still nothing. Checking for tracks, I found the unmistakable prints of where he had run down the road; then on a bend a few hundred metres later, they veered off and disappeared into the bush. I began calling his name, trying at least a couple of dozen times until fear dried up my mouth, and soon I could no longer utter a sound. There was no response, so I went back to the last track I could find, hoping for a clue as to the direction he took. It was really hot now and the midday sun beat down bright and brassy, quite possibly the worst time to try and follow spoor. This only added to my anxiety.

Thinking he may have headed back to camp by taking a shortcut through the bush I drove home and started the generator and water pump, hoping he would be guided home by the familiar sound of the thumping diesel motors. Then, not satisfied with the noise level, I began hooting in desperation (something one doesn't do in the bush): this brought my concerned staff in from their lunch break to find out what the problem was. Even before I'd finished explaining what had happened they groaned in sympathy; everyone there knew what Shilo meant to me.

The Timbavati Game Reserve bristles with large predators, so I knew despite Shilo's bush sense that a domestic dog had no chance of survival out there – I had to find him. Almost in tears at the thought of what could happen if I didn't, I climbed back into the Land Rover and headed out to look for him again. In those days Motswari didn't employ trackers or game scouts at the lodges and there wasn't time to hire one from elsewhere. In my impatience to get going, the wheels of the vehicle spun as I tried to get traction on the loose quartz gravel of the road surface, and this brief delay allowed the camp gardener, Phinias Sibuyi, to step into the road and motion me to stop.

'I can help you find Shilo, if you show me where you left his tracks,' he said.

In situations like this, one clutches at straws: I was happy for any help at this stage, even the gardener's.

Arriving at the spot where I'd last seen Shilo's tracks, I pointed them out to the 'gardener'. I wasn't expecting much more than a sympathetic pair of eyes to help me scan the bush for Shilo ... well, that was until Phinias took the spoor – and he literally did 'take the spoor'. Cupping his hands on either side of one of Shilo's prints, he scooped the soil that had contained the track and put it in a small plastic bag which he promptly pocketed. 'We will not lose him now,' he said.

I remember thinking how weird that was, but as I had a much more pressing issue to worry about I decided on adopting an 'any-port-in-a-storm' attitude, which thankfully didn't last for long. As Phinias proceeded I began to detect a definite change in his attitude and the way he moved. Despite his baggy, soil-stained overalls and oversized gumboots, there were subtle behaviour-isms that were hauntingly familiar – then it suddenly dawned on me. Years before in the Sabi Sands game reserve, I'd seen game scouts with the same mannerisms conjure the same magic ... I was witnessing a master tracker at work. This man was no longer the humble labourer tending a garden, which at best was what the warthogs and crickets didn't want to eat, or the man who depended on me for a meagre wage each month. I was clearly in the hands of an expert and totally dependent on him now for something no amount of money could buy.

Clasping his hands together behind his back and bending over slightly, Phinias studied the spoor. He proceeded frustratingly slowly, but with such confidence that it completely renewed mine. An hour later he turned to me with a broad grin on his face: '*Nangu*' (there), he said, pointing to Shilo, who lay softly panting in the cool shade of a magic guarrie bush. Besides a sheepish grin that broke into a toothy smile which made him sneeze when he saw us, he looked rather comfortable, this despite the heat that had driven him to search for shade which he'd found a few hundred metres from the road. This is probably where he would have lain until it cooled down later in the afternoon, and who could blame him. It was I who was to blame, having horribly under-estimated the heat that day ... and it was I who should have been wearing a sheepish grin.

Realising Phinias's extraordinary talent, I immediately promoted him to the position of game scout, with commensurate salary. I then went on to institute a change: all the rangers at Motswari and Mbali would henceforth conduct game drives and walking trails using a tracker, and it didn't stop there. Five years later Phinias Sibuyi made history: he became one of the first black rangers in the country to take international guests on safari as a qualified Ranger at Motswari. Would I still have promoted him had he not found Shilo? ... Watching him tracking that day had me convinced of his talent long before we found my dog ... plastic bag filled with sand and all.

Phinias continued to work at Motswari for many years until his premature death from a lung infection in September 2004. South Africa had lost one of its finest trackers, a proud Shangaan and a true spirit of the bush.

Having gained first-hand experience from working with these men in the field, I would like to share some of what I was taught and what was learned. I will also throw in a little of my own experience and observations in the hope that I spark an interest and draw you closer to understanding something most people regard as magic. For the purpose of the foregoing, I will concentrate on the tracking of animals, as I have limited experience tracking men, although the transition from one to the other would be effortless as far an expert tracker is concerned.

Observing an expert tracker at work doesn't elicit material for an action movie script or moves for Jackie Chan to emulate, and unless you question them when they're tracking, there is nothing to hear. It is essentially a gentle, intricate art where clues from nature are skilfully analysed and then used to achieve success ... a little like fly-fishing (sorry, I just had to bring that in). I have often been asked what it is that makes some people better trackers than others. Considering the seemingly infinite variables and circumstances involved, there could never be a definitive answer. However, of all the possible attributes, there is a trait common to the best trackers I've known, which I believe lends itself to the art, and incidentally is extremely rare in First World people ... patience.

There are fundamentally two types of tracking, namely systematic tracking and speculative tracking (Liebenberg, 1990). The former is a systematic, painstaking gathering of visual information that tells the tracker where the animal was, what it was doing and which way it is headed. This method is most useful in hunting situations where a specific animal is being tracked either to be hunted or put out of its misery after being wounded. The latter is broader intelligence gathering based on knowledge of the animal being tracked and the terrain or feature it is likely to head for, the nearest waterhole or shady riverbed for example, also known colloquially as leapfrogging. This tactic is used extensively in game viewing operations with great success. Some of the best men I've worked with would combine the two methods, and depending on the circumstances it was usually a 70 per cent systematic approach, with the balance relying on gut feel, and a thorough knowledge of the animal and the area. The best results are obtained by using two trackers, one leapfrogging speculatively while the other systematically plods on. I fondly remember two trackers I worked with on Letaba Ranch who complemented each other in this way, producing excellent results, particularly when we needed to track the same animal for more than a day, or when wind direction precluded a strictly systematic approach.

Having said this, a good tracker is unlikely to assume or guess where an animal may be found: even if pressured by clients he usually remains circumspect, and for good reason. A lucky guess is not good tracking, nor is raising false hopes based on guesswork. A good tracker will stay focused on the signs left behind, combining these clues with his knowledge of the animal's behavioural traits. From this he will paint a mental picture and make calculated guesses in his mind all the time. I must admit that, even though I prefer the finesse of this approach and admire its complexity, there have been times when even 'systematic' trackers have needed to speculate and tell me what they were thinking or how the animal they were tracking might be 'thinking'. This information is vital when following dangerous game in thick bush.

From the outset I should make it clear that seeing a full print when tracking is a bonus: invariably the tracker is guided by signs that are far more subtle. Often the signs are not recognisable print impressions; rather they are minor disturbances sometimes unrelated to the footprints of the animal being followed, but indicating the animal's passage as a whole, through a specific space. Trackers will walk next to the line of tracks so as not to smudge any clues, and in order that should they momentarily lose the spoor, they can backtrack and pick it up again. Tracking is not a hurried affair, however; when a good tracker gets to an easy section he will move through it quite quickly, often at a slow run. This saves time and crucially maximises the light advantage: leaving a trail to go cold overnight greatly reduces the chances of finding the animal the next day.

Here are a few basic examples of the signs a tracker looks for:

- The most obvious of course is spoor, with the clues derived from the various surfaces they're found on and the forms the imprints and marks subsequently take. Any characteristic that gives an animal a unique identity is stored in the tracker's memory bank, helping him to single out the subject from among others – for example, a chipped hoof, a skew toe or, as in the case of a lion, mane hair length and colour.
- Urine and faeces can often provide the most accurate information on the age of the track.
- Insects found on the track that were inadvertently killed or injured by a hoof or paw, an ant lion reconstructing a recently trodden on pit-trap, for example.
- When close enough to certain animals many trackers are able to identify their proximity on scent alone; they can smell them long before they see them (Young, 1986).
- Disturbed vegetation in the form of bent foliage and grass springing back as the track ages, scuffed bark, broken twigs and crushed or discoloured leaves.
- In the case of a wounded animal, a blood trail helps with identification in the beginning, but as the droplets get progressively scarcer, other longer-lasting clues need to be looked for and memorised. Blood spoor can tell the tracker a lot about the wound: droplets of dark blood will indicate a flesh wound, and

larger amounts will indicate a bleeding artery or vein. Pinkish, frothy blood, sometimes with larger bubbles, will indicate a lung wound. Blood from a gut wound is often watered down with stomach contents and the distinctive smell of rumen matter in ungulates is unmistakable.

- Secondary signs include the reaction of other animals in the vicinity. Game birds like francolin and guineafowl can be quite raucous when disturbed, and the chirping of oxpeckers, a bird usually associated with large game, is also a giveaway. Alarm calls from prey animals, if not directed at you, may indicate the presence of a predator.

One evening around the campfire hoping to pick up a tip or two in general conversation, I asked Phinias how he had learned to become a good tracker, He looked at me with a sort of embarrassed sideways peek, then broke into a broad grin and admitted that as a child he was actually a naughty boy, and that as important as the responsibility was, he disliked tending the family's livestock. He said he preferred hunting and playing with the other herd boys and so he would allow the livestock to wander where they wished for most of the day … but as we spoke it became apparent that this was not the main motivation, there was something else. In those days Mum didn't pack the Twinkies and Melrose cheese sandwiches in a neat little lunchbox, nor was there a tuck shop to run to with your lunch money. Other than a bowl of maize porridge in the morning, he'd be out in the open air all day with nothing to eat; needless to say he remembers always being hungry – and as we all know, they don't come much hungrier than a growing child. There's nothing that demands your attention quite like real hunger does. The anticipation of a mouth-watering morsel being grilled over an open fire was enough to keep him sharp and focused; he told me he ate whatever he could track and kill that was edible. He soon realised that the better he understood the behaviour of the animals in that environment, the better he could track them. This made him a better hunter. The more he hunted, the more he had to eat … simple.

In addition to playing and hunting for food, come late afternoon, Phinias needed to find his father's livestock before the light faded. He quickly learned how to tell his own herd's footprints apart from the many others in the area, then he'd track the scattered animals, round them up and take them home. At the time he was unaware of the technicalities of the two types of tracking he was employing, tracking the cattle and goats each day is where he learned so much about speculative tracking. This was after having spent much of the day concentrating on the finer systematic aspect of tracking which was necessary to find the smaller more elusive animals he hunted for food. So, as a youth, he was already perfecting the two main aspects of tracking. Later in life he often combined the two, using them as circumstance dictated, making him one of the most skilled and versatile trackers I've known.

No one is born a good tracker, just like nobody is born able to dance like Nureyev or play the guitar as Eric Clapton does. Tracking is an acquired skill honed over time; how proficient you become depends on the dedication and natural ability of the pupil. Although the San Bushmen and the Shangaans of Southern Africa are tribes with a reputation for producing good trackers, not all of their members are good at it. The elite few with whom I have had the privilege to work, acquired their skill when it was passed down from one generation to the next: they were taught. So then, in theory at least, anyone committed enough can learn to be a good tracker. Although there is no formal book learning or written exam to pass, the practical training required, if it were to be documented, would fill volumes and you could live a full life tracking every day and never uncover all of its mysteries. It is a fascinating and challenging art to try and master; there is no greater sense of accomplishment than when you successfully locate an animal you are looking for by tracking its spoor.

Sadly the art of tracking is a dying one – and not for lack of demand, far from it. The Ecotourism industry and related facets still provide many employment opportunities in this field and the demand is ever increasing; however, there are fewer young men coming through the ranks who can track like their fathers could. Aspirations have changed. Today the majority of young

Shangaan men, even those living within sight of the Kruger National Park, don't have the faintest clue how to track; worse still, they are not interested in learning. The blame for this can be placed squarely on formal education and modern lifestyle values. Compulsory schooling no longer allows for young boys to spend their days in the bush tending livestock and hunting, thereby effectively denying any potential trackers the very foundation activities which hone tracking skills from an early age.

Having worked as closely with nature as I have over the last 35 years and by taking an intense interest in learning the unwritten secrets of this mythical art, I could at a stretch push the description of my tracking ability to include the word 'competent'. However, I'll be the first to say that being able to get across the dance floor without tripping over someone's feet doesn't make you a dancer. Strangely enough, many of the Nureyevs of the tracking world I so admired were a little like the dancer himself, slightly temperamental by nature, often small wiry men, but with hearts of lions. This aside, it was their talent for seeing the invisible, their patient persistence in finding what everyone else had given up for lost, and finally, when they turned to me and whispered, '*nangu*' – that's what made them giants in my eyes.

For those interested in learning more about the science and theory of tracking, I recommend that you read *The Art of Tracking* by Louis Liebenberg. From a guide to tracking perspective, this book will only provide you with the absolute basics, the bare bones as it were, but it is a start. Look at this as being much like the little book of road signs your daughter studied and the subsequent test she took to pass her driver's license. While you have to accept she is now legally a 'driver', in your heart you know the acid test is going to be out there on the highways, shoulder to shoulder with 20 ton articulated trucks and doped-up wannabe Schumachers, or bumper to bumper in the concrete jungle with that impatient animal known as peak-hour traffic. Mastering it is going to be a lifelong learning process – as will tracking …

Good luck!

Not Just Another Buffalo Story

JANUARY 2008, RECALLING AN EVENT FROM 2004

According to the blurred illuminated dots of my Swiss army watch, it was just after 2 am. I groaned, not just at being woken at this hour, but because these early morning calls were usually from the Phalaborwa-based regional head of Spoornet's train drivers. Few phone calls received at this unearthly hour bring good news, unless someone you know is phoning from Brisbane, or some equally far-flung place, and miscalculates the time difference. When Spoornet calls late at night or early in the morning, it is always bad news, invariably to do with a train colliding with some unfortunate animal.

We have a working protocol that in the event of an animal being struck by a train, the reserve's management will be informed immediately, irrespective of the time of day or night. Basically, this ensures that if an animal is badly injured, it can be humanely despatched or if already dead, the carcass can be removed from the tracks as soon as possible. This is to prevent predators and scavengers attracted to the immediate area becoming secondary casualties when the next train comes along. Here on Olifants, we are well-equipped and experienced in using our labour force and heavy machinery to do what is necessary. The staff know the routine and are more than willing to help at odd hours, and as an added incentive, although it may sound a touch both gruesome and opportunistic, there's often the chance of collecting meat from the carcass. In this instance, the message was that a buffalo had been hit. According to the driver's report, it was caught a glancing blow and knocked head-over-heels down a steep embankment. The rest of the herd of about six or so were apparently unharmed.

I always keep the equipment at the ready for just such events – a powerful hand-held portable spotlight, a Petzl headband lamp, camera, hand-held radio, binoculars and a heavy calibre rifle. So, within minutes, I was loaded and on my way. Normally, I would take someone with me to shine the spotlight, which leaves my hands free to operate the rifle, but for some reason in this case, I thought it unnecessary to wake Meagan.

The previous time I'd been called out was for a hippo with a broken jaw – and in that instance my daughter Eleana bravely shone the light for me while I put the poor animal out of its misery.

The train drivers are usually spot on with the incident site, giving the number on the kilometre-marked pylons along the tracks as a reference. This time-saving process meant it wasn't long before I was on the scene.

Climbing onto the tracks and shining the spotlight, I could clearly see the disturbed gravel where a small group of buffalo had crossed. The embankment down which the buffalo had fallen was about eight metres high and had a pitch of about 35 degrees. I scoured the area with the spotlight hoping to pick up an unnatural shape or the reflection of an eye, but ... nothing. Switching off the light, I sat in silence on the tracks, listening for laboured breathing or any sound of movement, but besides the odd Mozambique nightjar and the distant drone of the Phalaborwa mine, silence reigned. After about ten minutes, I turned on the spotlight again and did another sweep – and again ... nothing. I walked up the railway tracks for a couple of hundred metres and then down again in the opposite direction with the same negative result. There was not much more I could do, so I decided to go home and come back first thing in the morning to study the signs at the scene properly.

Subsequently, a follow-up visit revealed that a buffalo had indeed been hit before tumbling down the embankment. The precise nature of his wounds could only be revealed by tracking him, but all indications from the spoor showed he was favouring his left front leg and although not quite in 'buffalo 4x4', he still managed to cover a considerable amount of ground on three-and-a-half legs. He was certainly able to keep up with the group and as buffalo are notoriously tough and resilient I gave him the benefit of the doubt, as he was probably only temporarily lame and would be fine in a couple of days.

A few days later, a camp attendant at one of the properties down-river radioed in to say he had a buffalo in camp that was acting out of character. I went to investigate and found the buffalo had moved into a virtually impenetrable thicket of riparian bush. As this was on a neighbour's property, owned by a part-time professional hunter, I telephoned him and suggested he follow up on the buffalo.

I also suggested he take the tracks the following day, by which time it should have moved out from the thicket allowing for positive identification, as it would be disastrous for a healthy animal to be destroyed in error. Two days later, despite a concerted effort, he had not managed to get a clear sighting of the buffalo, and having other commitments, had to abandon the pursuit.

A day later, one of my staff members staying on the next-door property casually reported to me that there were tracks of a lone buffalo bull near our northern boundary. The spoor pointed to behaviour totally out of character for a healthy buffalo. As it was already mid-morning, I thought there was no point in doing anything immediately, and with the morning weatherman having said the day was going to be a stinker, I decided to tackle the problem the next day.

The next day was no different. A typical summer lowveld day, when not a leaf rustled and midday temperatures hovered around 40 degrees in the shade. Besides the mournful hooting of emerald-spotted wood doves, the still air was punctuated only by the shrill, ear-piercing staccato of cicadas. The only sensible thing to do was to chill out, take it easy and stay as cool as possible. But out there somewhere was an animal that was suffering, while I lay sprawled on my comfortable couch in an air-conditioned house watching Schumacher practising to bring Ferrari home to victory yet again. It just didn't feel right.

Unable to relax I filled a five-litre container with ice-cold water and placed it in my back pack. I tied a bandana around my head under my bush hat to stop the sweat from running into my eyes, picked up my rifle and binoculars and drove to the last set of tracks near our northern boundary. It was a Saturday afternoon and my game guards and trackers were off duty. They were doing the only sensible thing under these conditions, taking a siesta. I didn't expect them to jump at the opportunity to track for me, and so I didn't ask.

Once I'd made up my mind, there was no stopping me. I would find the buffalo myself and put an end to this matter.

My mind would not contemplate procrastination, so neither the intervention of logic nor the consideration of reasons for delay would be tolerated. I'll never know why I had such a bee in my bonnet. I had horribly underestimated the effect of walking in this kind of heat and so it wasn't long before I was forced to take a break that I didn't want to take. The midday sun, shining directly into the spoor, didn't throw much of a shadow, which made the tracks difficult to discern, and so I needed to concentrate that much harder. This proved to be both tiring and thirsty work, so I stopped again. Leaning my rifle against a small raisin bush in front of me, I unshouldered my backpack. Taking the water out, I noisily gulped down what must have been at least a litre!

Something I did or a subtle shift in the wind must have alerted the buffalo, because when I took the water container away from my mouth, he was standing broadside on to me about 50 metres upstream of the small gully in which I was standing. His nose was in the air testing the wind and he then swivelled to face me. I could see him favouring his left foreleg as he did so. In any other situation it could have been mistaken for a little stumble, but in this case it was precisely what I was looking for. I grabbed the rifle and took aim, whereupon he snorted and ran. Quickly reaching the spot where he had been standing, I could see from the spoor he was definitely favouring his left front leg. This was the injured buffalo we'd been looking for.

Tracking a wounded buffalo while keeping a look-out for potential cover where it could seek refuge or from which it could charge is not very practical. I was straining my ears listening for red-billed oxpeckers, as these little birds are in constant attendance, gleaning parasites from a host of large game. Although excellent early warning systems for a buffalo, their shrill chirping often gives away its whereabouts. The stark reality of being on my own in a precarious situation then hit home. I would need every bit of help I could get.

It started to cool down, not dramatically but perceptibly. I didn't need the bandana anymore and my sweat-soaked clothes started to work like a cooling radiator.

I knew I should ignore these comforts and stay focused. I proceeded cautiously, taking time to scour the bush in front of me, bending down every now and again to look below the browse line for the buffalo's legs. Basically, I was hoping to see him before he saw me. The area through which we were moving is known as 'Klipheuwel' (Stone hill), and I thought how aptly named it was. At times the terrain was so rocky there was no visible spoor to follow. In these instances I relied on instinct, experience and a dash of luck, and made a calculated guess as to which route he had taken. Looking for tracks in the soil between the stones, I carefully placed my feet on the larger rocks to deaden my approach. This tactic worked, and as I rounded a small stony kopje something made me look up.

Looking straight at me, not more than five metres away, was the buffalo! Again he snorted and turned to run, but this time I'd anticipated his move ...

The sun was sinking low and I had only a vague idea of where I was. Climbing to the top of the little kopje, I made out the single power lines in the distance. The thick bush and fading light were of some concern to me as the carcass needed to be loaded before predators found it. At the same time, I wasn't sure that in the dark, I'd find the spot where the buffalo lay. I needed something to mark the way and the only material light enough in colour to use was my underpants. Off they came, and I cut them into strips. These were tied to prominent trees and bushes until I reached the single power line road so I would be able to use them to guide me back in on my return. Tightening my shoelaces and placing my backpack against the pylon, I began the slow jog home.

In less than half an hour, we were on our way back to collect the buffalo. Bringing the vehicle in wasn't easy and it was almost dark. But, as I had the game scouts with me, I felt more confident. It took all of 15 minutes to slowly pick our way through the bush, guided by the occasional strip of my underpants, and we found the buffalo easily enough. Everybody wanted to have a look as natural curiosity takes over when you're able to touch and feel such an awesome animal. We were just getting the vehicle into position to load, when I saw one of my trusty trackers, Jabulaan, shake his head and smile.

'Come and look here, Zutini,' he said, using my Shangaan name. He was standing about 15 metres down the slope from where the buffalo lay and was pointing to a road. Even though the 'road' was more of a track than a real road, it was perfectly serviceable, and I felt foolish for having led them through a gauntlet of thick bush, following pieces of my underpants. Had I known exactly where I was, I would have been able to take us straight to the carcass, but I had concentrated so hard on tracking the buffalo, hoping to see him before he saw me, that nothing else mattered.

Later, back at camp, while butchering the buffalo, an autopsy revealed that the poor animal had a broken shoulder, bruised spleen and a haemorrhage on the left lung, hence he couldn't lie down comfortably to rest and chew the cud – it was no wonder he had lost condition so rapidly and had been reported acting in ways atypical for a buffalo.

Although the events of this story culminated in a fortunate outcome, both in terms of the suffering of an animal being brought to an end, and my walking away with only the loss of my underwear, it could so easily have gone the other way, and sometimes it really does do just that, go the other way.

This all happened a while ago and until now I have not discussed it much, let alone put it in a newsletter. However, something I read recently changed my mind and prompted me to share this with you.

Ask anyone who knows and they'll tell you that taking on a dangerous animal, particularly a Cape buffalo, alone and without consideration of the consequences, is extremely dangerous. Taking on an injured or wounded buffalo alone is total madness. This revealed a side of me of which I was ashamed, and upon which I have subsequently reflected occasionally and uncomfortably.

Given my experience, I should have known better. It is difficult to understand what makes rational people act irrationally and impulsively, doing things that in the light of coldly analytical hindsight seem so careless and irresponsible.

This frame of mind remained until I read *Into the Wild* by Jon Krakauer. It's a factual account of an intelligent young man, Chris McCandless, who is so driven by his love of remote places, particularly Alaska, that his single-minded passion culminates in an emotional state that clouds all rational thought. As a result, he carelessly fails to prepare properly, and neglects to take the necessary precautions.

Some say this showed that he lacked the necessary respect for the Wilderness. Although nobody will ever really know, I suspect I gained a deeper insight into Chris McCandless' psyche than many may have; I think I understand the way he felt and why he did what he did. I pretty much did the same. The only difference is that I didn't pay for my actions with my life. Tragically, he did.

The Olifants Annual Game Census ...
Is it Necessary?

OCTOBER 2003

The cost of a helicopter game census seems prohibitive. There have been times when the necessity of doing an annual game count using this method – in comparison with, say, the fixed wing option – has been questioned. Dr Petri Viljoen, a wildlife ecologist who specialises in census methods and models throughout Africa, was consulted for his expert opinion. His recommendation was that a helicopter grid count be conducted in reserves of 50 000 hectares or less. He told me that this was particularly important in the thick bushveld and topography that is so typical of lowveld reserves.

As a warden tasked with the efficient running of a game reserve, I am often asked if this cost is justified, and my answer is the same as always. 'Is taking a monthly stocktake in a retail business necessary, or, is the Pope a Catholic?' The answer is, of course, yes, it's necessary! The fact of the matter is that, on average, the costs incurred equate to less than 0.00017 per cent of the total market value of the property, and less than 0.0003 per cent of the value of the game being counted. Meaningless figures perhaps, but it does put things in perspective in terms of the cost-to-value ratios.

In order to keep a handle on the real state of affairs on Olifants, to implement appropriate conservation management techniques, and to help make informed decisions on how best to manage our game populations, we need accurate and reliable data. Without the knowledge of what is on the land, it's down to guesswork, and this can be a big problem in a relatively small reserve. As it happens, our annual game census, our 'audit', is no longer an option as it is now required by law as part of a management plan. This plan has to be complied with and submitted to the authorities before any permits are issued or the removal or hunting of game can take place.

The logic is simple. If you have no evidence of 'stock' how can you possibly know how much to market in the hunting sense, or if there is no proof of abundance or overpopulation, how can you expect to obtain a permit for capture and removal of surplus stock. Most importantly, this formality encourages landowners to actively move closer to the holistic approach and further away from the ecologically terminal '*Myne* syndrome' and manage their properties in a cohesive and responsible manner by replacing thumb-sucking with science.

Two sets of numbers sit at the heart of the required data. There are the game count figures, which indicate larger herbivore biomass, and then there is the analysis of the vegetation monitoring plot data, conducted by members of the same team, which determines vegetative biomass. This is the crux of the statistical base of our management. The data are definitive. They give you a very good idea of what your veld is carrying in terms of animal biomass, and what you should be carrying, relative to what there is available for that biomass to consume.

Of paramount importance and key to reliable data is consistency. Consistent light conditions, veld conditions, counting apparatus and personnel are essential. This year's census was delayed by a few weeks in order to allow the vegetation to dry and thin out more, thereby approximately replicating last year's conditions when the count was done. This variable is unpredictable and the most difficult to control, but with the identical counting apparatus and the same professional team that have been doing our counts for the last 16 years, we were at least assured of excellent control in this regard.

Nonetheless, you cannot expect to count every animal on the reserve; the best we can hope to achieve is a pattern of trends, which is reliant on being as consistent as possible. The most uncontrollable variable in the equation, besides the weather, is the human factor. Even a consistently average-to-poor spotter is better than someone who has good days and bad days. Worse still, if counters change frequently, your results may not be an accurate indication of what is happening on the reserve.

I'll stick my neck out and say for the last 16 years, Olifants has probably compiled some of the best and the most consistent game census data in the lowveld, largely due to the consistency of our team.

Mike Peel, with his recently obtained doctorate behind him, heads up the team and has done so since the beginning. His brother, John, and colleague, André Jacobs, are the counters. Mike Pingo, the pilot, is so familiar with the area that he even remembered the tree in which they had spotted a leopard last year that had now been flattened by elephant. I don't think there's been another pilot ever to have flown this team on our reserve. You cannot beat this for continuity.

The jump-seat in the rear of the Bell Jet Ranger helicopter is usually reserved for the game warden or ranger of the reserve or region being counted. There are times, however, when this privilege is given up to allow an enthusiast the opportunity to 'help' with the count. This generous offer can also be a discreet way out of a rather embarrassing affliction suffered by some of the most rugged and burly of rangers. These individuals, despite trying really hard to hide their weakness, can be identified by the slight bulge in their top shirt pocket. Invariably, this contains a sturdy zip-lock plastic bag which is reserved for later use during the flight. Almost always near the end of a counting session as the chopper settles on the ground, the bag is rapidly deployed to receive that morning's breakfast. It always fascinates me to see how many rangers eat diced carrots for breakfast. Maybe Jiffy could manufacture 'game ranger sick-bags' that aren't see-through, perhaps in khaki or camouflage ... and, of course, they would have to be biodegradable.

Riding in the jump-seat of the chopper and low flying for hours with the doors removed is for most a once-in-a-lifetime opportunity. Choosing who gets to ride is difficult, as there have been times when the occupant of this seat has had a noticeable effect on the outcome of the count. On one such occasion there was an inexplicable blip in the data, an unaccountable buck in the trend (no pun intended). It was the year that a rather attractive young woman occupied the jump-seat between John and André. After a post mortem of that day's data we learned their focus was not where it should have been. Given the Freudian fact that men cannot concentrate on two subjects at once, this statistical hiccough was sympathetically put down to human error.

Easter is the Best Time

EVERY YEAR!

We are fast approaching what is arguably the most beautiful time of the year in the South African lowveld. The autumn months of April and May produce a climate that is hard to beat anywhere in the country, in Africa, in the world. In our neck of the woods, this usually translates into pleasant and comfortable weather conditions in which to view game and enjoy the bush. The days are clear and sunny, and are pleasantly warm as opposed to hot. Midday temperatures gently taper off as you approach sundowner time, cooling suddenly as the sun sets; yet, you won't find it cold enough to need more than a windbreaker to stay comfortable. When evening sets in, the fire in the boma becomes the focus of warmth and sustenance, and soon the soles of your boots get really warm as the flaming hardwood turns to glowing hot coal. Then it's time to sit back with a glass of your favoured tipple in hand, and take it all in.

Insect numbers start to dwindle. There's no more moth with your mouthful of merlot, and no supplementary squadrons of stinkbugs spicing up your starters. The boomslangs have beaten it back into the bush, bloated with a bellyful of bats that they slithered into your roof to get. There are fewer red veld rats to rasp through your vehicle's wiring harnesses. The Mozambique spitting cobra which these rodents attracted has now done its pest control job and is curled up out of harm's way at the bottom of the woodpile. Mambas are less active, and unless you have a late brood of squirrels in your roof, you're unlikely to see one until next season.

Oh yes, I'd say it's a good time to visit the bush.

Woken by the first francolin's harsh cackle, invariably the raucous Natal spurfowl, you don't mind, because the crisp fresh mornings fill you with eager anticipation. There's something to get up for, and for once, it's not to try and beat the traffic to work. You feel an urgency to get out early, before the game quench their thirst and seek shade.

As you head out, you cannot help but notice the myriad animal tracks, scuff marks and tell-tale signs in the soft sand on the roads. The detail is sharp, because there's not much wind to round off the edges at this time of the year. There is no dearth of information out there, and if you take the time to learn the language, it can be read like an early morning edition of 'Bush News'. Not only are the happenings and drama of the night before revealed, but important clues as to where to concentrate your search for big game can also be gleaned from this evidence.

The characteristically undulating topography of our reserve allows for some commanding views from which to survey the bush. Sitting quietly on one of the designated vantage points, or on a personal favourite, you watch as the pink haze of dawn gets brighter, the sun rises and the day begins. Sipping a mug of hot coffee and dunking a rusk, you plan your game drive route, the strategy of which may or may not be influenced by the lions you can hear roaring in the distance.

Only the wiliest of last season's youngsters have come through the lambing and calving season. Having survived the relentless attention of predators, they are beginning to hint at the promise of maturity. Wildebeest calves have begun to change colour, going from juvenile fawn to the darker grey-brown of the adult, and are now beyond their most vulnerable age. The longer they live, the wiser they get, which improves their chances of survival exponentially.

Impala youngsters have now grown by more than five times their birth weight in less than three months, and have all but lost their gangly-legged cuteness. The adult bulls and rams prepare for the coming rut, which peaks in May or thereabouts, and will spend most of the day eating, rapidly putting on condition now, because later there's going to be no time for eating when the serious stuff starts. The grass begins turning the colour of ripe wheat, reaching maximum protein content, which provides the nutrition necessary to help hedge against the lean winter months that are just around the corner.

Tamboties are among the first to show that autumn is approaching, their leaves turning a deep red. Bush willow leaves begin to pale, never quite turning the classic deep autumn orange, with their leaves remaining edible and nutritious late into winter, even eaten off the ground, as crisp and dry as cornflakes.

Dry, cool air also signals the start of the biltong season, and for those who secure supplies of this year's game biltong and *droë wors* at the local butcheries, or like to hunt and make it themselves, there isn't a better time of the year to do so. Having just come through the height of the growing season, the game is in excellent condition. This is the lowveld's harvest time in every sense of the word.

The Olifants River, having transported millions of tons of waterborne silt during the summer months, begins to fine off, running progressively clearer each day. The release of clear mountain water from the Blydepoort Dam supplements and maintains the flow right through the winter months. Large-scale yellowfish can now be clearly seen, their golden flanks glinting in the sun as they writhe and twist, gleaning minute invertebrates and algae off the water-worn river stones with their thick rubbery lips. Pel's fishing owls, fish eagles, otters and herons use this opportunity to maximum advantage. Fishing conditions couldn't be better. If you happen to be a keen fisherman, as I am, this is as good a time as any to take advantage of St Peter's Promise, that God does not subtract from a man's lifespan the time he spends fishing. Unfortunately, in order not to make a mockery of this pledge, no one is allowed to fish in the Olifants River, because we know that the crocodiles here have definitely not read the Gospel according to St Peter!

If you can tear yourself away from the bush during this time, why don't you head out to the coast or the mountains and wet a line ... what have you got to lose, except maybe a big one? It really is a good time to be outdoors anywhere in the country, whether you're searching for fish or game. Somehow, however, I suspect most of you would rather be in the bush thinking about fishing, than be fishing thinking about the bush. Similarly, I suspect you'd rather be in the bush thinking about golf rather than playing golf thinking about the bush, even though I am told golf is a different ball game altogether. But nothing can compete with Olifants around Easter.

Orphaned Rhino

The planned relocation and establishment of the three white rhino to Olifants North was going to take place later than planned. This was mainly due to the delay in the construction of the rhino holding pens on the North. Essentially, this posed no major problem as the selected rhino had already been captured and placed in our old pens at Sable Dam, and after five weeks had settled in well. My only concern was that they be moved in cool ambient temperatures. The longer the delay, the closer we moved the relocation date to December, so the hotter it would get and the riskier the operation would become. Consensus from both Olifants North and South was that the transfer should take place sooner rather than later, so every effort was made to speed up the erection of the holding pens on the North.

Having got two of their five pens ready, I suggested we move the rhino into the two that had been completed, and continue with completion of the other three at our leisure. The rhino would soon get used to the building activity and settle down.

At 4.30 am on 16 December 2003, the capture team arrived and preparations were made to move the rhino across the river. The bull we had named Tweedledee would be loaded first. The cow and her teenage bull calf would be loaded next. Everything was going according to plan until Johann Myburgh, the capture team leader, called me to the pen holding the cow and her young bull calf. He pointed to something that looked like a wet warthog. The salmon hue of the early dawn light hadn't quite penetrated the interior of the pen, so it took my eyes a while to focus. When

I realised what I was looking at I went numb ... it was a new-born rhino, not more than a few hours old. 'We can't move these anywhere,' Johann said.

To disturb the cow in any way might cause her to stand on and crush the baby. So we proceeded to load the bull as quietly as possible – well, as quietly as one can load a rhino bull. Tweedledee was safely transferred and relocated to the two pens on Olifants North. Although we felt disappointed that all three rhino could not have gone across at once, the members of Olifants North were even more disappointed, given their unbounded enthusiasm for the project.

The cow, her teenage calf and his tiny little brother were to be released back on their home turf that afternoon at 5 pm. The pen doors were quietly opened and the release left to take place passively. To minimise the risk of injury in the narrow gangway, the rhino had to move out in their own time and with no encouragement.

Mark Wolter, out on a game drive that evening, put out a general radio message to say that he had found a large lion and a lioness at Sable Dam. Knowing that our two pride males had been witnessed trying to catch baby rhino a few months previously at Hide Dam, I naturally feared the worst. Sable Dam is only about 300 metres from the pens, so it was logical that once out of the pens, the rhino would make for this waterhole for a drink and possibly a mud wallow at the inlet. Given Sable Dam's popularity with rhino and the fact they hadn't had a mud bath in over five weeks, this scenario was almost a certainty. I decided to go out and check on the situation.

Clad in a T-shirt, shorts and a pair of slip-slops, I grabbed a small torch and drove out to the pens. It was about 9.30 pm when I approached Sable Dam. Other vehicles had responded to Mark's call and were now following the lions as they moved off in the direction of Rhino Pan, away from the pens. Although relieved, I wasn't completely satisfied, as no one had been back to the pens since the doors were opened at 5 pm, so I decided to go and see if the rhino had managed to move out on their own. Arriving at the pens, my headlights made out the grey flank of an adult rhino moving in the bush outside the main enclosure. This was really encouraging! I quietly made my way to the entrance of the pen; using the torch, I threw a low beam virtually at ground level. Light being cast over tracks at an angle like this helps to lengthen and increase visibility of the shadows, making the impressions stand out more clearly. The reverse of this, incidentally, is tracking when the sun is high in the sky, when discerning impressions is relatively far more difficult. Now I needed to make sure that the rhino tracks outside the entrance had come from the pens and not just from an inquisitive outsider.

Satisfied that they had left the enclosure, I decided to close the doors of the pen. There's nothing like the idea of bumping head-on into a rhino cow and her calf in a passageway 1.2 metres wide to keep you focused, so as a precaution, I shone the beam of the torch through the gaps between the upright poles forming the pen walls. At first, I saw nothing. It was eerily quiet, with the shadows cast by the poles making it difficult to see clearly. Then, something in the peripheral light caught my eye; I focused the beam directly on the apparent movement and my heart sank into my slip-slops. It was the baby rhino! I hoped to see a large protective mother's head appear in the gap any second, but it didn't materialise.

The realisation dawned that the mother had abandoned her calf. I reacted instinctively: if I could get the little chap outside the pen, the rhino I saw in the bush might be his mother, and she might be hanging around and would return for him. Anyhow, I had to give it a try. Walking up to the baby rhino, I placed the torch in my mouth and began to move him towards the exit some 40 metres away. This was easier said than done. I remember thinking how loose his skin was and how warm the little body felt. I also remember that the more I shoved him, the more he fearlessly shoved me back. He used his little stump, where one day a formidable horn would grow, in surprisingly powerful upward thrusting movements. His excellent aim made me wish I had a cricketer's box in place, and I wondered how I'd explain the bruising in that area to Meagan. His huffs and puffs, punctuated with the occasional squeal, didn't help matters either; visions of an enraged rhino cow coming to his rescue gave me the extra strength to try and get this over with as quickly as possible.

To make matters worse, the dung and urine that covered the floor area combined to make for a very slippery surface indeed. I soon slipped right out of my slip-slops, which are, incidentally, useless in the bush. If they were bio-degradable I would have gladly left them there to rot.

Now barefoot and covered in you-know-what, I was the epitome of some poor unfortunate standing too close when, as the saying goes, 'the s**t hits the fan'. Nonetheless, I eventually managed to get the little guy to the entrance. Now it was my turn to huff and puff. Although I imagined myself reasonably fit, the rhino, which was less than one day old, stood there defiant and committed to an apparently endless game of 'you shove me, I shove you back'. Fairly quickly, I became exhausted. Leaving the rhino outside the pen, I closed the entrance to the passage with a large pole, climbed into the Cruiser and drove away. A concerned Meagan tried to console me when I arrived back home at about 11 pm – albeit from a distance of two metres and with her nose curled up. Ah well, it's the thought that counts.

After a good bath, tired as I was, I expected to fall asleep quickly, but I couldn't. Concerned about the rhino, I was unable to sleep, tossing and turning, much to Meagan's annoyance, so I decided to go back and check on him. It was now 3.30 am. Arriving at the entrance to the pen, there was no sign of the rhino calf. Thinking positively and admiring the strength of motherly instinct, I approached the enclosure confidently. Stepping over the pole I had lodged in the entrance to the passageway, I made my way to the door to the pen itself, this time with a large torch and wearing a decent pair of boots. I swung the torchlight around the empty space of the first holding pen. As the light penetrated the far dark corner, it fell on a familiar shape and there, curled up fast asleep, was the baby rhino. He had jumped over the pole I had used to block the passageway and made his way back into the pen where he felt safe. There was no 'ag shame, how cute,' just my immediate resignation to the fact that this rhino's life now depended entirely on human intervention. Faced with this responsibility and the need to make decisions and act quickly, the process began.

Despite the urgency, we thought it unfair to wake anyone at four in the morning. An hour later, we thought it totally fair, so I phoned our game capture operator for advice on to whom we could take the rhino. His immediate answer was, 'Karen Trendler'. Karen is world-famous for her rehabilitation work, in particular for her success in rearing orphaned or injured rare species, including black rhino.

We gave Karen another half an hour to sleep and then Meagan woke her. Without hesitation she accepted. Then, as now, I was reminded what a wonderful person she is; the world can do with a few more like her. As Karen's Care Centre is on the other side of Pretoria, we had to make suitable preparations for the seven-hour journey. An hour later, we had the rhino comfortably crated and Meagan and I comfortably stocked up with coffee and sandwiches, so we headed for Pretoria. As apprehensive as we were about the well-being of our cargo while in transit, we were also looking forward to seeing Karen again, as the last time we'd seen each other was in Botswana's Tuli Block in 1984.

Concerned about hypoglycaemia, I telephoned veterinarian Dr Pete Rodgers of Hoedspruit, and asked if he would please give the baby rhino a quick once over. Perhaps he would recommend a mild tranquilliser for the journey, or whatever he thought appropriate. When he heard the predicament we were in, he suggested we save ourselves a long journey and take the rhino to Kapama. He had been their full-time vet for years prior to opening his own successful practice, and thus had first-hand knowledge of their capabilities. 'Kapama Game Reserve has an excellent track record of rearing orphaned wild animals, particularly young rhino, and they have all the necessary facilities,' he said.

We couldn't ignore his advice. We thought that Karen was the best, but the reality was that she was seven hours' drive away. We decided that as we had to drive right past Kapama to get a permit from the Department of Environmental Affairs, we would give it a go, and arranged to meet Pete at the rehabilitation facility on the reserve.

The fact that Pete offered his personal assurance of his commitment to the veterinary care of the rhino was also a major deciding factor. The reception at Kapama was overwhelming. The little rhino was treated like it was the last one alive. It was then moved into what I can only describe as a stable, in which I would be happy to sleep ... something akin to the cosy, welcoming environment Joseph and Mary came across a couple of thousand years ago, except now complete with infra-red lamp and a sheep for companionship.

An enthusiastic Juliette Ersdick, as pretty as she is dedicated, would be in charge of the rhino's care. Taking it in shifts with other trained staff, they would bunk down with the little rhino as it would need regular feeding and monitoring. Pete examined him and gave the thumbs up. Seeing the team fussing over the orphan, Pete and I quietly agreed that in our next life we would like to come back as an orphan rhino at Kapama ... we could lose the sheep, though.

'Roger', yes, 'Roger the Rhino', as he is now known, is doing very well indeed, thanks to the dedication of Kapama's staff and their excellent facilities.

FOOTNOTE

It is well known that white rhino calves run in front of their mothers, while black rhino calves run behind or follow. It is feasible, then, that white rhino calves not only run or walk in front of their mothers, but that they may actually lead them. We suspect this is probably what happened when the rhinos were released from the pens. The cow may not have had enough time to firmly bond with the new calf while the existing bond between her and her 'teenage' calf was still intact. When the doors were opened, he simply led his mother out of the pen – and in so doing, she inadvertently left little Roger behind. Little Roger, being instinctively a leader and not a follower, stayed put. Why then did we not leave them in the pen to establish the vital cow/calf bond? There is no simple answer, except that the risk of injury to such a small, delicate animal in the confines of a small pen was high, and this overriding concern outweighed other considerations.

Black Rhino

HISTORY IN THE MAKING, 2009

When Ron Thomson, well known conservationist and author, visited Balule a few years ago, he was quite taken with the rugged Commiphora woodland and broken hilly terrain that the Olifants River ran through. This habitat, which makes up approximately 40 per cent of the reserve's total area, features a rich variety of *Acacia* and *Grewia* species, the latter forming thickets and stands wherever the soil was a little deeper. For the most part the substrate is characterised by rock-strewn valleys and undulating terrain with relatively shallow soils. Hard country even by African standards, though the world's biggest waterbuck are found here, but this is not what intrigued Ron. He recognised something about this bush that none of us were aware of. He could see the excellent potential of this area for black rhino, so much so, that he said a more suitable habitat for black rhino would be difficult to find in the lowveld.

Although Ron had spent an enormous amount of time studying these animals in Zimbabwe, his assessment of our area with regard to suitability for black rhino was based on gut feel, his knowledge of their habitat preference and what he had seen driving around the reserve rather than specific research in the Balule area with this prospect in mind. Little did anyone know at the time that years later his ecological prophecy based on his experience, keen observation and evaluation would be unequivocally endorsed by the experts on what constitutes good black rhino habitat … the rhino themselves!

Recently a unique opportunity to exchange two black rhino

313

bulls for three white rhino was presented to the APNR. Three of the four reserves making up the association, namely Timbavati, Klaserie and Balule, would each offer one white rhino. A simple enough exchange, but we're not talking about marbles for peanut butter sandwiches here. For this to happen as planned would require the special effort of dedicated professionals – but even this initiative was influenced by politics, which always have a way of interfering. Sometimes this can be a good thing; mostly though it isn't, so it was understandable that a high-profile project such as this would elicit some political debate.

Where should the rhino be released, on which reserve – and more specifically, on whose property? The wardens, on the other hand, were more concerned with the practicalities; we needed to decide whether the rhino should be penned in bomas for a while prior to release, or simply be 'wild released'. Fortunately, in consultation with the veterinarians tasked with the co-ordination of this introduction, the decision was made easier when we adopted a pragmatic approach, focusing primarily on the release method in the best interest of the rhino themselves.

Olifants offered our 20-year-old but serviceable rhino pens for this purpose if the rhino were to be penned. The consensus among the wardens and the veterinarians involved was that the rhino should be wild released. Looking objectively at the bigger picture and the value to conservation in the APNR, the wardens and non-landowners were in the best position to make the necessary decisions on the ground. Kudos to Colin Rowles, the warden of Klaserie, who played a leading role in the co-ordination of this project and for choosing the release sites with total impartiality. They would be released in the southern part of the Klaserie, far enough from Kruger and yet central to the three biggest of the four reserves in the APNR. From here the rhino could choose to fan out into the greater area without obstruction, in whatever direction they chose. In hindsight, this was the correct decision, as the rhino have made up their own minds and have decided without any unnatural interference.

Finally all the t's were crossed and all the i's were dotted and the day, or rather the night, arrived. The two black rhino had endured the ten-hour journey from Swaziland to the Klaserie safely and in good health, thanks to constant monitoring of this precious cargo by two of the industry's most capable vets. We were on tenterhooks awaiting the actual arrival and even though we were sent a whole series of text messages updating us every hour of their progress, the journey seemed to take forever.

Coincidentally, one of the Olifants shareholders, Janine Scorer, had invited Karen Trendler up to the reserve for the weekend. Even though the road journey up from Johannesburg had been long and tiring, she jumped at the opportunity to witness conservation history being made. Karen has reared so many orphaned black rhino calves, she's lost count. It was a privilege to have her there to be part of the release of animals with which she has such empathy.

The rhino were released in the Klaserie Nature Reserve on the farm Copenhagen, at two separate locations approximately four kilometres apart, not too far from the old Enoch's Gate (a primary access gate to Olifants that was closed 17 years ago). In an atmosphere belying the significance of what was happening, the two rhino were gently released and quietly left to explore their new home. A couple of days later, the younger of the two bulls moved straight into Balule down the Brakspruit (Mohlabetsi) riverbed and under the train bridge onto Drifter's and Ukhosi. After a few more days there, he moved across onto Olifants near the old Lion Pan, then down to Nature's Valley, from which he strolled onto the floodplain of the Olifants River. He then walked past lodge 56 and back onto Ukhozi.

Possibly the lack of mud wallows in the vicinity prompted the rhino to move further west where there was a higher waterhole density as well as suitable habitat. The younger bull has been relatively easy to follow as its radio telemetric transponder is working well, while the older bull's does not work at all. Nevertheless, the movement of the older bull has been monitored by trackers on foot, who take up the spoor each day from the last waterhole visited by the rhino.

And, in case you were wondering, yes … the sightings of black rhino have been officially recorded in Olifant's game sightings register at reception – twice so far!

On 27 May, nearly a month after their release, I received a call from Colin to say the older bull that they had been tracking on foot had now moved onto Olifants near the bottom end of Lisbon under the Four Pylons, heading for the Sable Dam/Rhino Pan area. After visiting Hide Dam and Nkonkoni Dam, the rhino moved to Sable Dam and then a couple of days later moved south past the old rhino pens and across our cutline onto Venice.

As I write we have received confirmation that this bull has crossed the railway line road heading west along the Brakspruit riverbed ... incredibly this was the identical route the younger one took two weeks previously! The latest position on the younger rhino is that it appears to have settled in the Olifants west/Ukhozi area, near the old main gate. This appears to be where the older bull is now heading – the very heart of the habitat that years ago Ron Thomson had said was ideal black rhino country.

A little more about these wonderful creatures. Black rhino *Diceros bicornis* are smaller than their 2 200 kg white cousins, in fact, they are approximately 900 kg lighter, weighing in at a maximum of 1 350 kg. To get a better idea of this proportionately, consider that a big buffalo bull can weigh about 900 kg. Other obvious differences are that the black rhino holds its head higher than the white and I also noticed the other day how relatively big and more rounded the black rhino's ears are, a dead give-away to its position in the thick winter bush. As far as I'm concerned that's all I have to see of the animal to confirm it's a black rhino.

Although black rhino can go for a few days without drinking and will travel up to 28 kilometres to water, they love to wallow and if water is available will drink daily. Contrary to popular belief that they are more content living a solitary existence, they are also known to enjoy semi-social acquaintances, as do white rhino, and up to 13 have been recorded in one group. Their lifespan and gestation periods are similar to the white rhino's, 35–50 years and approximately 16 months respectively. I'm not forgetting they are supposedly more aggressive than the white rhino, although the couple of times we've come across the two new recruits their response appeared to be one of curiosity rather than aggression. It may be possible that they were still feeling some of the residual effect from the tranquillisers.

Black rhino are primarily browsers with pointed prehensile lips which are perfectly adapted to their feeding habits. They are able to utilise over 200 species of plants, showing a preference for leguminous herbs and shrubs.

It is interesting to note that they also have a penchant for Tamboti, *Spirostachys africana,* and are also able to utilise certain *Euphorbia* species, both plants that have a toxic latex. The square-lipped white rhino is essentially a grazer, which has historically confined this species to specific habitat types and a narrow distribution range with a mean rainfall of 500 mm per annum. Black rhino, on the other hand, enjoy a much wider distribution in Africa, being more versatile, and able to inhabit rugged desert habitats which, with the exception of goats and camels, are unsuitable for domestic stock. Early records by ivory hunters and explorers verify this, indicating that they occurred in healthy numbers and were encountered frequently in a wide range of habitats. Sadly, mainly due to poaching and poor conservation administration in the countries to the north, the tables have turned completely. White rhino numbers are steadily climbing in South Africa while black rhino numbers are threatened and declining rapidly elsewhere in Africa.

Coincidentally, whilst writing this chapter, I received a call from Ian Black, one of our shareholders and a keen conservationist who has close ties with the veterinarians working for 'Back to Africa'. This organisation is mainly concerned with the re-establishment of rare and endangered animals to their former homes and countries. They had recently brought in two black rhino that were born and bred in the Berlin zoo to be released in Tanzania, where they were now virtually extinct in the wild. How sad that a country which not too long ago had thousands of these animals has now sunk to this level. At the same time, it's so encouraging to hear of committed organisations really contributing to the re-establishment of threatened species.

Leaving a Bloodline – Legacy or Liability?

I know an Englishman who is the quintessential exemplar of tradition, and who has been a good friend of the family for a number of years. He is also an accomplished author on the history of the Fens, having written two books on this interesting area in the heart of Lincolnshire. Prior to the ban on fox hunting, he was master of the hounds for the Fitzwilliam pack, so I suspect that the breeding of dogs and horses had always been an important part of his life, and may have influenced his philosophy and preoccupation with tradition and bloodlines. So, when on one of his visits to Africa Rex Sly told me the most important thing we can leave behind when we die is a bloodline, I put this down to melancholy contemplation lubricated by a couple of rather stiff gins as we watched the sun set on another beautiful day in the bush. However, he elaborated, saying that although the importance of leaving the legacy of your family name when you die appears to be less of an issue these days, he firmly believes it is a most worthy duty. Having said this, he also said it is a quest fraught with obstacles, as if sent to test the worthiness of the continuance of the very name itself, and as things go, it all starts by having a son. No further thought was given to this, until something happened not too long ago that had his words ring in my ears.

Meagan and I were seriously beginning to doubt our ability as parents. Our son Dino was just a toddler when he fell and badly injured his little toe on the pathway from the house to the office. He had wandered down on his own looking for Mom, which prompted us to fence the yard, not to keep the lions and elephant out, but to keep the happy wanderer in! Not long after this, on a trip to the highlands to do a spot of fishing, he dropped out of his seat restraints into the steeply cambered gutter of the main street in Lydenburg. We picked him up out of the street as quickly as we could, collected his things and awkwardly bundled the now crying child into our arms. The 'drop' didn't go unnoticed; a crowd of bystanders had already gathered at the scene, most of them curious, some concerned. However, the look of disdain we got from a couple of middle-aged women, who by all appearances were experienced mothers, and who had probably given birth to and raised at least a dozen children single handedly, was hurtful. In a small conservative town where sex is frowned upon because it may lead to dancing, the cry of an infant elicits more than a casual interest; it was as if the residents knew the cry of every baby, and here was the sound of a strange child that needed investigation. No one laughed when I tried to make light of the situation and joked that we were thinking of calling him 'Guttersnipe'.

It took another two years to realise we weren't entirely to blame for the mishaps that befell our son.

Now a little older, but still not quite ready for school, Dino would accompany Meagan and I when we attended board meetings in Johannesburg. We would also use this opportunity to take a couple of days' leave, do a little shopping and catch up with family and friends. Dino really looked forward to these Jo'burg trips, it was a time to play on the escalators at the mall, and to meet up with his cousin Gareth and his friend Greg, who were about the same age. This particular trip was planned to coincide with the Reserve's annual general meeting in June of that year. We were invited by Greg's parents, Alistair and Michelle McKenzie, to stay with them in their charming home situated in their village of Kosmos near Hartbeespoort dam. We'd stayed there on previous occasions and loved it. Besides the McKenzies' congenial warm hospitality, the location made it the perfect base for Meagan and me; it was also ideal for Dino as he and Greg really enjoyed each other's company and would play together in relative safety for hours on end. This sleepy hollow is situated in a semi-tropical zone and most of the houses have beautiful, well-established indigenous gardens creating a comfortable country feel, yet it is less than an hour's drive from the city centre. ... And, oh yes, this was also where residents have seen the odd leopard in their gardens from time to time. These beautiful animals come down from the surrounding hills occasionally, and besides the odd stray cat or dog that is taken, the majority of their prey is confined to small antelope, rock hyraxes and ground birds, which are abundant. To date there have been no incidents of leopard having posed any physical danger to people in the area. But I digress – back to Dino.

Being a year older, Greg was already attending crèche until midday, so until he came home Dino had a few hours to while away each morning. Having done the escalators and walked the busy malls to his heart's content, we thought it was time to do something else, something less mindless, and something he could learn from. Then I remembered the Hartbeespoort Dam snake park close by, where as youngsters we would bring in snakes we had caught in the surrounding areas or rescued from being stoned in chicken coops. Turning to Meagan, I said it would be interesting to visit the park after all these years. I'd also heard they now had a wider variety of reptiles as well as many other interesting animals, and was sure that Dino would not only find it fascinating, but also learn a thing or two.

Midweek is usually the perfect time to visit these parks. You basically have the place to yourself and if you get there early you will often get to see management and staff at work as they go about feeding, cleaning cages and moving animals. We have also found that with fewer people around the staff are generally more amenable to answering questions from curious kids.

We arrived at the ticket office very early on a cool Tuesday morning, and although everything was still closed we could see someone inside shuffling a few papers around and fiddling around with keys 'n things. Then a minute or so later the window slid open and a man with a cheery face greeted us

'Good morning, how many tickets?' he said

Meagan had noticed that children under 12 were half price. 'Two and a half,' she said, sliding our credit card across the grubby counter.

'Sorry, we don't take cards, cash only'

I turned to Meagan: 'How much cash do you have on you?'

Scratching in her handbag amongst the usual paraphernalia necessary to keep a child clean, hydrated, medicated, fed and occupied, she managed to assemble enough loose change for the tickets. Collecting the change and placing the tickets in her bag, she turned to me: 'Where's Dino?' she asked.

As if in answer to her question, a scream from inside the snake park left us in no doubt of his whereabouts; his cries filled the early morning air, obliterating any peripheral sound; there was nothing else my hearing would allow into my brain. Apparently my reaction time could have been measured in split seconds; despite this I was numb with fear, but not paralysed by it, and I distinctly remember how slowly everything appeared to be happening. I will never forget that even though I was wearing top-of-the-range running shoes, I found myself wishing I was barefoot, because it felt like the technical cushioning of the shoes was too spongy and slowing me down. I just couldn't get to the source of the scream fast enough … and worse, I could hear Dino but couldn't see him.

If my memory serves me right, the open-air demonstration pit was approximately 30 metres from the ticket office and entrance. The structure consisted of an oval pit which covered an area of some 40 square metres which had been sunk about one-and-a-half metres below the surrounding ground level. A well-tended short grass and boulder-strewn island of about 15 square metres, encircled by a one metre wide dry concrete moat, was located in the middle. It was on this island that the snakes were kept and where the snake venom milking demonstrations and educational talks were held. This was usually done on weekends while spectators watched in awe and wonder while standing safely behind the chest-high wall surrounding the pit.

Reaching the pit, I leaped up onto the perimeter wall and lay with my torso on the broad lip. Looking down I could see

Dino sitting on the edge of the island; how he had ended up in this predicament was also clear to see. Having climbed up and onto the polished surface on the top of the wall, he must have slipped off the lip and fallen into the pit, landing on the concrete. Thankfully he took quite a tumble and hurt himself when he fell, otherwise he would not have cried out when he did. The worst realisation was that if he wasn't compelled to stay in one place crying and hurt, I know he would have gone exploring the island, which was littered with at least a dozen poisonous snakes. Fortunately there were no snakes on the relatively cold concrete surface of the moat where Dino had landed. The cool weather of the previous evening had kept them confined to the grass, where they lay around waiting for the sun to warm things up.

He was still crying miserably and only stopped when he looked up and saw me reaching out to him.

'Grab daddy's hand!' I yelled, trying hard not to focus on the huge snouted cobra that lay less than an arm's length away from him. These relatively thick-set cobras can attain a length of well over two metres and are amongst the largest and heaviest in Africa. In addition, the venom of this species is potently neurotoxic. Two puff adders as thick as a man's forearm, which if stretched out would have measured at least a metre, lay dead still and tightly coiled only a little further away. Their blunt arrow-shaped heads belied their lethal weaponry, which comes in the form of 20 mm long hypodermic fangs capable of injecting potent cytotoxic venom deep into their victims. Although sluggish movers, puff adders have the fastest strike rate of any snake, measured at nearly 20 metres per second! … Even an experienced Indian snake charmer could never pull back from that, so what chance would a child have?

Holding onto the lip of the pit wall with my left hand and reaching in, my lower abdomen on the rim to make up the reach necessary, I grabbed hold of his outstretched arm and yanked him out of the pit in one smooth adrenalin-powered pull.

Placing Dino on the relative safety of the pathway, we removed all his clothing to check for fang marks. This was also a good opportunity to check that nothing got damaged in the fall, but it wasn't easy – Meagan and I were fumbling for the same buttons and zips, but once we had our shaking hands under control we were able to check his naked, shivering little body for damage. There were no visible marks on him, well, not at that stage anyway. A few moments later, when I involuntarily smacked his backside in a knee-jerk reaction telling him to never just run off like that again ... the red hand-print was now as clear as a tattoo on his white but slowly-turning-blue-from-the-cold bottom. This time, however, he didn't cry.

Only the largest specimens of snouted cobra and puff adder were used in the snake pit arena, both for crowd appeal and to collect the highest volume of venom. Also I suspect that the larger snakes are easier for the handlers to see, enabling them to keep an eye on them when they moved about demonstrating the milking technique or giving an educational. Had Dino been bitten by one of those cobras, he would have died in minutes. The puff adders were also so big that the sheer volume of their venom injected into a child of his size would have overwhelmed his system before any treatment was possible. The nearest hospital was in Pretoria, over an hour's drive away, and nobody at the snake park at that time of the morning was qualified to administer antivenom. Had Dino been bitten by either species, he would have died!

Besides the park staff going about their routine daily chores, we were still the only visitors in the park. We decided to move away from the reptile section and progress to the area where the big cats were kept. They're always interesting, but I particularly wanted to see the rosettes on the black leopards, which would be clearly visible with the morning sun on their coats. On our way to the leopards, we stopped at the lions. There were two barred cages, each housing a pair of magnificent lions: in the one there were two beautiful 'Kalahari lions' and in the other, a pair from the lowveld. The only difference I could make out was that the one male had a darker mane than the other. I also recall being totally unimpressed with the housing of these enormous carnivores, but impressed with the size and condition of the lions. The cages were the old prison bar type enclosures, where the animals would typically pace back and forth in front of the bars all day, but these lions weren't pacing, in fact three of them were lying sleeping on the rock ledges which had been built in to create a little more of a natural environment.

The large black-maned male was lying on the floor up against the front of the enclosure, one of his enormous paws sticking out through the bars. With his eyes closed lying there asleep, he looked like a huge house cat in the morning sun. Although the invitation to reach out and stroke him was enticing, we knew better, nobody in their right mind would ever dare ... Except Dino, that is. The incident at the snake pit all but forgotten, he was now straining against the protective railings in an effort to get closer to the lion, something I guessed most kids would do. However, when he began reaching out as far as his short little arms would stretch to try and touch the lion's paw, I picked him up, put him on my shoulders and turned to Meagan: 'That's the last straw, let's get the hell out of here before the Cesare bloodline in Africa ends with us today!' I said.

Elephant Field Tests a Tyre

AUGUST 2003

There are aspects of man's modern throwaway society which have disgusting side effects on wildlife, I have seen warthogs living near human habitation with pieces of PVC piping stuck on their legs, usually just above the hoof. This is a result of the animals stepping through off-cuts as they rummage around feeding. Their predicament becomes more life-threatening as the animal grows and, if not removed in time, will result in a painful build-up of pressure due to impeded blood flow. The final outcome can be the eventual loss of the hoof, infection and possibly even death. I have seen photos of a tree monitor with its head stuck inside a tin can which, had it not been removed, would have caused the animal to die a slow death from starvation. The list of man's garbage finding its way into the environment causing untold damage to wildlife, particularly in our oceans, is seemingly endless. The following incident is a manifestation of our disgraceful disregard of the consequences of our thoughtless throwaway habits, and, horror of horrors, it happened right on our doorstep!

An elephant was observed to be wearing what appeared to be a tyre on its right front foot. It had been seen in the vicinity of our southern gate by a number of people entering the reserve and obviously required immediate intervention so was reported to the manager of the area to obtain authority to gain access to the elephant and then attempt to remove the hazard. The elephant had been seen on numerous occasions and all the feedback indicated that he did not appear to be suffering or to be unduly hampered by the tyre.

What was of concern however, was that not only was it un-natural and unsightly, but the elephant was a young animal, with some growing to do. The steel belts that reinforce the tyre would tighten as the diameter of the elephant's foot increased. This natural process would eventually impede blood flow, leading to complications that could well end up gangrenous.

As this animal found itself in this predicament as a direct result of man's pollution of the environment, we needed to intervene, and try to remove the tyre as soon as possible. Fortunately we were busy with a zebra capture operation at the time, and so had immediate access to a helicopter. I suggested we postpone the capture for a couple of hours and commission the pilot to locate the elephant. Once it was located, we could then bring in a vet, dart the elephant and remove the tyre.

Everyone agreed and the wheels were set in motion. The elephant, a young bull of approximately 18 years of age, was located not far from the reserve's railway gate and then was duly darted. The terrain through which he was now moving was very rugged, uneven and strewn with rocks. The elephant was running at a fair pace, and I was worried that he would trip and fall. Despite staggering and tripping over the rough ground as the drug started taking effect, he managed to stay upright until the toe of his back foot hooked the back of the tyre on his front foot and pulled it off, much like you would remove a muddy gum boot. After a few minutes he began slowing down until finally he stopped, staggered a little more, and then fell, stiff-legged, over onto his side.

While the elephant was tranquillised, we used the opportunity to take routine blood samples. Everyone present, mostly young students, had a unique opportunity to touch his rumpled skin and marvel at the delicate eyelashes blinking over hauntingly intelligent brown eyes. To see and feel such a massive animal up close for the first time is a memorable experience for anyone. Lying on its side, an elephant appears anything but the formidable icon of Africa that it truly is. It looks vulnerable, and, of course, it is just that in this situation.

As soon as the blood samples were taken and the necessary

checks completed, the elephant was revived and released. Within 30 seconds of the drug being reversed, he began to get up. A minute later he was on his way. He now leads a more natural life cruising around on his God-given all-weather slicks, with naturally self-replenishing tread which is 100 per cent bio-degradable, to boot. Later, we back-tracked the elephant to retrieve the tyre he had so unceremoniously removed. It was a radial ply Dunlop SP 73.

Olifants Rangers Versus Poachers Disunited

INSPIRED BY AN AUGUST 2001 NEWSLETTER

Any career, occupation or sport needs to be stimulating and challenging, especially if physically demanding and carried out in adverse conditions. Being a member of the anti-poaching squad on Olifants has its own challenges, its own highs and lows. The following illustrates the emotion these men have to deal with most often, and that is frustration.

Members of our anti-poaching team take their job seriously. Years of regular hot-pursuit action and less regular apprehension of poachers have kept both sides on their toes and this has honed our team into arguably the best anti-poaching squad in the area. Numerous awards and certificates of commendation bestowed upon this unit from the SAPS and DEAT bear ample testimony to this claim. On the other hand, this has also made our adversaries proportionately more wily.

The poachers have become like the black-backed jackals of the Free State and Northern Cape, which, after years of persecution, have adapted to their circumstances and developed survival skills far surpassing those of their game reserve cousins. This makes our task that much more difficult and we have to keep abreast of their latest devious techniques all the time. Frustrating as this is, it poses an ongoing challenge for our anti-poaching unit.

There is no one better on your side in the fight against poaching than an ex-poacher who has turned 'state's witness'. I have often thought about the poachers we've caught who are now in prison. Some of these men are experts in bush craft, and having them languish in prison is, to my mind, a waste of valuable bush knowledge. It would, surely, be worth developing a way to use these skills appropriately or pass them on to students in some way or another. The overall benefit to conservation could be significant.

Of course, those of them who are plain good-for-nothing bastards deserve being locked up for a long time, but these could be weeded out, I'm sure.

Outwitting the poachers, locating and removing their deadly snares, finding their supply caches and determining their probable escape routes are some of the challenges with which the team is routinely faced. Since the incident some two years ago when a poacher was shot and wounded by our patrol, poaching activities have slowed down somewhat, especially on our side of the river. But criminals are criminals and it appears that they have rather short memories. So, we can't become complacent.

Finding snares and bringing them in as tangible evidence of a successful anti-poaching patrol is getting more and more difficult. We have to maintain the sense of achievement and job satisfaction that comes with walking into the office after a couple of days' work with a collection of cable and wire snares that would hold back a Springbok rugby scrum. But, to achieve this sort of end result, our team has had to resort to hot-pursuit operations which sometimes take them beyond our boundaries.

No names, no pack drill, the tracts of state-owned land across the river, in the vicinity of the railway bridge, are targeted by poachers. Although the game density is relatively low, the threat to the few animals that do inhabit these areas, as well as those that move across the Olifants River during winter from our side and get snared, is not acceptable. Knowing that the poachers are plying their trade of deceit and destruction merely yards away, and being separated from our anti-poaching team by mere political geography, can be understandably frustrating at times.

The arrogance of the poachers was becoming increasingly apparent; these 'unproclaimed' tracts of land appeared to afford them a degree of safety, a false sense of security – and, dare I say it, they appeared to be treating this like a big game. This unsatisfactory state of affairs did not sit well with the anti-poaching team. Due to their dedication to keeping our area 'clean' and ensuring there was not too much of a build-up on the other side, they decided to go across and sweep the area, removing as many snares as possible. Although the situation was pretty well under control, our team couldn't take their eye off the ball, so to speak, so our anti-poaching measures had to be stepped up a notch or two. In addition, they would make their presence felt by conducting regular foot patrols, thus making it obvious to the poachers that they were not going to be allowed to re-group.

The majority of our anti-poaching patrols are conducted by pedal power. The rangers each have a bicycle of which they are extremely proud. Considering the rough terrain they need to cover and the constant maintenance needed, these bikes are kept in tip-top condition. The area on the other side of the river, however, is rougher still, with virtually no roads to speak of and mostly bush tracks and game paths, which makes foot patrols in this terrain more practical and effective than cycling. Once across the train bridge, the men would normally park their bikes and proceed on foot. These routine patrols were really working and for weeks there were only 'clean' patrols to report. It began to appear that our team was getting to the top of the league in this deadly game.

One evening just after supper, Meagan noticed there was someone at the back door, although I hadn't heard anyone knock. I opened the door to find our anti-poaching team standing there looking tired and dejected. Joachim Timani, one of my top anti-poaching rangers and a former officer in Mozambique's Frelimo army, came forward. Without lifting his eyes off his boots, he spoke.

'*Tina yenzile lo mastek*,' he said, which is Fanagalo for 'we have made a mistake'.

I went cold when I heard this, thinking they had shot another poacher, and by the expression on their faces, it didn't look like they had only wounded him this time. The dejected hang-dog look, the foot shuffle, the avoidance of eye contact and the body language usually meant really bad news. As the conversation went on and the full story came out, I lightened up, but held back the urge to burst out laughing, as this would only have added insult to injury.

What had happened this time round was that in this particular home game of Olifants Rangers against their traditional opponents, Poachers Disunited, the poachers had cheekily demonstrated new tactics and confidence to great advantage and had scored an away goal.

One of our ranger's bicycles had been stolen by a poacher. He had doubled back on their tracks like a wounded buffalo, then, finding where the bikes had been left, took one and pedalled off into the sunset. The poacher would no doubt brag to his friends about his newly won prize – and because it isn't a floating trophy, he would probably make full use of it in future poaching forays.

It wasn't a problem replacing the bicycle, but it would take more than money to restore the wounded pride of our team. However, a valuable lesson in the dangers of complacency was learned and they now lock their bikes together when they leave them unattended for any length of time.

I cannot help wondering what will happen when our team catches up with the bicycle thief one day. Knowing these men as I do, I only hope they remember that we are living in a democracy and that even bicycle thieves have rights to a fair trial. More to the point is that in today's justice system, carrying out the punishment happens after the trial and after sentencing as opposed to the traditional bush system, in which summary judgement and immediate punishment can be the norm.

Final score: Olifants Rangers 0 Poachers Disunited 1.

Lost in the Bush ...

FROM NOTES MADE IN THE LATE 1990S

It takes a while to get to know your way around the reserve, especially if you don't visit frequently. There are over 250 kilometres of roads and bush tracks making up the network on Olifants, and to the casual observer most of them look alike. To complicate things further, the vegetation growth changes from the way you remember things, which can make a quite dramatic difference from one season to the next. Long before, too long before the advent of GPS navigation, as a young ranger, whenever I drove or walked in unfamiliar territory, I always made a habit of making sure that before sunset I was in a specific area well known to me. When the light goes, so do all your reliable reference points. The shadows from your headlights or Q beam create strange and unfamiliar shapes which can throw your built-in direction finder way out of kilter. The bush can be daunting at the best of times, but at night it is especially so.

Although one can never get totally lost on Olifants, or any private reserve in the lowveld for that matter, it can be an extremely uncomfortable or embarrassing experience if you can't find your way home or back to camp. At worst, you may need to spend the night in your vehicle and try again in the light of day.

Late one Friday evening, I received a radio call from one of the shareholders, who said she was lost and needed assistance.

'Whereabouts do you think you are?' I asked. I then continued by being a touch more specific: 'What side of the railway line do you think you may be on?'

'I have no idea,' she replied.

I then told her to continue driving until she saw something un-natural or man-made, something like a name board or a pump, whatever. About ten minutes later, the radio burst into life again, and this time the voice had a lilt of optimism in it.

'I've found a sign,' she said excitedly, and repeated, 'I've found a sign on a tree!'

'Excellent!' I thought.

'What does the sign say?' I asked.

'Hang on, I'll go and have a look,' she said. A couple of min-utes later, still excited, she reported, 'The sign says *Lonchocarpus capassa* – Apple-leaf tree.'

I didn't know whether to laugh or cry, but knowing how it feels to be lost, I led her to believe she had found a huge clue, and would soon be out of the woods, if you'll pardon the expres-sion. I had a fairly good idea where the reserve's amateur bota-nist, Graham Vickers, had nailed most of these little green tree identification tags which he had printed. Unfortunately, though, there were at least a dozen apple-leaf trees out there with his tags on them. The good news was that at least she was still on the reserve, so it was back to gut feel and guesswork.

'Is there an open area close by, or are you surrounded by thick bush?' I asked.

'On my left there is a large open area and on my right it's very thick,' she replied.

The odds had improved, and I now had a rough idea where she was, but it was still a gamble. I told her to keep driving, keeping the clearing on her left, until she reached a junction. It proved to be a good guess, because before long she drove out onto the railway road. As this is the main access road into the reserve, it was familiar enough to allow them to get home … but it's not always as simple as that.

If you have ever had the experience of hearing an African lion roaring up close, I'm sure the following incident will get your sympathy and understanding. There is no animal sound on earth that commands a person's undivided attention like that of a lion's roar. It is difficult to believe that flesh and blood is capable of producing such an awesomely powerful sound. Once, in a disco, I had the misfortune to be trapped too close to one of those monster speakers. I could feel the sound waves hitting me each time a drum beat reverberated outwards. The same power and resonance produced by those enormous speakers is produced from a tiny little bone in a lion's throat – and to hear two lions roaring in unison is a humbling experience.

Whether you're a stockbroker from New York or a seasoned game ranger living among lions, the primeval fear and respect this sound evokes is indelibly tattooed on our DNA. Nothing else captures the ambience of wild Africa quite like it. Something is missing in my life if I don't hear the distant roar of lions at least a couple of times a week.

Depending on terrain, wind direction, humidity, and one or two other variables, a lion's roar can be heard by the human ear for up to eight kilometres and quite a bit further by other lions.

Early one evening, just as we were sitting down to supper, which is the precise time that chance and coincidence invariably combine, I heard some broken chatter over the radio. Even though I wasn't on duty that evening, I hadn't turned the radio off, and as it turned out, it was a good thing I hadn't. I was asked to help locate people who were stuck out in the bush with their vehicle broken down and no one, including themselves, knowing where they were. To add to their predicament, their battery was running low, and although they had managed to get one last message through over the radio, they still couldn't give us any idea of their location. Just before they lost all power, however, they said they were viewing lions. Their very last communication sounded ominous, that as it began to get dark the pride became bolder, moving closer all the time to the point that some of the lions had completely surrounded their vehicle. To add to the already tense situation, they said, the two large pride males were roaring.

I learned later that their radio hadn't received my response, which was that lions are naturally more confident at night, and also that the younger members of the pride can be very curious, but not to panic, keep noise and movement down to a minimum, and I was on my way. No power meant no light. It must have been terrifying for them, sitting in an open vehicle, not being able to see the lions, but able to hear them roaring a couple of metres away. Ironically this is what helped us find the stranded group and eventually rescue them. The only clue we had as to their location was that they were sitting with a pride of lions. We drove out to the highest central point on the reserve, switched off and sat quietly, listening for the lions to call. I reasoned that if we could locate them by homing in on their roars, we'd find the vehicle.

After 20 minutes we'd heard nothing except a couple of black-backed jackal serenading each other on the open plain below, so we decided to move on to the nearest prominent water point. Being winter at the time, there was a good chance the lions would not be far from a waterhole. But which one? There were five in the area to choose from. I made a calculated guess and headed straight for one of them. Switching the vehicle off the moment we arrived, we again sat in silence, waiting for the lions to call. This time we didn't have to wait long. Within minutes of stopping, they roared, and judging from the sound, the lions were approximately two to three kilometres away near one of the other waterholes. Most importantly, we now had both the direction and estimated distance. Stopping once more, we were guided even closer by the roaring lions, and now knew exactly where they were.

Shortly afterwards, the vehicle and its six hapless occupants were found, and as described, they were still surrounded by 11 lions, who lay around like overgrown golden retrievers waiting for someone to throw a stick. We managed to get the vehicle started and on the go again. I took a moment to explain that they should not use their one million candle power spotlights when the engine was turned off, otherwise they would flatten their battery and get stuck again. In a cautionary mood, I added, 'And next time, you may not be lucky enough to be surrounded by a pride of lion!'

Tannin: The Tree-saving Kudu-killer?

BASED ON A WARDEN'S REPORT MOTIVATING THE REMOVAL OF
FENCES – 2004

Somebody once said that game farming is actually veld or grass farming, with game being just by-products. This may be true to some extent, but whoever coined that phrase is probably of the same ilk as those who deride impala, regarding them as little more than 'goats of the bush', or is of the conviction that all you need to manage a game reserve is a rifle and a box of matches.

While specific statements or global generalisations may have some merit, they're usually simplistic and superficial. The functioning of a typical ecosystem is complex beyond our full understanding, and even the most basic ecological management requires the help of science. Odem, in his book *Fundamentals of Ecology*, finds it incomprehensible that space explorers plan to create self-sustaining life-supporting ecosystems in outer space, yet nobody fully understands the workings of a fish pond ecosystem here on earth!

Although we are not strictly a game farm here on Olifants, the following reminds us of the value of feed quality and the importance of veld management in terms of the available vegetation-to-animal biomass ratio, even in a relatively large reserve such as ours.

In the days prior to the removal of fences, we were obliged to supplement the winter feed for our rhino and so had stockpiled a huge store of lucerne expecting to feed them for a couple of winters. Buying early and storing the fodder can save up to 50 per cent on the cost price as demand increases dramatically later into winter. However, that season and the next, we'd received very good rains and so had no need to feed. By the time we needed to feed again, I was sure our old lucerne stocks would now be too dry to be of any value as feed for the rhino. To the eye it appeared to be unpalatable and possibly even unhealthy for them.

We decided to dump it on Kudu Plains near Hide Dam, and if the resident hippo and numerous other animals that frequented the area felt like a nibble – good ... if not, at least the termites would certainly use the cellulose. When the lucerne was initially left out in the bush, I didn't expect many animals to utilise it, but it was hard for me to simply destroy what may still have some food value; I'd seen too much suffering and starvation in drought years to become wasteful. So when a couple of rhino moved in to make use of this old fodder, I was amazed, particularly as there was still a fair amount of grass on the reserve, and much of it was still green. Once the word got out, every rhino on the property was happily munching away on this three-year-old lucerne within a few days. Why then was this dry and slightly mouldy old feed eaten in preference to what surely was, in our opinion, equally available and more palatable grass?

I believe the answer may lie in the fact that our assessment of palatability or nutritional value in relation to free-ranging wild animals is not as cut and dried as we would like to imagine. How are we able to determine palatability, particularly when deciding for palates other than our own? I have watched kudu eat over two kilograms of bitter aloe at a time and appear to enjoy it. Did you know there are people out there who eat and enjoy rhubarb! So, you see, there's no accounting for taste.

Many of you may be aware of the defence mechanism in plants and how this affects both the survival of the plant and that of the game that feeds on it. For interest's sake I have included a brief summary which also goes to show that sweetness and palatability may be relative. In desperation, animals will eat unpalatable and/or bitter vegetation in order to survive. This in itself is survival adaptation. But, if the bitterness is due to high levels of tannins, and they can tolerate the bitterness, it will be to their detriment. In harsh fact, if they continue to utilise this source of food, they will eventually die of malnutrition, which I will explain shortly. On the other hand, bitter aloe, for example, will provide nutrition because although the aloe is extremely bitter, it contains relatively little tannin. As a bonus, I suspect the ingestion of this plant may also help ward off disease-causing parasites which are more prevalent during times of stress.

About 25 years ago, the game farmers of the North West province found that their kudu were dying. Subsequent autopsies revealed that they had full stomachs containing green, apparently nutrient-rich vegetation. Mysteriously, this was happening even at lower-than-normal recommended stocking rates. Although the mystery has since been solved, this phenomenon had scientists dumbfounded for years. Fenced-in game farms were a relatively new and fast-growing concept and a lot of what was stocked in these areas depended on the all-important carrying capacity – which, depending on the veld type that predominated, was determined by the Large Stock Unit-to-hectare ratio, to which I refer in more detail in the chapter 'Management of game populations'.

The kudu-per-hectare ratio in these instances was within limits and in some cases, lower, according to this formula. Basically what was happening was the kudu that were now restricted by fences had to utilise the same vegetation, more specifically the same trees and shrubs, repeatedly over a short space of time. All trees and shrubs have a built-in protection mechanism against getting 'eaten to death'. When browsed on, they begin producing tannin, the amount being produced dependent on the type of plant and how vigorously it is being browsed.

The next time you watch a giraffe or kudu browsing, you will notice that they nibble for a while and then move on. Why do they not stand in one spot and nibble all the leaves off the bush or tree? The reason is the production by the plant of tannin, which occurs to a far greater extent in dicotyledons (woody plants) than in monocotyledons (grasses). One of the effects of tannin is that it discourages further feeding by making the leaves progressively more bitter and unpalatable the longer the animal feeds.

When confined to a smaller area, the availability and choice of shrubs and trees is reduced. This lack of choice forces kudu to browse the same bush or tree more frequently than they would have, thereby ingesting higher than normal levels of tannin. Were they able to choose alternative browse with lower tannin levels there wouldn't be a problem.

How then is this chemical responsible for the death of an animal? The ingestion of tannin has a dramatic effect on the digestive process in that it inhibits the enzyme and microbial action that helps break down the cellulose in the rumen. Thus the production of protein, and the absorption of protein in the gut, become severely inhibited. This process is vital in allowing nutrients to be released and absorbed by the animal. Simply put, if their rumens are filled with nutrients that cannot be absorbed, particularly proteins, they will paradoxically die of starvation with full stomachs.

The bottom line is that in fenced-in areas in particular, the carrying capacity has to be very carefully determined. What makes this extremely difficult is veld that appears lush to the eye, but which may not contain the nutritional requirements necessary to carry large numbers of animals on a continual sustainable basis. Without the possibility of rotational browsing, at intervals long enough to allow the tannin levels to drop, you have problems. Thus it is better to have fewer, but healthier, animals because they are able to derive maximum benefit from the vegetation, without the risk of losing condition or worse. The million dollar question is, 'how does one determine the optimum number?' Having slightly fewer, but healthier animals that are carefully monitored over time can provide some guidelines. However, as most of these farms are run as businesses, 'moderate' or 'minimal' are not words you hear that often in terms of stocking.

In summary, tannin is there to protect the browse from destruction by making it unpalatable and not by causing the death of browsers. In open systems I suspect that tannin-related deaths would be unheard of. However, it has been the result of man's confinement of high numbers of browsing animals in closed systems that has proved to be a fatal combination.

Witchdoctors!

BASED ON A WARDEN'S REPORT IN 2002

If it doesn't have a logical explanation, and/or cannot be scientifically substantiated, I don't buy it. I am particularly sceptical about those theological phenomena involving spirits or ghosts or anything to do with the supernatural and superstition. Yet, I am perfectly comfortable with the miraculous healing powers of certain plants and herbs if the claims are backed by science.

I suppose I have to admit that at times, I have been dragged kicking and screaming to a homoeopath, which to me is pushing my faith to its absolute limits!

I don't believe in witchdoctors, shamans or traditional healers. I never have and I doubt I ever will. By the same token, I don't underestimate the power that witchdoctors and sangomas and others of similar leanings, talents and positions, have over their followers. Nor do I underestimate the incredible faith some have in the often vile concoctions they're required to ingest, which are put together from pieces of unmentionables, and mixed with ground-up untouchables!

The respect these healers command and the results their muti mixtures produce, has to be seen to be believed. Recently, I used this unquestioned faith by believers in the power of the sangoma to help save a man's life.

A delegation of representatives of the Olifants work force asked me to convene a meeting to discuss a matter of grave concern. Among these men were my trusted and loyal anti-poaching rangers, game guards and security staff, as well as the formally elected shop stewards of our workers' union, in all twelve men. One of them, acting as spokesman, came forward and with a sombre expression I've not often seen on this man's face, got straight to the point and said that a member of our staff was changing into a baboon at night and entering some of the women's rooms. Even though the doors were locked, he reported, this baboon-man managed to get in and have his way with them.

'How does it get in?' I asked.

'Under the door,' he replied.

'That's impossible,' I said. 'It's far too narrow a gap for any-thing to squeeze through.'

'This baboon has magic powers and he gets in easily,' they in-sisted.

Now came the question I knew I had to ask, but was dreading. 'Do you know who it is?' I asked.

'Yes,' he replied and gave me the name of one of our most prominent members of staff, to whom I will refer as 'baboon-man' from now on.

He said that the rest of the delegation demanded that I chase him away or they would. I told them that in terms of the Labour Act there was no proof of any misconduct to warrant dismissal. This legalese fell on deaf ears, because they merely repeated their ultimatum and a standoff ensued.

To try and convince me how strongly they felt, they offered another means to confirm this man's guilt – and that was to consult a witchdoctor. This, they said, would weed out the guilty person and confirm their suspicions. I agreed to their proposal provided they were prepared to pay for the services of a sangoma as I knew they didn't do any pro bono work. As we were required to get an out-of-town witchdoctor, in an effort to ensure a measure of objectivity, I offered to help with the transport costs.

We managed to get two witchdoctors for the price of one, with the older man appearing to be the sangoma. He not only looked the part, but was considerably older than the other, though I didn't have the courage to ask whether the younger chap was an apprentice. I was just happy to get the 'bones rolling', so to speak. They negotiated the contract, comported themselves in a most professional manner and were punctual, arriving on time at the pick-up point in a late model Mercedes-Benz. Both men were dressed in modern suits, with their traditional garb being brought along in an old leather suitcase, like those used by wealthier travellers in the 'forties and 'fifties.

The mood amongst the staff back at the village was nervously apprehensive. Everyone believed in the power of the sangoma and they all knew the seriousness of what was about to unfold. As far as they were concerned, this was where the buck would stop.

Without too much delay, the two men emerged, both looking the part in leopard skin capes, feathered headdresses, wildebeest tail switches, sticks, bags of bones and bits and bobs off some animals I'd only ever seen in a museum. Then, in a well-rehearsed ritual, they stepped into the circle and began the chanting and bone-throwing almost immediately. They created quite a spectacle. Any twinge of guilt out in the crowd, however small, would show on the facial expression and in the body language of those subjected to the process, which would no doubt give them away. Even if only fractionally implicated, the fear and belief is so strong, that anybody knowing what to look for and watching for these signs would pick up subtle clues. I suspect that this was one of the main reasons why there were two witchdoctors so that while one ranted and chanted, the other observed the crowd. I remember thinking that this was an excellent strategy.

The wildebeest tail switches went swishing back and forth and up and down to the collective chant of '*Siavuma*!' Bones and other bits were thrown in a loose heap, accompanied by throaty, guttural words I couldn't make head or tail of. This must have gone on for the best part of an hour. Then suddenly, the tempo slowed, ending abruptly with a finger-pointing accusation that left no doubt as to who the sangoma had singled out. Surprise, surprise, it was the same man accused by the delegation a few days previously. There were no dramatics, just quiet acceptance, some head shaking and mumbling, nothing more. But the drama wasn't over. There was more to come.

Their job done, the two gentlemen, sweating profusely from their performance, began to pack up their gear. This they did slowly and with the same methodical indifference a plumber employs when he packs his tools away after unblocking your drain. Having showered and changed back into their suits, they came down to the office where I handed them their cheque for the agreed R3 500.

Thinking that wasn't bad for less than two hours' work, we drove them back to Hoedspruit. But, my problems, and particularly those of the baboon-man, were now further than ever from being solved.

Confirmation from the sangoma gave the staff confidence and renewed their determination: they were now adamant in their demands. They wanted this man gone, to which they added that if I didn't fire him, they would 'fire him' literally, using the infamous 'necklace' method! They were absolutely serious and I knew that unless something was done to stall them, they would act out their threat. This man's life was in real danger. Calling him into my office, I suggested he take leave and get off the reserve for a while until things cooled down.

By now I had established that there was, perhaps, some substance to some of the accusations against him, but it was certainly not serious enough to die for, or even lose his job over. He was adamant he was going nowhere, but asked for a ride into town, which I gave him.

Later that afternoon, he returned with the police, who sat down in reception. From there they sent for those who were threatening him to appear. They did not appear. Draining the two Cokes we had given them, they politely thanked us and then drove themselves to the village. Ten minutes later, leaving a substantial dust cloud behind them, they drove out, making their way straight back to Hoedspruit. What transpired, I later learned, was that the delegation had, in no uncertain terms, told the police to go home, that this was none of their business, and if they interfered they would be sorry.

At that point I knew I had better think of something, and quickly. It was a shocking revelation for management to see how little respect our people had for the police. I knew from the reaction of the police that we were on our own, and that the solution would have to come from within.

The next morning, I called everybody to a meeting, and everyone except the baboon-man turned up. I'd had enough of this threat of intimidation and savage injustice, so I laid it on the line for them. Knowing that the threat of criminal charges didn't seem to faze them, I still needed to make them understand that the consequences of their threatened actions would be very far-reaching.

Firstly, I let them know that they were not going to kill anybody on the reserve while I was in charge. Secondly, I reminded them that the shareholders had known this man for many years; he had watched their children grow up, and, I said, if you murder him, the shareholders would live in fear of you, and so, would not use your services.

'Think of it,' I said. 'How am I ever going to tell them the man guarding their lodge is a murderer, or the maid in their lodge was party to a gruesome murder?'

Suddenly the penny dropped. They asked me for an alternative solution to this problem. I told them to leave it with me for the time being and that I would get back to them soon. Although they agreed reluctantly, I had at least managed to buy some more time.

Even with these people of legendary patience, I knew that time was of the essence. I had to get help from someone who had first-hand experience with this sort of thing as soon as possible. Calling in a favour from an old friend in the forestry business, he put me onto a labour lawyer who dealt with tribal law issues, and who had knowledge of a similar case. What a relief this was, and when I was told of the possibility that a solution could be achieved by using another witchdoctor, to clean the 'dirty spell', I knew there was hope. This would cost another R3 000 or so, I was told, but that was the least of my concerns at that stage.

What was of real importance was that this fee had to be paid by the accused himself, as a demonstration of good faith and, I suspect, as an admission of guilt. So, I called in the baboon-man and put the proposition to him. He accepted without hesitation. I then approached the rest of the staff, who appeared relieved that there was a possible solution and that at least it involved the accused having to fork out a pile of cash. Most importantly, however, it included a witchdoctor's cleansing ritual.

The following day, our driver went to Ohrigstad to collect the 'cleansing' sangoma. Again for reasons of impartiality, he needed to be from as far away as possible, and we all agreed that 100 kilometres was far enough.

This witchdoctor was a younger man and proceeded without too much fanfare and paraphernalia. He was taken to some of the lodges at his request, on which he systematically performed a simple cleansing ritual. He then did the same in the staff village and compound area. The ritual appeared to be based on a mixture of water, a little soil, and something else from his bag of tricks; he then took small amounts of this potion and dabbed it on the door, while chanting a few words. Although this took a lot longer than the previous witchdoctors' two-hour ritual, he only charged R3 000.

I was surprised that no effort was made by the sangoma to consult with the baboon-man: surely logic dictated that this would be the first port of call? Anyway, I knew better than to question these things.

The following morning, the witchdoctor phoned the office to enquire if all was well. When we advised him that everything was fine, he simply replied, 'That's cool!'

We didn't really know how to interpret either that comment or the need for the phone call in the first place. I had difficulty believing it was a classic example of after-sales service, a follow-up from a true professional, rather positioning it as part of the mind games employed to perpetuate superstition, fear and belief to his own advantage. Being a sceptic, I also assumed he was checking up on the effect of the ceremony and the perceived value of his dubious muddy concoction. The reality was that the materials he used had no potency whatsoever in a physical sense.

Although I remain sceptically unconvinced of any of the individual elements employed by any of the witch doctors, they achieved results which neither I nor the police could achieve – and that's what mattered. Over time I have asked many believers and supporters of the role of the sangoma why witchdoctors have no effect on me whatsoever. The answer is always the same.

'But, you are a white man ...'

Signs of Elephant Running out of Space?

NOVEMBER 2005

When the elephant began moving into the Balule area, they did so with purpose, and although it wasn't a surreptitious infiltration, they were in amongst us before we could wipe the sleep out of our eyes. The majority of the population comprised breeding herds, some of which numbered up to 60 individuals at that time, though we have seen herds of well over 100 elephant since. Accompanying these large herds, but not integral to them, were young bulls in the age group 18–35 years old, moving in smaller bachelor groups of up to 16 strong. At this stage, there were only a handful of older bulls in the age group 35–45 years old on the reserve. The significant numeric observation is that the total number of elephant in Balule had risen from a couple of dozen to nearly 500 in about five years!

Understandably, there was a spate of exploratory forays to all corners of this new area, but these were mostly undertaken by the young bull herds. The cows were less inclined to investigate, especially if this involved crossing barriers or obstacles. The older bulls, being more experienced, were more habitat-selective. They also chose to stay on the periphery of the breeding herds, except when in musth, at which time they would move with the herd and seek out potential cows for breeding. Essentially, these were new elephant colonising a new area, 'pioneer elephant', for want of a better term.

As in all settling-in periods, there were bound to be teething problems. How we went about trying to solve them became an all-consuming management effort. This was particularly prevalent on the reserve's western boundary, which effectively was now the Greater Kruger Park's new western boundary, and where most of the elephant kept on breaking out. The potential danger to motorists on the R40 which lay almost immediately beyond the fence was a major concern, as most of the break-outs occurred at night, and this is a high-speed and popular route with commuters to and from the mining town of Phalaborwa. Can you imagine five tons of dark grey, non-reflecting elephant on a dark grey road, and you're doing 120 km/h ... it's good night!

One morning, driving through from Nelspruit to White River, I heard a general alert on Radio Jacaranda warning motorists of three elephant on the section of this road between Mica and Phalaborwa. I immediately got on my cell phone and with the help of the Balule regional wardens and a local chopper pilot, co-ordinated an operation to get these animals off the road and back into the reserve.

A couple of hours and R12 000 later, the elephant were safely back in Balule. But I knew this would not be the last time, and the frustration was compounded by the knowledge that we could not contain them with the existing fence. Clearly, the situation needed immediate attention, without any delays that would be inherent in complicated and/or expensive solutions. We couldn't wait for any committee-based decisions.

The first priority was that motorists be made aware of the danger. That sounds simple; signage was the obvious solution. But, though we quickly decided to make up road signs that would get the attention of all drivers, we also had to come up with a design that was clear enough to explain in all eleven languages of this country that this road was used by elephant, day and night. In fact, given the use of the road by many international tourists, the signage needed to be universally understood.

At this point, the professionals got it all wrong. The first, and embarrassing, batch of signs produced used the unmistakable silhouette of Indian elephants! Working with elephant researcher and artist Melodie Bates, we promptly re-designed the signage using the African bull elephant's side silhouette and a standard caution triangle. This emerged as the image you see today on provincial road signs. The first acceptable batch was made up at the Phalaborwa Number Plate and Sign Company, with the bill being footed by Olifants River Game Reserve and Balule.

You may ask if the signs got the attention of motorists? Well, they certainly did. All bar two of the first batch we put up were stolen within a week! One of the remaining two must have been copied by the provincial road authorities as, in a matter of weeks, official road signs were erected using our artwork, a great indirect compliment to Melodie's artistic talent. Not an official word of thanks or acknowledgement, mind you!

Fortunately there were no vehicle accidents involving elephant. On the other hand, there were a number of casualties resulting from breakouts, and all of them involved the young elephant bulls themselves. When they broke out of the reserve, they were classified as problem animals and then destroyed, but, if they weren't too far from the reserve's boundary, we would get a stay of execution, and then in most instances, at huge cost, chase them back in by helicopter.

Some of these elephant would wander great distances, often too far to try and get them back. A few of them even reached the citrus estates near the Blyde River's confluence with the Olifants River, some 35 km from the reserve's western boundary. Once they had gone this distance, they reached the point of no return, and were summarily destroyed by the Department of Environmental Affairs and Tourism (DEAT). In one year, 14 elephant were shot in these circumstances, and all of them were bulls roughly between 14 and 30 years old. However, to date not a single cow has been reported outside the reserve.

Under increasing pressure from pro-elephant lobbyists, the department officials were becoming more inclined to try alternatives to killing elephant, but they were also aware of the farmers' predicament. The possibility of confrontation and the associated danger that these young bulls posed in the relatively high people density zones or residential areas was also a serious concern.

One day I received a call from our local nature conservation official appealing for our help. Five elephant had broken out of Balule and were in the Hoedspruit Air Force base residential area.

They had been there for a few days, arousing much curiosity and interest from the residents, most of whom had no idea of the potential danger involved, so there was understandably increasing concern for people's safety. He went on to say that they had been using Air Force helicopters to try and move the elephant out of the area since the day before, but had been unsuccessful, and that possibly a co-ordinated ground and air effort might just do the trick. I agreed, and mustered all the regional wardens and their game guards, then arranged to meet with the official in Hoedspruit to discuss strategy.

We planned to have the helicopter move the elephant slowly towards the northern fence line of the Air Force base, where we would cut down 50 metres of game fencing. We would lay it as flat as possible then chase them over it into the game farm next door. If this went according to plan, we would then simply lift the fence back into place and repair it. With the elephant safely out of the residential area, they could then be directed without threat to human life, first back to the main road, then across back into Balule. Everyone agreed and the operation commenced.

Taking my bolt cutters, we cut the fence and laid it flat in a matter of minutes, though some of the expanded metal used along the bottom section of this particular fence was springy and didn't lie as flat as I would have liked. We could hear the chopper getting closer and knew by the throb of the rotor blades that it was bringing the elephant towards us, so we didn't have time for too many last-minute adjustments. Getting into position upwind and out of sight, we sat and hoped for the best, ready to shout and yell in case the elephant needed encouragement or were off line.

Everything so far had gone according to plan; they were coming in at a gentle run and were being skilfully herded towards the gap we had cut in the fence. The first four went over the flattened fence without a problem, but as the fourth one crossed the line, the toenail on his back foot caught, and momentarily lifted, the flap of expanded metal. This was enough to alert the fifth elephant, which immediately put on the brakes, turned around and ran back the way it had come! The pilot had to maintain momentum and keep the others moving until they were in far enough to allow him to backtrack and try and get the other one rounded up for a second attempt.

Despite a concerted effort by the pilot, I knew this wouldn't work. The fifth elephant now knew there was something fishy about the fence line, and would never cross at that point. Nevertheless, we had to give it a try. In fact, we tried repeatedly, even employing the vehicles in an attempt to narrow the passage and force the animal through. All we succeeded in doing was to increase the elephant's stress levels to the point where it was becoming aggressive.

At this point, the Air Force helicopter's gearbox began overheating, not being designed for this tight manoeuvring. It was also rather heavy on fuel, so had to return to the airfield to fill up prior to the move of the other four as planned. As warden of Balule at the time and responsible for ground operations, I was instructed by DEAT to shoot the elephant. While I knew that this was an innocent animal, acting instinctively out of fear and confusion, and did not deserve this fate, so did the official. This must have also been a tough call for him, but after two days of effort he decided that saving four out of five was the best that could be done.

As emotionally difficult as it was, and with increasing pressure from the circumstances as they played out, there were just no options left. Although I dreaded the instruction to act as executioner, I understood the decision and its beneficial effect on the remaining four elephant. They were not then herded back into Balule as initially planned; instead they were darted and translocated to an 'elephant-back safari' outfit in Polokwane. Incredibly, they all settled down and within two weeks, one of the young bulls was apparently allowing his mahout to ride him! Knowing the trauma they had been through, I found this news yet further proof of the adaptability and intelligence of these wonderful animals.

In all honesty, I have mixed feelings regarding the elephant-back safari industry. It's not the concept per se that worries me, but the ability of the operators to provide the long-term commitment necessary to provide a life beyond the working period for such long-lived creatures. In this instance, however, the choices were extremely limited, and we were grateful that someone could provide a home for these four elephant.

Since this report, the fence on the western boundary of Balule has been replaced with one erected to the latest specifications. The result is that the number of elephant breaking out has been drastically reduced and the need for our signs has also been reduced.

This last comment is not to be interpreted as an invitation to help yourself to one of 'our' African elephant traffic warning signs, no matter their investment potential.

Pigeons and Prisoners

Long before the concrete highway sliced through the Johannesburg suburbs of Sunninghill Park and Rivonia, where it now crosses the Jukskei River, there used to be a small seven-acre estate known as The Lychgate. Set amongst the poplars and willows on the bank of the river, you could not imagine a more idyllic setting for a country home. At the time, a good friend of mine, Irving, was lucky enough to practically live there, it being owned by his Aunt Mavis and he being her favourite nephew. I recall spending some of the most interesting times of my youth in Sunninghill and surrounds. Having spent all my life stifled in suburbia, this was the closest I ever came to experiencing the taste of traditional country living.

I loved any time I spent at the The Lychgate, but the autumn and winter days were particularly memorable. There was an atmosphere of history about the place that is difficult to describe, a feeling that was enhanced by the impressive array of antiques, old military weapons, swords, spears, and the like, boys' stuff mostly. I well remember the beautiful old stone and thatch house, which had the cosiest, most lived-in lounge this side of the Cotswolds. In winter there was always a log fire going, so the whole house smelled pleasantly natural, permeated with a subtle blend of wood smoke, the wheaty odour of thatch and a hint of creosote.

The cheesy-smelling old gun dogs, lying on the hair-covered couches or in front of the stone fireplace, were an almost permanent feature. They'd loll about languid and lazy until you picked

353

up a shotgun, when, without having to say a word, there would be three instant volunteers, tails wagging, ready to go hunting.

On the mantelpiece was Uncle Mike's assortment of old smoking pipes and his Erinmore flake tobacco, with a pinch of rum and maple. Next to that, a pile of old books always accumulated and always needed to be returned to the study. This was also where the gun-cleaning kit was kept, so there was never an excuse for a dirty gun. It contained the nicest-smelling gun oil, which apparently did everything from cleaning through to preventing rust to acting as an insect repellent on human skin.

One day I had just placed the kit on the coffee table and was about to open the leather case containing a pair of WW Greener shotguns to start cleaning them, when Aunt Mavis appeared.

'Mario, would you and Irv be darlings and shoot a few pigeons for me, a dozen or so should be fine; I have a dinner party tomorrow night and want to do them for starters,' said Aunt Mavis.

'No problem, Aunt May, I'll wait for Irving to get home, and then we'll go out and try our luck,' I responded as the dogs pricked up their ears in parallel response.

It was Irving's influence and the pages of *The Old Man and the Boy*, Robert Ruark's classic, that taught me the etiquette of conduct in the field and the ethics of wing shooting. This book is a must for anyone aspiring to train and use gundogs in field sports; it contains nearly everything you need to know and although set in North Carolina, the associated guidelines, ethics and philosophy are universally applicable.

Being the middle of the highveld winter, it was chilly but not unbearable, only occasionally dropping to below zero. Most of the willows and poplar trees were bare and from the paddock in front of the house you could see the Jukskei River glinting through their silver-grey branches. This tree-lined river course was a popular flight path for hundreds of speckled pigeons, which we called 'rockies', going to and returning from feeding. Even though it was late in the season, the birds were plump; their crops were stuffed full of ripe sunflower seeds from the outlying fields where the farmers were busy reaping what was left of that season's harvest.

It was a beautiful winter's afternoon with clear blue skies and there wasn't a breath of wind. The crisp air began to cool rapidly as the late afternoon sun dropped lower on the horizon so we picked a suitable spot and settled down to wait, concealed in amongst some low scrub facing the river. The shooting conditions could not have been better, and it wasn't long before the first couple of pigeons came hurtling through, jinking and twisting just above tree-top level.

After many thousands of years of dodging peregrine falcons, arguably the fastest predators on earth, speckled pigeons have evolved into one of the quickest and most evasive tacticians on the wing. They have earned the respect of both man and raptor, both hunters having to be wide awake to bag one. Irving was first off the mark and with a practised swing, collected the first bird, which folded in a puff of feathers. Before I could call out, 'Good shot, Irv!' we heard a man shout. Slowly, out of a grey shroud of windborne feathers, a policeman, cap in hand and with a few feathers sticking to his spotless uniform, emerged from the grove of poplars along the river. Apparently they didn't use camouflage overalls in those days.

Red-faced from anger and effort, he came straight to the point, explaining somewhat breathlessly that prisoners had escaped from Leeukop Prison, which was not far from there, and that he was part of a massive police manhunt for the convicts. They had been making steady progress along the river, he said, when the pigeon Irving shot had almost fallen on him. He angrily demanded to know what we thought we were doing. I simply told him the truth, and said that we were trying to shoot a few pigeons for the pot. He then asked us how old we were and when we told him, he informed us that by law we were not allowed to shoot unless over 21 years old, or in the company of someone of that age or older. He went on to say that if he hadn't been tied up with the search, he would have confiscated the guns and fined us. However, if we took the guns home and stopped shooting, he would consider this as a formal issue of a warning.

Thinking back, that shot going off must have alerted any escaped prisoner hiding within 100 miles, which wouldn't have done their search effort much good, so it was no wonder he was so livid. We didn't need a second prompting; we were off back home in a flash, just in case he changed his mind. How we would ever have told Uncle Mike that his cherished Greeners had been confiscated, I have no idea. One thing, though, the policeman was not a happy chappie, but he did let us keep the pigeon. Back at the house, Aunt May was busy in the kitchen bottling her delicious homemade preserves and jams to sell at their farm stall down the road.

Greeting us with her usual broad smile, she enquired how many pigeons we'd bagged. When we showed her, she was more than a little disappointed, and it wasn't until we'd told her the whole story that her smile returned. In a mischievous half-whisper, she told us that Mike's mother, who happened to be visiting at the time, was well over 21; in fact, she was 82. Surely then, if she were to come along with us boys, everything would be legal and above board?

The next day we gently bundled Uncle Mike's mom into the Land Rover, packed a small cooler, and drove to the same spot from which we'd been chased the day before. I set up a comfortable chair we'd brought along and sat her in it. Hardly was she settled with a stiff gin and tonic in hand, when she called in the first pigeons, 'Here they come, Irving.' With her remarkable long-distance eyesight apparently unhindered by her oversize bush hat and ear muffs that almost covered her whole head, the pigeons didn't stand a chance of sneaking past us. In a short while we had bagged our quota, and the game old lady, having grown up on a sugar estate, so no stranger to a shotgun, had thoroughly enjoyed herself out in the open air that afternoon.

The pigeons were prepared to perfection, casseroled in a white wine and mushroom sauce, with a slice of streaky bacon wrapped around each breast and held in place with a toothpick. Not much was said as the guests began the meal. All I can remember is that at the start of the second course, not a bird nor a trace of sauce was left in the dish and Aunt May's dinner party was, typically, a great success.

Most of what I know about snakes I also learned from Irving. I would accompany him on as many of his snake-hunting expeditions as possible, which, besides forays in the Honeydew and Kyalami area, also took us into the wilder areas in and around the Magaliesberg. For me, it was never just about catching snakes, it was the real enjoyment of getting out into the bush. Irving would capture certain snakes for his own collection and others would be given to snake parks, the Reptile Park at Hartbeespoort Dam being one of his main recipients. He had a tremendous respect for reptiles, and remains one of the only collectors of snakes I've known who was never bitten. We caught snakes, did lots of fishing and enjoyed the bush, but it was our decision to rebuild a Series 1 Land Rover that changed things.

This was a 'chassis-up' project that captured my undivided attention. It and the resulting focus of regular bush trips kick-started my desire for the bush, the lowveld in particular, where I would end up living, never to return to Johannesburg except when I just couldn't avoid it.

We used to call them 'Four hundred rand Landies' and they were barely able to get you home from where you bought them. This didn't bother us too much, as we'd be rebuilding this one from scratch, something that was easier said than done. Undaunted, we persisted with boundless enthusiasm. Irving was a skilled movie camera technician, so his fastidious attention to detail when having to improvise proved invaluable. We begged, borrowed and stole, and everybody who could help, did help. Soon, the aged little classic began to take shape; just three months after wheeling a heap of junk into the garage, we were driving our reconditioned and rebuilt short wheel base Series 1 Land Rover out onto the road. A couple of weeks later, after sorting out all the teething problems, we began packing our gear for the few weeks we'd planned to spend in the Timbavati Game Reserve. We loaded everything we thought we'd need, but as there's not too much space in a Landy 'Shorty', we had to think about what were necessities and what were nice-to-haves.

By the time the rising sun compelled us to drop the visors, we were already approaching the half-way point near Middelburg.

The Land Rover wasn't exactly fast, and I was impatient to get to the bush, the anticipation being almost unbearable. I was about to realise the dream I'd painted on my bedroom wall a few years previously. This would be my first time in the 'real' bush where the Big Five roamed, there were two of us in a Landy 'Shorty' and when we lit a fire this evening against the backdrop of a setting sun, the picture would be complete.

Doug Jackaman was the warden of the reserve at the time, and was based in the southern Timbavati, most of which was then owned by Hans Hoheisen. We would be staying in a bush camp with Doug's son Dave, who was a friend and former colleague of Irving's. The next morning over breakfast, Doug asked us to count all the wildebeest, elephant and buffalo we came across. My coffee cup wasn't cold and I was already in the Landy ready to go, and this time my impatience was rewarded. We hadn't driven more than 500 metres before I saw my first wild lions. I will never forget that sight, or the impact it had on me for the rest of my life. There were 13 of them, mostly sub-adults and females, lying on a dam wall, and I remember there were no big males. As it happened, these would be the last lions we'd see for nearly a week.

There were always plenty of hyaena around though, and Dave would call them right up to the vehicle by cupping his hands to his mouth and bleating like a lost calf. We were less successful with leopard sighting, as they are hard to spot anywhere, but although we didn't see any, we found a freshly killed common duiker hoisted way up into a knobthorn tree. Unfortunately, this was on the main dirt road through the reserve that took you to the Kruger Park's Orpen Gate in those days. Leaving really early the next morning, we hoped to catch the leopard feeding before the traffic disturbed it. Our efforts were in vain: when we arrived, the kill was no longer in the tree. According to Dave, the bicycle tracks under the tree left no doubt as to what particular predator ended up with the duiker.

The farms Spring Valley, Morgenzon and Kempiana, straddled a generous section of the Timbavati River and made up much of the area we drove in. The predominant veld type featured thick bushveld and knobthorn/marula woodland with beautiful, relatively large open seep lines. These black, cotton soil plains were studded with wildebeest and zebra made up of smaller family units in herds of up to about 60 individuals. In those early days, we would often mistake the black masses of wildebeest for buffalo when they were far off. The total number of wildebeest in the Timbavati at the time was estimated at well over 3 000. Giraffe, too, were abundant; we saw them all the time, but although we regularly came across fresh evidence of elephant, we never saw one in over two weeks. According to Doug, the total population of elephant in the reserve was about 65. We also didn't see any buffalo in the time we were there, although they too left evidence of their presence. The number of buffalo was thought to be around 180 at the time. Today, 35 years later, the Timbavati has well over 600 elephant and 3 000 buffalo, but fewer than 150 wildebeest! Yet the physical habitat, except for tree damage by elephant and a moderate amount of bush encroachment, appears to be relatively unchanged from what I remember all those years ago.

What is so amazing – or, more accurately, so concerning – is not so much the drastic differentials in animal numbers, but the ecological 'blink of an eye' in which all this has happened.

All good things come to an end. But, when it was time to leave, I don't recall feeling sad at all. I felt content, summarising the emotion by turning to Irving with a confident, prophetic announcement. 'One day, this is going to be my job and my life,' I said.

FOOTNOTE

Hans Hoheisen has since passed away, leaving his property and its management to the South African National Parks Board. The Hans Hoheisen Wildlife Research Centre, which he conceived, founded and built, is situated near the Orpen Gate to the Kruger Park and stands in honour of his contribution to conservation. Sadly, however, this institute is now a mere shadow of the wildlife research and environmental education centre that he had envisaged.

In similar realistic and perhaps disappointing vein, when I went back to visit The Lychgate nearly 15 years later, I found the old place had long since been swallowed up by progress, and a restaurant-cum-conference centre called

Falcon's Crest had been built on the estate. You could see the developers had tried to maintain the old charm and atmosphere by having parts of the house incorporated into the new structure, but sadly to no avail. Sunninghill was completely built-up, the river was littered with plastic bags and other detritus of humanity and The Lychgate and its surrounding countryside as I remembered it were gone forever. It even smelt unfamiliar and strange.

I never did find out if they recaptured those escaped prisoners, but as for the speckled pigeons – well, in and around the mushrooming suburbs of northern Johannesburg there are more of them than ever. Aunt May and her guests continue to dine forever in my imagination, still leaving not a scrap of pigeon nor a drop of sauce.

My Way with Leopards

FEBRUARY 2010

I don't think there is a game ranger out there who hasn't at some stage in his or her career fantasised about having a dangerous wild animal as a pet, and the reasons for this may be as varied as the individuals themselves. By way of example, on the one extreme, the thought of taking a 200 kg lion for a stroll in the bush while your city-dwelling counterpart takes his dog for a walk in the park may appeal to the machismo of some or the fantasy of others, or to those who simply love lions. However, this has proved to be both impractical and unsustainable; eventually something has to give, and invariably it is the animal that draws the short straw. Like all marriage, these journeys start out with every good intention and without contemplation of failure. Yet I have never seen a domesticated lion that was successfully rehabilitated into the wild once the relationship ended – and unfortunately, like some marriages, they do.

Raising orphaned wild animals is not something that ordinarily 'comes with the territory' of being a game ranger. However, the very nature of our jobs and where we live means that we're often the first door that gets knocked on when an animal needs help – and needless to say, that door is always opened. However, despite the best intentions, not all the creatures brought in are able to be accommodated. Time and expertise are required to nurture some of these orphans; they take dedication and a thorough knowledge of their needs. Not everyone is cut out to be a good mother and once the novelty wears off, many young animals are not given the appropriate care they need. More often than not, it is the sudden realisation of how much hard work it actually is, and then due to the caregiver's work commitments and time constraints or lack of knowledge in this field, many animals are simply neglected. Then there is the emotional preparation needed in order to face the inevitable day the foster parents need to release animals that they have become attached to, or in the worst case scenario, bury those that have died, for whatever reason. Some people find these aspects, as realistic as they are, the most difficult to cope with.

In the 35 years I've spent in the bush, my experience has been that for every successful release there are at least a dozen unsuccessful attempts. Artificially reared wild animals, habituated and dependent on humans, invariably end up in disaster; in fact I can count the success stories on one hand. But we're human and that's what makes us keep trying; and despite the hard lessons, we won't accept the status quo. There will always be a belief among some of us that this time it will be different and we will make the breakthrough.

It was a rather quiet afternoon at Thornybush Game Reserve. We had only just finished lunch and were contemplating fishing for tilapia in the river below the camp when the party-line telephone rang our ring, two shorts and a long. Frank, the Reserve manager, picked up the call, listened for a minute and then cupped his hand over the mouthpiece. 'Do you want three leopard cubs?' he asked. 'What a question, of course!' I replied without a second thought. I was 20 years old at the time and had no idea what I was letting myself in for … leopard cubs are just like big kittens, right? Little did I know at the time that this would be the start of an intimate relationship with three of the world's most enigmatic big cats, and as predicted nothing was going to be predictable.

The leopard cubs, two females and a male, were orphans of a female that had been poached on a farm close to the Manyeleti Game Reserve. Peering into the cardboard box that housed them, we were greeted by three spitting and snarling bundles of fur, their eyes barely open. Was this a promise of things to come? One thing we knew for sure, we now had our work cut out for us.

The 'we' side of the deal didn't last long. When Frank saw that trying to feed three uncooperative wild leopard cubs was dirty, difficult work, the romance wore off a day into the relationship. Although I was left holding the babies, I loved it. As the days went by, they began to feed well on a prescribed milk formula which they appeared to enjoy and the snarling was soon exchanged for contented slurping as they drank greedily. Very soon they began to associate me with food and love, and were now beginning to respond in such a way that it was clear they had accepted me and depended on me. Not able to spend as much time with them as I would have liked, I missed not being with them and began looking forward to feeding time almost as much as they did. I also found myself becoming quite possessive; I didn't want to share the care of these precious bundles with anyone else.

As a single young ranger my quarters were rather small so sharing them with three rapidly growing leopards began to leave much to be desired in the sanitation department. In short, my room stank so badly of cat pee and poop that the decision to move them was non-negotiable. There was no space to move without standing in something, so their paws were quite dirty; in turn the scratches on the back of my hands from their kneading claws as they clutched me while they drank turned septic. Yes, it was time for bigger, cleaner quarters ... for the leopards, that is.

Frank's mother lived in a large farmhouse with an enormous garden a few hundred metres away from the main lodge. At the bottom of the garden was an old but nevertheless, lovely two bedroom thatched cottage where Frank had stored most of his bulky possessions, and he agreed the leopards could be accommodated there for a while. We moved everything into the one bedroom, leaving the other bedroom and the living room for the leopards. I made the room as comfortable as possible by stringing up an old tyre on a rope; I dragged in a beautiful old leadwood log for them to climb on and to stretch their tendons on. A couple of empty 44 gallon drums were placed in the corner and the insides lined with hessian, and a large litter tray was placed in the opposite corner to their water bowl. These small features were not only fun to do but they were necessary. The leopards were becoming playful and active now, they needed the stimulation and exercise to develop and appeared to love the layout: when I was unable to play with them outside the cottage, which I did as often as I could, they would happily romp around on the indoor props we had provided for them.

At the time a popular TV series 'The New Avengers' was being broadcast weekly and I fell in love with 'Purdy', played by Joanna Lumley, so I named the cutest little female after her. The other female, however, was not to be trusted; a vicious attack on Frank one day left me in no doubt as to what we'd call her, so she was named Delilah. Bulu, the big floppy male, was like a young bull – cumbersome but strong, foreshadowing the animal he would one day become.

As the cubs grew bigger they became more like the big cats their parents were, energetic and extremely powerful for their size. They were now almost as big as a large house cat and would soon need to be weaned onto meat. At first I began slowly with a mixture that included liquidised liver, then they progressed to mince, which we kept them on for a couple of weeks, and soon they were eating small pieces of meat, but meat alone was not ideal. Roughage and trace elements are also an important part of a carnivore's diet: this would mean having to feed them a whole carcass of an animal – hair, teeth, toenails and all – so we started by giving them a dead tree squirrel to share ... Beeeg mistake! They attacked each other with such ferocity that fur flew amidst blood-curdling guttural growls I'd never heard them utter previously. I was shocked; I also knew that from that day on they would never eat together again.

While we decided on what we would need to construct in order to keep them separate at feeding time, I happened to go into their room on a routine litter tray inspection. Suddenly my legs went tingly and cold, looking down I saw my lower legs were covered in a black mass, which closer inspection revealed was thousands of fleas; I'd never seen or felt anything like it in my life. Calling for Frank to come in and see for himself, I wasn't surprised when he emerged a few seconds later: the look of horror on his face said it all. He was equally disgusted. 'Flea powder is not going to work here,' he said, climbing into his Land Rover, 'but I think I know what will. I'll be back in a few minutes, in the meantime get the leopards out of the cottage,' he shouted over his shoulder. Then he started the vehicle and drove off in the direction of the lodge.

The leopards were having a whale of a time in the bush outside the flea-infested cottage; they always loved the outdoors where they would play cat and mouse games with each other and the occasional grasshopper. Interestingly, they never wandered too far away from me and would come bounding back if they heard a sudden strange noise, particularly if their curiosity had taken them beyond the usual perimeter, which grew as their confidence did.

Frank returned a little while later with a gallon of diesel in his hand. 'This should sort those bloody fleas out once and for all,' he said. The idea was to create a low smoky flame. A quick burn on the concrete floor would kill the fleas by roasting them and the smoke generated would kill those trying to escape in crevices and hidey holes. Honestly, I had never heard of this eradication technique before, but it sounded as if it would work and we needed to get rid of this plague quickly. However, being pioneers in this field we needed to be sure of the quantity to use, how long it would burn for and so on – essentially we needed to experiment first, do a practical test.

Deciding to use the concrete floor of the stoep as a control, we sprinkled the diesel sparingly over an area of about three square metres and lit it. The result was a sluggish unimpressive flame that rose to no more than the height of our boots, but which burned long enough to ensure the fleas would be well done. Perfect!

I removed their water bowl, but otherwise left the leopards' room exactly as it was, then Frank sprinkled the diesel onto the floor, threw a match down and set it alight. At first all went much as it did outside on the stoep, then suddenly the flames began to get higher, and even though we had moved outside we could hear the fire. Somehow the draught through the open door and window had produced a drawing effect, causing the diesel to burn with much more intensity than we had anticipated! Realising there was nothing we could do to put the fire out and that the cottage was doomed, we resigned ourselves to making sure the leopards were safe and then doing some damage control.

With the leopards playing on the shorter grass on the edge of the clearing, safely out of harm's way, Frank and I could now focus on getting his belongings out of the other room. Old elephant tusks, a piano, furniture, a couple of zebra skins and so much other paraphernalia that he had accumulated over the years was dragged out and thrown onto the lawn surrounding the cottage. Up until now I'd kept one concerned eye on the burning cottage and the other on the leopards, but I needn't have worried. It was only when the tinder-dry thatch caught alight and started spitting and crackling that the three otherwise bemused cubs showed anything more than mild curiosity. Even though this was their first experience of fire, they appeared to have no real fear of it; in fact they were more interested in the animal things and skins that came out of the cottage, which made an interesting play heap on the lawn. Some of the skins that we'd draped over the furniture took on a realistic impression of the animals that once wore them, and as young as they were, the leopards' interest was more than casually aroused.

In less than an hour all that remained of the cottage were the white walls and a few blackened timber poles. Years later when I flew over the lodge, the charred remains still stood as a stark reminder of the day two pyromaniacs were let loose with a can of diesel. The cottage was never re-built … and even though some 35 years have since passed, some say the ghosts of a billion roasted fleas haunt the old place to this day.

We urgently needed an enclosure to house the leopards; in fact we needed three separate pens in one. So, housing them temporarily in the Lodge's enclosed vegetable garden, we spent the next couple of days building their new homes, which turned out very well. They could now eat without fighting with each other, and it was also a lot easier to give them individual attention when we needed to, as each one had a distinct character and reacted differently to various stimuli. I could never allow myself to lose sight of the fact that however tame they became, they were still leopards and pound for pound arguably the most dangerously powerful felines on earth.

As the leopards grew, so did my love for them, but I knew that one day they would need to go back into the wild, which was something I had absolutely no compunction about. Even so, letting go was going to be tough … it always is. Unlike most large carnivores, a hand-reared leopard, like a domestic cat, can be released into the wild without being taught how to hunt. The ability to kill prey is an instinctive natural progression as they develop; they are masters at adaptation and survival and their capability to eke out an existence in marginal territory is legendary. It appeared nothing could stand in their way, and that all the boxes for their survival were ticked – however, this was not to be.

Our relationship very nearly came to a premature end one day when we were paid a surprise visit by the conservation authorities. Somehow the word got out that three leopards were being held captive in an enclosure, and truth be told, we didn't have the required permits to keep leopards in captivity. In this instance the two officers used their discretion and judgement. They could see we had the leopards in decent enclosures; they also knew the cubs were dependent on care until their release. Taking these factors into consideration, they decided that confiscating the cubs would serve no constructive purpose and pending the permits being issued we could keep them. Clearly these were men with a broader outlook and conservation sense. This observation made at the time materialised years later when both of them went on to do their PhDs and become leading conservation figures in this country. One is a world-renowned expert on large carnivores and game census techniques. Sadly those now filling the shoes of these men are a mere shadow of the conservationists of yore, and I sincerely doubt whether this department has officers today that can spell the words 'discretion' or 'judgement', more's the pity.

When the leopards were about nine months old, I left Thornybush to take up a long-sought-after post at Letaba Ranch. Frank took over their full-time care and by all counts did an excellent job, but it was not all plain sailing. One day, arriving at the enclosure, only Purdy and Bulu rushed up to greet him: Delilah's body lay cold and stiff on the dew-covered grass at the back. Subsequent autopsy results revealed heart and respiratory failure as the cause of death; this finding confirmed she had been bitten by either a black mamba or snouted cobra.

At the age of 22 months Bulu and Purdy were released to fend for themselves. The easy part for them would be hunting for food; the hard part would be keeping from becoming food! The reserve had its own resident leopards, lions and hyaenas, all of which would kill a stray young leopard in a heartbeat. Until the young leopards' confidence levels improved it was felt that a more gradual or phased release would be preferable, so Bulu and Purdy were allowed to come home to their enclosures on occasion and get the odd free meal.

As time went by Bulu grew into an enormous animal; soon his sheer size would be enough to intimidate potential rivals and allow him to mark out a territory for himself. Both he and Purdy would spend increasingly more time in the bush, at times two or three days at a stretch. Neither leopard was fitted with a radio collar, in hindsight a huge oversight, but then again radio telemetry was not as developed in the early seventies as it is today. Also, I suspect everyone assumed they would simply melt away into the wilds of the African bush once they were confident enough to leave on their own. Reports of their movements from neighbouring landowners indicated they were definitely exploring further and further away. Apparently Frank was asked one evening by a neighbouring lodge owner to please come and collect his leopard. Purdy had found a perfect tree to snooze in, but unfortunately it happened to be in their boma, so the chef wouldn't do any cooking for their paying guests while she was up there.

To be able to see and touch a beautiful apex predator of such enigmatic and elusive qualities is an animal lover's equivalent of a religious experience, and a once-in-a-lifetime privilege for most wildlife enthusiasts. For some she was not much more than a novelty, a conversation piece to impress overseas visitors and friends, and at times regarded as a 'bush lodge accessory'. Eventually, however, her lack of fear for people, wanderlust and easygoing nature were to be her downfall. A visiting hunter on the property next door out looking for impala one morning was confronted by Purdy. Unaware of her status, the man suspected the leopard boldly approaching him in broad daylight to be rabid, so he understandably but tragically, shot her.

Bulu became the leopard nobody thought a leopard could become, predictable to a fault and affectionate, the antithesis of his late sister Delilah. Once he'd fed he would play like an overgrown kitten, his movements at this stage typical of those produced by immature muscles sometimes over extended and often with more power than was necessary. Bulu was rapidly developing into a huge tom leopard and at two years of age he weighed nearly 60 kg! Each time a new cell divided in his growing body, it made him stronger, faster and more limber, and soon it became difficult to play with him without getting hurt. It was time for him to move on and fulfil his rightful role as a wild leopard. Discouraged from staying by the cutting off of food, he slowly began to get the message, within a few months his return visits became less frequent and of shorter duration, and soon he didn't come home at all ...

About a year later word filtered back on the whispering leaves of the bushveld, that a large leopard had been shot by a trophy hunter on the farm next door, known as 'Mossies nest'. I have since often wondered what trophy room or hearth Bulu's trophy now adorns and whether the hunter even knew the history of this magnificent animal he killed. Somehow I doubt it. However, what I do know is that the outfitter of that hunt most certainly did.

FOOTNOTE

Most of the time this task of caring for and rehabilitating wildlife orphans is best left to those who know what they're doing. I refer to the likes of Karen Trendler, for example, and the other Mother Theresas of the animal world too numerous to mention here. Committed individuals who are prepared to accept the responsibility of raising orphaned wild animals or nursing those with injuries back to health, and then the challenge of rehabilitating them if necessary ... However, back to cold cynical statistics. After 35 years I can still only count on my one hand the success stories I know of involving hand-reared and rehabilitated wild African animals – but that doesn't mean we should be discouraging those who care from trying ... we wouldn't be human if we didn't give in to our emotions from time to time.

Man-eaters

AFTER A WORKER WAS ATTACKED BY LIONS ON OLIFANTS NORTH – 2008

An unprovoked attack on man by wild lions motivated by hunger elicits the most primordial fear in all of us. Being stalked intently by predators, hunted with the express intention of being devoured, and the final horror of being eaten alive, has got to be a fate worse than death. It takes us back millions of years to when we were lower down the food chain, to when we were considered just another prey item on the menu. It conjures up long-dead memories of a time when we ran in fear of these big cats and their larger predecessors, typified by the sabre-toothed tiger.

Our ancient forefathers' days and nights must have been filled with constant fear: as if the daily challenge of finding enough to eat wasn't bad enough, they had to duck and dive, but mostly climb, to stay alive.

Although a lot of water has since flowed under the bridge of evolution, and thankfully the tables have largely been turned, lions still need to be treated with the utmost respect. One on one, an unarmed man would have less chance of staying in one piece against a lion than a bleeding seal would have of getting across False Bay! Physiologically, lions are the same awesome predators today that they were all those years ago, though the scales of fear have since tilted in our favour. Millions of years of evolution have seen man advance in intelligence and survival stratagems to the point where we are now feared predators in our own right. Consequently, these big cats now show a grudging respect and deep-seated dread of man, avoiding confrontation whenever possible and usually only attacking under extreme provocation.

So what makes a man-eater a man-eater?

Before you start believing that the Tsavo man-eaters' genes have migrated 3 000 km south to the lowveld, I need to delve into the background of some circumstances that could drive a lion to attack and become a man-eater.

Let's take the best-known case of man-eaters in Africa, 'The man-eaters of Tsavo', and scratch around beneath the everyday surface of the story, seeking the less romantic stuff that doesn't make for box office appeal. In this brief explanation, 'hype' has no place, and although speculation and hypotheses could fill volumes, here's my attempt to give you, concisely, some insight into my take on things as gleaned from the recollections of men who were employed to hunt the man-eaters down, in particular the famous hunter, JA Hunter.

Construction of the Tsavo railroad, also known as the Lunatic Express, began in 1896. Incidents of lion attacks started to escalate until, two years later in 1898, 28 Indian workers and an unknown number of African labourers were killed and eaten by lions in less than a year. But it didn't end there; in fact the terror spread and lion attacks on people continued at isolated railway stations for the next two decades. The line between Athi River station 25 miles east of Nairobi and the aptly named Simba station, was one of the most notorious for man-eating lions. Given that records for the number of people killed by lions in the Tsavo area are less than reliable, I wouldn't place too much store on the accuracy of data recorded for the number of man-eating lions shot in retaliation. However, reading the various hunters' accounts, and allowing for the 'fisherman's tale' factor, it is apparent that many blameless lions were hunted down as potential man-eaters and indiscriminately shot. This is substantiated by the fact that professional hunters were employed on a full-time basis to tackle the problem and part of their remuneration, or incentive if you like, was the cash they earned for the skins.

The Tsavo railroad project needed over 2 000 workers for its construction. Try to imagine the logistics necessary to maintain discipline, health care, safety and hygiene when dealing with so many illiterate labourers, the majority of whom had never worked in the bush or seen a lion in their lives. Given the technical constraints and the remote wilderness in which the Tsavo line was built, it must have been one helluva job for the supervisors and engineers. I know how much management a field staff of around 30 people requires nowadays, despite modern technology and current logistical support options. Trying to manage so many people in a testing environment under primitive conditions must have been extremely difficult.

I'd guess that a major portion of their day-to-day routine was adapted ad hoc to meet the needs of an ever-changing situation, with new challenges to be met on a constant basis. Inevitably, this meant that things slipped through the cracks now and then.

Unfortunately, the lions were quick to capitalise on any weakness or lapse in discipline. For example, the latrine facilities and waste disposal procedures were informal. Everything was 'done and dumped' in the bush, and this alone would have attracted scavengers. Labourers shirking work, hiding in the bush and sleeping in the open no doubt provided more opportunities for confrontation between lions and man by attracting interest from predators prowling the bush on the periphery of the camps. Nocturnal and social movement of workers between the tented accommodation areas would certainly have led to over-indulgence at times, resulting in dulled senses and increased vulnerability. In lion country, there's only one outcome to the equation: (Dulled Senses + Lion) x Darkness = Death

Medical facilities, if available at all, were crude at best. A work force of this size, living cheek by jowl under such primitive and unhygienic conditions, would inevitably succumb to illness sooner or later. In order to prevent contamination, those with fever or infectious diseases were left in the bush with little or no medical attention to either recover or die. In 1896, an unseasonably wet year, 500 labourers went down with malaria alone!

Although illness and death were accepted occurrences under these conditions, it was the post-death procedures that left even more to be desired. The often hastily dug, shallow graves were easily excavated by predators and the bodies unearthed and scavenged.

Very soon the predators realised they didn't need to wait for the burial ceremony; they could speed things up by simply taking the hapless victims from their makeshift beds while they were still alive. From there, the progression was inevitable: healthy individuals became a menu item for predators.

Some aspects of the foregoing slice of history are being repeated in our neck of the woods in the twenty-first century. Perfectly healthy lions are being conditioned to become man-eaters. Mozambican refugees and illegal immigrants are attacked and eaten by lions as they attempt to cross the expanse of the Kruger National Park into South Africa on foot. According to members of our staff who have run the gauntlet unscathed, these journeys are almost always undertaken on full-moon nights to avoid detection by daytime ranger and anti-insurgent patrols.

Most of these people are young adults, but middle-to-old-age men and woman also attempt this perilous journey, often in poor health and unable to keep up with the main group. Many have some ailment or affliction that slows them down and as they lag behind they become progressively weaker until they are in no condition to take evasive action or defend themselves against lions. I heard of one woman who had difficulty walking, who apparently paid to be wheel-barrowed across the park. The pusher must have tired after a while and simply left her at a waterhole in the middle of the reserve! An upturned wheelbarrow, some bloodied clothing and a pair of shoes was all the patrol found a few days later.

This was, yet again, a classic case of an incapacitated person finding themselves directly in the path of a predator, with the consequences being a foregone conclusion. But it doesn't end there ... the next migrant who kneels down to drink at that waterhole now stands an excellent chance of being taken by those same lions if they happen to be in the vicinity, of which there is a good chance, lions being territorially bound. The difference is that this time a fit healthy human will be taken by a fit healthy lion whose fit healthy cubs now also become eaters of man. And so the cycle begins.

Migrants are known to follow the power line pylons through the Kruger National Park. This became such a popular route with illegal immigrants that fully functional prides of lions lay in wait for them. Some of these lions became conditioned to this source of easy prey in much the same way as the huge crocodiles that wait for the annual wildebeest and zebra migration across the Mara River in East Africa.

Subsequently, a number of healthy lions, including cubs, some of which could have been weaned on human flesh, were destroyed by rangers in the park. This phenomenon is tailing off as more relaxed border controls are reducing the numbers of illegal immigrants walking through the Park.

In conversation with an ex-Kruger game ranger, I learned that he had personally destroyed 15 lions thought to be man-eaters. This was made up of a pride of eleven and another two unrelated pairs; even so, the total number of lions destroyed is much lower than we were led to believe, probably less than 20 individuals. This represents a very small fraction of the nearly 1 500 lions in the Kruger. I examined one of the skulls of a particularly large man-eating lion that he had kept as a memento and, of course, it was very interesting, as skulls always are. What was so striking, though, was not so much the size, but rather the excellent condition of its teeth, indicative of a healthy animal in its prime. When I remarked on this he said that nearly every man-eating lion they shot was found to be in good condition. This pretty well proved that very few lions turn to man-eating because of physical impediments.

So, we're getting closer to the true source of the problem, and as you might have already guessed, there's only one answer.

Question: 'What makes a lion turn man-eater?'

Answer: 'Man!'

Wild, free-roaming lions have an innate fear of man. As always, however, there are those of us who take advantage of this, pushing the boundaries to the point where our arrogance and disdain gives us a feeling of superiority, and therein lies the problem. Some of us have been lulled into a false sense of security, lacking the necessary respect when in the proximity of such incredibly powerful animals, and there is no time when we need to be more aware of this than at night. Most of Africa's larger predators come into their own when darkness falls, and lions are certainly no exception.

Recently, a construction worker was attacked by lions on Olifants North. Instead of using the designated toilet facilities, he chose to go into the bush late at night without a flashlight and was severely mauled when he inadvertently stumbled over seven lions in the darkness. Moving from a relatively well-lit area into the contrasting darkness, his eyes would not have had enough time to adjust properly, so he couldn't see that he was heading straight towards the lions lying in the bush on the perimeter of the compound.

Six million years ago, he would have done his ablutions from the branches of the tree in which he was roosting, knowing full well that if he ventured on foot into the bush at night, he'd be instant cat food.

So why did this man, today, take the risk? Complacency, that's why, and as human beings, I believe we're all guilty of allowing familiarity to breed contempt at some time or another. In this particular case, details are sketchy as to whether he was squatting or standing when his motion was abruptly interrupted. This is understandable, as getting attacked by a lion is usually a shockingly quick and violent event and there's no time to think about it. Being within earshot of the main accommodation block probably saved the man's life; his screams were heard by his fellow workers, who managed to mount a mass action and chase the lions off. By the time they had arrived on the scene, however, he was already on the ground and had been bitten through his hands and on his back. Apparently, only one of the seven lions was responsible for initiating the attack.

Scant evidence gleaned from the tracks indicated that the lions were inside the section of the enclosure where the fence was still intact, and thus were unable to move through. I suspect that this was a spontaneous attack, an instinctive defence response borne of fear; after all, they were stumbled upon by man, not vice-versa. Elephant had broken the enclosure's fence a couple of weeks previously, and it had not yet been repaired. The lions apparently entered at this break, but appeared to have had difficulty finding their way back out, which would have caused them to feel trapped. No matter the explanations, it was clear that had the man used the designated facility for his ablutions, close to the accommodation block, this 'attack' probably wouldn't have happened at all.

The contractor's site foreman only became aware of the incident the following morning when he noticed that the man couldn't hold a shovel properly. Not until he asked what the problem was, were the details of the attack revealed. Incredibly, up to that point no one had raised the alarm or said a word. More than 12 hours had elapsed since the lions had attacked him! The man was immediately taken to hospital, where he received numerous stitches, some potent antibiotics and a tetanus injection. There aren't many legitimate excuses out there that can beat this one for a couple of days off work, so why he kept his misfortune so low profile and didn't capitalise on it, remains a mystery. Perhaps shock and post-traumatic stress had more than just a little to do with it.

The events surrounding the attack were thoroughly investigated. The compound fence was repaired, various preventative measures were implemented and discipline was more rigorously enforced. But, obviously, that was the 'man' side of things and the 'lion' side of the story had yet to be told. Due to the relatively high density of game viewing vehicles traversing the area, the lions responsible for the attack were sighted almost on a daily basis. Being able to monitor this particular pride for any signs of unusual behaviour, and finding none, we concluded that, as initially suspected, this incident occurred as a result of a natural reaction by animals that felt threatened or cornered. Nothing suggested that the lions had stalked or hunted the man with the intention of killing him for food. These were not man-eaters, not at that stage anyway, so there was no merit in declaring war on all the lions in the region without ascertaining the facts first. We also managed to identify with reasonable certainty exactly which lions were responsible. Seven of the 13 lions, mostly young animals, had a tendency to hang around together and their inexperience and lack of pride back-up may very well have made them feel unduly defensive, which is another mitigating circumstance. We were also reasonably certain that the two pride males, Hang-lip and his ally, were not present at the time of the attack, probably fortuitously for the victim.

Of all the abiotic (non-living) factors that affect these big cats, ambient temperature has the greatest influence on the activity levels of lions. They're often encountered on the move in overcast or relatively cool daylight conditions. However, there is something about the night that allows all cats to come into their own; besides being cooler, the darkness significantly boosts their confidence; they become much bolder and consequently more dangerous. Therefore, although this isolated spontaneous attack should not be taken out of context, it nevertheless demonstrates the need for anyone visiting any Big Five reserve to be ever-vigilant, and not to underestimate large predators or take their normal behaviour patterns for granted. Walking to or from the braai, the boma or the vehicle in the carport at night should never be done without a good flashlight and a thorough check of the surrounding bush in advance.

A local anti-poaching and security company, well known for the excellent service they provide, particularly to reserves needing help with wildlife security issues, recently lost a man to lions. He and a colleague were on a routine anti-poaching patrol on a game reserve close to the Timbavati Private Nature Reserve when the incident occurred. Many of this company's anti-poaching units are made up of ex-members of the old South African Military 32 Battalion. These are tough men, au fait with the bush, expert trackers and no strangers to hardship. These are men who have a healthy respect for dangerous game, and know how to operate in Big Five reserves, yet despite all their training and experience, one of them was dragged out of his tent, killed and eaten.

The circumstances leading up to the attack are unclear, as apparently both men were in the tent asleep when it happened. We can only imagine the terror of waking up from the pain as your foot is clamped in the jaws of such a powerful predator, held in the grip of canines from which there's no escape. Any attempt to prevent your insignificant 75 kg body weight being dragged away by a lion that can drag a 300 kg zebra with ease, would have been futile. The man's screams, the darkness and the confusion as the tent collapsed in a claustrophobic shroud, must have been too much for his companion to handle with any semblance of meaningful assistance. He couldn't see well enough to help; he had no idea how many lions there were; he had no idea where they were. This man, who had only ever known how to track down and tackle other, dangerous men, must have realised that against lions at night he stood no chance – and so he crawled out and ran for his life.

Daylight revealed the horror of the attack. The man's remains were found a short distance from the tent, partially concealed in some thick bush. Knowing that lions would sometimes do this if they intended returning to feed, the remains were left in situ in the hope that the man-eater would return. This wasn't an easy decision to make, but it was necessary in order to ascertain which lion or lions were responsible, so that only the culprits were destroyed. The decision turned out to be a good one, and it wasn't long before a single lioness emerged and confidently approached the body. She was summarily destroyed without a moment's hesitation. Closer examination of the tracks and the amount of flesh eaten revealed that only one lion had been responsible. This fact was confirmed a short while later, when the gruesome autopsy of the stomach contents was made. The lioness exhibited no impediment or handicap. She was a healthy, well-nourished individual in her prime. What made this animal turn man-eater remains a mystery.

Besides the famous white lions of the Timbavati there were two other well-known lions in the region, known as 'Mama Cass' and 'Waiter-eater', so named because, respectively, one lion's relatively big rounded face supposedly resembled that of the famous singer, and the other, because she ate a waiter! It's not really a joking matter as, seriously, she partially ate one of Motswari Game Lodge's best waiters. These two lions were otherwise perfectly normal in every respect and went on to provide thousands of overseas guests with not only exciting lion viewing, but also an incredible, rather macabre, story to relate when they went home. Why then, wasn't the man-eating lion identified as such and destroyed according to accepted protocol?

Well, I'll elucidate, giving you the facts as they happened in the hope that you reach the same decision, or at least gain an informed insight as to why the decision was made to let her live.

Before teaming up with 'Mama Cass', 'Waiter-eater' was a loner, whether out of choice or due to lion dynamics in the area, nobody knows. As far as lions were concerned, she was always approachable, wary but not skittish, in all a rather agreeable individual. At the time, I guessed this lioness to be about four years old, and although relatively young, she was well developed and in peak condition, which no doubt contributed to her success as a hunter. The airstrip at Motswari was one of her favoured hunting grounds, where she would target the numerous prey animals, mainly wildebeest and impala, which congregated there at night. More often than not, her hunting forays would culminate in a kill, something we were privy to on more than one occasion.

At that time, Motswari Game Lodge and Ingwelala were the largest employers of service staff in the Umbabat Nature Reserve. Their respective administrative offices were situated approximately three kilometres apart as the crow flies, which meant that any socialising between the two staff compounds required having to walk through the bush. There was a safer alternative, taking the main access road, but that entailed walking an extra two kilometres. Needless to say, repeated warnings of the dangers of being on foot in the bush at night fell on deaf ears, and it was extremely frustrating to see the disdainful attitude adopted by some members of staff. Eventually, we resorted to threats of dismissal and punishments just short of public execution for those caught using the shortcut. Despite our efforts, the already well-worn human path just got wider with increased use. Unfortunately, the evidence left in the soft sand indicated that this convenient route was not exclusively used by humans.

Late one evening, the owners of Motswari were returning from visiting a neighbouring landowner, when their headlights fell on a man staggering in the road near the Ingwelala/Motswari shortcut. Pulling up alongside the man, they recognised him as their head waiter on his day off. Apparently he had been drinking heavily, so they insisted he climb on their vehicle and ride back with them.

Belligerently refusing, I suspect partly out of sheer embarrassment, he incoherently mumbled something, then picked up the pace, stumbling and weaving along the shortcut. It was so dark that attempting to follow him would have been pointless as he was quickly swallowed up by the darkness and the density of the bush. When dawn broke a few hours later and the waiter had not pitched to do the early morning wake-up calls, the ranger on duty and a couple of trackers were sent out along the shortcut to find him.

Nothing escapes a Shangaan tracker's eyes. As far as they are concerned, if it doesn't fly or swim, it can be tracked, so when drag marks were seen leading into the bush from the path, they bent over to examine the scene more closely. It wasn't the drag marks that turned their faces an ashen grey, but the lion tracks on either side of them, indicating that a lioness had dragged something into the bush. A few moments later, the lifeless body of the unfortunate man was found some 15 metres from the pathway. As horrific as the scene was, it was not typical of what was usually found at the scene of a lion kill. Besides a torso bloodied where the lion had begun to feed around the abdomen area, the man's body was intact. What was more puzzling was that the lion had left the body hours before they found it; neither we nor the trackers nor other predators had disturbed her, so the question now was – what caused this lion to stop feeding and leave the scene?

Backtracking carefully to the point of departure from the path, the evidence lay clearly for the expert trackers to see. Waiting for the police to arrive before disturbing anything, the trackers began to piece together what had happened. When the authorities arrived they were able to show how the man had made his way along the path, stumbling and weaving until he could no longer maintain his balance. They pointed out where he had fallen down and passed out in a drunken stupor. The lioness, which had subsequently happened on the prostrate man purely by chance, had cautiously circled him a couple of times before approaching. Then, straddling his torso, she gripped him firmly by the head and proceeded to drag him off the path.

The barely perceptible trailing marks left by the man's hands as he was being dragged indicated he was either unconscious or dead at that stage. There were no signs of a struggle; he literally hadn't twitched a finger.

This fact was later confirmed at the autopsy, which revealed the man had died almost instantly when one of the lion's canines penetrated his skull as she bit in to get a good grip on the head. What made the lion stop feeding was ascertained when closer examination revealed she had bitten into the man's stomach, releasing the alcoholic contents, which then spilled over the rest of the abdominal area. At this point it appears that all interest in feeding ceased, and nothing else on the man's body was touched. Further forensic analysis showed that this alcohol was a local concoction known colloquially as 'skokiaan', an illegal, potent kind of moonshine, often pepped up with anything from industrial spirits and antifreeze to discarded PM9 and PM6 batteries. It seems that this was why she lost interest in feeding and moved off.

To determine which lioness was responsible wasn't too difficult. Game lodge rangers and their trackers know the lions in their area better than anyone else, and these guys were no exception. There was only one lioness that was known to move on her own at the time, and this event occurred right in the heart of her territory, so she was the prime suspect. Why she wasn't hunted down immediately and destroyed as a man-eater has been the subject of heated debate ever since; after all, technically she was responsible for the waiter's death. Objectively speaking, however, there were extenuating circumstances to show this was a marginal call.

Walking fully erect is exclusive to man. It elicits a reaction of alarm and fear among wild animals; the posture is instinctively recognised as unique, associated with danger and, for the most part, out of place in the wild. On the contrary, when we are lying prone, animals are unable to make the association; they do not recognise us as human. Experiments have also shown that even when we adopt a sitting or crouching position, it confuses all but the wiliest primates. For a carnivore known to scavenge as well as to kill for food, finding unguarded 'meat' lying in the bush is an opportunity not to be missed.

The animal will react spontaneously and its survival instinct will compel it to take advantage and eat. So, when the lioness happened upon the man lying on the path, passed out in a horizontal position, to her he represented 70 kg of flesh, not a human being, not man.

As the autopsy revealed, death occurred when her canines entered his brain as her powerful jaws clamped down to secure enough purchase to pull him off the path and into the bush. This certainly did not constitute an attack. She had not stalked and intentionally killed the man; therefore, strictly speaking, she could not be labelled a man-killer. Everything pointed to the fact that the poor man was probably already deeply comatose from the poisonous concoction he had drunk, and in all probability, he remained unconscious until he died.

We were persuaded by the unfolding facts of the tragedy to believe the assessment and subsequent verdict were correct. Confirmation of this decision was that 'Waiter-eater' never behaved out of character or looked hungrily at another human being for the next nine years. Early one evening she and 'Mama Cass' crossed over the Umbabat's southern cutline heading into the Timbavati, for the last time. We never saw either of them again.

It had been the right decision not to label her a man-eater and to leave her to her life without further interference from man, intentional or otherwise. Recently I spoke to the highly respected Dr Dewalt Kheet, a veterinarian with the Kruger National Park, on the subject of man-eating lions. His vast experience with man-eaters in Kruger showed that the majority of lions which had killed man in an opportunistic circumstance, 'Waiter-eater' being a classic example, invariably returned to their natural prey;

they didn't become habitual man-eaters. This further confirms that the decision was the right one at the time.

Ten years later and a mere two kilometres from where the waiter was killed, another lion attack occurred. A weekend social visit between the caretakers of two properties neighbouring Ingwelala in the Umbabat Nature Reserve ended in tragedy when a man decided to walk home alone through the bush in the dark.

According to the statement from his friend, he and the unfortunate man had enjoyed a few drinks together, possibly a few too many, which no doubt gave him the Dutch courage to attempt what no unarmed, sober person would have even contemplated.

Unarmed and walking alone in his state of inebriation in this reserve, particularly at night, was tantamount to playing Russian roulette with two or more bullets in the chamber instead of one. Another 500 metres or so and he would have been safe; he almost pulled it off. But ... The pride of five lions had an unsuccessful night's hunting on the Ingwelala airstrip. Dejected and hungry, they moved onto the main access road where they lay around for a while to regroup and plan the next hunt. Eventually the need to continue hunting, driven by hunger, got them back onto their feet, and from there they walked down the track that led directly to 'Goedehoop', the same track the man was on.

The pride of lions and the man were moving towards each other, and it wasn't long before the inevitable confrontation occurred. Having vastly superior night vision, the lions saw the man long before he was aware of them. Crouching in anticipation, two of them lay flat on the track while the other three moved into the bush on either side. As the man got closer something must have warned him of their presence. I suspect that when the lions were sure this was man, they instinctively growled as they often do when confronted by man on foot, though usually the growl erupts into a short grunt as they run away. At night, unless your response is convincing, this is not always the case. Realising the danger he was in, the man instinctively retreated and then tried to climb the nearest tree – which, unfortunately, was only a small mopane. This didn't give him anywhere near the height clearance he needed to safely clamber out of reach of the lions. The big cats soon overcame their initial fear of the man, replacing it with curiosity and opportunism ... the consequences were inevitable.

Roy Keeler, artist, freelance ranger and resident of Ingwelala at the time, was one of the first people on the scene the next morning. According to him, all that was found was a section of the man's femur and the ball joint and, in one of the pockets of a larger remnant of the man's bloodstained overalls, a six-inch nail.

Man-eaters Can Swim, Too

A TRAGEDY IN NOVEMBER 2000

African or Nile crocodiles don't get anywhere close to the size of their Australian saltwater cousins, which can attain an inconceivable length of 11 metres! It's incredible but true, and you need to actually pace out 11 metres to see why this measurement has got to belong to something prehistoric. African crocs may reach a maximum of some seven metres – smaller, sure, but no less deadly. The largest specimen was found in the Lake Victoria area and measured a shade over 22 feet (6.5 metres). The largest croc I've ever seen on our section of the Olifants River would probably measure a little over five metres, which is more than a metre longer than the man-eater I'm about to tell you about.

Incidentally, the way I measure the larger females is when they are guarding a nest, which will invariably be in some soft sand on the riverbank. The first thing you do is wait until she isn't there and isn't likely to reappear in a hurry. Then, by taping the distance between her chin mark in the sand and the tail sweep line as she moves off, you can get a measurement within a few centimetres of dead accurate, good enough for me, anyway. Don't ever try to take these measurements on your own; always have someone guarding you from the protective mother, who may assume you're there to steal her eggs.

There cannot be many happier moments in a young man's life than the day he finishes school. It's a time for celebration and partying before serious preparation for the rest of your life begins; a time when caution, responsibility and discipline are temporarily set aside; a time to let your hair down and enjoy the moment. What better way, then, than to grab a few beers and some meat, and head down to the river for a picnic and braai with your friends. The venue chosen by a group of students for this particular celebration was a neighbouring game reserve's designated and popular picnic site, situated about 500 metres downstream from Olifants' clubhouse. This well-chosen spot on the northern bank of the river lies in the shade of some of the most magnificent sycamore fig trees found along this stretch of the river.

December in the lowveld is usually an uncomfortably hot month, and is often punctuated with early seasonal rainfall. The combination of these factors leads to high humidity, creating conditions that can become almost unbearable. Swimming becomes a practical, fun way to cool down, and where more enticing than the Olifants River, only a few metres away? So, as the sun climbed in the sky, the day got hotter, the dwindling beer supply got warmer and the languid, steadily-flowing river became more and more of a magnet to the group of students. At the time, the river was slightly swollen with rainwater from high up in the Blyde catchment, but it wasn't carrying the red ochre-like silt load normally associated with flooding in the highveld and iron-rich region of Roossenekal. The water resembled weak coffee with a dash of powdered milk, not unlike the stuff we were served up in the army which we called 'Cofftea' because you couldn't tell whether you were drinking tea or coffee, and like the water in the river, it was just murky enough to hide the tip of a teaspoon.

The mini vortexes and swirls associated with under-water structures were noticeably less in the slower sections of the river, indicating deeper water. Potentially, these would be where the better swimming pools were, so it wasn't long before someone went in to try it out. Shouting for his friends to join him, the intrepid youngster was trying to convince them how refreshingly cool the water was. Some of them made up their minds and began to strip down in anticipation of the swim. None of the students were old enough to remember when only a few hundred metres upstream, Steve Jablonsky, a well-known local builder, lost two large dogs to crocodiles, and that the late Jack Colenso, a former Olifants shareholder and owner of property across the river, had erected a memorial to one of his trusted servants who went fishing one afternoon and never returned.

Something dark and sinister that had hatched before these students' parents were born, imprinted with millennia of instinct and evolution, now remembered ... and reacted as its genetic memory insisted. No one noticed the huge crocodile that slowly slid off the opposite bank into the water and was now making its way towards the group of teenagers partying on the distant riverbank.

Initially, the reptile may have been disturbed by all the activity, which normally would have caused it to move off. However, the lone swimmer who was now concentrating on staying afloat and swimming against the current had triggered its natural predatory response. For the croc, there was no turning back.

Suddenly the young man swimming in the river screamed out in Afrikaans, '*Iets byt my!*' (Something's biting me.) In the next instant, arms flailing, he disappeared under the surface and into the murky depths of the pool. Initially his friends thought he was joking, playing some sort of aquatic 'cry wolf' game. That all changed when he briefly reappeared on the surface, further downstream, and this time his incoherent screams were cut horribly short as he was dragged under again. Paralysed with fear, they stared hopelessly at the water for an indication of where he could be, but there was nothing to see, the river gave no clue and nor did the crocodile. The croc had been big enough not to need any surface battle and show itself, it simply came up from underneath the hapless lad, grabbed him and pulled him under. There was nothing anyone could do; he never came up again and it was the last anybody saw of him.

The crocodile thought to be responsible was approximately four metres long. This makes it a not particularly large individual, but apparently large enough to become a man-eater. There are quite a number of crocodiles in our section of the Olifants

River that are at least this size and there are a couple of specimens closer to the barrage which may be nearly a metre longer. This particular crocodile could not be singled out as a man-eater because, as horrific as this tragedy was, the reality remains that all large crocodiles regard man as natural prey. Crocodiles are not in the same category as lions, for example. Killing a man-eating crocodile would simply be revenge, an act of vendetta, as you're not going to solve anything. The vacuum you create will be quickly filled by another, equally efficient crocodile that is also a man-eater by nature.

Nowadays, there's a swimming pool at the Olifants clubhouse. It may not be as romantic as the river, but it's a whole lot safer.

Besides the Nile crocodile, there are no water-dwelling man-eating creatures to fear in the bush. I would be prepared to leave it at that ... unless of course, I am reminded of an exceptional swimming creature that can be added to the list, depending on where in the African bush you find yourself.

Although you won't meet one on Olifants, the Zambezi shark *Carcharhinus leucas*, also referred to as a bull shark, is a species listed as extremely dangerous and known to attack and eat man. More scary is that these sharks are one of very few shark species that can tolerate fresh water.

The bull shark in particular is equally at home in fresh or salt water, and is regularly seen in the Zambezi River and its tributaries. It can and does live comfortably for months on end hundreds of kilometres from the briny, so much so that some specimens have been recorded in the Kruger National Park! If you find this phenomenon difficult to swallow, the incredible tolerance of this ocean creature for fresh water has again been confirmed, when in late 2008 a three-metre bull shark was found in the Zambezi River nearly 400 km from the Indian Ocean! Can you imagine the dumbfounded look on the face of a wildlife trails guide when asked by tourists what the fin-shaped thing scything through the pods of hippo was?

Marula Madness

BASED ON A WARDEN'S REPORT – 1990

The marula tree *Sclerocarya birrea* is to Southern Africa what the chestnut tree is to Europe, the date palm to North Africa and the olive tree to the Mediterranean. People are dependent on these gifts from nature, and in some communities the fruits provide an essential source of vitamins, energy and oils. In Africa, particularly the bushveld areas of Southern Africa, the marula fruit is not only coveted by its peoples, it is also a staple sought after by many species of wildlife from the smallest tree squirrel to the largest African elephant. In addition, myriad invertebrates are entirely dependent on this resource to complete their life cycle. For the most part, however, utilisation is complementary and discretionary, ensuring that there's enough to go around – that is, until man and elephant cross paths. When both species compete for the fruit at common focal points, the competition inevitably leads to conflict.

One such incident occurred in the Umbabat Nature Reserve a few years ago. An exceptionally good rainy season had produced a magnificent marula crop that year. Swollen with juice, and now too heavy for their delicate stalks, the ripe fruit fell and lay strewn under the trees in a pale yellow carpet. Marulas the size of golf balls were being gathered and eaten, but there were so many that most of them lay uneaten, slowly fermenting. Warthogs, baboons, vervet monkeys and elephant would spend hours selectively feeding, resting and then feeding again. Porcupines, which are usually nocturnal creatures, were observed feeding during the day. As the mid-morning sun began to warm things up, the baboons that had been feeding on the fruit since early in the morning were now satiated. Sitting on their haunches, they only moved now and then to scratch a flea bite, or yawn. Mostly, they sat in the shade with their arms hanging down either side of their bloated abdomens, resembling a bunch of beer-drinking spectators on the last day of a five-day cricket match.

Elephant were also making the most of the harvest; in fact, eating so much of the fruit that there was often not enough other vegetation being consumed to bind their stools properly. Their droppings would collapse and break when they hit the ground, falling in a loose heap. The partially digested fruit now supplied food to a host of smaller animals, particularly those that didn't care much for the pulp but were more interested in the oil and protein-rich kernels housed in the large pit, which the elephant's digestive system is unable to process.

Despite the numerous species of animals that eat this fruit, one immediately associates elephant with the fruit of the marula, and for good reason, as these enormous animals find it impossible to resist. High in sugars and rich in vitamins, as well as containing twice the vitamin C of an orange, marulas are highly sought after primarily as food rather than for the mythical intoxicating effect they have on certain wildlife so comically depicted and made famous in the movies. For man, however, the alcoholic qualities are of prime importance, as when distilled or brewed properly, marulas can make a variety of excellent drinks. As if to entrench this association between the marula fruit and elephant, they take the starring role on the label of the popular 'Amarula' liqueur.

Marulas are used by indigenous people primarily for the production of marula beer, therefore fruit that is high in sugar would be a bonus, the key to a richer fermentation process and in turn a good brew. And so began the fever; word on the dusty streets of the region soon got out that this year's harvest was particularly good in the lowveld, better than it had been for many years. This caused a mini-stampede of people from the surrounding communities, who moved into the area by the taxi load to harvest the bounty. Unfortunately, efforts to co-ordinate the gatherers as fairly as possible proved fruitless. (Pun intended.)

Clouded by greed, caution was thrown to the wind, as bags of the fruit were gathered in a frenzy much like the out-of-control half-price sale mentality that shoppers can display at times. There was little rational thinking; reserve boundaries were ignored and, due to lack of respect for the dangers of entering big game country, the consequences were inevitable. It all led to direct conflict between man and elephant, or, more accurately in this instance, a clash between women and elephant, because nine out of ten people gathering the fruit were middle-aged women.

We'd had a particularly busy couple of months. Tourists had flocked to Africa to escape the winter in Europe, and a good number had visited the bush. As the onslaught waned and the bookings slowly began to taper off, Meagan and I decided to take a break. The hot summer had been taxing and we were looking forward to a few days up in the cooler high country of Dullstroom. There's nothing like leaving the humidity and ambient temperatures hovering in the high thirties, then a couple of hours later and some 2 000 metres higher, lighting a log fire for warmth and atmosphere. It is such a contrast ... and we love it.

I like to start any road trip as early in the morning as possible, and this day was no exception. Having packed the car the night before, we were already heading out as the francolin started calling, and although the first pink hue of dawn had begun to light up the eastern sky, it was still dark enough to need headlights. I negotiated the patch of thick sand on the road as we left the lodge, curbing my impatience, as driving in sand is one of those things you cannot rush. If you rush, you'll usually end up spinning your wheels and digging yourself in, so not wanting to delay this trip by getting stuck, I took it easy.

As it turned out, had I gone any quicker, I might have driven head-on into the lampless bicycle and its rider that were heading straight towards us in the middle of the road. The bike was wobbling and weaving from side to side as the rider struggled to keep it in a straight line in the loose sand, with one hand on the handlebars and the other frantically waving us to stop.

It was 'Wednesday', our gate guard on the Umbabat east gate; no prizes for guessing what day of the week he was born on.

Clearly in great distress about something, he was babbling incoherently between gasps for air. Listening carefully, I got the gist
of things from the odd key word here and there accompanied
by his frantic gesticulations. Apparently his mother, who had
come to visit him and collect some marulas, had been gored by
an elephant!

'Where is your mother now?' I asked.

'She is in my room at the gate house,' he replied.

'Is she alive?'

'Yes,' he answered.

'When did this happen?'

'Yesterday evening,' he said.

'Why didn't you come over to the lodge and tell us immediately?'
I asked. He explained that that there were a lot of elephant about
so he was too afraid to move in the dark.

We were fortunate to have recently employed a competent
young ranger, who, amongst his many noteworthy attributes,
had been a medic officer in the army, where he had seen his
fair share of blood and injuries. Waking the young man, we told
him his skills were desperately needed. Briefing him on what had
happened, I suggested that he take the lodge's minibus and follow us to the gate, as not only was this vehicle comfortable; more
importantly, with the seats folded down it had enough space for
a mattress. We needed to be prepared for anything, and none of
us knew the nature or extent of the woman's injuries.

Arriving at the gate house, we opened the door and peered
into the semi-darkness of the candle-lit room. A small woman
lay on a blood-soaked mattress, blinking in the sudden light as
we pushed the door wide open. Wide-eyed, with a slow nod of
her gashed and bloodied head, she acknowledged that we had
arrived and were there to help her. We were to find out later that
her head wound was a scratch compared to her other injuries. At
that point, the three men stepped outside, allowing Meagan to
examine her, as even at this life or death stage, we felt that while
Meagan was there, we should respect the woman's need for a little privacy and to be examined by another woman.

Meagan emerged shortly afterwards and relayed the diagnosis

to us in graphic detail, whereupon we wasted no time loading the woman, blood-soaked mattress and all, into the minibus. The only sound the woman made was when she was moved, and it was little more than an exhausted moan.

Having bravely tolerated her agony for the whole night without painkillers, the additional pain as we repositioned her and the movement of her cold and stiffening wounds must have been almost intolerable. We had advised the doctor in Hoedspruit of the emergency and so he was ready and waiting for us upon arrival. He came out to meet us, took one look at the injured woman's wound and, without hesitation, administered a powerful painkiller. He then connected her to a drip and told us to take her to the hospital immediately and he'd let them know we were on our way.

Once Wednesday's mother was stabilised, we left the hospital and drove him back to the Reserve. On the way, he gave us more detail about the incident as it had been relayed to him. From his account and the nature of the injuries his mother had sustained, we were able to piece together a fairly accurate version of the events leading up to the attack.

The sweltering heat and high humidity of that day had proved to be an energy-sapping combination, and so no marula-collecting was done in the heat of the day. She and her friend from a neighbouring property were certain that they would make up for lost time and collect more marulas when it cooled down later. With renewed energy, but starting rather later that afternoon than anticipated, they began filling their bags. Before they knew it, darkness fast approached. Undaunted, they placed their respective loads, which must have weighed at least 20 kg, on their heads, and started walking home. Following the well-worn path that would eventually bring them onto the road, they were confident of getting home in 30 minutes or so. Staying on the pathway required a little more concentration than usual now that the light was fading, and even though their eyes were beginning to adjust to the low-light conditions, neither of them saw the dark grey shape of the elephant until it was too late.

From out of nowhere, without warning, the elephant charged

the two women, its shrill, ear-piercing trumpeting shattering the peace typical of that time of day. Dropping their loads of marulas, the two terrified women ran blindly through the bush in opposite directions, but unfortunately for Wednesday's mother, the elephant chose to pursue her. In a desperate effort to evade the animal, she plunged herself head first into a bush, but couldn't get in far enough, resulting in her rear end protruding. The elephant went straight for the target she'd unfortunately presented. One of its tusks penetrated her vagina and with a flick of its powerful head, the elephant then flung her through the air like a rag doll. She landed hard and her forehead was gashed open as she struck a rock. She was instantly knocked unconscious.

A while later she came to, in agony and shivering from shock and blood loss. Despite her condition, she managed to crawl over 300 metres to the road, where she was able to get her son's attention by screaming. What possibly saved her life after being gored and thrown was the fact that she had been knocked out on landing. Seeing her lying there in a heap, unconscious and motionless, the elephant may have thought she was dead, and lost interest.

Another aspect of her relative good fortune and what saved her from dying of the wounds inflicted by the elephant's tusk, was that being a small, light person meant there was relatively little weight resistance when she was tossed. If any more force had been applied, for example if she had been heavier, getting her airborne while pivoted on that tusk would then have caused massive internal damage. The ripping and tearing wounds thus inflicted and the subsequent bleeding resulting from them would almost certainly have proved fatal. In this case, although the tusk had entered her vagina and caused a ghastly wound, it was not as bad as it could have been. Not only was the penetration relatively shallow, the tusk went in at an angle where it broke her hip, whereas, had it gone a little deeper and straighter, it would have ruptured her peritoneum.

Meanwhile, her friend had made it home in one piece, shocked and scratched, but OK. She, like Wednesday, had been too terrified to venture out looking for help that night, and had no idea how badly injured her friend was until the next day, when the bush telegraph was abuzz with the news.

Six weeks later, Wednesday's mother returned to visit, and although a little stiff and tender, she had recovered completely. When asked how she was feeling, her reply dwelled only briefly on the recent trauma she had suffered during the elephant attack. In fact, she appeared to be more concerned – or disappointed, rather – that a good marula season had been missed. However, her smile lit up her face again when she announced that she was already making plans to return the following season. Well, I thought, by then she would have had ample time to get over the emotional and physical trauma of the attack. But before I could develop this thought process, she interrupted it.

'Next week,' she said with a grin, 'I will be collecting mopane worms!'

Initially I thought she was joking: everyone knows that elephant also have a penchant for mopane trees, the leaves on which the mopane worms feed exclusively. I admit to being a little apprehensive at the time, and tried in vain to explain to her that the risks were not worth it, especially in her frail condition. But it was clear that the natural bounty of nutritious and delicious mopane worms was regarded as on a par with a good marula harvest, and that outweighed any call for caution or revision of plans, never mind the abandonment of plans.

As far as we know, there were no further near-tragic incidents in Wednesday's mother's life. Accordingly, we have no plans to follow 'Marula Madness' with a chapter entitled 'Mopane Madness'.

Bibliography and references

Alexander, G and Marais, J, 2007. *A guide to the reptiles of Southern Africa*. Struik, Cape Town.

Bekker, P, 1971. *Peoples of Southern Africa – their customs and beliefs*. The Star, Johannesburg.

Bertram, BCR, 1978. *A pride of lions*. JM Dent and Sons Ltd, London.

Bolwig, N, 1959. A study of the behaviour of the chacma baboon, *Papio ursinus*. *Behaviour* 14:136-63.

Bosman, HC, 1971. *In the withaak's shade*. Human and Rousseau, Cape Town.

Bosman, P and Hall-Martin, A, 1986. *Elephants of Africa*. Struik, Cape Town.

Bothma, JP, 2002. *Game ranch management*. JJ van Schaik, Pretoria.

Broadley, DG, 1983. *Fitzsimons Snakes of Southern Africa*. Delta Books, Johannesburg.

Bromilow, C, 1995. *Problem plants of South Africa*. Briza, Pretoria.

Bulpin, TV, 1954. *The ivory trail*. Cape and Transvaal Printers, Cape Town.

Carruthers, V, 2001. *Frogs and frogging in Southern Africa*. Struik, Cape Town.

Clark JD, 1959. *The prehistory of Southern Africa*. Whitefriars Press, London.

Coates Palgrave, K, 1977. *Trees of Southern Africa*. Struik, Cape Town.

Collier's Encyclopedia. 1971. Vol.5. Crowell-Colliers Educational Corporation.

Delsink, AK *et al.*, 2006. Regulation of a small discrete African elephant population through immunocontraception in the Makalali Conservancy, Limpopo, South Africa. *South African Journal of Science* 102: 403-5.

Douglas-Hamilton, I, 1987. African elephants: population trends and their causes, *Oryx* 21: 11-24. Oxford University Press, London.

Estes, RD, 1995. *The behaviour guide to African mammals*. University of California Press, USA.

Frison-Roche, R, 1969. *Hunters of the Arctic*. The Chaucer Press, London.

Gibbs Russell, GE, Watson, L, Koekemoer, M, Smook, L, Barker, NP,

Anderson, HM, 1991. *Grasses of Southern Africa*. Memoirs of the Botanical Survey of South Africa.

Grzimek, B and M, 1960. *Serengeti shall not die*. Hamish Hamilton, London

Hamilton, WJ, Buskirk, RE, Buskirk, WH, 1975. Chacma baboon tactics during inter-troop encounters. *Journal of Mammalogy* 56: 857-70

Henning, MW, 1932. *Animal diseases in South Africa*. CNA, Pretoria.

Herbert Marie, 1973. *The snow people*. Book Club Associates, London.

Herne, B, 1999. *White hunters*. Henry Holt and Co, New York.

Jamison, R, 1989. *A rifleman's handbook*. PJS Publishing, Illinois.

Leakey, LSB, 1935. *Stone-age Africa*. Oxford University Press, London.

Laws, PC, 1975. *Elephants and their habitats*. Clarendon Press, Oxford.

Liebenberg, L, 1995. *The Art of Tracking*. David Philip, Cape Town.

Maberly, CTA, 1960. African bushpig. *Animals* 9(10): 556-59.

Maclean, GL, 1978. *Roberts birds of Southern Africa*. John Voelker Bird Book Fund, Cape Town.

Marshall Thomas Elizabeth, 2006. *The old way*. Sarah Crighton Books, USA.

McBride, C, 1977. *The white lions of the Timbavati*. Paddington Press, London.

McKenzie, A (ed), 1993. *The capture and care manual*. Wildlife Decision Support Services and The South African Veterinary Foundation, Pretoria.

Morris, J, Levitas, B. 1984. *South African tribal life today*. College Press, Cape Town.

Mills, MGL. 1974. Carnivores of the Kalahari, Part 1. *Custos* 3(7): 3-42.

Odum, EP, 1971. *Fundamentals of ecology*. Philadelphia Press, USA.

Palmer, D. 2006. *Seven million years – the story of human evolution*. Phoenix, London.

Pooley, E, 1998. *A field guide to wild flowers – KwaZulu-Natal and the eastern region*. Natal Flora Publications Trust, Durban.

Porter, RN, 1964. An ecological renaissance of theTimbavati Private Nature Reserve. (unpublished).

Selous, FC, 1881. *A hunter's wanderings in Africa*. Reprint. Belmont Printers, Bulawayo.

Schaller, HNR, 1972. *The Serengeti lion. A study of predator prey relationships*. University of Chicago Press, USA.

Shaller, HNR and Lowther, GR, 1969. The relevance of carnivore behaviour to the study of early hominids. *Southwest. Journal of Anthropology* 25: 307-41.

Sheldrick, D, 1973. *The Tsavo story*. Collins and Harvill Press, London.

Skelton, P, 1993. Freshwater fishes of Southern Africa. Southern Book Publishers, Johannesburg.

Schmidt, E, Lotter, M and McLelland, W, 2002. *Trees and shrubs of Mpumalanga and Kruger National Park*. Jacana, Johannesburg.

Smithers, RHN, 1979. *The mammals of the Southern African Subregion*.

Pretoria University Press.

Smuts, G L, 1978. Interrelations between predators, prey and their environment. *Bio-Science* 28:316-20.

Smuts, GL, 1982. *Lion*. Macmillan, Johannesburg.

Sollas, WJ, 1924. *Ancient hunters and their modern representatives*. Macmillan, London.

Stevenson-Hamilton, J, 1929. *The lowveld – its wildlife and its people*. Cassell, London.

Tainton, NM, 1981. *Veld and pasture management in South Africa*. Shuter and Shooter, Pietermaritzburg and University of Natal Press, Pietermaritzburg.

Tannehill, IR, 1947. *Drought its causes and effects*. Princetown University Press, USA.

Tinley, KL, 1979. Management ecology of the Sabi Sand Wildtuin. (Unpublished report.)

Thomson, R, 1992. *The wildlife game*. The Nyala wildlife publications trust, Durban.

Turnbull-Kemp, P, 1967. *The Leopard*. Howard Timmins, Cape Town.

Van Wyk, E and Van Oudshoorn, F, 1992. *Guide to grasses of Southern Africa*. Briza, Pretoria.

Van Lawick, H, Goodall, J. 1970. *Innocent killers*. Collins, London.

Weavind, CHO. A brief history of the Klaserie area. Saxonwold. (Unpublished.)

Young, JZ, 1962. *The life of vertebrates*. Oxford University Press, London.

Acknowledgements

We know that an organism is the product of its environment, and that we are not above this law. The influence of this law and our response and adaptation to it over time is what shapes and moulds us. In the same way, this book is the product of the environmental and social stimuli that have surrounded me in my youth and beyond and the way they have influenced my life. These influences have inspired me and helped shape the person I am, the way I think, and the way I perceive that which is around me, and for this I am deeply indebted to far more people than I will be mentioning here. To those who know they have touched my life but appear forgotten, please know you are indeed remembered and you live through my words somewhere in the pages of this book.

Thanks first to Meagan, my loving wife and companion, a colleague, a shoulder to cry on and on occasion the voice of reason in a cacophony of chaos. Without her capacity for patience, her keen eye for detail sometimes outside my awareness and her support through the rough patches, this book would not have been possible. Even after a long day in the administrative hive of the Olifants office, she would find the time and enthusiasm to work with me. I couldn't type a word when I began the book, but her persistence paid off, and now I can operate the keyboard with two fingers. My children, Eleana and Dino, who patiently supported me and understood that there were times when I needed to focus on the task at hand ... what can I say, I am truly proud of them.

Thanks go to the present chairman of Olifants River Game Reserve, Quentin Sussman, to his predecessor Bev Humphris, and to the board of directors past and present for entrusting me with the guardianship of their precious reserve. Special thanks are due to Neil and Morag Hulett, whose weekly game drive published on the Internet keeps me and their fellow shareholders up-to-date on game sightings, and to Janine Scorer for the excellent job she does managing the Olifants website: www.olifantsreserve. com.

I am grateful to Balule's regional wardens past and present – Rian Ahlers, Crispian Barlow, Wynand Brits, Craig Ferguson, Marius Fuls, Ken Hartman, Timothy Hedges and Phillip Sheuer, also to the regional chairpersons of Balule – Andy Dott, Jurgen Elbertse, Jerry Gibbs, Steve Hearne, Gerry Morse, Ian Owtram, Lawrence Saad and Quentin Sussman, for placing their confidence in me as warden to represent Balule PNR. Thanks also to the APNR committee, past and present, for their support and co-operation.

Thanks to all my family who never saw much of me since I left for the bush over 30 years ago, but were always there when I needed them, as were my close friends who, since our childhood, have always been happy to take second place to my first passion – André van Vollenstee, Stuart and Desmond Russell, Tyrone Stevenson, Barry Ryan and William Watson. Thanks also to Irving Stevenson for introducing me to the Timbavati, a turning point in my life. Special thanks to: the late Edward Engela who unselfishly took me in as one of the family, he also loved the outdoors and was like a second father to me; to Howard Walker for his loyal friendship and for introducing me to fly fishing's doyen, Tom Sutcliffe, along with the late Steve Kruger, who unwittingly were in many ways my mentors, as was Desmond Prout Jones, who never doubted I would make conservation my life; to Arlene Fortune who against all odds put her faith in my ability to manage a safari operation in Botswana; to Dawid and Willem van den Berg, thank you for a lifetime's access to the finest waterfowl habitat in South Africa.

I count myself privileged to know Mark Jevon, whose respect for the environment and ethics afield with rod or rifle is enviable. To the ARC team Mike Peel, John Peel and André Jacobs, thank you all for your friendship and assistance on the ecological side, a relationship that is now seventeen years old. To my colleagues past and present, notably: Roy Keeler, Ian Ruddiman, Glenn and Karin du Toit, Ron and Cindy Hopkins, James and Olga Rankin, and the late George and Bernadette Carroll, thank you.

Thanks also to the unsung heroes of the bush, those brave and dedicated anti-poaching rangers, Jabulaan Makhubedu, Jose Ngoveni, Paolo Makhuvela, Joachim Ntimani and Januarie Mahlula.

To the finest trackers I've known, John Sibuyi, Kimbian and the late Phinias Sibuyi, go my acknowledgements to their timeless skills.

My apologies to the family heirs of Carl Weavind, who, despite diligent search, I was unable to locate. I wish to thank them for his account of the history of this area, which I researched.

Thanks go to Tony and Mandy Burgess, former shareholders of Olifants River Game reserve, who enthusiastically took on the editing of the first limited edition of this book which was privately printed under the name 'Olifants – The river runs through it'. Thanks also to Tony and Lynn Wright, and Graham Hickson and Sandy de Witt, who spurred me on and initiated the idea for me to write a book in the first place, and to David and Mary

Baker, who happily shouldered much of the financial burden of the first printing. That the book has now taken on a new incarnation owes much to David Ball's encouragement and support. I have left for last a big thank you to all the shareholders and their partners who make up the family of Olifants River Game Reserve, who, by response to my newsletters over the years, inadvertently inspired me to write this book.

My grateful thanks are due to the team at Jonathan Ball Publishers. In particular, my sincerest thanks go to publishing director Jeremy Boraine, who through his interest in the wildlife and wilder places of this country, recognised the potential in this publication. To production manager Francine Blum, my heartfelt thanks for her kindness, wonderful sense of humour and warmth, while maintaining a firm but gentle pair of hands on the reins of production. I am especially grateful to editor Frances Perryer for her meticulous approach to this undertaking, inspired in no small measure by her love of animals and passion for wildlife conservation, and to Valda Strauss for proofreading over 400 pages with words like 'Colophospermum' to decipher and my unorthodox style to contend with. The beautiful layout and design is thanks to Kevin Shenton, who has done so much with so little. The word is out that this book's cover will make you want to curl up with it in front of a fireplace, or on a couch or in bed ... which is exactly what I hope everyone does with it: thanks go to Michiel Botha for creating this perception in its design.